The Perreaus and Mrs. Rudd

DONNA T. ANDREW
and RANDALL McGOWEN

The Perreaus
and Mrs. Rudd

*Forgery and Betrayal
in Eighteenth-Century London*

UNIVERSITY OF CALIFORNIA PRESS

BERKELEY   LOS ANGELES   LONDON

University of California Press
Berkeley and Los Angeles, California

University of California Press, Ltd.
London, England

Library of Congress Cataloging-in-Publication Data

Andrew, Donna T., 1945–.
    The Perreaus and Mrs. Rudd : forgery and betrayal in
eighteenth-century London / Donna T. Andrew, Randall
McGowen.
        p.   cm.
    Includes bibliographical references and index.
    ISBN 0-520-22062-5 (cloth: alk. paper).
    1. Perreau, Daniel, d. 1776—Trials, litigation, etc.
    2. Perreau, Robert, d. 1776—Trials, litigation, etc.
    3. Rudd, Margaret Caroline, b. 1744 or 5—Trials,
litigation, etc.   4. Trials (Forgery)—England—London.
5. Forgers—Great Britain.   I. McGowen, Randall, 1948–.
II. Title.

KD372.P47 A53   2001
345.42'0263—dc21   00-066655

Manufactured in the United States of America
10   09   08   07   06   05   04   03   02   01
10   9   8   7   6   5   4   3   2   1

For Rachel

—RM

For Emily, Eleanor, and Marion

—DTA

That, for which many their Religion,
Most men their Faith, all change their honesty,
Profit, (that guilded god) Commodity.
He that would grow damned Rich, yet live secure,
Must keep a case of Faces.

THOMAS DEKKER,
If This Be Not a Good Play, the Devil's in It (1611)

CONTENTS

Illustrations follow page 84

ACKNOWLEDGMENTS

THIS BOOK ORIGINATED in a casual conversation that took place in the Huntington Library gardens more years ago than we wish to remember. At some point one of us suggested to the other that we might collaborate on a short piece on one of the century's "causes célèbres," the case of the "fascinating Mrs. Rudd and the unfortunate Perreaus." Here was an episode, seemingly so quintessentially eighteenth century, that everyone had heard of but no one had bothered to examine with care. We thought it deserved more attention. In this blithe manner we embarked upon an investigation that soon came to obsess us as much as it did English men and women in 1775. A pleasant diversion turned into a full-length study as we sought to answer the riddle of this case's appeal and complexities.

We jumped into this project with no sense of the difficulties of collaborative scholarship. Fortunately the pleasures have exceeded the pitfalls by a wide margin. This book is truly a joint effort; we shared the tasks of research and writing. Our friendship has grown as we watched this manuscript slowly, and sometimes painfully, take shape. We wish to thank each other for patience and good spirits during this long effort. Equally important has been the encouragement and enthusiasm of overlapping circles of friends and scholars, whose support was crucial to the book's completion. Many people listened to us talk about Mrs. Rudd and the Perreaus. For their assistance we would like to thank Ben Barker-Benfield, Gregory Claeys,

Natalie Zemon Davis, Simon Devereaux, Margot Finn, Richard Gorrie, Carla Hesse, Henry Horwitz, Joanna Innes, Heather Jackson, Peter King, the late Colin Matthews, Andrea McKenzie, John Money, Robert Nye, James Oldham, Ruth Paley, Stanley Pierson, Nicholas Rogers, John Sainsbury, Veronica Strong-Boag, Amanda Vickery, Dror Wahrman, Martin Wiener, and Bill Zachs, consulting editor of the James Boswell project at the Yale University Press. McGowen's research was aided by a grant from the American Society for Eighteenth-Century Studies and the McMaster University Library. Andrew profited from the opportunity to present some of her research at the universities of Warwick and London. We would like to acknowledge the support of the Humanities Research Centre of the Australian National University, which provided us with a happy setting in which to complete the production of this book. The manuscript benefited from the comments of Thomas Laqueur and an anonymous reader for the press. We would also like to thank Sheila Levine, of the University of California Press, for her constant support for this project, and Dore Brown and Marian Schwartz for their skillful editorial assistance. Above all, we owe a special debt to John Beattie. He not only introduced us but offered sympathetic readings and advice at crucial junctures in the composition of this work. He has been a friend and mentor to us both.

INTRODUCTION

LONDON NEWSPAPER readers were startled in March 1775 to see the first reports of an extensive forgery. This crime always attracted attention in eighteenth-century Britain, if for no other reason than that a conviction almost certainly carried the offender to the gallows. The English financial system at that time was held up to a great extent by faith in the individual's word. If that faith was broken—as it was each time forgery was committed—the authorities felt compelled to punish the transgressor severely.

From the first, this was an unusual case. Two respectable men—identical twins, in fact—and an elegant woman stood accused of the offense. No doubt the social status of the suspects, and the revelations of various sordid details of the conspiracy, would have excited gossip and drawn the attention of the news-hungry press at any time. Still, the sensation created by this episode was without parallel. At each turn events followed an unexpected path. Daniel and Robert Perreau sought to fix sole responsibility for the crime on the woman, Mrs. Rudd, while she insistently proclaimed her innocence and accused them of perpetrating the scheme. Even as the bewildered authorities sought to get to the bottom of the affair, the public debated the guilt or innocence of the accused. Through the brothers' trials in June, and then in the months before Rudd's trial in December, the controversy filled the papers. The case of the Perreaus and Mrs. Rudd, one correspondent wrote to a newspaper in June, "is lately become the topic of general conversation, from the high department of state down to the microscopic atmospheres of every petty coffee and porter-house politician."[1] Discussed in pamphlets, debated in letters to the press, with illustrations of the participants in the major magazines, the celebrated affair was impossible to avoid.

The Perreau-Rudd case preoccupied the public between March 1775 and February 1776. At first glance this attention is puzzling. Britain had, after all, entered a period of imperial crisis, one of the century's defining moments. The nation was slipping into a civil war with its American colonies. The trials of the brothers in June coincided with the first reports of bloodshed at Lexington and Concord. Yet the public was at least as much taken up with the tangled stories of the Perreaus and Mrs. Rudd as it was with the fate of empire. "So very extraordinary an affair," one pamphlet declared, "as has lately been discovered, is not to be parallelled in the history of any time or any country."[2] Such hyperbole was typical of these self-serving publications, yet it must have come close to the truth for contemporaries reading competing newspaper accounts day after day. To more reflective commentators the attention accorded to this squalid business appeared dangerously excessive. The space given to reports of Mrs. Rudd's antics suggested that a spirit of whimsy had gripped the nation or, more darkly, that some fatal corruption had overturned notions of decency and common sense. These protests failed; the appeal of the case was irresistible, in part due to the peculiar personalities of the individuals involved, especially the inimitable Mrs. Rudd. There was also the perplexing question of where the truth lay in this murky affair. Glamour and a good mystery usually make an extraordinary trial the compelling topic of conversation. The obsessive quality of public interest in this case, however, suggests that it was more than a harmless diversion from the anxieties of the moment. Not merely an innocent preoccupation, its confusions and complexities served to compound the growing sense of a crisis of confidence brought on by difficulties at home and in the colonies.

This book attempts to explain the fascination that the affair of Mrs. Rudd and the Perreaus exerted over the country. It also offers a glimpse into neglected corners and hidden relationships within that society. The decade of the 1770s has most frequently been studied in relation to imperial concerns and their impact upon the political institutions of the day. We intend to draw a different portrait of the period, making the cause célèbre our point of entry. Familiar figures such as John Wilkes and George III, Lord Mansfield and Sir John Fielding people our book, but so do those less well known, speculators and courtesans, as well as judges and politicians. The neat categories of "respectable" and "unrespectable" do not capture the complexity of this society. When the public read about the Perreaus and Mrs. Rudd, they saw them not as aberrant types but as neighbors and acquaintances, people who embodied striking features of the age.

What was it that people recognized as they read with mingled curiosity and uneasiness the details of the case? Forgery cases often involved tales of individuals who aimed high and fell hard when they were detected. Frequently some clerk or merchant turned to crime after living a life of dissipation and extravagance. In the present instance both motives, luxury and ambition, appeared to operate. The principals, like so many Londoners, came from various corners of the British Isles. They had been drawn to the metropolis by the prospect of connection, opportunity, and advancement. London was the capital of a great empire; it was the vibrant center of trade and finance, the residence of the court, and the seat of Parliament. Coming from relatively obscure backgrounds, the Perreaus and Mrs. Rudd, in their various ways, sought to vault to the upper rungs of London's finely graded social ladder. Their biographies carry us back and forth across the city. They aspired to the glamorous world represented by the fashionable West End. Here, among the squares where the nobility and upper reaches of the professions shared addresses, the scene was composed of opulent display, polite conversation, and polished manners. To gain access to this enchanted realm required wealth. The brothers looked to the City, where stock speculation seemed to promise a shortcut to riches. Between the City and the West End lay the Covent Garden area, a world of courtesans, actresses, and prostitutes. Here was a more ambiguous neighborhood of illicit but tolerated pleasures, where beauty and wit provided another avenue to success—or, more often, a road to misery. In its midst was Bow Street, where a magistrate's court attempted to maintain order in this unruly district. Bow Street belonged both to Covent Garden and to the legal structure of the metropolis. The magistrates sent those accused of serious crimes to Newgate, the most important house of detention in the metropolis. From there delinquents were carried to trial at the Old Bailey, where eight times a year judges and juries handed down verdicts of acquittal or guilt, life or death. The condemned traveled west to Tyburn Hill, once on the edge of town but now increasingly surrounded by prosperous new streets and shopping districts. London was still intimate enough that much of what the papers offered appeared to be shared gossip rather than hard news. The Perreau-Rudd case was a metropolitan story, not only in the sense that its participants lived and operated within the town but also because its themes and emotions spoke of the quality of life there.

If the story offers a panorama of London, it also provides a gauge for tracking the shifting currents of the period. For the case captured the mood and feel of the 1770s—a mixture of folly, silliness, and excess, yet also of challenge and decision. Having gained possession of its first great empire by the conclusion of the Seven Years' War, Britain almost immediately faced intractable political and economic problems in managing these outposts. By the mid-1770s, in both its American and Indian dominions, crises of administration and finance had erupted that raised doubts about the viability or very survival of this empire. Furthermore, at home, Britain's own political system was being tested and the claims of established institutions questioned. For many contemporaries these divisive issues found expression in savage satires on the conduct of powerful personalities. The public turned to discussions of the character and even the physiognomy of individuals as a way of understanding contemporary events. In the most obvious sense, the Perreau-Rudd case fit this pattern; it presented a morality tale, expressing the disquiet felt about current social trends. Here were ambitious people, seduced by the lures and charms of the fashionable life of London, who had resorted to unscrupulous means in a desperate effort to get ahead. The catastrophe that overwhelmed the Perreau family, whatever its origins, provided a sobering lesson in the midst of a drift into war.

Seen in this light, the tale echoed themes found in a much longer tradition, often expressed in literature but especially on the stage, of dismay or outrage at the consequences of new forms of wealth. The epigraph to our book comes from a line in a 1611 play by Thomas Dekker. A familiar attack upon trade, it decried the influence of London in spawning a particular kind of character and conduct. The play's villain, in recommending a "case of faces" for anyone who wished to grow very rich yet remain secure, advised them to acquire a box of masks, alternate personae that could be changed at will. Success required ruthlessness; safety, duplicity. Seemingness, shifting identities and loyalties, were thus recognized and feared as the sine qua non of the ambitious Londoner. This anxiety is the leitmotif that runs through our case. The three principals, to different degrees and with varying success, acted different roles. As the case unfolded, evidence was offered that revealed that these handsome, well-spoken people were not as they seemed. Each week exposed some new instance of Mrs. Rudd's art. But hints of misconduct swirled around the brothers as well. The case, however, would not have been so unsettling had it amounted to no more than this, the disclosure of unpleasant truths that lay behind seemingly pleasing appearances. It was not merely another instance of duplicity exposed. What made the public especially uneasy was that while much was revealed, much else remained hidden or obscure. Even what was in plain view was susceptible to different interpretations. There seemed no way to make sense of the affair, to know, finally, who was responsible for the crime that had been committed. This was, after all, not a play; it was a legal case, one that promised a fateful outcome. The Perreau-Rudd trial was a "case of faces," both a revelation that fair might well be foul, but even worse, that it might not be possible to determine which was which. Doubt and a grim fatality haunted its progress, even as contemporaries surrendered to its spell.

One

TO THE HANGING TREE

THE WINTER HAD BEEN as severe as any in recent memory. By the new year, England was in the grip of cold and snow. The Thames was frozen above Fulham. The papers contained stories of people perishing on the roads. "Raw, cloudy day," the American loyalist Samuel Curwen noted in his journal. "Hourly accounts of the damage by the excessive snow that has been falling more or less for these ten days now, higher than has been known within the memory of any."[1] Still, a crowd estimated to number forty thousand gathered early on January 17, 1776, hoping to catch a glimpse of the condemned. "An infinitely larger number of spectators than ever was known waited at the Press-yard of Newgate," one paper reported. They "lined the streets from thence to Tyburn, and filled the different galleries and sheds erected for the purpose of enabling the curious to observe the agonies felt by men who die in sacrifice to public justice."[2] People came in carriages, on horseback, and by foot. Artisans and apprentices, laborers and street vendors all trudged toward the place of execution. And so did the fashionable, the writers, and the politicians. A public execution was an ambiguous event, both dreadful and festive, a holiday and a day of retribution. It was meant to put people in mind of the uncertainties of life and the terrible grandeur of death.

Londoners were familiar with such scenes. They occurred eight times throughout the year. In the decade between 1765 and 1774, some 278 people were executed for various crimes in London and Middlesex.[3] Although the biographies of the condemned contained few surprises, people were still attracted by the interesting stories. They were also curious to see how an individual would behave—with dignity or indifference, with submission or rebellion. Yet even for London this execution was different. Seven men were to be hanged, all for property offenses. But it was the identity of the condemned rather than their number that was unusual.

At nine the procession set off from Newgate for the hour-and-a-half trip to Tyburn. It formed, one correspondent wrote, "a variegated and solemn assembly." First went the city marshalls, followed by a cart containing Lyon Abrahams and Saunders Alexander, convicted of burglary, and George Lee, a handsome eighteen year old condemned for highway robbery. A hurdle, the sledge reserved for those condemned for treason, followed the cart, carrying two coiners, Richard Baker and John Radcliffe. After them came a number of sheriff's officers.[4]

Interesting as this spectacle was, most of the crowd had braved the cold in hopes of catching a glimpse of the two remaining men. Part of what made their presence among the condemned particularly interesting was their social status, marked by the mourning coach in which they rode, accompanied by the Ordinary and a sheriff's officer. The grant of a coach was rare. But then the twin brothers, Daniel and Robert Perreau, represented unusual participants in the Tyburn fair. They were men of fashion from a respectable family. Unlike the others, who were hustled to the gallows after their December trials, the Perreaus had been hoping for a pardon since their convictions in June. By now many of the assembled knew the story of the apothecary Robert and his "amiable" wife, who had "lived together for the space of eighteen years,—in perfect harmony and conjugal felicity, heightened by three hopeful and promising children, pledges of their mutual love."[5] The story of the brothers' crime and the controversy over their fates had filled the papers and preoccupied the public for months. Rarely had a criminal case generated such attention, such an outpouring of letters and pamphlets. Seldom had a drama opened so many details of fashionable society to public view. Even more was at stake, however, than the brothers' social identity, for the crime itself remained clouded in mystery. Although the brothers had been convicted of forgery, they continued to protest that they were the victims of a beautiful, intelligent, and dangerous courtesan, Mrs. Margaret Caroline Rudd.

When the crime was first detected in March, the brothers insisted on their innocence. They alleged that Mrs. Rudd, Daniel's mistress, had entrapped them. Although a jury convicted them both in June, their defense had established enough doubt in the minds of the judges that Mrs. Rudd was bound over for trial herself. Her acquittal in December set the stage for the execution of the brothers. Numerous wealthy and titled individuals had intervened on their behalf, but to no avail.

The trials had been unsatisfactory affairs. The participants told wildly conflicting stories and offered strikingly contradictory portraits of themselves. The public remained divided over the issue of who was guilty and who should be punished. There was great anxiety that innocent people were about to suffer, individuals known to a considerable number of society's elite. Many spectators watched intently for some key in the conduct of one of the parties that would unlock the truth. They hoped someone would clear up the whole business at last.

In the pageantry and ritual of the execution the authorities sought to teach a lesson, to make, in the often-repeated phrase, an example. The words of the clergyman and the confessions of the condemned reminded the assembled of the even more dreadful day of judgment that awaited them all. But not all contemporaries agreed that the event ever achieved this goal. In recent years there had been frequent complaints about the misbehavior of the crowd and the bravado of the condemned. On this occasion, the *Morning Post* complained that the "remorseless multitude behaved with the most inhuman indecency—shouting, laughing, throwing snowballs at each other, particularly at those few who had a proper compassion for the misfortunes of their fellow creatures." Other witnesses employed a less exacting standard of behavior. Most papers agreed the execution had gone well enough.[6]

Yet the papers found it hard to resist heightening the sense of drama associated with this extraordinary execution. They were filled with often conflicting accounts of the strange coincidences and accidents that marked the event. Newspapers competed with one another to offer the more fantastic detail. "Several persons were severely hurt by the fall of a temporary scaffold yesterday at the place of execution," the *Morning Chronicle* announced. "A soldier had his leg broken, by standing upon the wheel of a coach; another man was almost bruised to death, by being jammed between two coaches; and we fear many other accidents happened upon the melancholy occasion." The *Gazetteer* offered an even more melodramatic rendering of the mayhem. The scaffolding broke just as the "malefactors were turned off"; one person was squeezed to death and another trampled by a horse. It reported that perhaps a dozen people had died. A well-dressed woman, big with child and standing at Holborn in order to see the victims pass, "gave a shriek" at the very moment they went by, "was taken in labour, and delivered immediately in the street a fine boy." She was quickly transported to a home near the Mint.[7]

According to the *Morning Post,* a woman and two children died in the collapse of the stands, while another woman was trampled to death and still others were badly bruised. One child died when a woman dropped it from her arms as she strained to catch sight of the procession from a window.[8] The *Public Advertiser* cast doubt on the accounts offered by its rivals. It had not heard of anyone being hurt in the collapse of the platform. The only death had resulted from a man falling from the roof of a coach. Several days later, however, even this sober paper added the surprising information that the victim was only seventeen and stood heir to a fortune of £20,000.[9]

An execution was always theater, and the condemned chose various parts for themselves. "On leaving Newgate, Lee put on an air of vulgar heroism, exceedingly improper for so dreadful a situation." "The Jews [Abrahams and Alexander] and the coiners," one paper noted, "behaved with becoming decency." But the brothers understood, perhaps more fully than their fellow sufferers, the importance of the spectacle. They not only lent themselves to the purposes of justice; they sought to exploit the drama in order to save their reputations and family name. For their combat with Mrs. Rudd would extend beyond the grave. They played upon their uncanny appearance: they were identical twins, handsome men in their forties, so similar that even close acquaintances had difficulty telling them apart. On this day "they both appeared in new suits of black, and their hair dressed and powdered, and each of them without a hat." Their dress, as always, was very "genteel," and their hair and costumes were "exactly alike." They offered an image that they had presented from the first moment of discovery, one that claimed fashionable status while proclaiming their innocence and confusion in the face of evil.[10] But it was not only their appearance that carried this message. They followed a script that was faithfully reported by the press, a script that had as much to say about their social identity as it did about their innocence.

The Perreaus began their day at eight by attending a service in Newgate with the other condemned. A large number of influential people clamored for admission, but only six gentlemen, friends of the brothers, succeeded in gaining entry. Then their chains were knocked off and they were bound by a rope for the journey to the gallows. Daniel was composed until he saw this "same office" done for his brother, when he wept.[11] Aside from this one display of emotion, the brothers betrayed no trace of fear or dread. They emerged from Newgate "without any person holding their halters (as the custom usually is) and seated themselves in the coach." As Robert and Daniel looked out upon the spectators, "they recognized several of their acquaintances." Robert confided to the Ordinary, Villette, a concern that that "wicked woman," Mrs. Rudd, was among the crowd; "he should not wonder if she was." "Daniel appeared confident she would not" attend.[12] While their vehicle stopped as usual before St. Sepulchre's for the familiar verses, the throng pushed forward to get a view of the condemned men. Robert, on observing the turmoil, put down the window. Once people could see them, the disorder ceased.[13] The brothers were calm and dignified, demonstrating that they were worthy representatives of their class.

The press of people continued to the foot of the gallows. "It took three hundred constables to keep clear the space around the execution."[14] A dispute over the order of execution caused a brief delay. Although no one could remember such a circumstance to have occurred before, "the Jews [Abrahams and Alexander] were to be tied up by themselves." They had "a Hebrew priest" to offer them solace. The presence of the Perreaus may have played a role in these special arrangements. Villette said he had been happy to assure the brothers that such a separation would prevail, so that no "disturbance" would arise "from their opposite principles of religion." The difficulty arose because Lee then begged to be executed apart from the Jews as well. He was told that no other cart was available. The papers reported that he accepted this explanation, but perhaps reluctantly, as suggested by his striking his leg on entering the cart, causing himself considerable pain. A due respect for social hierarchy prevailed even at the gallows. "They all behaved," one account concluded, "with a proper firmness and decency, in proportion to their former characters in life."[15]

The Perreaus waited quietly until "everything was settled proper for their reception." As the time approached for their execution, Sheriff Newnham left his coach and came to the brothers to bid farewell. "The Perreaus very politely, and with an air of innocent complacency, returned the compliment." The crucial moment in their drama had arrived. They mounted the cart and joined with the Ordinary in prayer. They spent ten minutes conversing with him. Daniel put his right hand on his heart and looked to heaven, apparently swearing that he and his brother were innocent. The crowd watched carefully for such signs. It was usual at the gallows for criminals to confess their crimes and ask the assembled as well as God for mercy. The words spoken on such an occasion, in the face of eternity, took on great significance. Villette reminded them that "God knew all." In this muddy and tragic business, here seemed the moment when all might be revealed. Of course, none of the witnesses could actually hear what was said. All they could observe were the movements and general deportment of the brothers. So the Perreaus, in turn, took care to authenticate their final statements. When the Ordinary made the usual request, that they "acknowledge the justice of their sentence," they instead handed him written documents and added "with great seriousness and solemnity, 'that the contents were strictly true.'"[16]

In these statements the Perreaus did not confess their guilt, as was usually done in the genre of the "last dying speeches." Instead they repeated the charges that they had made at their trials, that Mrs. Rudd was responsible for the crime. They were, at most, guilty of credulity. She had taken them in, and now she had perverted the course of justice itself. Robert said his only mistake was in believing everything that his brother and Mrs. Rudd had told him. Daniel too declared his innocence "with my last dying breath." He said that his infatuation had led him to place entire faith in his mistress. It was by "her artifices" that he had misled his brother. She "was a very wicked woman, with an infinite share of understanding." Daniel hoped that his statement would have "sufficient force" to impress "conviction on the minds of the benevolent and unprejudiced." He made great play of forgiving "even her to whose intrigues I am now about to fall an innocent sacrifice." He added that it was only his brother's "kindness and fraternal regard for my welfare and interest, which I verily believe led him to take the part he has done in this fatal business."[17] Every action, every statement the brothers made repeated the claim that they were the victims, the sacrifice, the injured.

In a familiar gesture, Robert gave the hangman and his assistant some money. Then the two brothers kissed each other. "At about five and thirty minutes after eleven the caps were drawn over their faces." "When the cart drew from under them they joined hands together, and in that manner launched into eternity." "When they had been turned off about two-thirds of a minute, their hands dropped from each other, and they died without the least apparent pain, amidst the prayers of an immense commiserating multitude." "Thus the two brothers," observed one paper, seeking to underline the melodramatic point, "in the same moment quitted that world which they had entered together."[18] It was a death meant to inspire belief, but it left many questions unanswered.

Two
ALARMING CRIMES AND UNSETTLING STORIES

ALTHOUGH EIGHTEENTH-CENTURY London was one of the largest cities in Europe, in 1775 it still had no "police" as we today think of that institution. The apprehension and prosecution of criminals were largely in the hands of the victims, aided by various semi-professional local peace officers such as constables and watchmen. If the victim apprehended a malefactor or had a suspicion of who was involved in a crime, he went to the local magistrate's office. The justice of the peace then had a number of options. In some instances he offered mediation in an attempt to reconcile the parties in the case. He might carefully cross-examine witnesses and issue search and seizure warrants to collect evidence. He might commit the offender to prison to await trial or release him on bail. Many of these decisions were a matter of routine. The normal business of justice seldom attracted much attention from the press or the public.

From the outset, the crime reported to the magistrates on March 11, 1775, was anything but ordinary. Justice William Addington, one of the magistrates of the police office at Bow Street, was unsettled when, on Saturday morning, a well-dressed man appeared before him with an alarming story of fraud and deception. As an experienced magistrate at London's foremost police office, he was used to dealing with a wide variety of crimes characteristic of the Covent Garden area. Bow Street saw a steady stream of pickpockets, prostitutes, and petty thieves brought before the justices. Addington was also an authority on England's vast and complicated criminal law.[1] But his experience offered him little help when confronted with the peculiar tale he heard from the elegant and polished gentleman. This man, Robert Perreau, a prominent London apothecary, said he had information to give of an elaborate scheme of forgery. The mention of the crime was enough to excite Addington's interest. It was a rare but much feared offense, a capital crime that often carried its perpetrator to the gallows. No doubt Addington's first thought was that Perreau had come to the office to report a forgery of which he had been the victim. Such would have been the usual expectation. But once Perreau began to speak, it quickly became clear that here was an episode to challenge Addington's skill.

The story Robert Perreau told seemed far-fetched, but it was supported by Perreau's friend Henry Dagge, a well-known attorney.[2] Perreau claimed that he had negotiated a forged bond at the instigation of a woman named Margaret Caroline Rudd. While Perreau presented himself as the innocent dupe of Mrs. Rudd, he asked for immunity from prosecution before he told his tale, and he signaled his willingness to appear as a witness against her. This request for a privilege that was usually granted to a suspect in order to secure his testimony against a confederate put Addington on his guard. It suggested, at the very least, that Perreau knew his story would cast him in a suspicious light. The ambiguity of Perreau's account of himself was troubling. He proclaimed his innocence even as he confessed that he had been responsible for uttering the forged instrument. Deliberately passing a forged note was as serious an act, according to the law, as creating it.

Addington insisted that Robert reveal all he knew before he would agree to swear him. As Perreau told his version of events, he mentioned that the bankers Robert and Henry Drummond were in possession of the forged bond. Before he proceeded further, the justice thought it proper to send for them to corroborate the story. He also sent a constable to secure the woman Rudd. Perreau reported that she could be found in a coach at the end of King Street, St. James Square.[3]

Whatever the justice may have hoped, the appearance of the Drummonds did little to clarify the situation. Despite their being the target of the crime, they evinced little enthusiasm for getting to the bottom of the case. The presence of Mrs. Rudd further clouded the issue. She was a small but elegant woman, well-spoken and intelligent. Both she and Perreau assumed a posture of injured innocence. At first Mrs. Rudd denied that Robert had any role in the forgery. But once she heard the substance of his evidence, she told a different tale, one that made her the victim of a foul conspiracy. She claimed that Robert, in collaboration with her "husband," Daniel Perreau, had decided to make her the sacrifice to their villainy. To support her accusation, she offered a harrowing account of how she had become involved in the crime. She confessed that she had written the bond but now said she had only done so at the point of a knife, held to her throat by Daniel. She made such a pitiful object as she told her tale, and she related it with such sincerity, that the justice felt uncertain how to proceed. At one point Addington seemed prepared to commit Rudd for the forgery and Perreau on a charge of uttering. He hesitated when one of the Drummonds said that, from what he knew, Robert might, in fact, be an innocent victim. As each witness spoke, one newspaper reported, the "stories grew more intricate." As the details multiplied, "such things came out" about Perreau that the justice "did not think it right to set him at liberty." In growing frustration, Addington decided to detain both Mrs. Rudd and Robert Perreau. Daniel, who had quietly joined his brother soon after Mrs. Rudd's arrival, was allowed to depart the office, since nothing the Drummonds said implicated him in the crime. Addington sent to the senior magistrate, Sir John Fielding, to know what he should do next. Fielding, who was at his country home in Brompton, replied that he could not attend that day, but he indicated that there was enough evidence to hold both parties until he could attend.[4]

The following day, it fell to Fielding to try to make sense of the conflicting accounts. There was no more qualified official in England to assume the challenge. Fielding was the chief magistrate at Bow Street. Since 1754, when he had succeeded his brother Henry, he had been the principal magistrate for Westminster. Famed as the leading criminal investigator in the metropolis, he was frequently consulted by the government as it grappled with crime. During his tenure as magistrate he was a leading advocate for new measures to reform the policing of the capital. He possessed a particular belief in the utility of newspapers and a confidence that improved communications would aid in the detection of crime. Perhaps no man in the country could match his experience with or knowledge of crime. The Perreau case was to test his patience and ability, as well as his faith in the contribution the press could make to the solution of criminal cases.[5]

Fielding listened attentively as the various participants in the case told their stories. Blind since the age of nineteen, he had become expert at detecting inconsistency or falsehood in the words spoken in his office. But the testimony offered to him, although it revealed an extensive fraud, failed to establish who was responsible for the crime. Perhaps the polished phrases of the well-spoken suspects made the task too difficult. Or it may have been the confusing conduct of each of the participants, at one moment suggestive of guilt, and at another open to a very different reading. Surely everyone hesitated before the awful responsibility of indicting such attractive people for a crime that might carry one or both to the gallows. Yet these early proceedings took on great significance in the days and months that followed. Pages would be devoted to an analysis of each sentence, as lawyers and letter writers, as well as the defendants themselves, sought to cast an action in a particular light. These narratives became the "facts" of the case. But the facts proved slippery, as even the most straightforward detail, upon reexamination, was shown to be susceptible to quite opposed interpretations.

THE DISCOVERY OF A FORGERY

Henry Drummond, the Charing Cross banker, was called to describe the detection of the crime. He reported that on January 15 or 16, 1775, Robert Perreau came to him requesting a loan of £1400. Drummond said that he had known Robert for several years as an apothecary and that he had "seen him in two or three families." He added that he was "well spoken of, and perfectly well respected." Nothing about the request struck Drummond as odd. Robert asked the "favour" of a loan. In doing so he relied upon the social connections between them. He assumed Drummond would know something of his income and status from his clientele and social relations. Many of the financial transactions among the London elite were made like this, on the basis of polite requests, supported by knowledge of personal creditworthiness, in private conversations. The apothecary explained that he had lately made a purchase in Suffolk or Norfolk for £12,000 or £14,000 (Drummond could not remember the exact details), and that this transaction produced the necessity for the loan. The banker responded that the title deeds to the estate would prove more than adequate security for such a loan. He would be happy to extend the sum if Perreau would leave the deeds with him. Robert replied that he could not do so as the purchase was still to be completed in the country, and thus he did not have them in his possession.[6]

At this impasse he suddenly proposed to Drummond that "he had got a bond of a gentleman, whose name he was not at liberty at that time to mention, but, that if I knew the person, he was sure that I could make no objection to it." The offer of such a bond, pledging the credit of a third party in order to raise money, was a familiar device in London financial circles. A bond, signed by some man of worth, was perfectly good security for a loan. But, Drummond added, "every thing depends upon the name, for some men's bonds are as good as other men's mortgages." Since everything depended on the identity of the guarantor, he could not give the apothecary the loan without knowing the name of the person who stood behind the paper. Perreau refused to divulge the identity of his supporter. No doubt the obscurity of this discussion of the bond aroused some misgivings in the banker. Robert's reputation might secure him a private conversation with Drummond; it could not overcome Drummond's caution when confronted with such a mysterious request. Faced with this reluctance, Perreau decided to offer Drummond the mortgage on a house he said he owned in Cavendish Square, worth £4000, as security. The banker found this offer acceptable. The next day Robert returned with the deed for the property and received the money. Since Perreau said he only needed the money for ten days, the banker asked for no more formal record of the transaction. If he had found Robert's behavior at all unusual, he did not let it stand in the way of a polite agreement made between respectable gentlemen.[7]

Robert failed to keep his promise; it was March 7 before the banker saw him again. But in his testimony Drummond gave no hint that he was uneasy at Perreau's delay in repaying the loan. The apothecary apologized for not keeping his word. Instead of offering to settle the account, though, he now asked for a new loan of £5000. He proposed to use £1400 of that amount to repay the earlier debt. The circumstances of the delay and the sudden request for an additional sum no doubt suggested to the banker that Perreau was experiencing financial difficulties. The apothecary, most likely anticipating such objections, now announced that "he had got leave of the gentleman, whose bond he formerly mentioned," to tell the man's name. Henry Drummond felt so uncomfortable with this renewed request that he called in his brother Robert to consult with him on the "propriety" of lending so much money. Both men were startled when Perreau produced the bond. It was a note for £7500, seemingly signed by the wealthy army agent William Adair. The Adair family name, and that of William Adair in particular, was well known in London financial circles. The firm of Adair and Bullock had dealt in army contracts for a number of years. Lord Rockingham, Lord Albemarle, and the Duke of Newcastle all had close contact with the business.[8] Henry Drummond had himself been an army agent from 1753 until 1772. His brother Robert had only recently persuaded him to give up the business and devote himself to the family bank. While an agent, he had become acquainted with Adair, and the latter had been a customer of the Drummond bank.[9]

The Drummonds were astonished at the note Robert offered them. They had dealt with Adair and knew his handwriting. "As soon as we saw it," Henry later testified, "we both expressed a disbelief of its being Mr. Adair's bond." The handwriting did not appear "the least like that of Adair." This attention to handwriting was a characteristic feature of eighteenth-century commercial life. So many financial transactions were carried out by notes of hand that one's best security lay in knowing the hand as well as the reputation of those with whom one dealt. Businessmen learned to pay careful attention to the way an associate signed his name. It might be said that one knew the customer's hand at least as well as his visage.[10] So the Drummonds were confident that something was amiss, but in this instance it was the very ease of detection that gave them pause. Forgeries were supposed to be difficult to detect. The conduct and circumstances of the person offering the note, rather than the note itself, were supposed to indicate a crime. Here, however, the note gave the plot away, while the conduct of the utterer seemed to speak of his innocence. Perreau appeared utterly unmoved by the Drummonds' discovery. On the contrary, he pointed to the signatures of the witnesses, Adair's solicitor and servant, as proof of its validity. He explained that he was a "particular friend" of Adair's, "that there were family connections between them." He hinted that Adair had borrowed money of him and that the bond was a way of settling their account. When asked whether he had actually seen Adair "execute the Bond," however, Perreau admitted he had not. The bankers remained skeptical. Although they had not dealt with the agent in recent years, they were certain that his signature had been forged. Still, as one brother later testified, "there was a delicacy; we did not chuse to say he had brought us a forged note." They had to be careful before raising the cry of forgery. The slightest hint of scandal would cast doubt upon the most important aspect of a respectable businessman's character, his creditworthiness. Furthermore, if they made an accusation and it proved false, it might imperil their own standing and lead to civil litigation. They allowed the apothecary to depart but asked him to return the next day.[11]

Henry Drummond confessed his surprise when Perreau returned two hours later. The apothecary told him that the suspicion cast on the bond had so "alarmed" him that he could not "be easy" until he had talked to Adair. Fortunately, he reported to him, he had encountered Adair as he was about to go riding. The latter had calmed his fears by acknowledging the writing as his own. Perreau added that Adair explicitly requested the bankers to let him have the money and assured them that he would repay the bond two months before it fell due. As an additional proof of the intimacy between Adair and his family, the apothecary produced a letter which he claimed came from Adair and which was signed "W. A." The brothers remained unconvinced; they asked Perreau to leave the bond with them so that they could look more deeply into the murky business. Drummond later said that he understated his doubts because he was desirous of securing the bond so that he could find out "whether it was really a good bond or no." Perreau readily left it, promising to call at eleven the next day.[12]

The Drummonds spent the intervening hours doing what they could to discover the truth of the matter. They made discreet inquiries. They showed the bond to a friend of Adair's, a Mr. Stephens of the Admiralty. Stephens and one of the brothers called upon Adair. By the time Perreau returned to them, the brothers were convinced that the note was not right. What continued to confuse them was Perreau's behavior, his insistence upon the bond's validity, and the stories he told to uphold his claim. Robert "grew very warm" at their suggestion of its being forged. They were reluctant to believe that he could be a party to such a fraud. The brothers felt a good deal of discomfort at their situation, discomfort that came out months later at the trial. Perreau acted like a man whose integrity had been questioned rather than one with guilty knowledge of a crime. He had an unblemished reputation and highly respectable connections. The Drummonds seemed to feel their predicament more acutely than Perreau did his own.[13]

Finally the Drummonds announced that only a visit to Adair would clear up the confusion. Perreau readily assented, even volunteering his carriage since it stood first at the door. This offer struck the brothers, since once again it spoke of a mind entirely composed, even in the face of a frightening charge. One brother told the justice that he observed Perreau carefully as he made this proposal, watching for any reaction that might betray guilt. "I looked steadfastly on his countenance, and could not see him alter in the least." The visit, however, was to bring more surprises.[14]

Adair was at home and greeted the bankers warmly, but he bowed only distantly to Perreau, "as a person he had never seen before." Drummond produced the bond and Adair said it was not his writing. Only at this point did Robert express surprise, saying to Adair, "Surely Sir, you are jocular." Adair made no reply, "but gave him a contemptuous look." Henry Drummond spoke sharply to the apothecary, advising that no one would joke when a "man's life was at stake." Perreau appeared startled and, according to one account, said "he had been strangely duped indeed." He asked Adair "if he did not know Mr. P of Pall-Mall (meaning his brother) and if his wife was not nearly related to him." Adair replied that he knew "no such people." Drummond pressed Robert to explain "what could all this mean." At the trial he spoke of how, during this meeting, he felt "wonder and astonishment at what had passed." His brother Robert told Perreau, in words that would come to sound prophetic, that he was "either the greatest fool, or the greatest rogue, that I ever saw." "I do not know," he added, "what to make of you."[15]

The conversation continued for some time until Perreau said that he had received the bond from his "sister, Mrs. Daniel Perreau," a woman he called his brother's wife. She could be found at his house in Golden Square. A carriage was dispatched to bring her to Adair's. Her arrival dramatically altered the character of the discussion. It considerably unsettled the three older men. They found themselves in the presence of a woman of perhaps thirty, well dressed and attractive, vivacious and intelligent. At a later date a newspaper would explain that her influence was "by no means owing to her beauty, of which she has a very small portion." She was of "middling size," thin, and had a "sallow complexion." But she possessed "a dark piercing eye, and fine teeth." "Her dress and tone of voice" were distinguished and "captivating." She would, the paper concluded, "be an object of attention in the politest circle." To these qualities she added "an uncommon degree of understanding and presence of mind, which never forsake her on any exigency."[16]

The woman they understood to be Mrs. Perreau immediately seized control of the situation. She energetically defended Robert. When asked about the crime, she admitted giving the bond to Perreau, "and, in short, took the whole upon herself, and acknowledged herself to be the forger of the bond, and everything." She quickly added that "nobody was meant to be injured; that it would all be paid, that she never meant to injure us or any body." The

Drummonds expressed doubts that a woman had the ability to carry off such a scheme. They turned to Perreau, asking him to explain how he could have claimed familiarity with Adair if he was simply the innocent dupe in his sister-in-law's plot. "We could get nothing from him," the bankers reported, "but that he was an innocent man, and he did not mean to impose on us, and that his sister could explain all." Robert remained cool and reserved. It was his "sister" who animated the confrontation with her passion. She continued to take the crime "upon herself, expressed much regard for Robert Perreau, and begged that an innocent man who had a family might not suffer." She asked to speak to Adair separately, but he declined, saying that she was a stranger to him and that the Drummonds should be present at any interview. In an attempt to shake her story, Robert Drummond remarked that the bond appeared to be written in a "masculine hand." She instantly took a sheet of paper and showed them how she had written the note. The brothers were convinced by this proof but they were also uncomfortable with her spontaneous admission. The Drummonds hastened to reassure her that they had no intention of "ensnaring" her. Lest the paper be used to incriminate her and it seem that they had taken advantage of her openness, they destroyed it. Despite the proofs she offered to demonstrate her guilt, they treated her with great care. Three or four hours of continued discussion and much pleading on her part produced little that was new. Finally Perreau asked if her confession did not clear up the matter. When one of the Drummonds responded no, his level of agitation noticeably increased.[17]

In a quest for more information, the bankers and Adair sent for Daniel Perreau, in hopes that he could cast more light on these dark matters. As the brother of one of the suspects and the supposed husband of the other, he might have something material to contribute. Daniel, when he arrived at Adair's, solemnly declared "that he was quite a stranger to the whole affair." He "seemed greatly amazed," Robert Drummond later testified, "and shrugged his shoulders." "I do not believe he said ten words." The strange immobility of the brothers contrasted sharply with the energy of Mrs. Perreau. She acted as if she had the situation well under control. She spoke forcefully, elaborating her story, appealing to the three older men to believe her. They could not but be astonished at the ease with which she told a tale that could only put her life in peril.[18]

The Drummonds and Adair found themselves facing a conundrum that became increasingly unpleasant as the hours passed. Daniel's wife not only took upon herself complete responsibility for the crime; she even offered con-clusive proof of her role. Yet she presented an affecting portrait as the good wife and mother prepared to sacrifice herself to free her brother-in-law. Robert Perreau, on the other hand, continued to protest his innocence. Daniel said nothing to contradict either story. The older men, no doubt, found it difficult to accept the description of the episode offered by the Perreaus, since they had trouble believing a woman could occupy the chief role in such a business. At this juncture one of the Drummonds "signified his intention of troubling himself no further in the matter." There seemed to be clear evidence of an at-tempt to perpetrate a fraud, but given the class of people involved and the gender of the prime suspect, neither the Drummonds nor Adair showed much zeal for probing deeper. No money, after all, had been lent or lost, since the deed to the house covered the original loan. Robert Perreau in proclaiming his innocence, and Mrs. Rudd in announcing her guilt, seemed utterly sincere. Most especially, the insistent performance of the attractive Mrs. Rudd pro-duced a reluctance to proceed. The Drummonds had initially sent for a con-stable to attend them at Adair's, but once Mrs. Rudd confessed, they sent him away. Rather than prosecute her, the Drummonds "were willing to tread on the whole affair, as no person had been injured."[19]

When the three men permitted the Perreaus to depart, they probably as-sumed that this embarrassing episode was at an end. [20] It must therefore have been disturbing for the Drummonds, three days after their interview with the Perreaus, to be summoned to Bow Street to face the examination of a magis-trate. In all probability nothing more would have come of the episode had Robert Perreau not decided to go to the police office. His unexpected action produced as many conflicting interpretations as his conduct during the inter-view with the Drummonds. Robert later explained that he only wanted to clear his name. Others charged that he sought protection because he knew other crimes were bound to come to light. Whatever the explanation, his decision was a fateful one. Once the justices, and the press, showed an interest in the case, it could not be suppressed. Forgery was too serious a crime to ignore.

THE CRIME OF FORGERY

The crime of forgery presented its victims with difficult calculations. The authorities regularly pronounced the offense one of the most dangerous threats to the life of a commercial nation. The legislature repeatedly enacted measures to make the prosecution of the crime easier and to bring new sorts of forgery under the protection of the capital code. One pamphlet on the Perreau case spoke of forgery as "destructive to commerce and its welfare." It was "a crime of the deepest dye, as well as prejudicial to society in general." "Though it is not half a century since forgery was rendered a capital offense," the author noted, "yet even with the gallows before their eyes, forgers abound more than ever." Such was the danger that haunted a country growing richer, one where the vast circulation of paper instruments formed the life's blood of an expanding economy. One correspondent to a paper complained that "forgery, drawing and re-drawing, and frauds upon paper currency, particularly in the glare of life, are now pretty nearly reduced to a traffic, and notwithstanding the wholesome laws that we are possessed of, for the security of property, that property is always in danger of wicked invaders."[21]

As the Perreau case demonstrated, the crime struck at a personal level as well. A gentleman of business depended upon reputation in dealing with other men of property and standing. The signature on a piece of paper was the feeble and exposed link in many of the transactions among people of wealth. No doubt because of the absence of settled forms and institutions to reduce the risk, and because so many credit relationships were so personal, forgery touched the lives of the wealthy like no other crime. It suggested both the ease with which someone could appropriate the signature that protected one's property and the fragility of reputation, the only guarantee that one could depend upon in dealing with acquaintances in a city like London. The betrayal of a relationship and the calling into question of the entire system of trust based on reputation, not only that of the forger but also of his victim, sent shock waves through the public. A report of forgery often attracted special notice in the newspapers. Although only three or four forgery cases a year were prosecuted at the Old Bailey, they aroused an anxiety out of proportion to the rarity of the offense. Because the crime was viewed as so serious, the legal authorities seldom pardoned those who were convicted. Despite the fact that the condemned often possessed powerful connections who worked hard for a commutation of the sentences, such appeals rarely worked. Thus the punishment had the paradoxical effect of heightening the dread produced by the appearance of the crime, casting a gloom over the proceedings.[22]

While judges intoned about the seriousness of the crime, prosecutors, as well as those who witnessed trials and executions, felt more ambivalent toward such episodes. Those accused of forgery were often of the same social milieu as the prosecutor. The crime might be committed by a clerk, a business associate, or a neighbor. A prosecutor might experience uneasiness at the thought of hurrying an acquaintance to his death and a sensitivity to the judgments his neighbors might make. The effect of pamphlet accounts of forgery cases further increased this anxiety. The published "Lives" of forgers often told pathetic tales of advantaged and promising youths who fell afoul of the law. Through bad luck or, more frequently, the pursuit of an extravagant life-style, they were led into severe financial difficulties. They then abused the trust of others and their own skills in a desperate attempt to secure the funds that might save them. These tales touched the lives of respectable readers, who could easily imagine the circumstances and emotions that led the offenders to the crime. Repeatedly, in the early stages of this case, people expressed a reluctance to proceed. One rumor reported that an upholsterer named Bradshaw had received an order for £500 worth of furniture from Mrs. Rudd to be paid for with a bond from William Adair. She had told him confidentially that "she was his natural daughter." Bradshaw refused to believe the tale, but "he never mentioned the affair till now lest I suppose detection might be attended with trouble."[23] Similar qualms convinced the Drummonds to drop the matter after the first discovery of the forgery.

The Drummonds, however, were not always swayed by such tender feelings for the accused. On several earlier occasions they had suffered from forgeries. At the Old Bailey in October 1774, they prosecuted William Lewis for forging an order for the payment of £15, purportedly drawn in the name of John Pownall. The case was like many others of the period. Lewis was a young man who served as a draftsman in Lord Hillsborough's office. He "was far from an abandoned character" and lived with his mother. A skilled worker, he was "a most ingenious copyist, and could counterfeit copper-plate writing to astonishing exactness." The clerks at the bank had no trouble connecting him to the crime. His counsel offered no defense other than the testimony of several respectable witnesses that he was sober and honest. Despite their pleas, Lewis was convicted and executed. He died as all criminals were supposed to do, a fitting "example of penitence."[24] The Drummonds' rather different treatment of the Perreaus and Mrs. Rudd was testimony to the different light in which they regarded these suspects.

During his first session with the suspects, Fielding had made no more progress than Addington in making sense of this tangled business. But by the new week the case had assumed more alarming dimensions. It was revealed that, far from being a single instance, several forgeries had been perpetrated over a considerable length of time. Rumors circulated through polite circles and found their way into the press that Adair had been tricked out of £20,000, while Sir Thomas Frankland was supposed to have lost £9000. These sums and names indicated a more sinister scheme of deceit and betrayal. Fielding himself, as he was leaving town after examining the witnesses, encountered Dr. Brooke, an old friend of the Perreaus', who told him of having a bond of Adair's as security for a loan of £1500 to Daniel Perreau. Here was the first information linking Daniel to the crime. Fielding requested that Brooke carry this news back to Bow Street with a letter ordering that Daniel be taken up. Never far from his brother's side, Daniel was seized while visiting his brother in prison.[25]

The large number of forgeries increased the authorities' sense of urgency. But the sharp conflict between the stories told by the Perreaus and Mrs. Rudd made it difficult to decide who should be charged. The Perreaus had negotiated all the instruments, but they continued to protest that they were merely the dupes of Mrs. Rudd. Given the testimony of the Drummonds, it appeared that the notes were in her handwriting. Yet in her testimony to Addington she had claimed to be the unwilling agent of their plot. Further contributing to the confusion, she had called herself Mrs. Perreau, while the brothers insisted on calling her Mrs. Rudd. Most troubling of all, the magistrates found it hard to discover a motive for the tales they had been told. The justices encountered conspiracies every day. Typically they made a deal with one of the accomplices, who then agreed to testify against the other parties. In return the informant would be granted crown witness protection against being prosecuted for the crime. Usually in such cases the guilt of all the participants was clear. Here, however, the case was strikingly different. The parties each seemed to be maneuvering for protection, while claiming at the same time to be entirely innocent. The Perreaus and Mrs. Rudd acted as if they were deeply offended that they should be subjected to a criminal accusation. Each offered the most sincere protestations of innocence, coupled with charges of duplicity and entrapment on the part of his or her accuser.

Among the many disturbing aspects of the case was the uncanny fact that the brothers were identical twins. In a case where everything hinged on identity, key witnesses had a difficult time distinguishing the brothers. When the scrivener who had drawn up the bond was asked to indicate who had given him instruction, he paused a long time before answering, and then replied that he was not positive. He swore that he filled up the bond for one of the Perreaus, "but that they resembled each other so nearly, he really knew not which." One newspaper assured its readers that the witness was not being evasive in not identifying a customer who had been eight or ten times at his office. "The strong and exact resemblance the two unfortunate brothers bore to each other, both with respect to their features and figures, would render a mistake of the one for the other extremely probable." Even a tailor who had worked for Daniel for many years, on visiting the brothers in prison, "where both sat together," talked for a time to Robert, under the mistaken impression that he was Daniel.[26]

It was not until the following Wednesday morning that Fielding, joined by his two colleagues, held the formal commitment hearing. Although by this time the participants had repeated their stories several times, the case proved irresistible theater, especially to the rich and fashionable circles within which the Perreaus and Mrs. Rudd moved. Increasing numbers of people had descended on Bow Street to observe each successive stage of the pretrial proceedings. By this particular morning the press of the crowd had become almost unmanageable. "A great number of persons of rank and distinction sent their compliments to Sir John Fielding to procure places for them." "So large a Concourse of People assembled themselves," while "an amazing Croud still pressed for Admittance," that Fielding adjourned the business to the Guildhall in Westminster. This structure too was soon thronged with people; it was "so entirely full by a Quarter past Eleven, that the Magistrates with some Difficulty passed to the Bench." The newspapers made much of the assembly's social status, reporting that "a great number of noblemen and gentlemen of the first distinction" were in attendance. The case had captured the public imagination.[27]

Fielding, as imposing as ever, secured a "profound silence" and proceeded to interrogate the parties "in the closest and most solemn manner." The appearance of the accused made a striking impression. All three were fashionably dressed and coiffed, as the papers reported in considerable detail. Their costume as well as their poise suggested that they belonged among the well-heeled members of the audience rather than in the dock. Witnesses were called in order to provide the evidence upon which the charge would be laid. Henry

Drummond was sworn first. He repeated the story of Robert offering him the bond and described how Mrs. Rudd took upon herself the responsibility for writing it. A scrivener named Wilson was called to identify the bond. He testified that he had drawn it, along with eight or nine others, for a person he thought was Robert Perreau. The testimony of two further witnesses confirmed the rumors that the case involved a wider scheme of forgery. Dr. Brooke told of taking a bond in Adair's name for £3100 as security for a loan of £1500. Like the Drummonds before him, Dr. Brooke expressed his reluctance to prosecute, afraid, he said, that "it might hurt him in his profession." Fielding assured him, however, that the Bench was bound to act out of a sense of their duty "to promote public justice," and Brooke grudgingly assented. More surprising was the evidence of Admiral Sir Thomas Frankland, who spoke of accepting several bonds in return for loans to Robert Perreau. Frankland had a reputation as an astute businessman, and the court as well as the press were puzzled to know why he would lend Robert so much money without consulting with Adair, a man who "lives in London, and is every day to be seen." The admiral explained that the apothecary attended upon his family and he had always taken him to be an honest man. But Frankland confessed another motive that weighed heavily with him, and his admission lent substance to gossip that had been circulating since news of the case first broke. He reported that he had met Mrs. Rudd, saying she passed in their circle as Mrs. Daniel Perreau, and that he had "always understood" that she "was either a ward, or a natural daughter of Mr. Adair's." He had heard that Adair "was so fond, and so much attached to her, that he intended to do great things for her and her husband, and talked of a seat in Parliament, and purchasing him a baronetage." Frankland's testimony, with its hints of relationships still to be made clear, helps explain the ever expanding sensation created by the episode. But it also made the justices' decision about how to proceed that much more difficult.[28]

At this point in the hearing the accused were asked to explain their conduct. Robert replied that when he offered the various bonds to raise money upon them, he considered them good. He denied any knowledge of their forgery and particularly disavowed his participation in a scheme to defraud Drummond, Brooke, or Frankland. Mrs. Rudd was challenged about her acceptance of responsibility for the forgeries before the Drummonds and Adair. She responded that she had made the confession not because she was guilty but in the hope of saving Robert's life.[29]

It would take all of Fielding's skill to sort out responsibility for what seemed by now a clever and extensive scheme. Since forgery was an especially difficult crime to prove, as the actual act of writing was usually done in private, the prosecution had to be constructed out of circumstantial and fragmentary evidence.[30] The public act of uttering, or attempting to pass a forged instrument, was more easy to establish. It involved the suspect in an attempt to negotiate the bond, and a great deal was done and said at such moments, before witnesses, that might help to determine guilt or innocence. Nonetheless, since an individual might offer a note without knowing it was forged, the authorities had to exercise great care—often involving a psychological assessment of the accused's behavior and motives—before concluding that utterer and forger were part of a common criminal effort. Thus far in this puzzling case the justices had proceeded slowly, more fearful than usual of charging an innocent person. Their caution stemmed in part from the very stories told by the Perreaus and Rudd. Each attributed to the other party an extraordinary ability to play a false part and to deceive an unsuspecting observer. They also characterized themselves as having been led to apparently illegal actions by the most admirable of impulses, a noble if misguided loyalty and an excess of affection. Each spoke of how, only at this extreme moment, when life itself hung in the balance, did he or she recognize the horrendous error in judgment and the fundamental unworthiness of the person in whom he or she had placed such blind trust.

After hearing their responses, Mrs. Rudd's counsel, a solicitor named John Bailey, asked if "she chose to be admitted an evidence for the King, and to unravel the whole of this iniquitous business." She replied that "upon these terms," she would "tell all she knew." Here was the second fateful decision in the history of this case. These exchanges revealed that Fielding had decided to make Mrs. Rudd a crown witness. Critics would later charge that the justices, by their actions, had fostered the impression that "Mrs. Rudd could not possibly be the principal actor in this iniquitous business."[31] But Fielding had good reasons for following the course he did. He had become convinced that only the evidence of one of the confederates would bring the crime home to the participants. In choosing between Robert Perreau and Mrs. Rudd he was guided by legal custom. Women were often taken before London magistrates charged with serious crimes, but they usually appeared as the accomplices of men. In such cases the women were, for the most part, treated as the subordinate partner in the commission of the crime. This was especially true when the man and woman appeared to be husband and wife (even if the relationship had not been sanctioned by the Church). The law, one author wrote, assumed that the wife acted "by the coercion of her husband," and "such coercion is always presumed until the contrary appears in evidence." As many respectable witnesses had testified, Mrs. Rudd passed as the wife of Daniel Perreau.[32]

But Mrs. Rudd had more than judicial custom in her favor. Her spontaneous confession made to the Drummonds and initially offered before Addington might be overlooked, or rather recast in such a way as to substantiate the portrait she drew of herself as a woman of feeling whose actions were guided by her love for Daniel and regard for Robert. Her subsequent story of being forced at knife point to forge the bond accorded with male expectations of gender roles. From what the justices knew of the story, she might well appear to be what she claimed, an injured woman who suffered insult and abuse at the hands of ungentlemanly males. Certainly the behavior of the brothers seemed ungenerous, as they attempted to portray her as the sole instigator of the crime. It might be seen as treacherous, as one later commentator noted. After her attempt to lay down her life for them, one melodramatic version went, "they, with remorseless barbarity,—a barbarity more disgraceful and more detestable still, perhaps, than even the crimes with which they stand charged, would, in return for such exalted sentiments of generosity, have treacherously sacrificed that life, to save their own. To exempt themselves from the gallows," the author concluded, "they would coolly, and without compunction, have devoted to it an innocent and helpless woman."[33] This was an easier interpretation to accept than one that cast the Perreaus in the unmanly pose of naive and passive instruments of a more sinister intelligence. The effect of Mrs. Rudd's performance reinforced the conclusion. "She gave her testimony with a great deal of modesty, and without hesitation." One reporter remarked upon her "faltering, pathetic voice," while others were more impressed by her composure. Mrs. Rudd's attractive voice was uniquely adapted to appeal to the blind magistrate. Her story, by turns pathetic and angry, called forth a chivalric response among the men who heard her for the first time.[34]

The tale she now told, over the next two sessions, increased the sense of astonishment already expressed in press commentary. It was rambling and disjointed in part, full of miscellaneous detail more concerned with drawing a particular portrait of character or settling a score than with illuminating a crime, but nonetheless effective, largely because it coincided so completely with the impression she created. Rudd began by identifying herself as the daughter of "one of the first noblemen in Scotland." In her youth she had married

Mr. Rudd. The marriage did not work out and she soon parted from him but retained possession of a fortune worth £13,000. A short time later she became attached to Daniel Perreau, came to think of herself as his wife, and employed this vast sum to aid him. She said she never regarded him as "a man of fortune" but believed he had an income of about £300 a year. It was not his wealth but his person and manner that attracted her. All was well for a time, until the war scare over the Falklands. Then Daniel became "very uneasy and could not sleep at night," because, as he soon confessed, he had lost £1400 "gaming in the Alley." She heard him say that "he got his intelligence from, and was indemnified by William Adair." Soon she made other disquieting discoveries. She found out that he was a bankrupt who regularly ran into debt. Still, she suppressed her concern because he always had money, and "she believed he had large transactions in the funds." She continued to have a "great regard for him"; they had three children together, and, until lately, she "always thought he loved her." Only in recent days had she begun to suspect that Daniel might set her aside as he began to talk about finding a lady of fortune to marry. Before this time she had always felt at home in the Perreau family, adding that Robert, in particular, had treated her well. She had such a high regard for him "that till this last instance of cruelty in charging her with knowing any thing of these bonds, she would have laid down her life to serve him."[35]

When it came to describing the specific facts of the case, Mrs. Rudd told a riveting tale in exacting detail. Fielding "interrogated her in the closest and most solemn manner" about the actual forgery. Rudd said Robert Perreau had brought her a bond purporting to be Adair's, dated January 25, 1775. He also produced a letter and asked her if she could imitate Adair's signature. He told her that she must write the name, as his life was in danger if he did not raise £5000. He went on to say that he would have employed another to do the deed but that the man was away at the time. She told him to leave the bond and that night showed it to Daniel. He too urged her to sign it, saying that if she did not, their lives would be in danger. On several other occasions he repeated the request, and on March 6 he came to her insisting that there was no longer time for delay. Faced with this demand, she "professed a sincere inclination to serve either him or his brother, but on her knees implored him not to oblige her to forge the name." He then drew a knife and, in a violent rage, threatened to kill her if she did not sign. As he stood over her with the drawn weapon, she wrote the name. "She called God to witness, that this was all she knew of the transaction, and that she never once heard of a bond given to Sir

Thomas Frankland or Dr. Brooke." In discussing these other forgeries, she admitted that she had received £4000 from Robert, which he had raised from Frankland, but she assumed that the loan was simply from an old friend. She passed the money on to Daniel, she testified, who used it to pay for their new house on Harley Street, Cavendish Square. As she concluded her narrative, she swore to the truthfulness of all the information she had given.[36]

Extravagant as it was, Mrs. Rudd's testimony gained support when James Adair of Soho Square, an important dealer in Irish linens and a relation of William Adair's, was called as a witness. He said that she had come to him soon after the forgery was detected, told him the story she had related in court, and asked his advice. Adair knew Mrs. Rudd because, several years before, she had brought him a letter from her Uncle Stewart, a man with whom Adair dealt in the north of Ireland. She had first approached him for help in dealing with her husband, Valentine Rudd. Later she sought to renew the acquaintance and told him that she was living honorably with Daniel Perreau. She made strenuous efforts to deepen her relationship with Adair. At the later trial of Robert Perreau, a servant testified that she went "two or three times" to visit Adair, once ran into him at Soho Square, and had sent him a present of French pears. "Mrs. James Adair," he reported, "called once to pay her a laying-in visit."[37] Unbeknownst to Adair, Mrs. Rudd had made a great deal of their connection. Adair, when he saw her on that March day, only knew that he had resisted her attempts at greater familiarity. But because of her distress and his connection with her uncle, he heard her out. Only later, after he heard the reports of her claim that he had given her money, did his fury rise. He wrote a confidential letter to his son, a lawyer attending the assize circuit, on the Monday when the details of the crime first became widely known.

> It is extremely fortunate that your mother and I have so long stood out
> against the artful attempt which that wicked woman Mrs. Perreau has
> repeatedly made to bring on an intimacy between the two families. I
> believe you knew of an invitation to us all before you left town to dine
> with them and that we had declined it in such a manner as to prevent
> a repetition of it in future. It was well we did so, for we now find it
> was to answer a deep laid plan of imposing upon others by the appear-
> ance of such intimacy.[38]

Despite these private reservations, Adair's testimony tended to support the story offered by Mrs. Rudd. He simply answered the questions put to him, without volunteering his suspicions. He declined to make public his personal feelings for or knowledge of Mrs. Rudd but merely repeated what she had told him, "that her husband was a wicked villain, and had forced her to commit a forgery." Coming from Adair, a gentleman of recognized probity, these words had a decisive impact. They lent some substance to her claim of high connections and seemed to confirm that she had spontaneously told the truth before she had had time to consider the prospect of arrest and trial. His account swayed the justices, in part because it conformed to the conclusions they had drawn from the behavior of Mrs. Rudd. It completed a picture, supported by substantial circumstantial evidence, that cast Mrs. Rudd as an unwilling accomplice to the unscrupulous brothers in their scheme to obtain vast sums of money. The mysterious conduct of Robert in reporting the crime, the lies he told the Drummonds, the assumptions about male agency, the apparently cowardly action of the brothers in betraying Mrs. Rudd, especially in contrast to her seemingly heroic behavior—all of these considerations seemed to point in one direction. The brothers were bound over for trial at the Old Bailey and confined in Newgate.[39]

At the completion of the formalities, Mrs. Rudd was admitted to bail, entering into a recognizance for £200, finding two "respectable tradesmen," a poulterer and a butcher, to act as sureties in the sum of £100 each. Many, like James Adair, believed the rumor that "these men were procured for the purpose by others who did not chuse to appear themselves." He assumed that she would "go off," that there then would be insufficient evidence to convict the brothers, and that they would be acquitted. The more knowing assumed that the case would not culminate in the punishment of any of the parties. Some were puzzled at the plotters' seeming ineptness; they had missed two opportunities to escape the consequences of their deeds. They might have accepted the decision of the Drummonds to tread upon the business, or the suspects might have fled to the Continent, as other perpetrators of large-scale frauds had done. The *Gentleman's Magazine* cited a rumor that, "in their first agitation, it had been consulted either to make their escape, or, in case that should be found impracticable, that Mrs. Rudd should acknowledge the signature, as most likely to escape punishment, and procure for the two brothers their liberty."[40] This was not the story arrived at by the justices at Bow Street, but it was a version of events widely held among the more "worldly" in polite London circles. No one could quite believe that this affair would amount to anything more than another scandalous exposure of financial misdeeds among the fashionable that had filled the papers in recent years.

In the immediate wake of the hearings, the press was filled with praise for Fielding. "The great pains that was taken to come at the real truth of this business," editorialized the *Middlesex Journal,* "does singular honour to Sir John Fielding." The commendation awarded him was accompanied by a sympathetic treatment of the beneficiary of his decision, Mrs. Rudd. "The solemnity, that was with so much propriety assumed by the Bench on this occasion, joined to the plaintive tone of Mrs. Rudd's voice; the artless manner in which she told her story, and the decency of her whole deportment, produced a scene so truly pathetic, as drew tears from many of the spectators."[41] Despite the unseemly scramble for places at the hearing, which produced a good deal of hostile comment, the proceedings associated with this case seemed to vindicate British justice. For a brief moment the papers celebrated a process that not only delivered the "truth" but gallantly rescued a vulnerable and deserving woman. The brothers had already earned the appellation of the "unfortunate" Perreaus. This adjective said nothing about their guilt; it described their situation and the inexorable fate that awaited them. "Many people," one paper reported, "seemed affected at their unfortunate situation."[42] The phrase referred to an end people could already foresee. The story of the Perreaus seemed to belong to a familiar genre, popular gallows literature, according to which the brothers had fallen victim to their own cupidity. They had abused trust in a desperate effort to avoid ruin. They had been detected, and the law demanded their sacrifice, so that other people caught in a similar predicament would have an additional motive to avoid immoral behavior. Punishment in eighteenth-century England was excessive, and its excess was a crucial element in the theater of justice. The brothers were not simply "bad"; they were unfortunate. The poignancy of their situation was supposed to enlist the feelings of polite society.

ROBERT'S TRIAL

Early on the morning of June 1, the brothers' long awaited trial took place at the Old Bailey, the main criminal court for London and Middlesex. This court usually attracted an audience representing a cross-section of London society, but the Perreau case drew a more fashionable crowd, which convened early in hopes of gaining entrance. "There was a most amazing crowd," one paper reported; "every avenue to the court being filled with well dressed people; who offered very large sums for admittance; some of the gallery-keepers had the modesty to demand two guineas in the morning for admittance, and one guinea and a half was actually given." So intense was the competition for seats that the *Morning Post* told of an unseemly squabble between the London grand jury and the Lord Mayor over the control of the jurymen's gallery. The contest threatened to delay the trial; "the foreman … replied, that they determined not to give up their claim, nor would they do any business until they had possession of the keys" to the gallery. Not only did the cream of London society pack the court but, it was said, several gentlemen had traveled from Birmingham especially to attend the trial.[43]

Most trials at the Old Bailey were hurried affairs. Rarely did the accused have legal counsel; perhaps no more than 2 percent of defendants in 1775 had such assistance. Eighteenth-century English justice offered no presumption of innocence; the burden of proof lay with the accused to disprove the prosecution evidence. The belief was that, with the judge to guard against abuse, the court was most likely to learn the truth by observing the deportment, words, and character of the accused. "It requires no manner of Skill to make a plain and honest Defense," wrote William Hawkins, early in the century, "which in Cases of this Kind is always the best." Few defendants had the skill or self-confidence to cross-examine prosecution witnesses. Many remained silent or mumbled a few words about their innocence. More important was the quality of the witnesses a defendant could produce to sustain an alibi or testify to character. Thus trials tended to be short; "many could only have lasted a few minutes." The loud, seemingly chaotic courtroom, the businesslike actions of judges and clerks, the dazed appearance of the accused—this was the normal experience of eighteenth-century justice. The contrast between these usual trials and the Perreau proceedings could not have been more striking, in terms of either length or the quality of their counsel. Daniel's trial lasted two hours, while Robert's took nine, and few cases displayed such an array of legal talent. The parties to the case drew from the elite of the English bar, each side employing three or four barristers.[44]

Robert Perreau was tried first, an arrangement that may have hinted at a measure of favor accorded the brothers. Certainly after the trials Mrs. Rudd would charge that powerful forces had been at work behind the scenes to secure every advantage for the Perreaus. The challenge of convicting Robert appeared formidable. He seemed in every way to have a stronger case than his brother. He had a better reputation in respectable circles; his conduct and the words of Mrs. Rudd argued for his innocence.

At the outset the prosecution announced that it was abandoning the charge of forgery and would instead seek a conviction for uttering and publishing a forged note. They adopted this strategy because of the difficulty in proving the actual forgery. Uttering was always the easier offense to establish, for it was an act committed in public. The prosecution could produce witnesses who described details surrounding the presentation of the false instrument, and from such details it could assemble circumstantial evidence that suggested guilty knowledge on the part of the accused. Still, such a charge presented difficulties, for a jury had to be convinced that the inference of guilty knowledge was well founded. Forgery trials often produced a minute inspection of every aspect of a transaction, and any suggestion of nervousness was seized upon as implying a consciousness of guilt. The most important proof, however, was evidence that the accused had lied at any point during the exchange. In many forgery trials, a lie about one's name or address formed the crucial evidence that secured a conviction. A lie proved that the accused had something to hide and was capable of the kind of deception a forgery implied. It raised doubts about whether one's word or any other aspect of his appearance could be relied upon. And it created a powerful presumption of guilt.

The trial began with Henry Drummond repeating the story he had told at Bow Street. He spoke again of the many puzzling features of the case, including the fact that the writing did "not the least" look like Adair's hand and Robert's surprising nonchalance when the forgery was exposed. He told of Mrs. Rudd's appearance at Adair's, of how she took the crime upon herself and proclaimed Robert's innocence. He even described how she had proved to their satisfaction that the handwriting on the note was hers. For the most part the prosecution was content to let the evidence speak for itself. One spectator thought that its presentation was "the most kind and moderate I ever saw." But the lawyers placed great emphasis upon the false statements Robert had made to the Drummonds about seeing William Adair on the day he presented the note and about Adair being well known to him. The circumstances of the actual drawing up of the note also told against him. A scrivener, Richard Wilson, said that Robert had come to him in late February or early March with a request to draw up a bond. Robert gave Wilson specific written instructions for creating the instrument, and although the bond included no names, the directions mentioned William Adair. Wilson testified that the apothecary told him to date the bond for January 25. To prosecution lawyers this detail suggested an intention on Robert's part to make the instrument conform to the story he had told Henry Drummond at their first meeting in January. Still more damaging to the defendant, Wilson told the court that Perreau had ordered him to burn the paper after he was finished. Here was further evidence that Robert knew he had something to hide. The paper only survived because Wilson forgot his promise.[45] Having pointed out the suspicious aspects of Robert's conduct, the prosecution rested.

Robert Perreau's defense was managed by an exceptional group of lawyers. Joining John Dunning, a leading advocate of his age, were Edward Bearcroft, James Wallace, and William Lucas.[46] They were faced with the daunting task of constructing their version of events within the limits imposed by contemporary practice. In theory there were severe restrictions on the points at which defense counsel could intervene in the trial. In practice, and despite the relative infrequency of legal defense, talented members of the bar had developed effective strategies for circumventing the limitations on their participation. Robert's defense team showed how a clever lawyer could reshape the character of a criminal trial. Not surprisingly, they got Drummond to repeat his doubts about Robert's guilt when he first suspected the forgery. In response to a question from counsel about whether he complied with Drummond's request to leave the bond "as the most innocent man would have done," the witness replied, "Yes, readily." Drummond conceded that even after repeated expressions of certainty that the bond was forged, Robert "did not once ask to have the bond away with him." But his counsel went beyond such obvious tactics. Through a sophisticated examination of defense witnesses, they offered one shocking revelation after another concerning the background to the forgeries. They were not content simply to refute the prosecution case; their goal was to put Mrs. Rudd on trial.[47]

If Robert's defense was powerful and well orchestrated, his own speech was its crowning moment. Defense counsel were not permitted to deliver a summation. English practice adhered to the belief that the words and manner of the accused, speaking in his or her own defense, provided a unique opportunity for the court to assess the defendant's truthfulness. Just as Drummond had looked carefully at Robert Perreau when the banker challenged the bond, so the jury now studied Robert as he offered his statement. His performance "took above an hour" to complete, and the newspapers were full of admiration for the poise and eloquence of his delivery. He spoke in "a very masterly manner," offering "a long and well-connected defence." Holding his notes in his hands, he "made one of the most ingenious, classical, and best directed defences we recollect to have ever read or heard."[48] Few could have known at the time what became general knowledge later, that the statement had been written by the playwright Richard Cumberland, whose assistance had been enlisted by a friend of the Perreau family, Lady Frances Burgoyne. The speech submitted by Cumberland was deemed so compelling that, when it was shown to Robert's counsel, he had not altered a syllable. It is doubtful that his contemporaries would have been upset had they known the truth of its composition, though, for they judged the power of the performance rather than the source of the words.[49] The speech proposed, in the most persuasive terms, an alternative explanation of the facts that had become so well known to the public in the preceding months.

Robert began by explaining why he had gone to Bow Street in March. His concern with his reputation and his conscience had led him to bring this "transaction into [the] light." "I have voluntarily sought," he added for emphasis, "that imprisonment, which guilt never invites." He had looked forward to this trial for the opportunity it presented to vindicate his conduct. Many witnesses were ready to testify to the regularity of his life and the sincerity of his "calling." There was, he implied, no trace of the difficulties that usually led men into forgery. "I have followed no pleasure, nor launched into any expenses; there is not a man living who can charge me with neglect or dissipation." On the contrary, his life presented the very picture of a successful, happy, and upright existence. He earned a reasonable competence with which to support a wife and three children. "In short," concluded Robert, "we were as happy as affluence and innocence could make us, till this affliction came on us by surprise, and I was made the dupe of a transaction, from whose criminality, I call God, the searcher of all hearts, to witness, I am now as free as I was upon the day of my birth."[50]

Having sketched his own character, Robert next drew a portrait of Mrs. Rudd, along with a description of her activities. He was, he said, the innocent victim of an evil, scheming woman. "Honest undesigning characters have at all times been the dupe of craft and subtilty." He accused her of "consumate artifice" of a sort "scarce equalled in all the annals of iniquity." Now that the scheme had been exposed, he admitted, it would look ridiculous to many. But he sought to show how skillfully she had played upon the hopes of an ingenuous man to improve his own lot and that of his family. How could intelligent men have been tricked by such fantastic promises? "Now, that detection had broken the charm, they appear too glaring for imposition; but when they followed in the order of their conspiracy, prefaced as they were by every artifice that could engage my confidence, the facility with which the truth might have been discovered, became with me the strongest reason for never suspecting that it could have been so daringly transgressed." Mrs. Rudd offered so many tempting prospects for Robert's dear "twin-born" brother that he could not but be dazzled by this amazing turn of luck. Could anyone really criticize him for believing her? Society, he demanded, should not judge the case after the "trick" had been exposed, but imagine the position of one entranced by the "juggler." Mrs. Rudd worked upon them all slowly at first, building up their confidence in her. "The arts to which I fell a sacrifice, were not shallow and transparent." She first won his attention with her sad tale of woe, then she opened up to him the promise of a connection with the Adair family. "The full lustre of that fortune, which grew to be so dazzling in the end, was not revealed but with the utmost deliberation." His reason was gradually put to sleep so that finally he did not pause to think about the fabulous nature of her promises of a seat in Parliament, a banking establishment, and a fortune of £50,000.[51]

When it came time to explain the immediate circumstances that led him to go to the Drummonds, he told of her coming to him with a story that William Adair needed to raise money on a bond. Naturally he felt honorbound to assist the man who had become a patron to his family. The first few bonds were punctually paid and included what he understood from Mrs. Rudd to be the "most flattering thanks" from Adair. Since the money was put to use on his brother's establishment, he could only congratulate himself on being of assistance in such a happy project. So many of the early promises she had made had been fulfilled that he now believed even the most extravagant of them. He was "led from error to error by such insensible degrees." Every step she took only "strengthened" his "infatuation." He recounted the events of the days immediately before the detection, suggesting that he only told the Drummonds a lie because Mrs. Rudd assured him that she had seen Adair. He had felt no alarm at the objections raised by the bankers because he had already negotiated several bonds in the same manner with reputable figures who had never questioned their authenticity. His behavior testified, he now argued, to his utter reliance on Mrs. Rudd's word. This was the only assumption that made any sense of his actions. Going to Adair's was the decisive proof of his "fair and open" conduct. "It does not come within the bounds of common sense, much less does it fall within the possibility of guilt, that any man living should voluntarily, and with his eyes open, take a step so directly and absolutely centered in his own certain conviction." He was confident, he concluded, that he had shown how his own conduct was truly innocent, and that his only fault lay in his credulity at the artifices and intrigues of Mrs. Rudd, "the most artful of imposters."[52]

Here, at last, was the Perreaus' answer to the lengthy story told by Mrs. Rudd. Elements of the tale had circulated in the press before the June trial, but it took Robert Perreau's account to transform them into a convincing narrative. The story of an honest man whose very integrity rendered him vulnerable to schemes concocted by a worldly and corrupt individual was the stuff of the plays and novels of the period. The papers reported that Robert's statement had "such an effect on the hearers that the crowd which filled the bench, the galleries, and the area of the court, thought he would be acquitted."[53]

Not content with this powerful plea, the defense team proceeded to call witnesses to lend support to Robert's accusation that Mrs. Rudd had been responsible for the deception. Such a strategy was a gamble. It meant proving the innocence of the accused by casting suspicion on someone not on trial. The judges were divided as to whether this was a proper way of proceeding. Justice Aston, at first, "was unwilling to enter into" such evidence, but "he yielded" to his associate, Burland, who inclined "to Bearcroft and Dunning's motion for it."[54] Robert's lawyers then called servants and friends to describe transactions that preceded those associated with the forgery now on trial. This material was intended to complete a portrait of Mrs. Rudd as a skilled dissembler who had fooled an entire family. It opened up the Perreau household and family network to detailed examination, making the familial drama ever more central to the challenge of deciphering the crime. George Kinder, an Irish colonel, described as an "intimate acquaintance" of Daniel Perreau, testified that he had lived for some months with them. He swore that Mrs. Rudd told him that "she was a near relation of Mr. James Adair; that James Adair looked upon her as his child, and promised to make her fortune, and establish her in life." It was James, she told him, who had recommended her to William Adair, a relation of his. Kinder claimed that it was common knowledge in the household that Mrs. Rudd received letters from William

Adair. She had shown them to Robert Perreau and even to himself. Since Robert visited his brother as often as three or four times a day, he frequently heard her speak of these letters and the promises they contained. Kinder, as well as the brothers, had no reason to doubt these reports. Adair's letters contained glowing promises about the future. Mrs. Rudd said he was about to settle a yearly income of £2400 on Daniel and allow her £600 in "pin money." He was also busy arranging to set the brothers up as bankers, and even spoke of his plans to have Daniel made a baronet. Not surprisingly, Kinder disclosed, these messages composed a large part of the conversation at the house. Mrs. Rudd often entertained them with details concerning the progress of negotiations to secure Daniel a seat in Parliament. Her stories gained credibility because she spoke of visits to and from Mr. and Mrs. James Adair, as well as William Adair, though always made in the absence of others of the family. Occasionally a Perreau family member would express displeasure at not being permitted to visit them as well, but Mrs. Rudd always explained that the situation required tact and discretion and that the time was not yet right. Thus, according to Kinder, she cast an aura of mystery and expectation over the family. No one saw any reason to question such a fair prospect.[55]

Daniel Perreau's footman, John Moody, contributed darker details to the story of a household captivated by Mrs. Rudd's bright promises. If the Perreaus and their friends played the delighted audience for her tales, the servants, according to Moody, were called upon to assist her in a series of peculiar transactions. Why they participated so readily and did not betray their suspicions to the Perreaus was never made clear. Perhaps they thought it no more than a harmless game. Moody testified that he often observed Mrs. Rudd contriving to pass letters to the brothers. He also offered details about their source. Mrs. Rudd, he reported, sent him for special paper, "thick gilt-edged," and she had him mend the many different pens she owned. He observed her feigning a different hand from her own to produce letters that purported to come from William Adair. He swore that the bond in this case and the letter Robert showed to the Drummonds were both in her "feigned handwriting." He revealed that she had instructed him to deliver these letters to Daniel and to tell him that Adair had visited and spent an hour with her. On other occasions she instructed him to rap on the parlor door to summon her downstairs, so that it appeared, as she would later tell the Perreaus, that she had had a visitor. Mrs. Rudd cautioned Moody not to reveal the truth about these transactions, warning that Daniel would never forgive her. Moody was convinced that the entire family was utterly taken in by these activities. The servant's testimony gained additional support from the reading in court of the letter supposedly sent to Robert from "W. A." The note adopted a familiar tone and suggested a sense of obligation the writer felt toward Robert. "I am," the message ran, "more obliged to you than I can express, for the friendly trouble you take to get me accommodated." Soon he would "give you solid proof of my regard." He promised to "infinitely add to your favours." At the same time, he expressed a sense of urgency about the need to pay the money to Frankland. The letter, in the same handwriting as the bond, mingled familiarity and promise with instruction and urgency in precisely the ways that Robert had described in his statement. Finally, Catherine Perreau, a sister of the accused, swore that "she had seen a bond, supposed to be Mr. Adair's, for £19,000."[56]

Daniel Perreau was then called to testify to the events surrounding the bond for which his brother had been indicted. Mrs. Rudd's account of being forced to sign the bond at knife point had created a profound sensation at the commitment hearing. Daniel now sought to present a different version of the bond's creation. His story followed closely the line suggested by Kinder and Moody. He told of how, after returning from a visit to his brother, Mrs. Rudd had left him in the parlor, only to return a few minutes later. Almost immediately a maid brought in a letter. Upon reading it Mrs. Rudd informed Daniel that Adair "desired" her to apply to Robert to secure £5000 upon a bond, as "he had done before." The next day, after Robert expressed an unwillingness to go to Mr. Evans, a family friend, for the money, she told him to make the request of the Drummonds. "My brother, after a great unwillingness, at last agreed to it." Robert arranged for the bond to be filled in and, in the presence of witnesses, gave it to Mrs. Rudd. Daniel heard nothing more of the matter until the evening of March 6, when, as he prepared for bed, he saw a letter with the bond in it upon the table, seemingly now executed by Adair. The next morning Mrs. Rudd carried the bond to Robert and "desired him to go with it to Messrs. Drummonds." "My brother," Daniel claimed, "shewed a vast deal of reluctancy, and said it was a very unpleasant work." Nonetheless, he consented. Throughout his testimony Daniel sought to show that his brother had only with the greatest unwillingness participated in these transactions, and that he had done so only as a service to the woman with whom his brother lived. He cooperated with her only because he believed her "representation of her connection with Adair." Daniel concluded on a poignant note that both he and his brother had trusted her completely, "to my misfortune," he now added.[57]

The defense, having presented its story of deception and misplaced trust, had only to demonstrate Robert's reputation for integrity. It did so by calling upon his acquaintances among a wide circle of distinguished people. Character witnesses played a large part in every eighteenth-century trial. They spoke to the "trustworthiness" of the accused and revealed much about his past history. But Robert Perreau produced character witnesses of a quality and number that was rare at the Old Bailey.[58] Sir Thomas Frankland, whose testimony was no doubt strengthened by the fact that he was a major victim of the scheme, volunteered that his uncle had always referred to Robert as "honest" Perreau, and that he personally had the "greatest confidence" in him "as a man of honour and reputation." A long list of witnesses, some fellow apothecaries and physicians, others his wealthy clients, echoed these sentiments. Perhaps the high point came with the appearance of Lady Lyttelton, who called Robert "one of the best men I ever met with; one of the most upright, humane, and benevolent." Her adjectives were carefully chosen to complete the picture of a man who was so honest and straightforward that his only weakness was an inability to see through the web of deceit spun by a cunning creature.[59]

All in all, Robert's defense was a masterful performance. Despite the difficulties under which the accused labored, he and his lawyers constructed an alternative narrative of the events of the case, including much evidence of Mrs. Rudd's earlier conduct. They also presented an appealing portrait of Robert, one that could be tested against the powerful impression he made with his own statement. Most of those present in the courtroom no doubt believed that he would be acquitted.

Nothing remained but for Justice Aston to deliver his summation. Judges occupied the central position in the eighteenth-century trial, and their directions, especially in complicated cases, played a large role in guiding jury deliberations. The papers differed in their judgment of his statement. All agreed that it was an accurate review of the facts, but several felt it had not leaned "to the side of mercy." Others reported that it was delivered with "the greatest tenderness and precision" and with "great impartiality." A West Indian acquaintance of the Perreaus, John Baker, left a fuller account of this crucial aspect of the trial. Aston began, he noted, by venting his unhappiness with the strategy pursued by the defense team. He "spoke of the impropriety" of hearing the evidence against Mrs. Rudd. Although he had consented to it, "he said he was never more ashamed of anything." No doubt swayed by a feeling that he had allowed defense counsel too much latitude, he now sought to right the balance in his comments. He proceeded, according to Baker, to make "every remark against [the] prisoner." In particular, Aston said that "if Robert had come as an innocent imposed-on man to borrow money on a bond he thought good, there was no occasion for the false pretenses he made use of to obtain the money." The judge laid great stress on the four major lies Robert told in the course of negotiating the bonds: that about purchasing a country house, the one concerning his holding money for William Adair, the pretense that he had encountered Adair about to go riding, and the deceitful presentation of a letter that claimed a close familiarity with the man. "These palpable falsities (all of his own)," Aston concluded, "rendered his efforts to exculpate himself to no purpose." Baker found these remarks effective. They met head on the carefully contrived narrative Robert Perreau's defenders had developed on his behalf. Baker thought that it was also a mistake that, instead of addressing the issues of the lies in his own defense, Robert "sunk them and said nothing to them." The very length of the summation, well over an hour, worked to undo the patient efforts of Robert's counsel.[60]

Despite these explicit and damning comments, many in the courtroom seemed to expect that sympathy for Robert would triumph. By the time the trial came on there can have been few among the respectable classes, especially those likely to be called as jurors, who were unfamiliar with the details of the case. Juries were typically composed of men of the middling sort, men from social circumstances similar to those of Robert Perreau. Since the same men were called time and again for jury duty, they possessed considerable trial experience. In most cases at the Old Bailey, jurors huddled in the courtroom and reached a decision after two or three minutes' deliberation.[61] Not surprisingly, given the complexity of this case, the Perreau jurors withdrew to consider a verdict. However, the court was stunned when, after an absence of almost half an hour, the jury returned with a verdict of guilty.

Many observers were surprised and moved. One reporter observed "that one of the first comic actresses in the world held up her fan to her face, and for some minutes shed tears."[62] Apparently Robert was surprised as well; a paper reported that he had ordered dinner for himself to be prepared at his home at Golden Square for that evening. Word of the verdict quickly spread. "When

Robert's trial was ended," the *Morning Chronicle* confided to its readers, "two messengers were immediately dispatched to two well known men (whose names we do not chuse to mention at present) at the West End of the town." Even if his defense had not swayed the court, it seemed to have convinced many who read the press reports of the trial. Some wondered aloud at how the jury had arrived at a conclusion seemingly so at odds with the evidence uncovered by Perreau's lawyers. One of Robert's defenders would later argue that he had been convicted because the jury wanted to make an example of someone, and Mrs. Rudd appeared to have escaped justice. Several writers asserted that the jurors had overestimated the importance of Robert's "little" lies.[63]

DANIEL'S TRIAL

The trial of Daniel Perreau, which followed hard on the heels of Robert's conviction, provided further evidence of how unexpected that outcome had been. The Perreaus had staked everything on Robert's defense, assuming that if he were acquitted—and, by implication, Mrs. Rudd were held accountable for the crime—Daniel would be freed as well. Daniel, as his trial would show, was ill prepared to mount an effective defense. For technical reasons he was acquitted of the charge that resulted in his brother's conviction. There was no real evidence to show that he was guilty of forgery, especially since a momentous decision had been made not to have Mrs. Rudd testify. Instead he was tried the next day for uttering the forged bond for £3000 that was left with Dr. Thomas Brooke.

Daniel had been intimate with Brooke for several years, and there had been much visiting between the two families. On November 1, 1774, Brooke testified, Daniel came to him asking to borrow a sum of money. The doctor replied that he had only enough cash by him to cover the expenses of the house. Daniel, however, knew his friend's finances well enough to ask, "Let me have some of your Ayr bank bonds." Brooke was reluctant to agree, but Daniel was persistent. Finally, Perreau offered a £3100 bond from Adair as security. Brooke removed a roll of Ayr bonds and asked his friend how many he wanted. After some thought Daniel answered fifteen. Daniel filled out a receipt for the instruments and promised to deposit them at the Drummonds' bank. In the period between the loan and the discovery of the forgery, Daniel and Brooke continued to see each other almost every day. Although the bonds had not been deposited at the bank as Daniel had promised, Brooke did not press the matter, as he hoped to be useful to his friend. About the middle of December, when the interest on them was due, Brooke requested their return. Daniel replied that if his only concern was the interest, he would be happy to pay it to him. Brooke again decided, as he said at the trial, that "if it was any service to him he was welcome to keep them longer." He heard nothing further until the brothers were taken into custody. He could scarcely contain his surprise. "At first," he confessed, "I could not believe such charge against them."[64]

Daniel's defense followed the general outline of his brother's, but the effort was shorter and seemed to lack conviction. No doubt both Perreaus were dispirited. He had little to say in his own statement. He swore that he had received the bond from Mrs. Rudd and that he "did really believe it to be a genuine, authentic, and valid bond." He denied ever intending to defraud "any man of his property." After this brief comment, John Moody, his footman, was once again a witness on the defendant's behalf. He repeated his testimony of Mrs. Rudd employing him to deceive Daniel about the receipt of letters and visits from William Adair. "I entertained," Moody explained, "no other opinion, than that Mrs. Rudd wanted to make Mr. Daniel Perreau think, that Mr. William Adair was an acquaintance or correspondent of her's." He described her as "a very artful person for so doing." Another letter signed "W. A." was read to the court, and Moody once again identified it as being in Mrs. Rudd's feigned hand. Two additional witnesses, Elizabeth Perkins and Hannah Dalboux, servants of Perreau, testified to the ruses employed by Mrs. Rudd to suggest visits by Adair. Daniel, too, called "several respectable persons" to testify that he was "an honest, upright man, well respected both in the mercantile and genteel world." But, in general, his character witnesses were less impressive and had fewer specific details to offer about his life. After a trial of perhaps two hours, the jury took less than ten minutes to find him guilty.[65]

JUST STORIES

At every stage during the discovery and prosecution of the forgery of the bonds, the chief suspects confronted the legal authorities with lengthy, compelling, and intricate tales. Fielding, Aston, and the members of the Old Bailey jury were old hands at dealing with criminals and the feeble stories they told on the few occasions when the accused even bothered to make a defense.

But this case was different, not only due to the defendants' social status, but at least as much because of the narratives they related and the skillful way they delivered them. Forgery was a frightening crime. What aggravated the offense in this instance, however, was the accusation launched by the parties in the case that the deceiver, whether Mrs. Rudd or Robert and Daniel Perreau, now plotted to take the life of an innocent person by manipulating the judicial process. The case no longer concerned a simple forgery of a signature, one so poorly contrived that it had been instantly spotted by the Drummonds. It now involved a different kind of deception, that of assuming a fair identity and character. The participants assumed a variety of poses in an effort to sway the course of justice. Wildly implausible as their narratives appeared at some moments, at others they seemed compelling and disturbing. Over time they became so complex that it was difficult to keep the simplest detail straight. Just when a magistrate or reader felt on the verge of discovering a seemingly solid fact, the truth slipped away yet again. The participants in this case could spin stories that inspired belief. Their tales, time and again, forced the authorities to reverse course, creating the impression that the judicial process was not up to the task of discovering where the truth lay. Mrs. Rudd's story carried the day at Bow Street. Her plight and her performance played upon the chivalric instincts of the magistrates and secured for her the privilege that Robert had so awkwardly desired, that of crown witness. She won this protection in part because of the conventions of the usual London criminal tale, which allowed her to present herself as the injured woman to an audience who assumed that women were always subsidiary agents in any criminal activity. Once she had secured the grant, the Perreaus were burdened by the authorities' insistence that someone suffer in order to deter such a dangerous offense. In other words, the Perreaus had to counter her story under the most unfavorable conditions.

Robert Perreau had botched his first attempt to tell his story to Addington at Bow Street. Perhaps, as he later claimed, he was too startled by his discovery, too ashamed of how he might appear to the authorities, too anxious about the danger in which he stood. Perhaps he only underestimated the resourcefulness of the woman he accused. Given the odds against them, the Perreaus' success in eventually putting forth a defense that did raise doubts in many minds appears little short of miraculous. The publicity attending their trials, and especially the skillful exposition of evidence by Robert and his counsel, gave them the opportunity to disseminate a very different tale.

The brothers offered a portrait of Mrs. Rudd as a woman who was constantly concocting stories. This was not the harmless game of a women who read too many French novels. Rather it represented a more sinister behavior on the part of a more mischievous character. The Perreaus offered a story in which Mrs. Rudd's claims of exalted relations who were enthusiastic about doing something great for the Perreau family had enthralled them. Her hold over them was strengthened by the ever increasing sums she produced to support and expand her and Daniel's household. They had not thought it wise or polite to inquire too closely about the source of these funds. They presented themselves as puppets in her performances, bewitched by her cleverness in playing upon their hopes and fears. There were many witnesses to her feats. The Perreau servants spoke with one voice of the elaborate lengths to which she went to create an impression that James and William Adair were frequent visitors. They also added to the Drummonds' earlier testimony about the demonstration of her "masculine" hand, the evidence of her pens and paper. There seemed little doubt that she was the author of the bonds and most likely of the letters that purported to come from relations and connections. Daniel made much of the various men who passed as her cousins—John Stewart, Thomas Cairns, John Adair—all of whom initially lent credibility to her claims. Now that the plot had been discovered, they had all vanished. Here was evidence of a widespread and well-developed conspiracy of talented "sharpers." The Perreaus repeatedly proclaimed their innocence and appealed to their integrity as proof of it. They asked the jurors to imagine them as trapped by the cunning of a woman of great art, a woman who left letters on the mantle for Daniel to discover and had him called from coffee-houses to deal with Adair business. In their accounts she appeared the clever and resourceful instigator of all these complex undertakings. The brothers presented themselves as the alternately reluctant and dazzled victims of her ruses. Her "artfulness"—the word they repeated more than any other in describing her—put them off their guard. The term expressed at once her skill and pleasing aspect, but it also suggested her basic falseness and artificiality. The brothers offered their story as hard-won confirmation of the wider belief that an artful woman was a dangerous woman.

Throughout their accounts the brothers employed a sentimental idiom that was common parlance in their day. They were both, in their own accounts, sentimental heroes. They had been seduced by fair promises, but their wishes were not criminal, and their mystification followed from their ingenuousness and was a proof of their essential innocence. They were overmatched, they announced, not by the strength but by the beauty and cunning of their opponent. Their weakness testified less to a lack of character than to their honesty and trust in human goodness. Their claims resonated with some of the most familiar literary themes of the day. For a generation, a familiar plot of plays and novels concerned the danger innocence faced when confronted with the machinations of an evil individual more skilled in the ways of a corrupt society (whether defined by commercial unscrupulousness or aristocratic vice). In one of the most popular plays of the period, *The London Merchant,* the artful lady of pleasure, Millwood, ensnared the too-trusting apprentice, George Barnwell, leading him to commit a horrid crime that resulted in his destruction.[66] Often these seducers put forth wild schemes that no one could penetrate until the last moment. The authorities, inattentive or captivated by appearances themselves, too easily collaborated in the oppression. From *Jonathan Wild* and *Tom Jones* to *The Vicar of Wakefield,* this trope had been a staple of popular fiction. The melodramatic climax came when the heroes, trapped in prison or facing the gallows, seemingly without hope, stood revealed in all of their sentimental purity. Now the Perreaus offered themselves as a living tableau of such a narrative. A gentleman who was present at the first interview of Robert Perreau and his wife, one paper reported, "declares he never saw any thing so moving; the wretched objects beheld each other with speechless anguish for several minutes, not being able to address each other till many floods of tears had fallen from both."[67] In the accounts offered by the Perreaus, as well as in the situation they faced after their trials, life seemed to imitate art.

If their tale had a familiar ring, the appearance of the accused, identical twins possessed of similar dress and manner, proved far more disconcerting. The true nature of the relationship between the brothers was mysterious. Opinion differed about which one exercised the greater influence. First one and then the other was described as the "elder." They evidently shared ambitions; they had long coordinated their actions. Whoever was the stronger, they were obviously deeply attached to each other. Daniel placed loyalty to his brother above that to Mrs. Rudd. Robert appeared equally ready to sacrifice his reputation and risk his life to defend Daniel.

At the trial, the Perreaus attempted to take advantage of the interest aroused by their resemblance. They sought to downplay Daniel's past as they emphasized Robert's reputation. In taking up with Mrs. Rudd, Daniel had shown poor judgment and a vain pursuit of fashion. Robert was the honest, well-meaning, too-trusting brother who presented a picture of a happy home and a circle of admiring, respectable clients. They tried to minimize these differences by portraying themselves as equally innocent and equally deluded.

But the Drummonds' tale stood this picture on its head. Robert had been calm in the face of questioning, smooth in telling his "lies," while Daniel seemed dumbstruck by the fiasco he found at William Adair's. Despite later efforts to distinguish the responsibility of the individual brothers, their fates, like their identities, had become enmeshed. Though some had hoped that Robert's respectability might persuade the world to view his twin in the same light, it seemed to work the other way, and Robert was tarred with Daniel's faults.

Thus it was that several days after their trials the brothers were returned to court to hear sentence passed upon them. No one could doubt the outcome; the judge ordered them to prepare themselves for death. "Previous to the judgment," one paper announced, "they had a most excellent exhortation from the Bench, which lasted near fifteen minutes, and was delivered in such a pathetic manner as to draw tears from the spectators." He warned them solemnly not to expect mercy. The sentence of death in forgery cases was almost invariably carried out.[68]

But at this moment a dramatic surprise created both confusion and sensation in the court. Some hint of uneasiness on the part of the prosecutors appeared in their refusal to make use of Mrs. Rudd as a witness in either trial. No doubt rumors of her reputation, as well as the disturbing evidence that came out at Robert's trial, had persuaded them that she would make an unreliable witness. Some sources hinted that influential figures sought to aid the brothers. For whatever reasons, at the end of Daniel's trial, the Recorder ordered Mrs. Rudd brought into court, where he explained that they "did not think proper to admit her as an evidence." Instead the judges committed her for trial. The papers reported that the justification for this decision was that she had failed to tell all she knew and had not mentioned her part in the other forgeries. Justice Aston "spoke with much warmth on the impropriety of her having been admitted evidence for the Crown by the magistrates of the Public Office, an act he deemed totally unauthorized."[69] Clearly some on the Bench were outraged, feeling that justice as well as the Perreaus had been duped by a too-clever and immoral woman. Given what they had learned from the examination of various witnesses, they felt the only remedy lay in committing her for trial. Perreau supporters played upon this sense of frustration, for it was already obvious that their only hope of avoiding the gallows lay in whatever might be revealed at her trial. Nonetheless, this course of action held risks for the authorities. The chief disadvantage was that it seemed to violate the pledge given to Mrs. Rudd by the magistrates at Bow Street. These legal maneuvers appeared anything but regular. Far from convincing the public that at last the authorities were on the right path, their actions looked wrong-footed, and the mystery only seemed more obscure.

Sir Thomas Frankland made an affidavit charging Mrs. Rudd with forgery and entered into recognizances (a bond with a monetary penalty for non-performance) to prosecute her. There had been some delay in making the charge because he had "expected Mr. Drummond would have prosecuted her for the forgery of Mr. Adair's name." The judges, too, tried unsuccessfully to get the Drummonds to act as the prosecutors. Frankland's testimony in the trials of the Perreaus had played little role in their conviction, and there was reason to think he had a weaker case to offer. He had also revealed that he was a Perreau partisan when he appeared as a character witness for Robert. The Drummonds, on the other hand, had no link to any of the parties. But Robert Drummond refused to act; it was rumored that he felt "he could not, in honour, prosecute the person who had convinced him of her guilt." Justice Aston repeated this report. The general reason assigned early in the affair for why Mrs. Rudd was not prosecuted, "he understood proceeded from a point of delicacy operating on the Drummonds"; more specifically, it arose "between Robert Drummond and her, relative to her writing William Adair on a slip of paper."[70]

Mrs. Rudd appeared agitated when the court announced its decision. Her request for bail was denied, and she was told she must remain in Newgate until her trial. One paper repeated a rumor that she whispered to a friend "that her health would probably be endangered if she was detained for trial." The judges seemed little moved by such a plea. The friends of the Perreaus took new hope from this transaction that their story would yet prevail.[71]

Three

THE PRESS AND THE CASE

IN MARCH 1775 THE newspapers were full of gloomy reports about relations between England and her American colonies. Despite the occasional glimmer of hope—a report of an important defection among the rebels or a notice of some new gesture from the administration—most commentators recognized that the two sides stood on the brink of civil war. London papers reflected the several shades of English opinion. In general there was a good deal of controversy about the best way to handle the crisis, but most of the press, like much of the public, supported the increasingly firm measures being adopted by the government. For weeks the papers had been filled with stories of violent episodes and preparations for hostilities. Most of the news dealt with these issues: the introduction of bills restraining the trade of selected colonies, the need for national unity, the embarkation of a detachment of marines from Portsmouth. On the second Monday in March, two of the three letters to the printer of the *Morning Chronicle* concerned American affairs. The nation seemed preoccupied with the unfolding political and military drama.[1]

The first report of the forgery appeared on March 13, in a short paragraph almost at the bottom of the last page of news. It said simply:

> The same evening [Saturday] a very genteel woman, who goes by the name of Gild, was taken into custody, and brought to the Rotation Office, in Bow-street, she being charged with having a forged note,

on a banker at Charing Cross, to the amount of ten or twelve thousand pounds, a great part of which money she had received. She was conveyed to Sir John Fielding at Brompton, who committed her for farther examination. A great number of persons of fortune attended.[2]

Although the paragraph contained many errors of fact, it captured, even in its brevity, some of the essential features of the case: the mysterious woman, a forgery involving a very large sum, and the keen interest of fashionable persons. These unusual details would have attracted a reader's attention. Still, the modest space given to the report, and even the many misleading details, suggested limited interest in the crime.

By Wednesday, however, there was fresh evidence that the papers were competing to place new revelations before their readers. Four of the tri-week-lies essentially copied the first report of the case, but the *London Chronicle* introduced a more complete cast of characters. It noted that "two persons, a Gentleman and his reputed wife," had been committed to Tothill Bridewell for forging a note "on a distinguished English Admiral for £14,000 and the next day, the brother of the supposed offender going to see him was taken into custody, and detained as one of the parties concerned." This story, while fuller, omitted the names of the suspects and confused the relationship between the woman and the brothers. Still, several papers signaled their greater interest in the episode when they described the couple as living in the *beau monde*. The *Morning Post* made the same point when it characterized the accused as "two persons of credit, each of whom keeps his carriage." The *Middlesex Journal* promised its readers "a more particular account of the blow-up that has lately happened at the west end of town." Here were phrases calculated to pique curiosity. Any "fashionable" crime promised a *frisson* to the public, a hint of intrigue that more ordinary villainy could not match. The suspects' precise social identification left the implicit promise of disclosures to follow. The evident haste with which such stories appeared to be written indicated the press's feverish enthusiasm for the case.[3]

By the end of the week the London papers had seized upon the episode, giving it extraordinary prominence. Although the first rumors of the crime had spread by word of mouth, as demonstrated by the speed with which people hastened to Bow Street to hear the proceedings before Fielding, the London press increasingly became the medium through which the public followed the story, which soon became a staple item in the provincial press as well. Within a week of the story breaking in the metropolis, long articles on the crime appeared in the *Bath Journal,* the *Sussex Weekly Advertiser,* and the *Leeds Mercury.* By the following week it appeared as a major feature in the *Manchester Mercury* and the *Cumberland Pacquet.* The *Weekly Magazine and Edinburgh Amusement* supplied its readers with a particularly accurate narrative of events, and on twenty-five occasions over the next ten months it returned to the story. Before long extensive reports could be found in the *Gentleman's Magazine,* the *Westminster Magazine,* and the *Universal Magazine,* and by the end of the month a reference had even appeared in the notorious "Tête-à-Tête" section of the *Town and Country Magazine.*

The press, which loved the story, was to have a decisive impact upon how the case developed and how the public experienced it. The papers made it into a national sensation—an inescapable phenomenon, the story on everyone's lips. The press gave full accounts of all the official proceedings, but their contribution went beyond mere reporting of the major legal developments. They opened their pages in a novel way to the parties involved in the case and to the public. Both Mrs. Rudd and the Perreaus used the press to circulate their accounts. The antagonists and their allies flooded the papers with letters offering new accusations. They advertised the pamphlets that supported one side or the other. The papers played to and fostered the swelling interest. The public joined the fray by contributing letters on crucial issues raised by the controversy. Editors stoked the fires by passing on hints and rumors in short items from unattributed sources. In the fiercely competitive world of London journalism, publishers fell over themselves in an effort to satisfy the curiosity they had helped arouse. The tale of the forgery exploded at a pivotal moment in the history of English journalism. Although the papers helped make the case, the case also helped shape the press. Newspapers had long since ceased to be mere vehicles for advertising and a means of carrying on political disputes. Not only did they now convey news of foreign affairs and parliamentary business, but the areas expanding most rapidly were the sections offering news of high society, the doings of royalty and aristocracy, examples of poetry, and discussions of the arts. The revelations of the Perreau-Rudd case offered fresh territory for expansion. Through their handling of the case, the papers helped to produce a new genre, the sensational criminal trial.

There was a tendency on the part of the English by the 1770s to congratulate themselves on the character of their press. "The freedom of the press," one paper announced in 1780, repeating what had become the conventional phrase, "is the palladium of English liberty." "The liberty of the press," Blackstone wrote, "is indeed essential to the nature of a free state." Foreigners often shared this view. A vigorous press checked arbitrary government by giving voice to "the sense of the people." English liberty, de Lolme wrote, did not depend on "King, Lords, and Commons only," but on the "people at large." The crucial means by which the public expressed their views was through "liberty of the press." This freedom had emerged slowly, but now "time has perfected the system of printing liberty." Several major victories were fresh in readers' minds. Less than a decade earlier the government had failed to block the publication of the Junius letters. And only recently printers had won the right to publish parliamentary proceedings. These triumphs produced a kind of euphoria about the potential for social and political improvement that might flow from the rapidly expanding world of printers, booksellers, and publishers. Samuel Johnson expressed the conviction that a people without print was barbarous. "Knowledge is diffused among our people," he argued, "by the news-paper." The ever greater presence of newspapers in people's lives was one of the most marked and remarked-upon features of eighteenth-century London life.[4]

Everyone conceded the power that the press had secured by the 1770s, but not all were confident that it was for the best. Many thoughtful men doubted the exaggerated claims made by the newspapers when they considered the self-interested origin of the pronouncements. They looked upon publishers as low-born, impecunious fellows who would stop at nothing to secure sales. Papers, they argued, dealt in slander, spread lies, and appealed to "the ignorant classes." One commentator in 1785, looking back over the previous fifteen years, wondered "whether this progress from caution to daring, has been too rapid for the genuine purposes of real and honest information." Opponents of the press asserted that it encouraged a spirit of licentiousness that was sweeping the land. They criticized the values the papers seemed to offer. Even Burke, normally a defender of the institution, announced in 1770 that the issue was still undecided, "whether the liberty of the press be a curse or a blessing."[5] The treatment of the Perreau-Rudd case tested the confidence of those who praised the papers and provided fresh ammunition to those who lamented the consequences of popular journalism for the culture.

The most notable feature of the press world of the 1770s, both in London and in the provinces, was the rapid proliferation of papers. Recent years, one observer noted, had "wonderfully multiplied all kinds of public papers." By 1775 there were five dailies and eight or nine tri-weeklies in the metropolis.[6] Starting a newspaper was relatively easy, requiring only a modest amount of capital. Most London papers by this period were founded by a consortium of printers, booksellers, and shopkeepers who would then hold shares in the business. They were drawn to publishing, in part, by the lure of free advertising, but a successful newspaper also promised a profitable return, derived in large part from circulation. Thus they were sensitive to the interests of their audience and to any opportunity to draw new readers. This concern, at least as much as political commitment, led the papers to fight for the right to print the popular parliamentary debates. Papers also experimented with new sections and topics in an effort to draw a larger share of the metropolis's potential readers. Novelty and sensation sold well. "This country," Josiah Tucker complained in 1774, "is as much news-mad and news-ridden as ever it was popery-mad and priest-ridden." The possible readership for the press was growing rapidly in this period, but the number of papers battling for that audience increased even more quickly.[7]

These changes were not limited to London. The number of provincial papers was increasing as quickly. The early 1770s saw a particular rise, and there were as many as fifty papers by 1782. Even the London press was influenced by this expanding audience, as the large number of tri-weeklies reveals, since they were usually distributed outside the city. These papers were less innovative than those of the metropolis and were more careful in their political stance, yet they did not simply repeat London news. Improvements in transportation meant that the content of London papers was rapidly conveyed to the distant corners of the kingdom, but the relationship was not all one way. Most London papers made a habit of receiving important local papers and repeating the news they contained. In this way, as one observer on the English press noted in the 1780s, "private anecdotes [circulate] in the different country towns, and even find their way into the villages, where every man down to the laborer, peruse them with a sort of eagerness." "Every individual thus becomes acquainted with the state of the nation, from one end to the other; and by these means the general intercourse is such, that the three kingdoms seem as if they were one single town."[8] Provincial papers joined with the metropolitan press to spread London fashion across the country and to create an insatiable appetite for the doings of royalty and aristocracy.[9]

What all this meant in terms of the numbers of readers is difficult to say. By 1775 some 12.7 million papers were stamped each year. This figure is an imperfect guide, since some journals arose and quickly passed away, while others sought ways to avoid paying the tax. The sales level for individual papers varied, but one estimate puts it at between 1500 and 3000. One of the most successful papers, the *Gazetteer*, sold as many as 5000 copies on a regular basis. Henry Bate claimed an equal number for the *Morning Post*. In 1782 one contemporary thought that 25,000 papers a day circulated in London. A more cautious witness put the figure for the mid-1770s at 15,000–20,000. If we include the provinces, the volume rises to perhaps 34,000–35,000 each day. Given that the population of England and Wales in 1771 approached 7 million, while that of the metropolis was 750,000, newspapers may have reached one in every three or four people in London and 8 percent of the population outside that area. Illiteracy was probably less an obstacle to a wider readership than cost. The stamp tax ensured that papers were expensive. Thus the crucial question becomes how many individuals read each issue of a paper. In 1782 one well-informed political propagandist suggested that there were ten readers for every copy of a newspaper. Many people read papers at coffee-houses or in a small number of public houses. "Without newspapers," one editor wrote, "our Coffee-houses, Alehouses, and Barber-shops would undergo a change next to depopulation." Some publishers complained about news hawkers who lent out papers at a small charge. Papers could also be found at the lending libraries beginning to appear in many major towns. Sales varied considerably depending upon the events of the day. London papers sold more readily when Parliament was in session, either because the political news boosted volume or because the class that could best afford papers was in town. At any rate, if papers in the city passed through 200,000–250,000 hands, then the audience consisted not only of the wealthy but also of most of the "middling sort" as well as some of the artisan-class readers of London. While advertisers pitched their messages to the elite, publishers sought to appeal to a much wider population with their news and gossip.[10]

If the political disputes of the 1760s helped to increase the popularity of the press, they also had a profound impact upon the style and content of the papers. "The political controversy at the beginning of the present reign," one author wrote in 1775, "taught printers to feel their power." The press played a leading role in the violent contest between the established parliamentary groups and the government of George III and Lord Bute. Not only did it serve as an important instrument in this conflict, but the extent of journalistic freedom became one of the most significant topics of debate. When the central opposition figure, John Wilkes, employed his newspaper, the *North Briton,* to condemn the administration in scurrilous terms, a new and uninhibited style of journalism was born. Ministers were attacked by name, and their policy mistakes were jumbled together with attacks upon their character and abuse of their nationality. "We then first find personal abuse, unrestrained, stalk abroad, and boldly attack by name the most respectable characters." Editors soon found that these charges not only aroused political passions but also titillated the reader. In short, they were wonderful for sales. Much of the London press joined in the assault on the political establishment. Changes of government did little to still the controversy. The struggle climaxed in the brilliant invective of "Junius," the name assumed by an anonymous correspondent. Junius began publishing in the *Public Advertiser* in 1769, and for the next several years this propagandist dominated the newspaper scene. Fifteen years later one observer still marveled at the "virulence, the illiberality, and the froth of matter and manner which prevail in these letters." "Suffice it to say," he concluded, "they suited the taste of the times, and were more read than any letters ever published in a similar vein." The letters of Junius and the debates they spawned led the press to give increasing space to news, opinion, and letters. People rushed to buy the *Public Advertiser* or the *St. James's Chronicle* in order to catch up with the latest slander or sly innuendo that flowed from the pens of government critics.[11]

The papers mingled political commentary on contemporary events with personal calumny of leading figures. A spirited exposure of both was justified in the name of "true patriotism." Wilkes exploited the grossest satire of Scots; *The Whisperer* and *The Scotchman* mingled charges of ministerial misconduct with sexual innuendo concerning Bute and the Queen Mother. Such language drew public attention, as much for the audacity of the accusations as for the justice of the political opinions. If the press was transforming the political world, opening it up to observation and new forms of participation, it was doing so in part by pandering to a desire for the sensational and salacious. The *Middlesex Journal* not only afforded its readers radical politics but also exposed "sexual malpractice amongst the aristocracy" and a host of other instances of misconduct by justices, lawyers, and merchants. It did so with one eye on circulation. A transformation in the style of political debate helped to produce a change in the fashion for social reporting. The papers said pretty much what they wanted to, seldom troubled by libel law. Though often prosecuted for defamation, publishers usually paid a small fine or faced a brief imprisonment, in either case a small price to pay for increased sales. When the political furor died down, they easily turned their attention to "private anecdotes, which gratify a certain curious disposition," in an effort to hold their readers' attention.[12]

No doubt the founding of the *Morning Post* in 1772 solidified and exacerbated these changes. Under its editor, the eccentric and pugnacious Reverend Henry Bate, the paper sought to attract readers by offering them scandal as news. Its goal, one observer wrote, was "to diffuse private anecdotes, detail the varieties of fashion, and circulate the rumors of polite circles." "Success emboldened them, and they soon became the arbiters of wit and fashion." Bate skirted the line between news and malicious gossip, inviting lawsuits and challenges to duels. His efforts were brilliantly successful, and the paper's popularity was irresistible. "The paper was termed a polite paper, fit for the breakfast tables of distinction, who cared little for politics." Despite widespread condemnation of his tactics, other publishers, in order to stay competitive, were forced to follow his example. The *Morning Chronicle* and the *Gazetteer* found themselves especially hard-pressed. Bate's goal was as much entertainment as it was information. "Vivacity, point, and humor, distinguish its paragraphs and squibs." Scandal was a valuable commodity, and Bate had a genius for finding, packaging, and exploiting it. He was seldom fastidious about accuracy. He sold "gossip and abuse," which found an ever-ready and eager audience. Bate opened the pages of the *Morning Post* to whatever comments or slurs he thought might sell papers; he then quite cheerfully announced that it was all a mistake and warned against the possible unfairness of views he himself had printed. Whatever his lack of principles, his business sense was unerring.[13]

Bate's tactics may have won him readers, but they also inspired widespread condemnation, especially from those who suffered at his hands. "[The *Morning Post*] is full of lies and no news," complained Lady Sarah Lennox in 1778. In a pamphlet published in 1775, one author charged that "personal abuse in periodical publications was till late years almost unknown." Even after politicians became the targets of violent squibs, "domestic quiet was unmolested." But now the *Morning Post* had "brought abuse to its utmost perfection," pursuing people even "to our firesides." "Ought the language of the stews to be printed in a public newspaper?" Women, in particular, were singled out for malicious treatment. "Hints, innuendoes against the most lovely part of creation, expressed in such unmanly terms," filled its pages. "Will not the liberty of the press become a dangerous nuisance," he warned ominously, "if that time should ever come, when a man must either submit to be cheated by a rascal printer, or must be abused by him in a public newspaper for months together?"[14] The note of desperation in this complaint offers us a telling commentary on the perception and scale of Bate's achievement.

The tone and content of the newspapers of the day, the passion for tell-all scandal mark one of the distinguishing characteristics of the age. Authors acknowledged the seeming inexorable advance of such an appetite even as they bemoaned its consequences. The *Gazetteer*, in 1789, looking back upon the revolution that Bate had engineered, noted that the change had come "when some needy adventurers thought that a fashionable Paper, that is, a record of private and public scandal, would suit the taste of the Public, and fill *their* pockets." This author did not put all the responsibility on Bate, though. "The public *have been* to blame by encouraging such Papers. Many like the tale of a scandal." "The man of middling rank," he charged, "chuckled to read the amours and intrigues of Lords and Ladies, little thinking that his turn would one day come, his harmless actions be misrepresented, and his character blasted in a paragraph."[15] Even Johnson bowed before the power of the press when he remarked, at least according to Boswell, that fifteen years earlier he would have visited Mrs. Rudd, but he declined to do so now because "they have a trick of putting every thing into the newspapers."[16]

REPORTING SENSATIONAL NEWS

This history of the press between 1760 and 1775 does much to explain the eagerness with which the papers greeted the first revelations of the Perreau case. In their early enthusiasm, though, they had a difficult time getting the story straight. The first detailed report appeared in the *Middlesex Journal,* a triweekly, on Tuesday, March 14. The paper offered more of the particulars of the crime, especially a description of the mission of "a Mr. P an apothecary" to "Mess. D—, bankers at Charing-cross, to borrow £5000 upon a bond of

£7500 which he purported to be the bond of Mr. A——r, the agent." Although the story was the most complete to this point, it was scarcely longer than one-third of a column and contained numerous omissions and errors. It did, however, correctly name two of the main "victims," Sir Thomas Frankland and Dr. Brooke, and gave the amount of their losses. Yet it also mentioned Mr. B., a jeweler in Pall Mall, as having lost £4500 through a forged bond, a charge that would subsequently prove inaccurate. Understandably, given the confusion at Bow Street, the papers reported conflicting versions of who was responsible for the forgeries. The *Morning Chronicle* on Tuesday corrected its previous story, noting that "the capital forgery talked of yesterday in the public prints, was not committed by a woman, but by a Mr. P——, formerly an apothecary at the West End of town." However, even this new version repeated a mistake common in the earliest accounts; "Mr. P—— and his wife were sent to Tothill-fields Bridewell on Saturday," it asserted. The mysterious woman, whose presence ran like a thread through all of these stories, was not only misnamed but misallied by the press. Part of the difficulty arose from circumstances of the hearing; the noise and the crush of people trying to catch a glimpse obstructed those trying to take notes on what was said. The *Public Advertiser* informed its readers that its report was "a tolerably correct account; but the crowd was so excessive, and the inconvenience of taking it such, that small errors will be excused." These errors, however, included confusing Daniel with Robert at a crucial moment in its description of the transaction at the Drummonds'.[17]

These problems continued to trouble the press throughout the early part of the week. Another sign of the story's growing significance was its appearance on Wednesday in the *Daily Advertiser*, a paper almost entirely devoted to general advertisements. It usually reported facts without comment. Not only did it omit all names but, uniquely, gave no clues as to the status of the accused. On the same day, *Lloyd's Evening Post* carried a version of the *Middlesex Journal* account, albeit with a different ending. According to *Lloyd's*, the still-unnamed apothecary was detained when the forgery was detected at Adair's (which, in fact, had not happened). It also failed to mention accomplices. At the end of three days' coverage, much about the case remained unclear. The salient facts remained the sums of money involved and hints about the social status of the accused.[18]

Both the organization of the press and the tastes of the age meant that "news" often sounded like rumor, while gossip and false reports abounded.

"English newspapers," one aristocrat wrote in 1763, were composed of a "chaos of truth and falsehood." Although we know little about how news was gathered or stories written, papers of this period had few employees or staff. Much of the time they relied on "official" sources, government announcements, military dispatches, trial summaries, stories drawn from foreign papers, and articles submitted by the interested parties themselves. In some instances independent writers called "news gatherers" wrote stories that they then sold to whichever papers they could interest in them. The first regular reporters appeared in the 1770s, and they devoted themselves almost exclusively to parliamentary reporting. Editors were responsible for collecting the items that went into the paper. They were usually at sea until some reliable "source" provided an authoritative account. Often desperate for news, they were unembarrassed about plagiarizing from each other. Not surprisingly, one paper often looked much like another. Where they competed strenuously was in the effort to get a story out first or to introduce some novel detail. For this to happen, editors relied upon luck or a hint from a friendly informant to enable them to strike before anyone else.[19]

This informal, haphazard, and often frantic search for news led to mistakes and worse. There were constant complaints that misinformation or propaganda contributed to political crises. Stories about American events in 1775 contained numerous errors of fact. Since it was difficult to secure any news of the colonial politicians' activities and intentions, hopes and fears, often in the form of rumors, found their way into bulletins from dubious sources. The unreliability of the press was a familiar refrain during the year. By 1776 Thomas Hutchinson, the former governor of Massachusetts, was complaining bitterly about "the many palpable absurdities or impossibilities" that appeared in the papers. "The law against spreading false news" had lost all force. David Garrick expressed similar sentiments to a friend in a letter he wrote in June 1775. He hoped that his "nonsense" would offer his correspondent "a few minutes" relief from his cares, "amidst the Truth & Lies that are daily arizing about American affairs."[20] The papers promised news of distant events to a public with an ever expanding appetite for information. But what they actually offered fell far short of the extravagant claims they made for conveying facts and the truth.

The *Morning Post* was even less fastidious than most papers about the truthfulness of the reports that filled its pages. On the same day that the *Morning Chronicle* printed its initial report of the Perreau-Rudd forgery case, Bate offered his readers an uncannily similar tale, a story of financial imprudence, imposture, and discovery. A young woman, the paper explained, with a fortune of £15,000, had married the heir of a City business fortune "a very few years ago." Through a course of dissipation and extravagant living, the man had run through both their fortunes. As a consequence, he resorted to a ruse, setting himself up as Lord W— in the west end of the town, in order to continue his spending spree. At length he forced his wife, on pains of being "turned out of doors," to become his agent in such fraudulent transactions. When she was apprehended, her husband absconded. Like many sentimental stories printed in this paper, this tale turned out to be a hoax. Less than two weeks later, the indignant printer sought to put the blame on the anonymous correspondent who had sent it to him. By this time, though, the report had already been picked up and reprinted as fact by at least two provincial papers.[21]

The equally fantastic story of the Perreau brothers and Mrs. Rudd did not prove so illusory or ephemeral. Still, the papers could not help noting how many aspects of the case remained fundamentally implausible. Almost all the London press commented on the remarkable nature of the forgeries, noting that unlike other instances of the crime, which usually consisted of a single utterance, this scheme resembled a veritable "trade" in forged paper. At a loss to understand what could have been hoped for from this pyramid of false bonds, the papers continued to speculate about and, in a curious way, to celebrate the crime and the imprisoned suspects. They proved especially susceptible to the more melodramatic aspects of the case. Desperate for additional news, the press widely (and probably incorrectly) reported that Robert Perreau was trying to starve himself in order "to prevent an ignominious exit." When the Perreaus' trial was delayed from the end of April to the beginning of June, several papers speculated about the cause. "We hear," they wrote, "that a quirk in the law has been found out in the case of the unhappy brothers now under confinement in Newgate, which will turn out greatly in their favour; whether it is owing to this circumstance or not we cannot determine, but wagers to a considerable amount have been laid within these few days, that they will not be even convicted."[22] Occasionally the brief comments could be quite acerbic. Some of the papers raised doubts about the credibility of aspects of Robert Perreau's defense. For example, the promises that Robert claimed Mrs. Rudd had used to secure his cooperation were characterized in one paper as "a great deal of . . . romantic stuff, seemingly copied from the Tales of the Friars."[23]

However, there were few such skeptical comments, and the papers offered little to guide their readers toward a stable interpretation of the case. They were so eager to pick up any stray matter relating to it that they seldom bothered about consistency. Far from shaping opinion, they tumbled out any gossip or rumor they could pick up. This meant that the press was peculiarly susceptible to manipulation by the parties, especially once both sides reached the conclusion that public opinion might play a large role in determining the outcome of the judicial process. Mrs. Rudd moved first. Several papers rushed into print with the story she circulated even as the justices at Bow Street debated what to do. "Since this affair has blown up, they [the Perreaus] took from her a gold watch that cost her £60, her purse containing twenty guineas, and lastly, to leave her entirely penniless, they borrowed the only half-crown she had in the world to pay the coach-hire to Sir John Fielding's." Thus was she exposed and defenseless at the very moment when they were preparing to betray her. At the end of one day's testimony, the *Morning Post* concluded with another such poignant tale. When Mrs. Rudd visited her Scottish relations in 1772, the paper confidently reported, she left £1400 with Daniel for the household expenses. On her return she discovered that not only had the money been exhausted, but her clothes and jewels had been pawned as well. "She was obliged to borrow £70 of a friend, to get some of the clothes back to appear in." On another occasion Mrs. Rudd sought to complete the portrait of herself as a sentimental heroine, still trying to help the brothers. "A correspondent," the paper reported, "assures us that she hourly expresses the deepest concern for their fate, and has expressed an earnest desire to administer them all the consolation in her power."[24] Once such stories appeared in one paper, others tended to pick them up, and through repetition they gained conviction.

The battle for public opinion escalated dramatically when Mrs. Rudd, on March 28th, presented her "Case," in part to answer what she announced was a "conspiracy formed against my life by Messrs. Perreau." This scheme, she charged, used the vehicle "of anonymous newspaper paragraphs" to slander her character. Her response came in a long, two-part history of her life with Daniel Perreau, an account that was quickly published in many London papers. It built on the story she had told at Bow Street, but in a move that was fateful for the future development of the episode, she told the tale of her life as a way of establishing the truth of who she claimed to be.[25] Mrs. Rudd seemed to be the first to grasp that the newspapers would become an important battleground in the case. In their pages she might meet her enemies on more equal terms. She sensed instinctively that public opinion might influence the course of justice and that the central contest would take place over the representation of character.

Mrs. Rudd continued to exploit the papers, although usually in less than subtle ways, throughout 1775. One senses that she must always have been an avid newspaper reader. In addition to publishing her "Case" and numerous letters, she placed advertisements warning against the errors contained in pamphlets arising out of the proceedings. She announced a £300 reward for information about an anonymous letter writer, and a threat of legal action against anyone who dared buy her goods at auction.[26] Her actions were often guided by a desire to secure maximum publicity and to foster a particular impression. Early in August, for instance, Mrs. Rudd launched a new campaign, this time against her children's nurse, Hannah Dalboux, with whom the children had been living since Mrs. Rudd's arrest. She demanded that the nurse return her youngest child to her. When Dalboux refused, Mrs. Rudd "summoned [her] before the Magistrates in Bow-street, in order to make her surrender her child." Rudd's attorney, Bailey, represented her in this matter and, accompanied by a "peace officer," went to Dalboux's house for the child. Francis Dalboux, the nurse's husband, told them that she had left home with the child and refused to divulge their whereabouts. A day later Bailey charged the man with assaulting him with a knife and threatening to kill him when he demanded the child's return.[27] The story of the fracas filled the papers for over a week.

No doubt Mrs. Rudd moved against the nurse because she had testified on Daniel's behalf at his trial. Rudd now charged that Dalboux was part of a widespread conspiracy to deprive her of her life. The nurse, Mrs. Rudd reported, was in private communication with her prosecutor, Frankland, and had made frequent trips to visit the Perreaus. These connections explained "from what Cause and for what Views this Woman refuses to deliver up the Child to its Mother." The papers melodramatically described Mrs. Rudd as "the wretched mother, in a state of mind bordering upon distraction lest any injury should befall her child." Mrs. Dalboux denied all the charges; she still awaited payment for the child's care, and her husband had been far too ill with gout to present any threat to Bailey. The press, however, tended to accept the sentimental portrait of Mrs. Rudd as a desperate mother wanting only to be reunited with her infant. The episode was one of her more effective performances.[28]

Predictably, the *Morning Post* was exceptional in the amount of space it gave to the case and the editorial comment it offered. It was particularly willing to open its pages to correspondence. Seventeen of the twenty-two anonymous letters published during the period up through the Perreaus' trial appeared in this paper. It also provided the most sympathetic portraits of the participants, even while publishing the most vitriolic letters. Although it assumed no consistent position, its style, tone, and procedure for collecting news certainly favored Mrs. Rudd. For instance, in April the paper praised an elegy she was supposed to have written for Daniel. "What a pity," it lamented, "that a woman of such superior beauty and talents, should have been fatally betrayed into such complicated misery." In the wake of the revelations offered at the June trials, the editor sought to assure her "that she had friends, that are still persuaded of her innocence and merit." The next day the paper prominently displayed a letter which complained that "the malevolence of Mrs. Rudd's enemies has now uninterrupted play." "It is certain no person's life and reputation has ever been so cruelly struck at, as Mrs. Rudd's." The author appealed for justice from the "impartial public."[29]

The *Morning Post* also showed its loyalty through its selection of what material to include or exclude. Shortly after their trials, Robert and Daniel published their defenses in the press. Between June 7 and 14, their stories took up almost twelve full columns and appeared in four of eight issues of the *Gazetteer*. By contrast, the *Morning Post* gave their first-person narratives less than three columns and these appeared only in two issues. When, after she was detained for trial, Mrs. Rudd published a second account of her story in the press, the *Gazetteer* gave it less than three columns in one issue, while the *Morning Post* ran her full story, usually on its first page, for more than a week, over seven issues, and filled fifteen columns with her first-person narrative.[30] Yet Bate, like all editors, made a great show of his supposed impartiality and often demanded of other papers that they treat Mrs. Rudd fairly. She had made a great display of canceling the publication of the third part of her "Case" so as not, she said, to prejudice the brothers' trials. Bate bemoaned the fact that her opponents were not as generous with her. Criticizing the appearance of two pro-Perreau pamphlets, the paper thundered against "the cruel and unjust steps taken by the prosecutors of Mrs. Rudd." Seeking to "depriv[e] her of that *undoubted right* of every person in her unhappy circumstance, [to] an impartial, uninfluenced trial," it was to the "*everlasting disgrace*" of her enemies, the *Post* concluded, that they attempted to "influence the minds of the jury and the public at that *very critical and awful moment* the *hour of trial.*"[31]

The *Morning Post* did not limit itself to stories favorable to Mrs. Rudd. Bate fully exploited the advantage to be gained from airing private controversy in public. His nose "to the wind," he knew what the public wanted to read and never hesitated to provide it. He was not above baiting the audience and seeking to provoke heated exchanges. Thus, on March 23, the paper reported that "a correspondent assures us that Mrs.—, now at large upon bail, is not the saint she appears." In addition to the many "Jews and Christians" who have supported "her unbounded extravagance," the anonymous author assured readers that "she is well known in King's Court, St. James's, as the celebrated Charlotte Turf." Bate got what he desired when Mrs. Rudd responded to these sly hints. In a further example of her close attention to the press and its power, the day after this insinuation she had inserted in the *Morning Post* a paragraph begging "the impartial public ... to suspend their judgment concerning the unfortunate Mrs. Rudd, as a most particular and true state of her connections with the two Mr. Perreaus, will certainly appear in this paper on Monday next."[32] Bate and Mrs. Rudd made unembarrassed use of each other. Their alliance was more one of convenience than conviction.

Most other papers took a fairly even-handed approach to the story, happy to print any information that came their way. One paper, however, the *Morning Chronicle,* was outspoken in its antipathy to the woman. At first its sympathies found expression in what it declined to print rather than in explicit commentary. In explaining why he had not printed Mrs. Rudd's "Case" in the paper, its editor, William Woodfall, noted that "as Mrs. Rudd is admitted an evidence for the Crown in the prosecution of two men, charged with a capital felony, whose lives may be affected by her testimony, he conceives it not only improper, but wantonly cruel to publish any matter which tends to enflame the popular prejudice against the unfortunate prisoners, and which might create an undue influence in the minds of those on whose verdict their fate depends." In the aftermath of the brothers' conviction, however, the paper pursued another line, choosing to publish Daniel's narrative. One correspondent wrote to the paper, demanding to know "how shall we account for the very different treatment of Mrs. Rudd." He complained that the "paragraphs respecting Mrs. Rudd" were "disgraceful to humanity." Woodfall took the unusual step of responding directly to this challenge, in a passage that left no doubt about his feelings. He would not "wantonly aggravate real distress, nor add to undeserved affliction; but there are some characters so totally depraved, so entirely lost to every sense of truth, honour, and morality, that they provoke our execration." "To talk of pitying such monsters," he concluded, "would only betray our weakness."[33] The paper intensified its campaign against Mrs. Rudd in the wake of the brothers' conviction. "The voice of the public," it announced with obvious pleasure, "seems now much in favour of Robert Perreau."[34] Such active partisanship on the part of two leading London papers helps explain the intensity of the emotions aroused by the case.

THE PAMPHLET WAR

Although newspaper accounts dominated discussion of the case, they were supplemented by the several versions of events that appeared in pamphlet form. Newspaper publishers often printed pamphlets as well, inspired by the desire to profit doubly from a case attracting wide public interest. Some of the pamphlets were reprinted verbatim in the press; for instance, the *St. James's Chronicle* republished a portion of one pamphlet in May under the title of a "secret history," exposing the reputed "lies" that Mrs. Rudd had told.[35]

In 1775 there were perhaps 120 printers at work in London, and some 110 bookseller-publishers. The competition was intense. It was a precarious trade, and printers seldom scrupled about publishing works for which the public was clamoring. They eagerly took tracts prepared by allies of the Perreaus or Mrs. Rudd, or half-invented accounts written by Grub Street hacks. Within a year some 20 pamphlets relating to the case had appeared. The developing conflict with the American colonies, by way of comparison, saw 14 works in 1773, 88 in 1774, and 160 in 1775.[36] Many of the tracts associated with the case came from well-known presses in the metropolis. John Bell, printer and bookseller, was behind the founding of the *Morning Post*. John Bew, a prolific dealer in popular literature, also published the *General Evening Post*. George Kearsley, bookseller and printer, had been arrested for his role in publishing the *North Briton*. These publishers had little interest in regulating the content of the publications associated with the story. On the contrary, the speedy release of an inflammatory work was likely to secure them the best sales. The literary reviews thought little of the quality of such efforts; the *Monthly Review* described many of them as "a fungus, grown out of the newspapers." In the heat of the moment, few readers were bothered by such jabs.[37]

The first pamphlet in the field was *The Female Forgery*, published by Bew. It promised "the affecting and interesting narrative of the elegant, though unfortunate, Mrs. Caroline Rudd, as written and corrected by herself." Appearing even before the brothers' trial, it advertised itself as "a minute recital of the repeated cruelties she suffered for a series of years, from her first connection with Mr. Daniel Perreau, to the present crisis; to which is added a pathetic elegy, which she transmitted to him in prison some few days ago." Although it was credited to her pen, she sent a note to the papers denying authorship. She would not deign, she wrote, "to contradict a false, lying, scandalous pamphlet, published on Saturday last, called *The Female Forgery*, and basely asserted to be written by me, the whole of which I am totally ignorant."[38] Such contentions and disclaimers were the staple of controversy in the period, but in this episode they provoked particular anger, for they contributed to the sense of deception and false dealing that haunted the proceedings, confounding every attempt to get to the bottom of the business. The brazen lies of either Rudd or the pamphlet's author seemed a continuation of the very fraud imposed on so many respectable people in the days and months before the crime was exposed.

Even as controversy surrounded this pamphlet, it was quickly followed by *Forgery Unmasked*, attributed by some to Sir John Fielding. It promised to reveal new information on what had transpired before the justice and warned that "no other account contains the memoirs of the Perreaus, nor is any other warranted genuine but the above." These too were the familiar claims of the pamphlet writer—to special authority, privileged knowledge, and novel details. As an added incentive, the advertisements said, it "was embellished with an elegant copper-plate of Daniel Perreau threatening to stab Mrs. Rudd." The account it offered was essentially that told by Mrs. Rudd during the commitment hearing. The *Critical Review* complained that this work was no more than "an attempt to profit by the curiosity of the public."[39] This pamphlet was followed by the *Genuine Memoirs of the Messrs. Perreau*, a volume that condemned other pretended efforts "fabricated by some Grubstreet Gazetteer, in order to get a dinner, and impose upon the world" to the prejudice of the brothers. "The rapidity of yesterday's sales, in preference to all others," the announcement promoting the tract ran, "shows the authenticity of these memoirs, and may convince the public they are the only genuine ones."[40] But what really inspired this comment was the knowledge that another pamphlet, employing the same title, was about to appear. Indeed, advertisements for the two works appeared in the same issue of the *St. James's Chronicle,* along with one for *Forgery Unmasked.* The author of the second work, published by Kearsley, issued the virtuous disclaimer that he had hesitated to publish his volume until the brothers had been tried, but reassured by the knowledge that his work would aid their cause, he went ahead with publication. At the same time he confessed that he wanted "to send it forth before the rise of Parliament had thinned the town."[41] The authors of these various works announced pompously in their titles that they aimed to unmask or discover the truth of an alarming situation. They all proclaimed that only they were genuine and honest. Protestations of disinterest and objectivity regularly filled the opening paragraphs of these works. Yet no one was taken in by the claims. Contemporaries bitterly debated the guilt or innocence of the Perreaus and Mrs. Rudd as they had recently argued over the character and intentions of George III, Lord Bute, and John Wilkes.

DANIEL'S TALE

One of the more remarkable features of this case was the readiness of the accused to turn to print to spread their stories. In hopes of winning over public opinion and swaying the course of justice, they offered the intimate details of their domestic lives. If Daniel's defense at his June trial was half-hearted, within five days he had recovered himself enough to contribute another chapter to the Perreau version of events. He published a pamphlet with what he claimed was the complete history of his relationship with Mrs. Rudd. He explained that in anticipation of being tried first, he had prepared an account of their connection from its beginning. But when his brother's trial had come first and ended so dishearteningly, he had felt unable to present it to his jury. The tale he now offered under the pretext of completing and correcting what had appeared at the Old Bailey was full of disturbing hints about Mrs. Rudd's past. Like Mrs. Rudd in her "confession," only with the roles now reversed, Daniel presented himself as a trusting, if romantic, fellow, whose conduct, if not wise, was nonetheless sincere and even noble. He explained that he was drawn to Mrs. Rudd by her "engaging manners and behavior," that he had acted toward her with honor, and that he thought of their connection as a "union." He had, he said, placed absolute trust in her word and fidelity. If he now seemed to be disloyal to her, it was only because she had already betrayed him and had perhaps never thought of him except as an instrument in her scheme. He now wrote, he protested, from a sense of the duty he owed to his "family and connections."[42]

Daniel told of meeting Mrs. Rudd, who was going by the name of Mrs. Gore, at Mrs. Johnson's in Hollen Street, Soho, during the spring of 1770. He frequently visited her and soon "became much attached." In these coded phrases Perreau confirmed the rumors that she was a courtesan when he met her. At an early meeting he learned that she was financially embarrassed; one day she was arrested as a result of the lawsuit of a silk-mercer. Daniel gallantly paid the £60 she owed, but he had no sooner done so than he discovered that she had other debts as well. She was, he wrote, pursued by a milliner for £80, and in all she owed some £400. He formed the resolution of breaking with her, but in the face of her desperate pleas, he relented. During this period, Daniel claimed, he had no knowledge that Mr. Rudd was alive. In October 1770 she came to him in great distress, however, with word that her husband had been inquiring after her. Mr. Rudd, she told him, was "a most debauched drunken man, who had used her with the greatest barbarity." Daniel helped her to move to a new address (in Parliament Street, Westminster) and, after Christmas, welcomed her to his abode in Pall Mall Court. In conversations with him at this time, she frequently spoke of her family, of an Uncle Stewart, whom she represented as a man of fortune in the north of Ireland, and of James Adair of Soho Square, a relation who had helped her in her troubles with Rudd. When she talked of this connection, she expressed regret that she was no longer on visiting terms with Adair, but she was coy when it came to explaining this coldness. In these opening pages Perreau drew a portrait of an extravagant and fantastic character, a woman capable of inventing complicated tales, and a courtesan who was often only a step ahead of multiplying troubles.[43]

Daniel failed to heed the warnings. On the contrary, the birth of a daughter on July 30, 1771, cemented the connection. It was, he wrote, "an event which, added to the great satisfaction I received from her engaging manner and behavior, so captivated my affections, that I truly lamented the insurmountable bar which prevented a legal union with her." This birth inaugurated a period of "uninterrupted harmony." Before long, however, new mysteries began to circle around the "family." In the summer of 1772, John

Stewart, a man Mrs. Rudd represented as the son of her Uncle Stewart, arrived from Ireland. He expressed his entire satisfaction with her situation. Mrs. Rudd now informed Daniel that this visit had led Stewart to arrange a reconciliation between herself and Adair. She told him that she was to go to the home of another relation, Thomas Cairns, and that Adair would meet her there. Following this supposed meeting, she returned home and happily announced that Adair had received her with "an affection truly paternal." Thereafter, Mrs. Rudd spoke constantly of visits from Adair, of walks in the park during which he "interested himself most warmly in her affairs."[44]

It was at this time, Daniel now argued, that she developed her "horrid" plan. In July she gave him £500, which she said James Adair had given to her as part of her grandmother's legacy from her Uncle Stewart. Over the next few months she showed Daniel an additional £400, which Adair supposedly bestowed on their daughter. At the time Mrs. Rudd was pregnant with their second child. The stories she now told became increasingly generous in terms of future prospects but also evidenced a greater concern to regulate Daniel's conduct. She told him that Adair repeatedly asked whether her connection with Perreau was one of necessity or affection. After she told him that no one else could make her so happy, he promised her £2000 for their first child and something for the second as well. She added that Adair wanted her to begin using the Perreau name and to take on, "as far as was possible, the appearance" of Daniel's wife. If this wish were fulfilled, Mrs. Rudd told Daniel, he would settle a "pretty little fortune" on her and introduce her to respectable parts of the family in Scotland as well as to his own wife. Because of his affection for her, and with an eye to the "great advantages" that might flow from this "great and singular friendship," Daniel said he happily let her "assume every possible appearance of my wife." He informed his brother of the change in his situation and mentioned the possibilities they opened up for the entire Perreau family. To a few friends, such as Dr. Brooke, he hinted at the connection with Adair. Pleased as he was with these developments, he was also frustrated, he wrote, that he was not able to meet with Adair in order to thank him for his generosity. Whenever he brought up the subject, Mrs. Rudd always put him off with the comment that such a meeting was premature. At the time he thought this response odd, since she spoke of the many visits she had from the gentleman. Daniel admitted in his "Narrative" that this situation was "a most extraordinary piece of delicate singularity," but since she was adamant, he did not press the issue. The tie between them became stronger still when, in October, she presented him with a son. At first they talked of naming the child for Adair but at the last moment decided to call him Stewart, to honor her uncle.[45]

Soon after her son's birth, Mrs. Rudd announced that she was setting off on a trip to Scotland. Her Uncle Stewart, she said, had arranged for her to meet some of their relations. She also showed Daniel £300, which she said Adair had given her to cover the expense of the visit. While in Scotland, Mrs. Rudd wrote him regularly, filling her correspondence with the details of meetings with her illustrious relatives. Even as this fair adventure was unfolding, however, Daniel spoke of the disquieting rumors that began to reach his ears. Mrs. Rudd first introduced the issue when she reported one day that Adair had received "several anonymous letters, tending to traduce her character." She also expressed the suspicion that she was watched whenever she went abroad. While she was in Scotland, Daniel reported, he found the house "beset with a number of mean and impertinent enquiries," some asking for Mrs. Gore, others for Mrs. Rudd. He received letters in a similar vein, which seemed to imply a blackmail scheme. Since no name was affixed, he chose to ignore them. Another letter, however, addressed to Mrs. Perreau, attracted his curiosity, and when he opened it, a card from Mr. Salvadore fell out. A letter from one of the wealthiest men in London could not but attract Daniel's attention. The card reminded him, he wrote in his "Narrative," that Mrs. Rudd had spoken of "an epistolary correspondence with Mr. Salvadore, which afforded her more pleasure and amusement, than any comedy or novel she had ever read." When Daniel approached Salvadore for an explanation of this most recent letter, the latter told him that he only wanted to locate Mrs. Rudd's sister. When Daniel informed him that she had no sister, Salvadore refused to believe him. Upon her return, Daniel confronted Mrs. Rudd about her continued connection to Salvadore, but she denied having written to him since she had taken up with Perreau. She swore to him at that time that all these letters and stories originated with her enemies. "I must own," Daniel concluded, "this occurrence gave some degree of uneasiness, which was aggravated by the impossibility I found of unravelling the mystery."[46]

Mrs. Rudd worked hard to allay Daniel's concerns. In June 1773 she assured him that James Adair had seen through this web of lies and was once again her friend. What this came to mean, at least according to Daniel's narrative, was an even more extensive intervention in their lives. Mrs. Rudd soon informed him that Adair wanted them to take a house at Grosvenor Square, for which he would provide £1000 to be spent on furniture. At the same time she produced £150 to pay for a new coach and reported that Adair was going to supply them with £800 per annum until he could fix Daniel up in business. Daniel recognized that his audience might find his crediting these ever more complicated tales of a wealthy man, operating in secret, taking such an interest in his family, incredible. "But surely," he responded, "it cannot be wonderful that I should believe them true, when it is considered, that she gave me the most substantial proofs of her veracity, by the frequent sums of money she produced." He could not long sustain his doubts when, at regular intervals, she gave him so much money. How else could he explain this income except by believing her story? Two months later Mrs. Rudd came to him with the tale that Robert Adair, the surgeon, had been behind the malicious campaign of gossip conducted against her. "She in this conversation told me a long story of the horrid wickedness of Mr. Robert Adair." He stood revealed as the one responsible for her low state when Daniel first met her. Daniel encouraged her to go to James Adair and explain Robert Adair's evil machinations. Mrs. Rudd returned to him later to say that she had done so and that Adair had expressed his determination "to have no farther connection with so bad a man." He added, however, according to her, that this tangled family intrigue justified his care in keeping the favor he showed to her and the Perreaus quiet. It also served to explain his unusual financial proceedings. In early 1774 Mrs. Rudd told Daniel that Adair, resolved to make their situation easier, had enlisted his relation, William Adair, to assist them. Daniel said he felt no qualms about such transactions because Mrs. Rudd enjoyed a steady stream of visitors and correspondence that supported her endless discussion of her relations. One John Adair was often at the house, and he in turn carried letters from Lady Agnew's family in Scotland. Mrs. Rudd "regularly received letters," both from Scotland and from her uncle. The evidence of so extensive a network of wealthy and respectable connections convinced Daniel of everything she told him. His confidence and affection increased still further when, toward the end of April 1774, she gave birth to their third child, a daughter.[47]

From this time Mrs. Rudd spoke of William Adair as the chief agent in advancing the interests of the Perreau family. The gentleman, she assured Daniel, had taken their welfare to heart, so as to put right the injury inflicted by Robert Adair. Thus it was William who instructed Perreau to take his wife into the country to help restore her health. He also requested Daniel to keep the house in Pall Mall, so that he might have a place to meet Mrs. Rudd without arousing suspicion. The scale of the promises concerning what the Adairs would do for the Perreaus increased dramatically about this time. Mrs. Rudd confided these plans to Daniel and other members of the Perreau family and showed them letters, supposedly signed by William Adair, which spoke plainly of these promises. There was talk of setting the brothers up as bankers and securing for Daniel a seat in Parliament. Nor did James Adair neglect them. Just before they left town Mrs. Rudd gave Daniel £200, which she said James had given to them to purchase plate.[48]

"About this period," Mrs. Rudd showed Daniel another letter from William Adair asking that Daniel secure a sum of money upon a bond in Adair's name. Daniel denied that he had any knowledge of such instruments. Instead, he simply followed the very specific instructions contained in Adair's note. Adair wished it to be done "in the most private manner." So Daniel obtained two bonds from Wilson, and Robert negotiated them with Mr. Mills, a banker, raising £3260 on one and £4000 on the other. The brothers gave the money to Mrs. Rudd, believing that she carried it to Adair. A week or so before the bonds fell due, Mrs. Rudd returned the sums so that Mills could be paid. About this time Robert carried another bond to Frankland in order to raise £4000. This instrument was repaid in August. The ease of these transactions lulled the brothers into an easy acquiescence to Adair's unusual requests. Along with the bonds, letters arrived, purportedly from Adair, containing various promises and instructions. William Adair had come to take as detailed an interest in the household as James had earlier. He proposed to take over the annual allowance, increasing it to £1500, of which £1200 was for general expenses and £300 for Mrs. Rudd's and the children's clothes. A gift of £30,000 would guarantee this income. Another letter recommended the purchase of a new house; initially he specified Cavendish Square. When no suitable house could be found, he suggested one in Harley Square whose builder wanted £4000. During this period Mrs. Rudd often went to town, saying she had to meet Adair. One day she returned with a letter and a draught for £19,000, the funds needed to set up the bank. Before Daniel could cash it, Mrs. Rudd requested its return, for it seemed now that Adair would buy them an estate in Suffolk so that Daniel might qualify for a parliamentary seat. She followed this report with word that Adair's first effort had failed because Lord Sandwich had already promised a seat at Huntingdon to a Mr. Womble (George Wombwell). Additional setbacks followed; in November 1774 she told him that the negotiations for the bank had failed when plans for a house in Pall Mall fell through because Adair did not like the terms.[49]

By this time, Daniel claimed, his brother was fully involved both in the promising plans for advancement and, more practically, in the arrangements to secure the loans. When, in November, Adair had given them a bond to pay for the house, Robert wrote to Frankland, who was in Yorkshire, to borrow against it. Frankland replied approving the request and directing them to apply to his banker. They followed a procedure that had become routine; Daniel obtained the bond, gave it to Mrs. Rudd to have signed, and, when it was returned, passed it on to his brother to negotiate. The money, Daniel insisted in his "Narrative," always went to Mrs. Rudd. In December another bond arrived with instructions that Daniel use it to arrange a loan with Dr. Brooke. At first, he wrote, he hesitated, noting that the bond was the same one that had been proposed, but not employed, in the earlier transaction respecting the seat in Parliament. Soon a letter arrived from Adair seeming "to reproach" him for his delay. So Daniel went to Brooke, who responded that he was short of cash. Daniel, acting on information from Mrs. Rudd, reminded him of the Ayr bonds. He also hastened to assure Brooke that it was Adair who wanted the money, and that it would be returned in a few days. At the same time he told the doctor that he had no idea what the money was for and expressed his unhappiness at being sent on such a mission. According to Daniel, both brothers were getting weary of these transactions. In order to calm the brothers' fears, Mrs. Rudd told them that Adair wanted the money to satisfy a loan to the King, which had gone to make up the debts of the Duke of Gloucester. Adair, she added, had used the occasion to speak to George III about making Daniel a baronet. Lord and Lady Gower had lent their support. Daniel described how this sudden escalation in the bounty that seemed about to descend on them once again stilled their doubts. Since the house was soon to be ready, Adair sent word that Robert should employ another bond for £4000 to raise money with Frankland in order to pay the builder. With this payment they secured the house and moved in about the middle of January. It was soon furnished in a grand style. Mrs. Rudd now announced that William and James Adair would soon visit them. She cautioned Daniel, however, that no mention should be made at that time of any of the financial transactions, as any slip would embarrass all the parties.[50]

Daniel's summary of the events leading up to the forgery's detection supported that of his brother. Once again he stressed Robert's great reluctance to be involved in one more bond. "This is a very unpleasant business," Daniel quoted his brother as saying; "I wish Mr. Adair would not trouble me with it." He told of returning home to find Robert uneasy about what had transpired at the bank. Mrs. Rudd tried to reassure them by speaking of a visit to Adair, who, she said, had given her a letter to the effect that all was well, which she passed on to Robert. Daniel wrote that he knew nothing more of the matter until he was called to Adair's. Once faced with the alarming revelations he learned there, he was stunned. "For considering him as newly waked out of a delusive dream, and suddenly immersed in infamy, he well might be confounded—nearly dumb—doubtful what to say—so stupified as not to know what to think, much less to utter." After they left Adair's, Daniel claimed that he pressed Mrs. Rudd to tell all that she knew, but she continued to insist that the bond had been given to her by William Adair. He was the one, or so he insisted, who proposed that they go see James Adair in order to get to the bottom of the business. She persuaded him to let her see Adair first. When she returned she reassured Daniel that Adair had been shocked by her story but that he would clear it all up when he dined with William Adair that evening. Daniel, not content with this version, sent his brother to inquire of James Adair how matters stood. Robert learned from Adair that Mrs. Rudd had told him the bond was forged. When all three next met together, Mrs. Rudd urged them to flee the country. Daniel said that he and his brother refused to adopt a course they found dishonest and disreputable. Instead, on Saturday, having been advised by several friends about his course of action, Robert procured one of Fielding's men to apprehend Mrs. Rudd. Daniel could scarcely contain his amazement, he remembered, when she was admitted to evidence while he and his brother were committed for trial.[51]

Daniel concluded his "Narrative" with the defense he had prepared but had not delivered in court. It repeated, for the most part, the portrait of Mrs. Rudd that Robert had offered at his trial. Daniel began by painting in pathetic terms the confusion of a man reduced to misery "by a series of the most artful deception." He hoped that the court would recognize that "elegance of language, and perspicuity of expression seldom flow from the lips of a man whose head is overwhelmed with the most poignant grief, and whose heart is distracted by the horrors of his situation." He knew that "the silent fear is the truly persuasive eloquence of acute distress." Still, he felt his reputation required him to offer a fuller statement of his case. He hoped thereby to expose "the most wicked and treacherous artifice, under a mask of the tenderest and most faithful friendship, worn by a woman, who by her specious behavior, and the delusive appearance of virtues, which she was in reality, far from possessing, had so captivated my infatuated affections, that I reposed the most unlimited confidence in her integrity." He conceded his weakness but said the "frailty of human nature" often led men to place their trust in an improper person. His narrative, he hoped, showed how this "pernicious woman" had drawn him into a "labyrinth" through a "horrid train of fraudulent deception" building upon his misplaced confidence. Only after he was imprisoned was he finally undeceived about the scope of her evil.[52]

He swore under oath that he had no part in a plot to rob another of his property. "It is," he continued, "the peculiar unhappiness of my situation, that the treacherous woman with whom I have unfortunately been connected, has been mistress of such consummate artifice to transact even the minutest matters, through the whole of this dreadful business, with such circumspection and foresight, as to put it out of my power to adduce any thing more than presumptive evidence in my justification." How, he wondered, could he be expected to have unraveled the mystery when, against all reason, it provided "houses and furniture." Who would expect a criminal to act in this way? Although the scheme was clever, he encouraged the jury to see to the bottom of the villainy. He reminded them of the similarity of handwriting in all the bonds as the surest guide to guilt. Since Mrs. Rudd's "feigned hand" appeared in all the instruments and letters, this fact must destroy her claim that he had coerced her into forging only one bond. Her successful imposition upon Justice Fielding was the epitome of the craft she practiced on all men. He concluded with the hope that the jury would resist the designs of "a most abandoned woman," who imposed on "unsuspecting innocence, by concealing a disposition truly diabolical."[53]

LETTERS AND THE PRESS

If the pamphlets produced by the participants and their allies helped to create and sustain the atmosphere of contention and suspicion that surrounded the case, the correspondence in the papers became central to the shape and impact of the Perreau-Rudd case. Letters formed an important part of the eighteenth-century newspaper, accounting for a significant portion of the paper's content. They were often intermixed with more conventional reports and sometimes presented fresh information for the news-starved papers. Hard-pressed editors found that correspondence offered cheap filler. Three or four letters might appear on any given day. They also generated responses, thus offering the reader a sense of participating in an ongoing debate. Although they appeared to originate in the spontaneous decision of the writer, a clever publisher might select correspondence to stir up trouble or circulate a view he did not want to own directly. Thus the letters could become the news, especially in the case of more controversial topics. Foreigners were struck by this aspect of English journalism. "You may insert your opinions," Archenholz wrote, "on any public matter in the newspapers, with a certainty of being read a thousand times." "The reading of the daily prints," he added, "[is] an epidemical passion among the English."[54]

Most letters were anonymous. Proponents of a cause were free to advance their purpose without acknowledging their identities. The veil of anonymity, however, acquired constitutional significance in the eyes of many contemporaries. Modest persons had an opportunity to engage as equals with their superiors. The people might lecture their governors, it was said. The appeal to the public also implied the existence of a court of opinion that counted as much as England's traditional class-bound institutions. The pseudonyms attached to many letters were meant to reinforce their messages. The writer professed to speak for a wider group or the entire public, to embody a principle or speak with the prestige of some classical figure. In the absence of reporters who could vouch for the information they presented, correspondents claimed to represent more than personal opinion. They pretended to an authority for their pronouncements all the greater because they had no rivals. From the epistolary novel to the letters of Junius, the letter form served as a means for private individuals to demand the public's attention. At their best, the letters permitted open debate among a wide public on the important issues of the day. At their worst, they invited manipulation and permitted unrestrained expressions of anger or slander, with little risk of being called to account.[55]

The appearance of Mrs. Rudd's "Case" produced an immediate response, a short, abusive letter to the *Morning Post* on March 29 accusing her of gross improprieties. The name affixed to this letter, Harriot Grieve, reinforced the most serious charge by linking Mrs. Rudd to a case of fraud and deception that had startled London in 1773. In that year William Kidwell charged Elizabeth Harriet Grieve with defrauding him of £36. Claiming to be the first

cousin of Lord North, second cousin to the Duke of Grafton, and an intimate friend of Charles James Fox, she put an advertisement in the newspaper offering to secure people government employment for a small gratuity.
Elizabeth Cooper testified that her husband paid £62 for an office and that
he died of a "broken heart" when the promise proved false. "Some of the
above-mentioned parties would probably not have fallen a sacrifice to her
artifices, but that the sight of gilded chariots almost perpetually at her door
seemed to confirm her account of her great interest and connections." It transpired at her trial that she neither possessed any exalted relations nor knew
the people with whom she claimed friendship. Fox became a target of satire
because he was her foremost victim. Short of money, he had let himself be
persuaded by her that she could arrange a marriage for him with a West Indian heiress worth £160,000. Grieve duped Fox, securing his regular attendance upon her, and used his presence to advance her other schemes. Fox
became the butt of several satires for his credulity. "How Charles," one poem
went, "with all his wondr'ous wit and sense—with all his quickness, parts
and eloquence,—his tricks, contrivances, address and skill—prov'd a cat's-
paw to a woman's will."[56]

If the name attached to this letter pointed to a parallel with the present
episode, the hints it offered about Mrs. Rudd's past must have shocked anyone following the story. It charged that her "Case" was the "production of
your learned, eminent council and letter-carrier manufactured at the widow's
over a pint of hot, in Bow-street." If it sought to prove she was possessed of
£13,000, it left the public "to guess how it was obtained." By way of answering its own question, the correspondent listed a variety of schemes and ruses,
including "cohabiting" with Salvadore, securing money from him by forging
a letter "from our gracious" Queen, pretending to be a "natural daughter" of
the late Prince of Wales, an excursion into Herefordshire that included imposing on tradesmen under the name Lady Caroline Gore, "and many more
curious anecdotes."[57]

A flurry of other letters in the following days reinforced these dark accusations. "Shall Mrs. R—, with a *genteel mind*," one author challenged, "affect to
despise anonymous writers, who tell her disagreeable truths, avow her being
in a state of whoredom, that she has spent her fortune in the indulgence of licentious and guilty pleasure." He expressed particular indignation at her attack upon a "lady of fair and honourable character [Mrs. Robert Perreau]."
Another correspondent put a series of provocative questions: "What is be-

come of her husband, Mr. Rudd? How became she possessed of that large property she has so wantonly lavished on D. Perreau?" Were her associates respectable, and had she been guilty of no lapses in her fidelity to Daniel Perreau? These letters took a mocking tone toward her claims of "exquisite sensibility" and a "high sense of honour."[58] Yet another author wrote that "her story appears extremely contradictory and evasive: if newspaper intelligence tell truth, this woman had been in gay life (worse I ought to style it) long before she became acquainted with these malefactors, and was ever esteemed as artful a woman as any in England." She might say that she gave Daniel £13,000, but "no planet can influence me to believe it." "It seems, she has always been remarkable for her great powers in moving the passions, therefore it is not the least object of admiration, that the tone of her voice, the artless manner in which she related her story, and the decency of her whole deportment was so truly pathetic, as to lull the wisdom of the magistracy that examined her." The fact that she had escaped the gallows, this author concluded, was no reason why she should be permitted to deceive the public.[59]

These accusations climaxed in a letter signed "S. L." that appeared in most London papers between March 30 and April 8. The timing was crucial because it was widely expected that the brothers would come to trial during the first week of April. This letter was intended to sway the outcome of the deliberations. Although it revealed little that was new, it was longer and more detailed, as well as more carefully argued, than previous efforts. Yet the material it contained was equally inflammatory. The letter adopted the familiar heavy-handed satiric tone that marked much of the correspondence of the period. The author posed as the friend of Mrs. Rudd, someone whose only concern was to help her confront the nasty rumors circulating around her name. "I hope," he wrote, "in her relation of this story, she will be able to refute all the ill-natured and unjust aspersions at present thrown out against her." The correspondent then proceeded to rehearse these charges. Had she abandoned her husband for another officer? Did she disguise herself as a "foreign princess" to win the "embraces of a noted amorous son of Levi"? "Whether she did not pretend to be with child by this Jew?" "Whether she has not, at different times, personated many and various Ladies of the first quality and fashion in town, and in *their* names prostituted *herself*?" The letter fostered the impression that she was a master of disguise who had a long career of fraud and deception. And it broadly hinted that these "intrigues" were only a few examples among "numberless others."[60]

It was not in Mrs. Rudd's nature to allow such accusations to pass unremarked. Sometimes she responded under her own name, as when she announced in April that she knew "at this moment" that the Perreaus were "concerting abominable falsehoods, whereby they hope to blacken my character." "How falsely my enemies represented me," she complained, "how undeservedly I was persecuted and traduced by them." In May she answered one opponent, expressing the hope that the "glaring falsities he has advanced refute themselves, and recoil on their author the scandal he aims at me." Quite often, it seems, she employed a pseudonym when she challenged her critics. A letter to the *Morning Post,* most likely from her pen, sought to undo the effect created by the revelations of "S. L." "How easy is it," the author wrote, "for him to put a string of impertinent questions, full of inveterate spleen." The correspondent responded in kind, asking whether "S. L." "did not rob a man on Hounslow Heath," and if "under an assumed character" he did not fraudulently obtain goods? "Let him clear himself of these charges," the letter demanded, "before he meddles with the character of a woman who has suffered enough already."[61]

These letters flooded into the papers in substantial numbers, especially at crucial moments in the history of the case. From the end of March to the end of May, normally a slow time for the press, more than 30 letters appeared, defending or attacking Mrs. Rudd or the Perreaus. Several were signed by Mrs. Rudd, but the majority were anonymous, passing under such pseudonyms as "One of the Public," "Honour and Justice," "Candour," "Unknowing and Unknown," and "Justice." Before the episode drew to its close in early 1776, over 150 letters dealing with one or another aspect of the case would appear in the papers. They represented one of the most dynamic aspects of the episode, in some instances reflecting the shifting public mood, in others acting as crude efforts to manipulate opinion. Most of the information about the case that went beyond what appeared in the public record originated in this correspondence. But precisely because of its source, this "news," though avidly read, did little to inspire confidence or to settle the doubts in people's minds.

REACTIONS TO THE PRESS

This was surely one of the first instances in which the press's impact on the outcome of judicial proceedings came in for such thorough discussion.[62] It was unusual for a party involved in a criminal case to issue an appeal to the public before the trial commenced. It was rare for a woman to make such an appeal. The papers were condemned for the attention they gave to immoral characters and revelations of scandalous conduct. They were accused of airing biased portraits that threatened to make an impartial trial impossible. "Nothing is now a-days more common," one correspondent complained, "than the discussion, prejudication, and decision of the innocence and guilt of culprits before trial in newspapers." "The minds of the petty jury should resemble a sheet of paper, without spot, impression, or stain." Yet full accounts had been from the first offered of the entire case, "prejudicing the most impartial; nor can one man out of a hundred, when he comes to be impanelled as a juryman, get rid of the extrajudicial impressions which such accounts had left upon his mind."[63] Both correspondents and editors worried about the way the papers were caught up in the case and seemed to be influencing its development. "An impartial correspondent," writing to the *Craftsman,* thought

> that the unfortunate situation of the Perreaus, instead of wantonly inducing people to dissect their characters, which are, at present, under the cognizance of the laws of their country, should in no one respect become a subject for public discussion, other than as a beacon to that large class of people in this metropolis, who like them despising the government of their own reason, as well as the line of their circumstances, permit themselves to be swallowed up in the too general vortex of dissipation.[64]

The *St. James's Chronicle* expressed a similar concern about devoting so much space to the productions of the participants. It appended a paragraph at the end of one of Mrs. Rudd's longer efforts explaining its conduct.

> We shall not enter here into any disquisition on the propriety or impropriety of publications of this sort, how far they may be supposed to prejudice peoples minds, and of course to influence the opinions of a jury; whether the two unfortunate culprits are right in reserving their defense till the day of trial; or whether they ought to have counteracted her charges by an immediate answer. All we mean by the present publication is, without influence or prejudice to anyone, to lay her case, according to her own relation of it, and so far as it has appeared, entire, before our readers, which has hitherto been given only piecemeal to the public; omitting in our account of it such

reflections only as do not at all interfere with the narrative, and which may be better spared, as from the strength of the narrator's feelings, they occur, perhaps, too often either to please or inform by their repetition.[65]

But it was not simply whether it was appropriate or right for the press to discuss the case or open their pages to antagonists that troubled some editors and correspondents. The real issue was what this unhealthy interest in the case said about the condition of the nation. One of the earliest letters to the *St. James's Chronicle* complained of the morals of an age that devoted so much attention to so sordid a crime. The papers were full of such complaints and pious moralizing. In late July the *Middlesex Journal* attacked the amount of space given to the "Perreaus and Rudd." "As much attention," he noted, "is paid to the protestations of convicts and forgers as if their despicable contradictions were material to the public." One saw "as many columns filled with their stuff as with the preparations of Spain, the American War, or the fate of Britain." The papers might as well be "mere Tyburn Chronicles." About the same time, another correspondent drew a similar conclusion. "At this alarming period," when there was trouble in the colonies and threats from abroad, people were too preoccupied "in considering the case of two notorious swindlers, and an infamous prostitute." He pleaded that the country pay less attention to such trifles, which made England look contemptible in the eyes of Europe. There is no evidence that these observations had the least impact on the press's treatment of the case or the public's avidity for news of it.[66]

The case's novelty and its troubling character produced a measure of soul-searching even amid the scramble for further details. Early in the coverage of the episode two letters to different publishers sought to place it in a wider context. One written to the *Public Advertiser* by "Philo-Messala" bemoaned the public fascination with the forgery story. "I find," the author commented, "that the *important* Affair of the two Perreaus has, at length, driven the American Business out of all Conversation without Doors, and even within." Here interest in the case was contrasted with the neglect of more important public affairs; in such degenerate times, the writer implied, scandal commanded more attention than the welfare of the nation. The second letter, to the printer of the *St. James's Chronicle*, connected a series of shocking events (the Duchess of Kingston's bigamy trial, Lady Grosvenor's adultery and divorce case, George Germain's cowardice at Minden, the Fordyce bank debacle, a royal pardon for the murderous Kennedys) with the Perreau case and with the desperate situation of the empire. He compared the 1770s to the period of the Walpolean ascendancy and described both as characterized by servile self-aggrandizement as well as personal and political corruption.[67] It was a characteristic feeling that too much attention was being paid to the case. Yet the attraction was irresistible; the case moved from the papers into conversation, until there was no way to escape its presence.

The papers did not create the interest, but they certainly fanned it, not only by their extensive coverage but more especially when they opened up their pages to people's comments. Although publishers expressed a general commitment to fairness, objectivity, and honesty, the conditions of publication militated against their realization. Papers lacked the means to search out the facts, and given the absence of an investigative police, they printed what came to hand. In this instance they published rumors or worse. The more sensational the accusation, the more outrageous the fact, the more enthusiastic the reception. Nor did the papers desire to control the story or filter what went before the public. They did not have the recognized authority to rise above the struggle. They were not yet an institution that could regulate the shape and direction of a report. They were simply a place where competing opinions could be expressed.[68] It was for this reason that the press coverage of the case paralleled its treatment of politics. The case became a kind of political contest in which the innocence or guilt of the accused became the subject of intense partisan wrangling. Certainly the participants adopted the techniques and language of such contests. Personal abuse and a kind of clumsy satire dominated discussion in the newspapers because that was the dominant mode of newspaper debate in the 1770s.

M! ROBERT PERREAU.

1. Robert Perreau. "The most amiable character that the English language is capable of conveying." (Courtesy of the Bodleian Library, Oxford University)

M! D. PERREAU.

M!ˢ RUDD.

2. Daniel Perreau. "Ambitious of splendour and magnificence." (Courtesy of the Bodleian Library, Oxford University)

3. Mrs. Rudd. "Mrs. Rudd's appearance and behaviour was in every respect becoming and distinguishing." (Courtesy of the Bodleian Library, Oxford University)

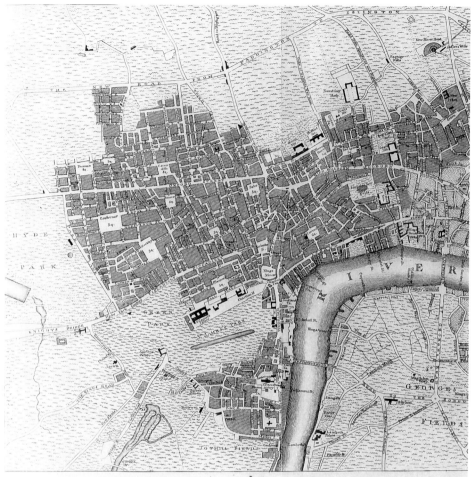

A NEW and Complete PLAN of LONDON WESTMINSTER

4. London at the time of the Perreau-Rudd scandal. On either side of Oxford Street were the squares of the West End, "the heart of British fashionableness."(Courtesy of the William Ready Division of Archives and Research Collections, McMaster University Library, Hamilton, Canada)

and SOUTHWARK, with the Additional Buildings to the Year 1777.

5. Mrs. Rudd's story. "On her knees [she] implored him not to oblige her to forge the name." (Courtesy of the Bodleian Library, Oxford University)

6. Sir John Fielding at Bow Street. "The great pains that was taken to come at the real truth of this business does singular honour to Sir John Fielding." (Courtesy of the William Ready Division of Archives and Research Collections, McMaster University Library, Hamilton, Canada)

7. Daniel and Robert Perreau at the Old Bailey. "Honest undesigning characters have at all times been the dupe of craft and subtilty." (Courtesy of the Bodleian Library, Oxford University)

8. Mrs. Robert Perreau visits her husband in prison. "The wretched objects beheld each other with speechless anguish for several minutes." (Courtesy of the Bodleian Library, Oxford University)

9. The Duchess of Kingston. "Possessed that gift of utterance for which ladies of spirit are sometimes so eminent." (Courtesy of the British Library)

10. Miss Jane Butterfield, the accused poisoner. "Butterfield was not a vicious wanton: perhaps few were ever born with sentiments so nearly allied to honour and virtue." (Courtesy of the British Library)

A New Scene for the Proprietors of India Stock

The Present times, or the Nabobs CL-VE and C-L-KE
brought to Account.
Deel awa wi em Au R-ques all alike, Bribers & Bribed

11. The financial crisis of 1772. "Oh what a Curse upon Commerce is
this modern Spirit of Speculation." Illustrated are Robert Clive, director
of the East India Company, and a "stock-jobber," who are chained to
the devil as they plead before a judge. (Copyright the British Museum)

MACARONI .GAMBLER

12. The fraudulent banker Alexander Fordyce, the "Macaroni Gambler."
"Disdaining the thought of mediocrity, without any moderation in his vast
desires, [he] aspired to be the richest commoner in Britain." (Copyright the
British Museum)

13. Mrs. Rudd at the Old Bailey. "She had a smelling bottle in her hand, which she often applied to her nose; and when she retired, she made a very low curtsey to the court, but did not appear in the least dismayed." (Copyright the British Museum)

14. Mrs. Rudd in prison. "What is the situation of the unhappy female . . . subject to all the little weaknesses of her sex." (Courtesy of the British Library)

15. Mrs. Rudd with pen in hand. "I am neither afraid nor ashamed of anything I do, say or write." (Courtesy of the Bodleian Library, Oxford University)

16. Portrait of Mrs. Rudd. Engraving from a painting by Daniel Dodd. (Copyright the British Museum)

17. Mrs. Rudd's trial. "The general deportment of Mrs. Rudd, in so awful and trying a situation, so far raised the admiration of all present, that every spectator became interested in her cause." (Courtesy of the William Ready Division of Archives and Research Collections, McMaster University Library, Hamilton, Canada)

18. Mrs. Rudd after acquittal, December 8, 1775. "Elegantly dressed, satin *couleur de rose*, her hair in perfect taste." (Courtesy of the Bodleian Library, Oxford University)

19. Daniel and Robert Perreau at Tyburn, January 17, 1776. "Thus the two brothers, in the same moment quitted that world which they had entered together." (Courtesy of the British Library)

Four

PASSING FAIR

DURING AND IMMEDIATELY after their trials, the Perreaus and their witnesses told of the fair promises that Mrs. Rudd had employed to secure their confidence. She had, they said, offered such a tempting prospect of advancement that they could be pardoned for naively acting as her agents. They were dazzled when she spoke of how her relations and their connections were at work to set the brothers up as bankers, buy them a country estate, make Daniel a member of Parliament and a baronet. Although the press, after the fact, characterized these promises as having a romantic or fairy-tale quality about them, Robert pleaded with the jury to remember the solid proofs she had presented to them. They had no reason to doubt her stories of distinguished visitors when they saw the letters that preceded and followed such visits. The frequent gifts of money lent substance to her tales. The startling accuracy with which she detailed the sums needed to complete these transactions, and the way influence would be applied to secure these honors, strengthened confidence in her veracity. After months of such talk they had become so enamored with their good fortune that they could no longer approach it skeptically. No one placed in a similar position, they suggested, would have looked askance at all this bounty.

To the brothers, Mrs. Rudd's promises had ceased to look fantastic. Nor, apparently, had they seemed so to Admiral Frankland or Dr. Brooke. Many in the Perreau circle responded to the rumors of the Perreaus' good luck with wonder but not disbelief. They took at face value the tales of mysterious interests at work behind the scenes promoting the family's rise. Even casual acquaintances had heard gossip suggesting this explanation for the sudden affluence of Daniel Perreau and Mrs. Rudd. Far from questioning this story, people sought to be associated with a family blessed with such connections, to share in the glamour it radiated. They did not consider Mrs. Rudd's offers chimerical because others had entered the world of fashion from origins more lowly, and in as improbable a manner as she promised. In fact, the man whom Mrs. Rudd claimed had beaten Daniel to the nomination for the parliamentary seat for Huntingdon, George Wombwell, was himself just such a person. Born only a year before the Perreaus, he had started life obscurely as the son of a Yorkshire grocer. Before his thirtieth birthday, however, he was a London merchant. He made a useful alliance in 1765 when he married Susanna, the only daughter of Thomas Rawlinson, master of the Company of Grocers and a former Lord Mayor. Wombwell served as a government contractor and army victualler, as well as a director of the East India Company. He won a seat in Parliament in 1774 and became a baronet in 1778.[1] Nor was he the only contemporary to have made so stellar a rise. Alexander Fordyce, bred as an Aberdeen hosier, left the north like so many other able young men, for the lure of advancement in London. After working as a clerk in Boldero's bank, he himself founded a hugely successful international bank.

Such stories of success had been a staple of London mythology since the Middle Ages, but there seemed a constant supply of fresh instances to sustain the dreams of the ambitious who flocked to the metropolis. The Perreaus would not have been the first Huguenots to have become successful bankers through a mixture of careful planning and good fortune. Claudius, the father of the founder of Amyand's bank, had been a Huguenot refugee who became a surgeon to George II. George Amyand set up as a London merchant with important dealings in Germany. His brother, Claudius II, held several government posts, which brought the firm substantial government business. A fortunate marriage to the widow of the Earl of Northampton helped to advance the family's influence. Like other successful financial families, the Amyands combined banking with government contracting, membership in the East India Company, and the acquisition of West Indies properties. George worked with Newcastle and Salvadore in supporting government financial measures, and he was an ally of the latter in the struggle for control of the East India Company. Rumor credited him, at the time of his death, with a fortune worth £160,000 sterling, in addition to other valuable assets.[2]

The metropolis drew the bold and adventurous from every direction. "London," Thomas Gisborne wrote, "is the center to which almost all individuals who fill the upper and middle ranks of society are successively attracted." "Business, interest, curiosity," he explained, "the love of pleasure, the desire for knowledge, the thirst for change, ambition to be deemed polite, occasion a continual influx into the metropolis from every corner of the Kingdom." "In most families of England," another author wrote in 1776, "if there be any son or daughter that excels the rest in beauty or wit, or perhaps courage, or industry, or any other rare quality, London is their north-star, and they are never at rest till they point directly thither." "At last," wrote the German visitor Lichtenberg in 1775, "I am in my beloved London, for which I have longed and schemed and pined."[3] Such incomers made the metropolis a city full of immigrants. According to one informal sample based on the records of the Westminster dispensary, only one quarter of the residents were natives of London, four-sevenths came from England and Wales, one in fifteen came from Scotland, and one in eleven from Ireland. The different backgrounds of the people involved in this case reflected the city's complex makeup. The Drummonds were Scots, as were Boswell and Mansfield. Joseph Hickey and the Adairs were Irish, as was Mrs. Rudd. Her one-time keeper, Joseph Salvadore, was a Portuguese Jew. Admiral Frankland's family estates were in Yorkshire, and Lady Frankland was a South Carolinian. Frankland himself spent many years in the Caribbean, as did John Baker, who had become acquainted with the Perreau family on St. Kitts. All came to London, the heart of British fashion, some to make their fortunes, and others to enjoy the fruits of wealth acquired elsewhere.[4]

Thus, before the disclosures at Bow Street, the Perreaus stood at the center of one kind of London story, that of rapid economic success followed by increasing social and even political influence. Once the case exploded, they figured in a different, though related, tale of overreaching ambition and collapse. These were peculiarly London stories, composed in equal part of aspiration, illusion, and cynical realism. They resonated among a metropolitan audience who shared the same ambitions and fears. Mrs. Rudd and the Perreaus were easily identified as individuals striving desperately to climb the slippery slopes of the capital's commercial and social world. Each new revelation only fixed them more firmly as kindred of the characters who haunted the London stage of the period. Men and women alike strove to get ahead. They pursued wealth and social recognition. In a world of outsiders, drawn from every corner of the nation or the empire, all wanted to become insiders. For every individual who had been born to or scaled the heights, there were hundreds of dreamers or schemers eager to join them. It was not always easy to tell the one from the other, amid the pushing and jostling for position. The few winners were admired and envied. Some of those who lost out crashed spectacularly; more typically, they simply slipped from view.

Although London in 1775 had a population of 750,000, with perhaps one in seven a member of what Wilkes called "the middling set of people," the participants in the Perreau case belonged to a much narrower social world. The papers from the very first gave the crime a precise geographical location that condensed a variety of social and psychological implications into a simple phrase. Daniel and Robert Perreau, they reported, "were both handsome, genteel men, and well known in the polite circles of the west end of town."[5] It had long been accepted that the metropolis was so deeply divided that "one end of London is like a different country from the other in look and in manners." The German visitor Archenholz wrote that the contrast between the City of London "and the western parts of the metropolis is astonishing." As the aristocracy and professional classes moved to the west, this area became the vibrant center of polite society. Here the houses were "almost all new, and of excellent construction; the squares are magnificent; and the streets are built in straight lines, and perfectly well lighted."[6] The social class who claimed the West End as their particular sphere consisted of perhaps 3000 to 4500 "gentle" families regularly resident in London, along with some 1000 families drawn from the elite of trade and banking. Altogether this "upper-income sector" may have amounted to 2–3 percent of the population. The Perreaus and Mrs. Rudd stood on the fringes of this class; for a time it looked as if they were about to launch a brilliant assault upon its upper reaches.[7]

One of the marked features of this case was the intimacy of the social world it revealed. People often knew each other, if not by sight then by reputation. They shared the same streets and squares. The aristocracy at this time dominated St. James Square and Hanover Square. Arlington Street attracted "ministerial" types, while Grosvenor Square contained the residences of Lord North and the Marquis of Rockingham. Several church dignitaries and judges, including the Earl of Mansfield, lived in Bloomsbury Square. Most of the leading figures in the case occupied residences in areas being abandoned by the aristocracy in the city's relentless march west. Robert Perreau lived for a time on St. Albans Street, but in 1770 he moved to no. 29 Golden Square, a fashionable address since the seventeenth century that in 1720 had been home to six members of the nobility. By 1740, though, only one remained, and the square had been taken over by a more professional and commercial population. One observer, in a slightly disparaging comment, remarked that there was "nothing remarkable in the structures." James Adair lived in Soho Square, still "largely inhabited by country gentry, dowager ladies and Members of Parliament, with a leavening of professional men." In the 1760s it housed Chevalier D'Eon, General Conway, and William Beckford, in addition to Adair. The Drummonds' bank was at Charing Cross, and William Adair lived among the shops and coffee-houses of Pall Mall. So did Daniel Perreau, who had rooms there at the time he met Mrs. Rudd. He also resided near Robert Drummond and within a few blocks of Dr. Thomas Brooke of Charles Street, St. James Square. Mrs. Rudd lived at various times in furnished rooms on Wardour Street and in Meard's Court, among the side streets of Soho. When she and Daniel purchased a house on Harley Street, they joined the movement of the fashionable to the north and west of the older squares.[8]

London was also a city crisscrossed by networks and alliances. The influence of family and kinship, professional grouping and personal favor, ethnic identity and neighborhood connection could be found at every turn. If at moments London looked like a society dominated by appearances, more often the metropolis provided glimpses of the structures and relationships that shaped individual destinies. The Perreaus and Mrs. Rudd were not unique; their lives and the tales they told echoed those of both the successful and the less fortunate. London gossip, like the London stage, was filled with stories of the lucky break, the advantageous connection, the secret operation of influence and favor. But everyone knew that these in turn worked through family, friends, and associates, any one of which could play a decisive role in transforming one's life.

THE PERREAU TRIBE

The Perreau brothers were members of a tightly knit Huguenot family. Their grandfather had been a native of La Rochelle, a principal magistrate of the town and the owner of a large estate. He abandoned his lands at the time of the revocation of the Edict of Nantes in 1685 and fled the country in disguise. His family joined the forty or fifty thousand Protestants who left France for England, the majority settling in London.[9] It was said that the Perreaus counted a number of "respectable French protestants" among their friends and relations in England and Ireland. Their father, Daniel, was born in Greenwich, one of the villages where the Huguenots established a school. Finding his prospects at home limited, he eventually went out to the West Indies to seek his fortune, becoming secretary to the governor of the Windward Islands. There he married a Miss Bretton, whose family came from Northamptonshire and whose father was attorney general of the islands. Through this alliance, the Perreaus became associated with an extensive clerical family. Miss Bretton's sister was married to the Archdeacon of Hereford, and both sisters were descended from the Bishop of Norwich's lady, Mrs. Reynolds.[10]

Daniel and Robert's parents had fourteen children, most of whom were born on St. Kitts. The brothers, the focus of family hopes, were sent to England to be educated, where they were "instructed in most branches of polite learning." The early deaths of both parents led to the return of most of the children to England. Unfortunately for all concerned, the family's social and economic situation was precarious. There was little wealth to go around, especially when it had to be shared among so many children. In this crisis, the extended family proved a crucial resource. The children were dispersed among a network of relatives. A cleric in Hereford took two nieces, while an elder sister stayed behind in the West Indies and married a doctor. Robert was sent to a man named Lloyd, who had married a sister of his mother's, and Daniel went to live with a younger brother of the archdeacon. Two of the Perreau sisters were trained as milliners; inheriting a small patrimony, they moved to the country, where they lived on their savings and what they made by their work. Their youngest brother, Samuel, became a lieutenant in the Navy, where, by one account, he was a favorite of Sir Peter Denis (a Huguenot himself) and Admiral Keppel. Samuel died, heroically it was said, in battle off the coast of India. A younger sister perished in going ashore at Madras, where she had gone to take possession of a fortune left to her by her husband, who had held a position in the East India Company. Like so many other families of the middling sort, the Perreaus looked to the empire as a means of repairing diminished fortunes.[11]

Whether far apart or nearby, the family frequently exchanged visits, letters, and assistance. Loyalty to one another was a supreme value. Daniel and

Robert visited with each other three or four times a day. Their families were often together. Susannah Perreau, their sister, said she was constantly back and forth to Robert's house from May through July of 1774. The sisters who lived in Wales exchanged frequent letters with their brothers and loaned them money. When danger threatened their brothers, they quickly rallied to their defense. Concern with the family name and reputation helped explain Robert's conduct throughout the events of the year.[12]

Such reliance on networks of kinship was common. Sir George Wombwell rose to public prominence with the help of his uncle and benefactor, who made him a partner in his banking house. Henry and Robert Drummond were introduced to banking by their uncle, Andrew Drummond, who got his own start through the assistance of an uncle, John Drummond, Dutch merchant, government contractor, and MP. Much of the Drummonds' early business came not only from expatriate Jacobite Scots (Henry and Robert's father, William, had been killed fighting for the Young Pretender in 1745), but also from dealings with other Drummonds. At least ten Drummonds banked with Andrew. During the Seven Years' War, Henry Drummond acted as agent for the 42nd and 46th regiments (both commanded by relatives), and the 98th (commanded by a family friend). During the mid-century wars, military contracting became a lucrative enterprise, if one possessed both organizational skill and political connections. Although this was not the source of their fortunes, the Drummonds, along with their acquaintance William Adair, "multiplied their fortunes several times by seizing the opportunity to feed Britain's soldiers and sailors." Andrew's son John married a granddaughter of the Duke of St. Albans, and both Henry and Robert married into well-connected gentry families. In his later years, Andrew viewed these marriages as the capstone of the family prosperity. "I have done great things, and have almost everything I could desire. My son is married into a noble family, and I have planted a colony of Drummonds round Charing Cross which appears to thrive."[13] Similarly James Adair, the Irish linen merchant who owned branches in Belfast and London, as well as a landed estate in County Down, wrote to his son James, the young lawyer and aspiring politician, that various family relations were using their influence to aid him. William Adair, his uncle, had been helpful. He encouraged his son to speak to Robert Adair, who might mention James's advancement to Dr. Hunter. He advised his son to have Robert mention that James was a relation. Only two of the fifty-three men who were made baronets in the decade before the case came from what their biographer has called "unknown parentage." At least thirteen directly owed this honor to estates they inherited from men other than their fathers. Thus, for most young men on the rise, family connections were essential to advancement.[14]

The Perreaus also employed a family-based strategy. Apparently, more was done for the elder brothers than for the younger children, perhaps in expectation that they, in turn, would help their siblings. In 1748 Robert was apprenticed to Mr. Tribe, a London apothecary, for eight years, at a premium of £80. He came to the profession at a time when it was consolidating its hold upon the treatment of less-serious medical problems. Apothecaries were frequent visitors in the homes of the middle and upper ranks of society, treating most commonplace complaints. Their prestige, along with their number, had increased considerably during the century. In 1783 there were 367 master apothecaries active or resident in the metropolis. The occupation's rising status was evidenced by the sharp increase in the price of apprenticeship indentures. Although its claims to gentility were uncertain, it drew in the sons of prosperous tradesmen. The career made an attractive choice because it guaranteed a comfortable income while demanding only moderately expensive training. No business, according to one witness, "requires so little money." Whereas, in the past, apothecaries had simply composed the medicines prescribed by doctors, they now scorned "to confine themselves to the dull scene of their profession." They no sooner set up a shop, one critic noted, "than they commence doctor." As relative upstarts in the competitive medical world, apothecaries provoked frequent satires on their pretensions. Dr. James, of the powder fame, "being once asked his opinion of the difference between a doctor and an apothecary, replied, it did not become him to decide on such a delicate point; however he would tell the company an anecdote which perhaps would elucidate the question." He told of a house where the mistress's pet monkey, observing the butler pull the spigot from a cask of ale in order to draw a glass, attempted to imitate the action. Although he was able to withdraw the spigot, he was unable to reclose it. Such witty characterizations did little to slow the advance of the profession.[15]

In London an apothecary could do well financially, the best-paid earning between £1500 and £2000 per annum. Their success inspired hostile comment. In 1748 one critic of the profession claimed that "few chemists and druggists ... build themselves fine houses, purchase country seats, and have large sums out at interest, or ride about in their chariots; & yet the honest apothecary can do all this in five or six years' time." Robert worked hard and, in due course, took over his master's business, establishing a reputation for mastery of his trade. He may not have been at the very top of his profession, but his assistant estimated that he earned at least £1000 a year. This same man argued that "the profits of so much business would have warranted a much greater expense than he appeared to allow himself in his way of living." No doubt Robert prospered because he had a pleasing personality. Such an attribute was widely believed to be more important than a large store of medical knowledge in a man who attended upon his patients day after day. Henry Drummond recalled that he had first met Robert at "Lord Egmont's, where he commonly was." Some charged that apothecaries were rewarded for being clever actors. "It is easy," one author wrote in 1773, "for the apothecary to deceive his patients, by a well forced gravity, pauses and nods, relating similar cases, with his happy success in them, which being interspersed with some terms of art, pass off the delusion very well." With his distinguished client list and a wide circle of acquaintances, Robert had achieved a solid if unspectacular place in the life of late eighteenth-century London.[16]

When Robert sought a spouse, he looked to his West Indian connections and married the daughter of Mr. Thomas, originally from Wales, but now a rector of the parish of Basseterre, St. Kitts, as well as a member of the Privy Council for the island. Robert and his wife, Henrietta, lived "in perfect harmony" for eighteen years. They had three children, the eldest of whom was a student at Westminster school, an institution famous for training the elite of society. The choice of schools is one of the few hints of Robert's social ambitions for his family.[17] Though his choice of partner was both suitable and (by most accounts) successful, it was not particularly lucrative or useful in terms of extending Perreau connections.

For men of ambition, like the Perreaus, marriage afforded a significant opportunity for social and financial advancement. A number of bankers owed a measure of their success to such alliances. The Childs, Coutts, and Amyand banks all benefited from strategic marriages. Sir George Colebrooke based his future prosperity at least as much on the £200,000 he received on marrying the daughter of a rich Antiguan merchant as on his uncle's bank. Alexander Fordyce consolidated his banking success by marrying the daughter of the Earl of Balcarres. Robert Adair, the surgeon, whom Mrs. Rudd declared was her special enemy, was known by his contemporaries as the "fortunate Irishman," for his good luck in having attracted, wooed, and wed the daughter of the Earl of Albermarle. This union led to his appointment as Inspector General of Military Hospitals and opened the way to his becoming a favorite of George III.[18]

If Robert had not made a lofty match, he nonetheless had achieved a significant measure of reputation and respectability. By the 1770s he seemed poised to imitate the success achieved by his neighbor in St. Albans Street, Joseph Hickey. Hickey had fled Ireland at the age of seventeen, arriving in London with a Dublin degree and little else. On application for assistance to an attorney named Bourke, a fellow Irishman, he was given a clerkship, which, five years later, led to his becoming an attorney in King's Bench and a solicitor in Chancery. Thanks in part to his connections, he soon prospered. By 1750 Hickey had an "immense practice," "having the honour of being consulted and employed by many of the nobility, and persons of the most exalted rank in society." Among his clients were Sir Joshua Reynolds and Edmund Burke. He banked with the Drummonds. Daniel Perreau, on several occasions, employed Hickey as his attorney. "[Hickey] lived," in the words of his son, "expensively, seeing much company, keeping a carriage and several saddle horses, and having a handsome country house at Twickenham." Among other family acquaintances were the Salvadores. Like others, Hickey used his influence on behalf of his sons. Through the interest of Lord Egmont, whom Robert was treating, Hickey secured a position in the Victualling Office for one son. He used his extensive East India Company contacts to help another son, William, to find a place in India. Sir George Colebrooke received Hickey politely and said "it afforded him pleasure to have it in his power to comply with his request." When William Hickey's first expedition to India ended in failure, the Burke connections arranged for him to go to Jamaica in pursuit of a career in the law.[19]

If Robert's career might seem to have paralleled that of Hogarth's "industrious apprentice," Daniel's was more checkered and shadowy. His history is harder to trace precisely because it possessed little of the stability or success that marked his brother's progress. Placed in a counting house in his youth, he soon revealed himself, in the words of one pamphlet, to be "a man of gallantry, having had several intrigues with some of the first rate demi-reps."[20] He was impatient with the slow advance in the career chosen for him and wanted, above all else, to "cut a fine figure." When occasion offered, he went to Guadeloupe, where he became a partner to a merchant of that island named Jollie. In undertaking this move Daniel was no doubt taking advantage of the English conquest of the island in 1759, for it was under military rule until the peace of 1763 saw its restoration to France. In moving back to the West Indies, Daniel not only renewed a family connection; he may well have sought to imitate the success of other young, ambitious men who found entry into London society through fortunes made in the Caribbean. No fewer than ten of the fifty-three baronets created in the previous decade had important West Indian connections.[21]

On Guadeloupe, Perreau and his partner set up shops on different parts of the island, and for several years they carried on a considerable business. Jollie was a careful merchant, but Daniel exhibited the extravagance that was to mark so much of his life. He "conducted his [business] in a very elegant and superb manner." He employed many clerks, lived in a grand house, and set a luxurious table. He was more attentive to the impression he created than to the details of trade. He had no inclination for the humdrum business of running a shop. The consequences were predictable; faced with mounting debts, the firm collapsed. Jollie wound up his part of the business honorably, but Daniel returned to England, leaving his affairs in total disarray. His creditors were so outraged by his conduct, one author noted, that they refused to allow him his certificate of bankruptcy.[22]

By all accounts, Daniel learned little from his reverses. When he returned to London to be reunited with his more successful brother, he showed no indication of emulating his industrious example. Instead, he almost immediately began to play the stock market. Daniel seemed to have lost none of his enthusiasm for an elegant life and no doubt was looking for a shortcut to wealth. There was no shortage of such men in London in the 1770s. Daniel was, in the words of one journal, one of those who, "ambitious of splendour and magnificence, place all their pleasure in ostentation, dress, equipage, and grand apartments." Handsome and possessing polished manners, he cut a dashing figure. Some writers suggested that it was Robert's unfortunate infatuation with his brother, and their deepening ties, that led him into trouble. The two seemed to draw closer together in the years after Daniel's return.[23]

By the time of his trial, Robert had become a "fixture" in the homes of many wealthy and powerful people and was able to produce witnesses of distinction who had been his colleagues, clients, and social connections. As one paper said, "an uncommon number of persons, high in repute, gave him an excellent character."[24] Captain Charles Ellis said he had known Robert and

Daniel almost from infancy. He thought Robert so honorable that he would have trusted his life and fortune to him. "I never knew him to spend an idle hour." He was "the best father, the best husband." "I always," Ellis concluded, "looked upon him to be in very affluent circumstances." His neighbors gave him a similar character. Richard Broadhurst said he was "a man that any body will do any thing for." Richard Brown spoke of him as "a good sort of man in his family as any in the world." Versions of this testimony would be repeated by every witness who appeared for Robert. They "not only united, as one man, to give him the most amiable character that the English language is capable of conveying, but likewise joined in deposing, that they could not believe he would be guilty of the crime laid in the charge." Nearly thirty witnesses supported this claim, and they offer a compelling portrait of Robert's social world.[25]

His profession rallied around him. Mrs. Tribe, the widow of his former master, testified that he had "performed his service greatly to my husband's satisfaction, and has bore a most excellent character." Some of the most distinguished medical professionals of the day spoke on his behalf. "I never," swore Caesar Hawkins, a leading surgeon, holder of a post at St. George's Hospital and sergeant-surgeon to both George II and George III, "saw a man more attentive, more diligent, and seemingly more desirous of doing everything upon the best principles; I do not know a man I have a better opinion of in private life." Surgeon Grindal said that if Robert had asked him for money the day before he went to Drummonds, he would have loaned it to him. Dr. George Baker, physician to the King and Queen, and soon to be made a baronet, told of knowing Robert soon after his arrival in London and of having the highest respect for his honesty. Dr. Schomberg, physician and author, said he could not imagine him guilty of such a crime. John Churchill, a popular London apothecary, brother of the poet and friend of Wilkes, also spoke highly of him.[26]

Robert's patients warmly expressed their regard for him. Sir John Moore, a distinguished naval commander, said that he had known Robert for sixteen or so years and thought he was one of the last who could be guilty of such a crime. General Rebow reported that he had "a universal good character." Captain John Burgoyne, a man of fashion and cousin of the more famous military officer, told of Robert's having paid money into his banker's hands for him. And, although she did not testify at the trial, his mother, Lady Frances Burgoyne (née Montagu) had secured the playwright Richard

Cumberland to write his defense. Lady Lyttelton, the second wife of the "good" Lord, gave Robert a complete endorsement. She added that he had had £4000 of hers, which he had restored and paid £90 interest without her keeping a record of the transaction. She could no more imagine him committing the offense than her doing it herself.[27]

While Robert's character witnesses presented a detailed portrait of a solid and respectable man, those who appeared on Daniel's behalf offered more ambiguous evidence. They were less distinguished and, for the most part, were drawn from among his West Indian connections. Their testimony, especially what it omitted, hinted that his past would not bear too careful scrutiny. They presented a less coherent picture of his history and character. Thomas Willis, a ship's master, said he had known him since 1761 and reported that he was respected. Peter Woolfe told of having known Daniel for three years in Guadeloupe, where he had a good reputation. Patrick Burke, a West Indian planter, who had known Daniel for seventeen or eighteen years in both the West Indies and England, said he "bore a general good character." General Melville was Daniel's most distinguished witness. He had helped in the conquest of Martinique and Guadeloupe and had served as governor of the latter island. His service in the West Indies, both in war and peace, had won him respect and honors. He said Daniel was "a very fair dealing, honest man." George Forbes, who had dealt with him since 1765, said Daniel had "always paid me very honourably and like a gentleman." John Sullivan told of trusting Daniel with £3000. Perhaps most revealing was the testimony of Captain Ellis, who had also appeared for Robert. He spoke of hearing that Daniel was honest, although he admitted that he was frequently abroad and so did not know the details of his private life.[28] Daniel's witnesses were not of "society," nor could they testify to his personal conduct. Still, they tried to make the same case as Robert's had, that he was an honest man, that he had been responsible in all his financial dealings, and that people had always respected his character. What made the case harder to prove was Daniel's lack of a profession or occupation, as well as the reports that he was a bankrupt and a "gambler on the Alley."

Though many may have thought the Perreaus the epitome of worldly success, both Daniel and his brother were missing several of the most vital indicators of solid social triumph.[29] They lived within a respectable but not distinguished social sphere. In the days before the discovery of the forgeries, they dined with Dr. Jackson and Dr. Brooke, Captain Ellis and the family of

Henry Evans—people of the same class as the Perreaus. In their accounts the brothers confessed, with some embarrassment, that they aimed higher. They aspired to ownership of a country estate and the acquisition of a bank, a seat in Parliament, and even a title. Since it was clear that, by his own efforts, Robert was unable to make that great leap, Mrs. Rudd's promises of banks, estates, and titles must have seemed irresistible to the ambitions of both men. For the fortunate aspirant to the world of fashion, financial prosperity opened a variety of doors: to membership in the large chartered companies, to government business and contracts, to the ownership of villas and estates. Although large amounts of money were necessary to enter into and live among the social elite, acceptance meant substantial and ongoing financial gains for the fortunate entrant.[30]

There was no shortage of examples to inspire imitation. Several banking families possessed large estates; the Childs had Osterley Park, and the Hoares, Stourhead. The prosperous distiller Joseph Mawbey acquired Botley in Chertsey, Sussex. Sir Merrick Burrell, like Mawbey a successful London merchant and MP, became a director of the Bank of England and acquired an estate in West Grinstead. Fordyce "purchased a large estate, with a most elegant villa, at Roehampton, where he aimed at surpassing Commissaries and Nabobs in grandeur and magnificence."[31] As a preliminary to his baronetage, the retiring governor of the Leeward Islands, George Thomas, bought Yapton in Sussex, while the former lieutenant governor of Dominica, William Young, purchased Delafield, Bucks, two years before being so honored.[32] By 1774 the Perreaus believed, or at least represented themselves as believing, that a lucky stroke would bring the symbols of social and economic success within their grasp.

HARLOT'S PROGRESS: MRS. RUDD AND THE DEMI-REP

Robert's respectability and Daniel's flair formed a base for the Perreau entry into West End life. They fell back on Robert's solid reputation in their defense against the charge of forgery. But neither brother possessed what it took to scale the heights to which they aspired. For this they needed something more—the vast sums Daniel hoped to make on the Exchange, or an advantageous alliance with a woman of fortune, as Mrs. Rudd seemed to be. Her wit, style, and taste made her a fascinating novelty within the Perreau social setting. She was the embodiment of fashion, both elegant and intelligent. She was an ornament and as such especially useful to the insecurely established Daniel Perreau. It was no wonder that he was attracted to her. But such attractions were not uncommon, and Daniel's decision to live with her, to pass her off as his wife, to share his name, fortune, and future, is not, on the face of it, explained solely by her personal charms. Mrs. Rudd promised Daniel, and by extension his brother Robert, the sorts of connections that might lead to familial wealth and advancement. First, she mentioned the intercession of various Scottish and English noble families, with whom she claimed to be allied by birth.[33] Second, she seemed to have access to and influence over a number of wealthy mercantile men, like the Adairs and Salvadore, whose insider information as well as capital could be vitally useful to the Perreaus. Robert said at his trial that he believed a connection with the "house of Adair" would do great things for them all.[34] Thus Mrs. Rudd brought to Daniel what a marriage to a genuine aristocrat might accomplish; she would provide them with the web of influence, money, and patronage requisite for entering into and living in good society. The most convincing proof of this was offered by Mrs. Rudd herself, who supplied not only gossip about the lives of her aristocratic connections but also astute knowledge of the structure and operation of eighteenth-century society.

Mrs. Rudd was not simply the vehicle for the fulfillment of the Perreaus' aspirations, however. She was deeply ambitious herself. Her every action, her every word, spoke forcefully of her desire. She meant to conquer London, to find her place in the "great world" of society. But at twenty-nine or thirty time was running out for her. As much as they needed her, she needed them to accomplish her objectives. If a man out to better himself in the world of fashionable society required connections, family, and money, a woman in the same situation required more; she needed a man to work through or with, and on her choice of that man everything depended.

Mrs. Rudd's supposed origins inspired rumors from her first introduction into the Perreaus' social world. The treatment of these tales hinted at sexual attitudes different from those espoused by conventional morality, attitudes at once more worldly and sophisticated. Frankland, when asked why he had lent the Perreaus so much money, said he had visited the family and had often heard mention of Adair. He was one of the many who thought that she "was either a ward or a natural daughter" of Adair's.[35] Neither illegiti-

macy nor adultery constituted an absolute impediment to social respectability among the fashionable classes in the 1770s. Either could be offset by
claims of wealth, kinship, beauty, or accomplishment. The three daughters
of Sir Edward Walpole all married well, even though their mother had
worked in a secondhand clothes stall and never married their father: the eldest to the son of Lord Albemarle, the second to Lord Waldegrave and, on his
demise, to the Duke of Gloucester, and the youngest to the son of Lord
Dysart. The mother of Winefred Thompson, who married Robert Drummond in 1753, was the illegitimate daughter of Sir Berkeley Lucy of
Charlecote. William Addington, the Middlesex magistrate first approached
by Robert Perreau, married Miss Lumley, the natural daughter of Lord Scarborough. Lord Chancellor Thurlow had three illegitimate daughters by Polly
Humphreys, the child of a coffee-house owner. He was devoted to them and
worked hard to secure their acceptance by society.[36]

Nor did Mrs. Rudd seem handicapped by another aspect of her background. In her earliest testimony, she had been vague about her past, insisting that only an unfortunate legal bar made it impossible for her to marry
Daniel. But in every other sense, she insisted, she was his loyal wife. However, even before the trial, a different picture of Mrs. Rudd began to emerge,
one that would situate her within the well-known contemporary context of
the demi-rep, or courtesan of fashion. The fact that she had entered into her
relationship with Daniel as his mistress, and still had a husband living, did
not prejudice polite society against her. The irregular nature of her connection with Daniel could be passed over, for it was common knowledge that the
sexual morality of the *beau monde* was more forgiving than that of the world
the Perreaus wished to escape. Like Mrs. Rudd, many of the demi-reps featured in the "Tête-à-Tête" section of the *Town and Country Magazine* had
checkered pasts, and yet, as long as they formed stable unions, set and kept
houses for their lovers, bore them children, and provided companionship as
well as sexual services, the *monde* was compliant and tolerant. Describing the
Duke of Seaforth and his mistress, Harriet Powell, as "the happiest couple
outside the pale of matrimony," the *Town and Country* celebrated the possibilities of domestic, though unhallowed, love.[37] Some of these women actually married their keepers when this was possible; Powell became the Duchess
of Seaforth before her early death, Lavinia Fenton became the Duchess of
Bolton after being Bolton's mistress for twenty-three years, and Mrs. Armis-
tead became the greatly loved wife of Charles James Fox. Ambitious men

such as the Reverend Doctor Dodd or the writer William Combe married the former mistresses of prominent men in the hope that such an alliance might advance their careers.[38]

The demi-rep inspired both praise and condemnation. "The Demi-Reps hold this intermediate station in the characters of females," declared one journal, "between the modest women and the women of pleasure; to both which they are in some measure connected, as they stand upon the utmost verge of reputation, and totter on the brink of infamy."[39] The most successful of such figures mingled with the elite at many splendid occasions. Kitty Fisher, one of the most sought-after courtesans of the 1760s, inspired even well-born aristocratic women to emulate her dress and poses. A painting of a beautiful demi-rep was valued almost as much as the woman herself.[40]

Journals like the *Town and Country,* which catered to fashionable taste, described such women without censure and their relationships without condemnation. The magazine said of the connection between W. W. Greville and Miss Philips that it would "not be of short duration; but that, probably, it may continue during the remainder of their lives." "A connexion of so agreeable, so rational a nature," wrote the magazine, describing the relationship between Sir Robert Keith and his mistress, "that it is almost beyond the reach of censure; and it is still supported with as much warmth and esteem on both sides, after several years duration, as the first hour it took place."[41] Archenholz expressed surprise at the familiar acceptance shown such women by "many people of rank." The better class of courtesans lived "very well" and occupied many of the houses "in the western part of the town." "Their apartments," he wrote, "are elegantly, and sometimes magnificently furnished; they keep several servants, and some have their own carriages." "Many of them have annuities paid them by their seducers." "All this," he concluded, "generally gives them a certain dignity of conduct, which can scarcely be reconciled with their profession."[42] Such a description certainly fit the circumstances of Fanny Temple, a courtesan much admired by William Hickey. "A finer woman in every respect," he wrote, "could not be." "She inhabited an excellent house in Queen Ann Street, and had besides neat lodgings in the country, pleasantly situated near the water side just above Hammersmith, and kept her own chariot, with suitable establishment of servants, the whole being paid for, as well as her domestic expenses, by a gentleman of rank and fashion."[43]

In this permissive, upper-class world of fashion in the 1770s, a world that gossiped openly about mistresses and affairs in a popular column called "Histories of the Tête-à-Tête," sexual standards were not strict. One "celebrity" who appeared in the column, a Miss Matthews, had had a career much like that of Mrs. Rudd. According to this account, she was the natural daughter of an army officer. She was sent to a boarding school, where, at an early age, she began to attract admirers. Duped into a false marriage by a military man, she came to London and took a series of lovers, the penultimate of whom was Robert Perreau. He took lodgings for her near Portman Square and set her up in lavish fashion. She proceeded to live in society in an extravagant style. During this period she met Mrs. Rudd, who passed as the wife of his brother. Matthews was at first surprised that the family would mingle so easily with Daniel's mistress, since she had learned that Mrs. Rudd had been married and had lived with Mr. Salvadore as housekeeper and friend for a period. Worried by the mysteries of the Perreau households, Miss Matthews took the occasion of a meeting at the opera with the Earl of A—m to make a break with Robert. She used the familiar strategy of having a lawyer arrest her for a sum, and when Perreau chose not to help her, she accepted the "advantageous" terms offered by her new protector. The decision was timely; her story appeared in the very month that the forgery case broke.[44]

Although Mrs. Rudd was never featured in these magazine tell-all portraits, her story resembled the tales told of other London demi-reps. Such stories mingled fiction with truth in liberal doses, entangling them so that it is impossible now to discern real from imagined. Yet these "histories" offer many points of comparison. For example, Mrs. Rudd came from the town of Lurgan, in the north of Ireland. At least nine of the sixty demi-reps featured in the five years preceding the case also came from Ireland. Rudd's father, Patrick Young (or Youngson), was, like Robert Perreau, an apothecary, while her mother, Margaret Stewart, may have been a "love child" of a Major Stewart. The major was a relation to the late Lord Galloway and so provided a basis for Mrs. Rudd's later claims to illustrious descent.[45] Among courtesans, her background as the daughter of an Irish apothecary was not extraordinary. Although many demi-reps came from lowlier origins (one was the daughter of a billsticker, another the orphaned child of a Surrey higler, while a third's father was a menial servant to a lawyer), many were children of middling types like Youngson.[46] Less commonly, these women claimed to be nobly connected; Mrs. Kendall professed to be the "natural" daughter of the late Lord P—t, Sophia Hunter of Lord B—, Mrs. Horneck of the late Earl of A—, and George Anne Bellamy of Lord Tyrawley.[47]

As an Irishwoman, Mrs. Rudd was born at a fortunate time. Before the eighteenth century the north of Ireland had been one of the poorest regions of the country. But by the time of her birth, in 1745 or 1746, the area was being transformed by the rapid progress of the linen trade. Linen exports from Ireland increased from 2.5 million yards in the 1720s to 8 million yards by the 1740s. Among those who prospered was Patrick Adair, described in 1744 as the largest importer of Irish linen. Adair dealt directly with Irish drapers and bleachers, providing credit and warehousing for their goods. Adair, Jackson and Company, located in Fountain Court, long remained a leading London firm dealing in Irish goods.[48] Despite the efforts of anti-Rudd authors to portray it as "a little obscure village in the north of Ireland," Lurgan was the center of the trade in the finest linens. When Arthur Young visited the town in 1776, he found a prosperous regional center where £273,000 worth of linen was sold in a year.[49] In 1764, one visitor praised the region as "that part of the kingdom whose inhabitants, in their manners and dialect, are the most like those of the English." The linen trade brought the two countries into close contact. Lurgan was, he wrote, "one of the prettiest little market towns in the north"; indeed, it had acquired the title "Little England" among inhabitants.[50]

No doubt this prosperity made it possible for Mrs. Rudd to acquire an education and a certain learned elegance—a great advantage to success as a courtesan. Demi-reps were not whores, but mistresses, and offered a good deal more than sex. A woman of any background could provide sexual services; only a well-educated, well-bred woman was capable of supplying that mixture of beauty, wit, and companionship that characterized the first-class Thais, the best and most successful demi-rep. If a woman wished to be taken into keeping, to form a long-term relationship with a man of wealth and position, she had to have more than physical beauty to offer, although good looks were doubtless a significant advantage.[51] Mrs. Rudd may have received a "genteel education" from her father, according to one account. Another proposed that, following on the death of her parents, she was raised by her Uncle Stewart, a farmer and supplier of linen, who sent her to a boarding school in Downpatrick. However acquired, her education supplemented her quick mind and lively conversation, which were to be her most desirable attributes. She proved "a delicate, agreeable girl, possessed of great vivacity," and when "she came to the years of maturity she had many admirers."[52]

Fate had to intervene before Mrs. Rudd could be transformed from local belle into London demi-rep. In 1761 the efforts of Thomas Rudd, a grocer, to secure a place in a regiment for his son, Valentine, finally bore fruit. The elder Rudd was a political agent for James West in his St. Albans constituency, "a difficult and expensive borough." West was the loyal follower of the Duke of Newcastle, a useful secretary to the Treasury and a man from a Warwickshire family who had benefited from a marriage to a wealthy timber heiress. Newcastle relied upon West for his knowledge of the City and its financial interests. Despite the importance of Thomas Rudd to West, and of West to Newcastle, the negotiations for a place were protracted and complicated, as was the way of most patronage in eighteenth-century England. Throughout 1760 the correspondence between West and Rudd contained pleas for the use of the former's "interest." Rudd urged action because he knew that it would be impossible to secure his son a commission "in a time of peace." Only shortly before his death did Thomas realize his ambition. Valentine was made a lieutenant and sent with his regiment to recruit in the north of Ireland.[53]

Not long after he arrived in Ulster, Valentine Rudd met the vivacious and enchanting Margaret Youngson. They were both young; she was sixteen at the time. One account reported that they married, after an acquaintance of ten days, in February 1762. The ceremony took place in an Anglican church, with John Stewart's consent. Before they departed for England, her uncle gave her a letter of introduction to a neighboring landowner, James Adair, thus inaugurating the fateful connection between Mrs. Rudd and that family.[54] Some accounts claimed that, upon landing in England, the couple went to St. Albans, while others reported that they went directly to London. Valentine became a half-pay officer, with his limited income supplemented by a small inheritance from the estate of his grocer father. The attractions of the metropolis were irresistible to the lieutenant and his wife. "The idea of the pleasures to be enjoyed in the capital," wrote Archenholz, "inspires the girls in the country with the most longing desire to participate in them. Imagination inflames their little heads, and presents every object under an exaggerated appearance." "The young people of both sexes," he observed, "who have been educated at a distance from town, imagine the metropolis to resemble that paradise promised to the Mahometans, by their great prophet. Is it to be then wondered at, that they form so many little projects to abandon their homes, and reside in the center of pleasure?"[55]

The Rudds lived together for several years, perhaps at Princess Street, Cavendish Square. They spent money lavishly, far beyond the means of Valentine's slender fortune. "Mr. Rudd," one newspaper letter commented, "soon found that a princely revenue was alone suitable to the elegant turn of mind his wife possessed." Mrs. Rudd had developed a taste for the fashionable life of London. In addition, her eye had begun to roam. By 1766 a Cornet Reid, living at the same address, won her attention. They ran off together and spent some months living in great luxury. Finally, threatened with debt, Reid fled the country. The angry creditors pursued Valentine Rudd, who was soon arrested for the sums owed by his wife and Reid. Ultimately he was forced to seek refuge in the district around the court, sell his patrimony to satisfy the creditors, and begin proceedings, in 1767, to divorce Mrs. Rudd. These proceedings failed because he could never secure proof of her adultery. However, in 1770 he took the precaution of putting an advertisement in the papers saying that he would no longer be responsible for her debts. This disclaimer proved inadequate. Shopkeepers regularly pursued him to recover his wife's arrears. One author claimed that the couple was briefly reunited; another said Valentine struggled to disentangle himself from her ongoing extravagance. Certainly at some point in 1770 or 1771 he tried to track her down. At a later date he was said to be living in Dublin. For the rest of his life he would suffer the consequences of the debts run up in these years.[56]

The pathetic tale of Valentine Rudd was frequently told in the months before Mrs. Rudd's trial. His ruin—debt, drunkenness, betrayal, a bout of madness, confinement—was offered as an augury of her relations with the Perreaus.[57] In this story Mrs. Rudd appeared the calculating adventuress who felt no affection of any sort and used men to secure her own advantage. It depicted Valentine as a young man, far from home, ensnared by an ambitious, lower-class Irish girl, eager to "extend her travels" and, through marriage, to "constitute her[self] a gentlewoman." When she had wrung all possible gain from him, she tossed him aside, leaving him to debtor's prison and dishonor.[58]

The history of Mrs. Rudd from the period of her separation from her husband until the time she moved in with Daniel Perreau is difficult to trace. She joined the ranks of the other "belles of Ireland" who served as companions and mistresses of the rich and powerful. In the wake of the brothers' trials, accounts appeared accusing her of every shade of evil and debauchery. There was no crime of which she was not capable, no deception in which she did not have a hand.[59] One particularly virulent critic said that she took up with a gang of swindlers and was detected in an attempted forgery. Another told of her liaison with yet another military man, a Captain Shee, while a third maintained that she had posed as the widow of a younger brother of Lord Annadale and gone to law to secure her property rights against her relations. It is difficult to accept all the exploits attributed to her, but there seems little doubt that, as one paper put it, "the lady by degrees stole into consequence." For a time she had a coach as well as a chair, and her name was connected with that of Lord D—. Another report claimed that she had received large sums from George Germain.[60] "There is scarcely a corner of the town," one author charged, "but what has been at intervals the scene of our heroine's residence and intrigues; and it is evident that she was peculiarly dexterous in assuming a variety of characters, as it best suited her schemes, and the urgency of the moment."[61]

Despite her successes, Mrs. Rudd never seemed able to manage her income or to secure herself an annuity from one of her lovers. "Though our heroine," one author explained, "had several good customers at her lodgings at Meard's court, yet from an unbounded extravagance, or the want of economy, her finances at intervals were exceedingly scanty." She flitted between addresses, found on side streets near the fashionable squares, that spoke to contemporaries of the shadowy world of prostitution. In addition to Meard's Court, she also occupied rooms on Wardour and Jermyn streets.[62] Mrs. Rudd seems to have been a courtesan of some note by 1770, but she was certainly not of the same standing as many of the women celebrated in the pages of the *Town and Country* as "eminent Thais." Perhaps she was too fantastical; perhaps she was simply doomed to attract men whose fortunes were precarious or in decline. Neither extremely beautiful nor on the stage, Mrs. Rudd lacked the attributes to carry her higher. Few of her lovers seemed themselves to possess the wealth, power, or talent necessary to establish her in the heart of the ton.

It was during these years that she made the acquaintance of Joseph Salvadore of the York Buildings. Salvadore was one of the most influential financial figures of the eighteenth century. His family, of Sephardic origin, came from Holland about the same time the Perreaus arrived from France. The

Salvadore family was to play an important role as a link between Jewish financial interests in Amsterdam and the financial markets of London. They were part of a small Sephardic elite within which marriage and kinship reinforced commercial interests. Along with the Medina family, they represented the dominant Jewish presence in the precious metals business. Joseph, after working with his father for many years in the Portuguese and Spanish trade, inherited the family business in 1754. He soon made his mark in the mercantile world. Although Jews had played a central role in the coral and diamond trade with India, Salvadore alone secured a significant position in the East India Company. His career illustrated the degree to which wealthy Jews were gaining acceptance in eighteenth-century English society. If they were denied place and honor, they still participated in the social and cultural, as well as the economic, life of the times. Salvadore used his political and financial influence to secure passage of the Jew Naturalization Bill in 1753 and fought an unsuccessful campaign to keep the measure from being repealed. The act brought to the surface the fierce anti-Semitic sentiments that would reappear during the controversy surrounding Mrs. Rudd. One paper attacked the measure as a reward to Jewish dealers, skilled in "the mysteries and iniquities of stock-jobbing," who had secured "vast estates by plundering the public." Salvadore's conduct made him a tempting target for such criticism. During the Newcastle years, 1757 to 1762, he advised the government on fiscal policy and was one of the twenty-two men who underwrote a government loan for £8 million. He took personal responsibility for £250,000 of that sum. After Sampson Gideon, he was the foremost Jewish financier of the period. Like Gideon he accommodated himself to English social life, but unlike him, he maintained his links to the Jewish community. He lived in an appropriately grand style and possessed an estate at Tooting, in Surrey. At one time he "kept" one of the most sought-after women in London, Kitty Fisher.[63]

The wealthy, lascivious Jew was a familiar figure in literature long before Richardson created his evil, licentious Portuguese Jew, Mr. Merceda, in *Sir Charles Grandison*. Because of their supposed venality, Jews, it was commonly said, had sold out English liberty and the Magna Carta. One cartoon of a Jew signing an anti-Wilkite petition in 1769, whose caption read, "Oh for a large portion of Scrip," may well have been of Salvadore, who did sign the document. There were frequent complaints about the transactions of wealthy Jews, like Gideon, who enriched themselves through government contracts and attempted to buy their way into society. A mark of popular anger and contempt for such wealthy foreigners was the well-known caricature of the ancient Jewish macaroni, dressed in extravagantly luxurious fashion, out for a night of fashionable though unorthodox enjoyment on the town. Jewish keepers were not uncommon among the demi-rep but were usually treated, often by the women themselves, with great disdain. Although several of the women had Jewish lovers at one time or another, it was claimed that, reluctant to enter into such relations with men whose persons they so disliked, they had been procured unwillingly by people whom they had trusted.[64] The revelation of Mrs. Rudd's connection with Salvadore called up these various comic portraits and unpleasant sentiments.

By the time Mrs. Rudd encountered Salvadore, he was an old man whose influence and wealth had greatly declined. He had lost heavily in several financial transactions in the 1760s, and the death of his wife in 1766 also seems to have been a heavy blow. Although he was far from insolvent, his situation was precarious. One measure of this liquidity problem was his embarrassing attempt to regain the money and jewels he had given Fisher. According to one author, Mrs. Rudd went to Salvadore pretending to have business to transact. Whatever the circumstances, she soon had him convinced that she was related to "a great personage" and promised him advantage. "A celebrated Female Adventurer," a Bath paper announced in March, "whose history is such a fashionable subject, had address enough to persuade an Israelite in the city, that she had it in her power to effect a match between him and one of the princesses of Mecklenburgh Strelitz."[65] Another report claimed that he soon succumbed to her stories and her tears. All accounts played with the comic vein of the tale of an unscrupulous courtesan ensnaring the wily Jewish financier.[66] She soon possessed some of his furniture and plate and filled her house in Soho with it. She discovered "his weak side, and played upon him so artfully, that in a short time she squeezed him near fifteen hundred pounds." It was reported that she regularly visited him, often pretending to be different women. Perhaps, some believed, she even kept up the connection after she took up with Daniel Perreau. After each visit to Salvadore, they revealed, she returned with a handsome present.[67] During this period she was alleged to have passed under different names: "Lady Caroline Gower, Mrs. Gore, Mrs. Gore's sister, the Countess of Moriencourt, a German princess, Mrs. Daniel Perreau, and Mrs. Roberts." In these various characters she was supposed to have "cozened and defrauded" Salvadore of a "large sum of money and effects."[68] For instance, she told him that she was returning to Ireland to be reconciled with her relations. She hinted that this visit might operate to his advantage. Before she left, she came to him in tears, complaining that she was ashamed to appear before her family dressed in rags. He immediately gave her clothes and valuable jewels. When she returned, she told him that her husband had surprised her in Dublin and seized the jewels she carried. One story reported that she had convinced Salvadore that she had borne his child, and thus extracted an even larger sum from him.[69]

Even as she played upon Salvadore's hopes of finding a match that might save his fortunes, she continued to search for a dependable keeper for herself. At the time she took up with Daniel Perreau, three men were vying for her favor. The most famous was Lauchlin Macleane, a friend of Burke and Wilkes, an adventurer who gambled heavily in the East India Company. Macleane had abandoned his wife in about 1768 and fathered several illegitimate children. Despite his debts, this dashing figure appeared an attractive catch. "You tried," Mrs. Rudd's servant wrote, "every art in your power to draw [him] into your net." But he was too wise to the ways of the world to be captured. Instead she ended up with Daniel Perreau, the least sensible and poorest of the men who sought her acquaintance.[70] Daniel wrote that they met at Mrs. Johnson's in Hollen Street, Soho, during the spring of 1770. He said that she was passing under the name of Mrs. Gore and was considerably in debt. An anonymous account presented a more romantic tale of their meeting. It reported that they met at a masquerade, in April 1770. She was dressed in a costume that represented day and night, while Daniel "appeared at Mrs. Cornelys' in an extraordinary garb, one side of which represented a skeleton, the other a proper handsome figure." The two seemed to take to each other immediately, Mrs. Rudd drawn perhaps to Daniel's double disguise as a successful, elegant, and available bachelor, while he, like Salvadore, may well have hoped "that something advantageous might by her means be done for the promotion of his fortune."[71] Thus they each looked to the other to repair past misfortunes and for advancement to new heights among the wealthy and powerful of London society.

LONDON STORIES

The biographies of our central characters, sketchy as they are, nonetheless reveal that they were not unusual or singular figures. They represented recognizable types in the vibrant, expansive world of eighteenth-century London. This imperial city drew to it ambitious individuals eager to make their fortunes. Men and women alike, although obviously under different constraints, made their ways, as best they could. Some, like Robert Perreau, chose the path of steady industry. Others, like his brother Daniel, hoped for a more spectacular and speedy success by playing the Exchange. Mrs. Rudd used her wiles and her beauty. But they all shared the same dreams and goals.

Moralists loved to complain about the dominant tendencies of the age. Many bemoaned the influence of fashion and the mad pursuit of wealth, as well as the obsession with display, that marked the period. One paper drew a sober conclusion from considering Robert's plight. It reminded its readers that the difficulties he faced should be a warning, particularly for those like apothecaries "who keep carriages and live elegantly." "Such men," it advised, "may dazzle the eyes of the public, live a few years in splendour, and leave their families beggars." "The company are immensely rich; great numbers of the individuals are also in affluent circumstances." But those who rode in carriages were not necessarily the richest, nor those who walked the poorest.[72] Another paper warned that even if the brothers had been deceived, they would not have been "dupes" had they attended to "a few sober maxims or right principles," rather than "studying elegance." Their fate should serve as a warning to others "to well know themselves" and to "cast away ambition."[73]

The very intensity of such laments demonstrated how futile these protests had become. The defense offered by the Perreaus asserted that their ambition was only natural and innocent. In this they simply echoed prevailing opinion. "Distinction," wrote Joshua Reynolds, justifying his own pursuit of professional titles, "is what we all seek after, and the world does set a value on them, and I go with the great stream of life."[74] "The desire of bettering our condition," concluded Adam Smith, "comes with us from the womb, and never leaves us till we go into the grave." The Perreaus and Mrs. Rudd could scarcely contain their ambition or regulate it by "the principle of frugality," as Smith advocated.[75] Daniel was the more impatient brother; he devoted himself to splendid display. But Robert's ambition ran deeper. He demonstrated more pride and took more concern to secure solid advantage for his family. Daniel might have fled when the scandal broke, but Robert had too much to lose. He had a place and reputation he was unwilling to surrender. He and his wife fought tenaciously, not only for his life, but to preserve the "genteel" status they had achieved.

For a woman like Mrs. Rudd, the choices were fewer and her resources skimpier. Everything depended upon the accident of birth and the chances of a favorable alliance with a keeper or husband. Although she could whiten the taint of her profession by hinting at illustrious aristocratic connections, the obstacles she faced and the abyss that threatened her were at least as ominous as the consequences facing the brothers.[76] In this desperate situation Mrs. Rudd made use of what arts she possessed and what expedients she could devise. She presented herself to the brothers and society as a channel through which influence, patronage, and favor could flow. All her energy went into fostering an impression and sustaining an image. Maintaining the appearance of polite connections through letters, visits, and gifts was vital to her advancement. She promoted the gossip that she knew circulated around her. Her talents and beauty could only carry her a short distance; she devoted all of her intelligence to sustaining belief in the one thing that could propel her into the circles in which she desired to move.

Although the moralist might argue that wealth sprang from effort and ability, this case exposed what everyone knew, that success was as likely to depend on other, perhaps less admirable, circumstances. Shadowy influences and dubious transactions could be found at work in the rise from obscurity of many families. And people of fortune knew the continued importance of such practices to the maintenance of their status. Family connections secured government contracts; easy access to loans depended on kinship networks. Even the hint of noble favor might open lenders' pockets. This situation paralleled the often-observed fact that extravagant display was as likely to establish one's credit as was more careful expenditure. The prolific author John Trusler, in a work that pandered to popular passion even as it reproved it, offered a passage from a "dispirited poet" as a guide to the leading tendency of his times: "Keep up appearances: there lies the test!/The world will give thee credit for the rest."[77]

For a time polite society credited the display as well as the rumors offered by the Perreaus and Mrs. Rudd. Few were suspicious of their great good fortune. During the heady boom of the early 1770s, the main thing was to get on.

Five

FASHION AND ITS DISCONTENTS

FROM THE FIRST MOMENTS when the news spread of Robert Perreau's arrest, the story drew a crowd. As a large number of people gathered at Bow Street, "each coach in the neighbourhood of Covent Garden was taken and the streets lined on both sides with persons of every denomination." Fielding's office was soon "filled with genteel people."[1] The fascination the case held for the elite and near-elite remained one of its most striking aspects. They were attracted for a combination of reasons: the suspects belonged to the fashionable world of London, and this fashionable world itself inspired deeply ambivalent feelings. Commentary on the case mingled curiosity and moralizing, the two impulses at war with each other. The reading public, composed in large part of people like the Perreaus, of the middling ranks who were trying to better themselves, could see in this case a tragic and salacious parable of their lives and their aspirations. For them the case offered prurient glimpses into the lives of those who aspired to live in the bon ton, while confirming their anxieties about the dangers of rapid social advancement and the ends to which such longings might drive its votaries. Thus the twin spectacles of desire and danger drew these readers to the conduct and fate of the ill-starred trio.

One of the earliest mentions of the crime hinted at its most distinctive feature; it attributed the forgery to "a gentleman and his reputed wife, who have for some time past lived in the bon ton."[2] This short phrase firmly fixed both the social and moral context of the story for its readers.

The character of the "bon ton" was so widely recognized that it needed no explanation. That year Garrick used the phrase as the title for a play, and it figured in countless poems and essays as a description of a class and a way of life. To many commentators the emulation of this influential group represented the most conspicuous expression of the wealth that had enriched some in the aftermath of the mid-century wars. To enter the ton, one had to live as though one were already in it. Style and fashionable consumption were its two leading qualities.

SPENDING LIKE A LORD

What struck everyone on first observing the Perreaus and Mrs. Rudd was the elegance of their appearance. Throughout the case the papers lingered over the descriptions of how they dressed and what they owned. All the parties were self-conscious about the images they created. The brothers often dressed alike, with elegance and simplicity, especially when their case came before the courts. This not only emphasized their fraternal bonds and loyalty but was part of their effort to shield Daniel by merging his identity with Robert's. Mrs. Rudd accented her claim to respectability by displaying her taste and feminine charms. The wealth and gentility of their clothing were meant to impress spectators.

When she appeared before Justice Fielding, Mrs. Rudd "was elegantly dressed in a striped silk night-gown, with a pink and ermine cloak, and a black laced bonnet." Later, at her first bail hearing, she appeared "elegantly dressed in a black silk Polonaise, and a white silk cloak." At her trial in September "she made a very elegant appearance," "dressed in a black satin sack and petticoat, a new polenneze silk cloak, her hair done up in curls and powdered, and her cap, of gauze, ornamented with black snailing, in the most fashionable style." Another paper described her outfit as "a suit of black satin, her cloak of the same, lined with white persian; her hair elegantly dressed; her Cap was Gauze, ornamented with small Knots of black Ribbon, and formed one of the handsomest Headdresses imaginable." The two brothers were just as fashionably dressed, one in brown and the other in a slate-colored coat, both with gold-laced hats. The papers reported that when the sheriffs of London and Middlesex seized the goods of Daniel after his conviction, they found that his wearing apparel alone cost £400.[3]

Just as important, the parties' manners and deportment confirmed the impression created by their dress. One report stressed how the brothers "behaved with great decency" at their examination. They spoke well. They were attractive men who displayed restraint and grace in all their actions. But it was Mrs. Rudd, in particular, who presented a compelling, fashionable portrait. "Mrs. Rudd's appearance and behavior," suggested the *Morning Post* of her attendance in King's Bench, "was in every respect becoming and distinguishing; and whatever may have been the *faux pas* of her former life, her present situation cannot avoid exciting a wish to have her restored to society, as there is no doubt but her uncommon understanding will point out such a plan for her future life as will restore her to universal esteem."[4] She entered the courtroom in September "with a modest firmness and made two respectful courtesies, one to the Bench and the other to the Jury and Company." "Though at her entrance and during the arguments, she possessed a decent composure and steady firmness that baffles all description," on being once again sent back to Newgate she "trembled much, and seemed greatly affected with her situation." "She had a languor in her countenance that seemed the consequence of long confinement and mental agitation; but, under all disadvantages, has much the appearance of the woman of unaffected dignity."[5]

The magazines hastened to capture these qualities for their subscribers in carefully drawn portraits. Such attractions were relatively new: the first fashion print had appeared in the *Lady's Magazine* just five years before.[6] Magazine editors sought to exploit the demand for illustrations of these defendants in order to increase circulation by inserting advertisements promising their portraits. The *London Magazine* in one notice promised it would publish a full account of the Perreaus, and, in another issue, that it would provide "likenesses" of Daniel Perreau and Mrs. Rudd. She was most frequently pictured. The *Monthly Miscellany* offered "a capital whole-length engraving of Mrs. Rudd," while the *Town and Country* advertised that its next issue would include an engraving, "drawn from the life, in the exact dress she appeared in at the Old Bailey."[7] The portraits of Mrs. Rudd were indistinguishable from the fashion prints offered elsewhere. Yet the number and variety of illustrations of her are extraordinary. The variety of scenes is also striking; several are drawn from theatrical tropes, and one or two juxtapose her fine dress and delicate gestures with the prison walls or sharp spikes of the Old Bailey box. Just as in print, she was imagined in different ways, located in different narratives. The early engravings allude to the narrative she told at Bow Street: the scene in the bedroom repeats a theatrical convention, with the violent husband threatening the woman, and the exposed bed a reminder of the relationship between them. The flamboyant portraits of her with pen in hand and of her as the distressed and thoughtful woman express moments in her own narrative. The most striking portraits, however, come from the period of her confinement and trial. No doubt they were meant to sell journals. They claimed to be "drawn from life," and they were widely advertised. Yet the figure portrayed in them resists easy capture. These were not repetitions of the same image (though there were family resemblances) as so many of the newspaper reports were. The varying dress and differences in physical features suggest she posed for different artists. And in contrast to the few engravings of the brothers, which seem vague and idealized, pictures of her capture traces of a carefully structured and constructed individuality. In most of these illustrations she seems self-possessed and immobile. There are no children about her. Her hands typically hold a fan, sometimes a pen, often a piece of paper. Her clothing is layered and rich, composed of a mixture of fabrics in intricate though elegant designs. Similar attention is devoted to her hair. Perhaps nothing so symbolized Mrs. Rudd's claim to fashionable status as her coiffure. In the 1770s, exotic hairstyles had become one of the most extravagant products of the quest for novelty among rich women.[8] Mrs. Rudd's "head"—her hair and its ornaments—displayed the restrained yet very expensive sumptuousness and tastefulness that characterized her personal display. The illustrations reinforce the idea of a woman skilled at projecting an image. Thin and small, she was not a fleshy presence; rather she relied upon the materiality of her clothing to convey the sense of who she was, as she did at her trials.

But it was not simply clothes, or stance, or hairdress, that attested to the tonish status of the three protagonists. One of the aspects of the case that made it such a sensation was the visibility and level of consumption achieved by Daniel Perreau and Mrs. Rudd. Robert had for many years risen slowly in fashionable London circles, until he could be found at some of the public functions put on by his aristocratic clients. He possessed such markers of gentility as a carriage, a respectable address, and entrance into some of the first residences of the West End. But Daniel and Mrs. Rudd offered a finer show and a more meteoric rise. They began modestly enough, but soon their level of expenditure marked them out. Each accused the other of the ambition and extravagance that now looked so criminal, though it is more likely that each encouraged the other.

In June 1773 they were looking for a house in Grosvenor Square, one of the West End's more prestigious new squares. In July, Mrs. Rudd produced the money required for one of the most significant status symbols of the day, a coach. "In this age of delicacy and refinement," satirized Charles Johnston, "the first thing thought of in genteel life is a carriage, which is so indispensably necessary to procure respect, that no eminence in science, no practice of virtue, is held in esteem, where that is wanted."[9] Soon after they took a house at Mill Hill, a fashionable country retreat where Wilkes had a residence as well. Mrs. Rudd did not like the country, so they then looked back to the West End, first seeking to buy something in Cavendish Square, before finally settling on Harley Street.[10] The end of 1774 marked a decisive period for the Perreaus and Mrs. Rudd. What had been modest affluence assumed greater proportions. The house in Pall Mall, once so superior, was deemed "a paltry place, and nothing less than the squares, or some of the best streets leading to them, appeared to be either the fit or the eligible situation."[11] Daniel and Mrs. Rudd began to acquire possessions on an entirely different scale.

"The house and furniture," one paper editorialized, "is exceedingly elegant, though the poor upholsterer is not paid one shilling for it."[12] Daniel Perreau and Mrs. Rudd spent thousands of pounds in the years between 1773 and 1775 on such items. By the time the fraud was detected, they owed vast sums to artisans and shopkeepers. During this period a steady stream of goods poured through their door, to the amazement of friends and neighbors.[13] Later, in a frantic effort to cover the Ayr bonds, Daniel disposed of some of his possessions, raising £1000 of the £1500 he owed Dr. Brooke, "and Sir Thomas Frankland had an assignment of my house in Harley Street, with the furniture and other valuables, which I conceive will fully indemnify him from any loss he may sustain on this unhappy occasion."[14] These sums testify to the splendor of their possessions. When Mrs. Rudd protested against the house transfer, she took out an advertisement listing the goods she claimed as her property and warning all potential buyers that she would contest Frankland's claim. Her meticulous account of each item, her intimate and satisfied knowledge of them, speak to her attachment. She listed a variety of her and her children's clothing: eight silk negligees, three silk nightgowns, five dozen shirts, two quilted satin petticoats, a complete suit of point lace, two fine minionet lace long aprons, several suits of minionet worked stays, cloaks, hats, stockings, handkerchiefs, and much more. She claimed all the household linen and china and much of the furniture, including "two mahogany side board pedestals, two mahogany card tables, a worked fire screen, several carpets, two India cabinets, a swing dressing glass, a picture of George II, twelve French prints in figures, eight varnished chairs without the covers, the beds, cradles, and carpet from the nursery." She described every-thing in loving detail. Her listing of wood, color, and fabric testifies to her passion for display and her desire to show that their possessions were the very best that money could buy. In the back bed chamber, there was a "bedstead, bed and bedding compleat, with blue and white striped Manchester furni-ture; window curtains, the same; two white quilts, one fine marcella, the other a fine white cotton; six armed chairs varnished; blue and white with cushions; a carpet in the front garret." She even had a special Hepplewhite dressing table made, and named for her.[15]

In January 1776, as the brothers awaited execution, the papers announced an auction of Daniel's effects. This became one more of the spectacles asso-ciated with the case. Curwen, the American loyalist, received a ticket from the auctioneer, Mr. Skinner, to enable him to view the goods of this house-hold before its sale, "none being to be allowed to be present at the auction but by ticket." On Saturday, January 13, Curwen visited the house "to view the superb furniture and house." There he "met a very large company of gen-teel, well dressed people most of whom were of the Feminine Gender, on the same errand as ourselves, to view the house and furniture, the former of which is in the highest and most expensive taste." He spent some time "pass-ing through the rooms, from the 4th story to the kitchen &c. below, and gratified our curiosity." "Amongst other articles of the latter are glasses each plate of 7 feet 3 inches by 4 feet 2 being by much the largest I had seen, a great quantity of tasty plate, china, glass, &c &c."[16] The papers reported the sale in similar detail. "Two large plate glasses sold for 185l. each; the plate sold for 7s8d per ounce, and the whole amount of the furniture in the dinning-room sold for £617." Eight cabriole chairs fetched 17 guineas; a commode dressing table of curious construction, 11 guineas; and an elegant bed and curtains, £42.[17] Curwen's response reveals how startled people were by the opulence of the Perreau household. The mirrors seemed symbolic of the self-consciousness of both Daniel and Mrs. Rudd, their preoccupation with image and presentation, their desire to produce a glittering stage for their performances. There was something almost obsessive about their acquisi-tiveness, as if it could ward off debt and doubt.

Both Daniel Perreau and Mrs. Rudd seemed to invest jewelry with special significance. They spent staggering sums on jewels. If there was something ostentatious about their display of valuables, most of their acquaintances seem to have been happily blinded by the glint. That was the point. When Daniel approached Mr. Belliard, a jeweler, about purchasing a ring, he wished it "to be of the finest lustre, and large, intending it as a family ring to descend to his future progeny." The ring sold for 2000 guineas.[18] Mrs. Rudd made even more of her diamonds. In her contest with Frankland over their property, she listed a diamond necklace, three "brilliant" diamond round pins, "a very superb" pair of diamond earrings, a pair of pearl earrings, and other jewelry. Belliard claimed to have been owed some £3000 by Daniel and Mrs. Rudd.[19] Her jewels figured at crucial moments in all of her stories. She made much of Daniel's pawning of them while she was in Scotland, and still more of her voluntary sacrifice of them to aid the brothers once the crime was discovered. The precious stones were not merely another form of her wealth. They symbolized her value, gave proof of her status, and secured her envy and admiration in the eyes of the world.[20] For her they worked as a talisman, a powerful reminder to people of who she was and a protection against the slanderous insinuations she knew to be collecting around her. At her trial, Admiral Frankland admitted that these jewels were valued at £2800.

Daniel Perreau and Mrs. Rudd adopted the habits of the elite, he with his daily ride in the park, she with her round of visiting her "connections." A French traveler, Grosley, marveled at the routine established by the London professional and banking classes. It conforms to the glimpses we get of the daily life of the two Perreau households and their constant visitors.[21] In their life-style as in their possessions, Daniel and Mrs. Rudd devoted themselves to enjoying leisure and acquaintances, to consumption and display. Many people had stories to tell about the elegant life they found at Daniel Perreau's. John Baker reported meeting William Neale, who told him "of his dining" there, in Harley Street. Dr. Brooke and "a young Scotch doctor" were present. Neale described it as "all superb"; there was "a porter at the door, 2 servants out of livery and four in."[22] The magnificence of Daniel's establishment was among the most frequently repeated tropes of the case. It was well beyond the means of most of the people in their circle and offered a hint of a half-hidden tale of extraordinary advancement. It lent substance to what must otherwise have seemed fantastic accounts of secret influences working to promote the Perreaus into the highest reaches of English society. Perhaps

Daniel and Mrs. Rudd conspired together to create this impression of wealth and influence. More likely they each separately played out a fantasy of boundless affluence. "In this luxurious age," Trusler wrote, "wealth is the only object of admiration, and to wear the appearance of wealth, we become expensive and extravagant in our manner of living." "If we cast our eyes upon the upper, on the middle ranks of life," another author commented in 1774, "we shall find that the principal business of men and women is the study of dress, and the pursuit of amusement. They lie down to sleep, and rise up to trifle ... changing one diversion for another, to fill up vacancies of time ... and lull their unquiet thoughts asleep."[23]

TWO FACES OF THE TON

The Rudd-Perreau case occurred in the middle of a period of particularly virulent debate about the nature and danger of the life of fashion. Laments about the corrupting power of fashion were no doubt conventional, but a convergence of factors—financial crisis, ministerial instability, popular unrest, and colonial violence—lent a special sense of urgency to the complaint. People's reactions to the case were no doubt informed and influenced by such discussions in this time of crisis. The debate filled the magazines, was widely presented in theatrical productions, and led to a proliferation of pamphlets and poetry.[24] Fashion, it was said, "governs the world: it regulates the morals, the way of thinking, dressing, eating, writing, entertainments, pleasures, every thing."[25] The swirl and glamour of metropolitan life obscured reality and disordered a person's values. "Fallacy," one poem warned, assumed "her mask," while it disarmed the unreflective individual.

> You'd scarce discover the deception,
> Unless endow'd with keen perception;
> 'Tis then you may detect the cheat,
> And all her super arts defeat.[26]

At the same time that fashion was being roundly chastised, and while few wrote in open praise of the morals of the beau monde, a vociferous readership was eager to learn more about its ways and its denizens.[27] The periodicals of the day worked especially hard to satisfy this customer curiosity and to stage the spectacle of fashionable life for those without its doors.

One of the first periodicals to cater to the appetite for "tell-all" journalism was the *Town and Country Magazine,* founded in 1769. What made this magazine novel and created competitive pressure on the others was its immensely popular monthly "Tête-à-Tête," the "affair of the month," complete with portraits of the featured fashionable couple. The column, as we have seen, offered an admiring look at the relations between wealthy men and their mistresses. This specialty of the journal is claimed to have raised its circulation to 14,000; the *Town and Country* itself argued that it was the "Tête-à-Têtes" that "so peculiarly distinguished this Magazine from all others." Whatever its sales, it was avidly read by those desiring to be in the know, to be up on the latest tattle and scandal, to be, albeit vicariously, a part of "the world of fashion."[28]

The market for these journals was expanding. New magazines like the *Town and Country* and the *Matrimonial Magazine* came into existence to satisfy a craving for gossip about fashionable society; they were read by the same people who were later to be so fascinated by the Rudd-Perreau scandal. Along with their more serious discussions of art and literature, periodicals offered an increased opportunity for a glimpse of the doings of the rich and glamorous. This fare was presented to a prosperous class of readers, a group Mrs. Rudd's "uncle" John Stewart was to call the "mushroom gentry," who sought to know about and imitate this elusive elite. The competition among these journals was intense as each vied to outdo the other. Few publications could resist the pressure to provide the public with fresh sensations. Even the usually sober *London Magazine* found itself swept along in the wake of these changes. Some editors made a feeble pretense of fulfilling a didactic purpose in offering a monthly sampling of scandal. Others insisted that they observed rules of delicacy and provided details of misconduct only to encourage morality. All promised "inside" information on the lives and loves of the *bon ton*. If it was not respectable to applaud the explicit stories of the amorous intrigues of the elite, readers were invited to indulge in and to be openly curious about such tales. In order to reconcile these opposing impulses, the journals adopted a tone of mild disapproval, but cloaked in a light or humorous vein that let the reader know that a more worldly or knowledgeable attitude was appropriate among the socially elect.

There was something deeply unsettling and unresolved about such coverage, however. The tonish life was undeniably attractive, and the space given to the details of high life in the magazines testified to this attraction. Yet the same journals almost without exception censured this life-style, condemning its falsity, corruption, selfishness, and deceit. In this way the periodical press mirrored the age's deep ambivalence about fashion: an infatuation with the subject, a sense of its irresistible power, and a troubled conscience about its expression. "Within the magazines, anti-fashion and anti-town contributions nestled uneasily amidst 'tête-à-têtes,' other city gossip features, and accounts of the latest dresses, nosegays, coiffeur, and cuisine."[29] Condemning the world of fashion on the one hand while providing an ever increasing dose of fashionable detail on the other, such journals encouraged the fantasies of tonish expenditure while deploring extravagance and ambition. Even after the *London Magazine* itself capitulated to popular taste and tried its hand at a monthly "history of gallantry," it still fulminated that "expensive furniture, elegant repasts, and rich apparel, are the ambition of the middle class of people; from these childish baubles they seek to acquire respect and esteem from the vulgar."[30] Many Londoners, themselves aspiring to social mobility and admittance to the *beau monde*, saw this double-sidedness in the Rudd-Perreau case, which seemed to combine the fulfillment of their most extravagant dreams in descriptions of the life-styles and acquisitions of the trio with the horrors of their greatest nightmare: crime, trial, and execution.

Magazines were not the only popular form to concern themselves with representing the life and manners of London's social elite. Exactly a week after the appearance of Robert Perreau at Bow Street, David Garrick's *Bon Ton* opened at Drury Lane in London and became one of the most successful theatrical pieces to appear that year. The farce expressed Garrick's own critique of the world of fashion, while simultaneously displaying that life on stage. In the play, Lord and Lady Minikin represented the fashionable marriage, based not on love but convenience. The action centered around the attempt of each to discover the extramarital affairs of the other, less from love than from injured pride. In the laughable exploits of this couple Garrick staged a satire on the manners and immorality of the fashionable. No one meant what he or she said; honesty and morality were condemned as vulgar. Each character surrendered to his or her pursuit of a temporary pleasure, becoming increasingly ludicrous at each turn. All of London society, the play argued, was infected with such vices. It was only the seemingly silly, but in truth sensible and sound, Sir John Trotley who saw through the "deceit and delusion." He represented the rough, plainspoken, non-Londoner who exposed their vices and condemned their pursuit of urban, foreign ways. By the end of the play he had abandoned London in disgust, but not before dealing out a kind of rough justice to all parties. And he carried off with him the "distressed damsels" he had rescued "from those monsters, foreign vices and Bon Ton, as they call it."[31]

A number of popular plays took up these themes. Fashion, these productions sought to show, produced a mirror world in which every behavior and value was shown to be its opposite. By its very seductiveness, it captured the innocent, taken in by its glamour, and led them through debt, deceit, and debauchery, ultimately to death (if they were not miraculously saved). So ran the plot of Richard Cumberland's *Note of Hand*, a 1774 play about a young man of good nature who was "corrupted" by "fashion"; led into gambling and dissipation, he was only saved by the intervention of a watchful uncle and a loving woman.[32]

Such satires as *Bon Ton* could not disguise, even as they tried to resist, the desirability of that world. Garrick was far too sensitive to the market to transgress the line between polite criticism and painful jeremiad. He produced a comedy, not a tragedy, albeit an ambiguous one that could be considered in contradictory ways. On the one hand, O'Keefe thought *Bon Ton* "too hard against the upper classes ... the satire ... is more poignant than any that appears in the comedies of Colley Cibber, Congreve, Farquhar, or even Shakespeare."[33] Yet denizens of the ton could attend these plays easily, for before the end, their target always shifted from fashion itself to those other vulgar pretenders to the real thing. Thus in hitting their target they missed their mark. No one left the theater shaken by the message. Too deeply implicated, culturally and economically, in the fashionable round to be forthrightly critical, theatrical productions of the 1770s combined satire with display, criticism with the latest in hair design and costume. To be too severe or too personal meant risking censure or worse. Garrick, unlike Foote, was not prepared to include specific contemporary references in the comic pieces presented at Drury Lane. In a letter to Hugh Kelly rejecting an unidentified and probably destroyed play of his, Garrick, after commenting on the inadequacies of several characters, noted that "the Widow [Keenly], which seems ye favorite female Character has the most abandon'd Mind, & tho she does not forge bonds, Yet she forges falsehoods to carry on her Schemes, & falls but little short of what is suppos'd of Mrs Rudd."[34] Clearly this was not the sort of drama that Garrick was prepared to stage.

If magazines and theaters tempered their criticism or included the latest in fashion while condemning its influence, the pamphlet literature of the period was thunderous in denunciation. This condemnation of fashion became especially intense in the 1770s, as the maintenance of empire seemed to demand a stern martial (and marital) preparedness. Commentators bemoaned a social world dominated by imposture and dissimulation. "Beware of counterfeits," one writer warned, "for such are abroad." The plague of the present times was the ubiquity of "imposters," who threaten "people in every part of the world." Though phrased in universalist and transhistorical language, the message of the *St. James's Magazine* was both timely and pointed: "But as mankind in general seem to act the imposter, I think we may with equal propriety compare human life to our modern masquerade." It was the American rebels who were characterized as "men disguis'd," "Ambiguous Things," and "men undefin'd by any Rules," but many believed that the men and women of the mother country were also masked and equivocal beings. William Crawford wrote that "dissimulation" was a vice "which prevails almost universally in the fashionable world" and added that "it destroys all confidence, fills the minds of those with whom we are connected, with suspicion and distrust."[35] The *Reflections on the too prevailing Spirit of DISSIPATION AND GALLANTRY shewing its dreadful Consequences to Publick Freedom,* published in 1771, was only one of the many pamphlets to make this connection between fashion and liberty plain. Slowly, over the course of the 1770s, the portrayal of the world of the ton shifted from affectionate jest to more tragic representations. According to Jonas Hanway, retired merchant, philanthropist, social activist, and moralist, it would be dangerous to underestimate the fateful effects of tonish vices. The fashion for fashion, he argued, was responsible for the spread of England's weakness and would lead to national disaster and imminent Divine retribution. "In many instances," he warned, "this TON seems to be so insignificant in their sight who have a moderate degree of understanding, as not to be worthy of a serious pen: But the event proves it has so many fascinating qualities, and attractive powers, it draws the heedless into a variety of pernicious practices, and hurls vast numbers into ruin!"[36]

In a world of hungry acquisitiveness, even neighbors, relations, and friends might fall victim to fashionable dissimulation. The very proximity and intimacy that allowed for their frequent intercourse made it possible for deceit and fraud to be more easily perpetrated. In the Perreau-Rudd case, both Dr. Brooke and Admiral Frankland were old friends and neighbors of the Perreaus, and Brooke lent Daniel his Ayr bonds gladly because of their past warm relationship. Thus the case exposed the duplicity, false-facedness, and false-heartedness not only of the Perreaus but, by implication, of many of London's most private and valued relationships. It seemed a confirmation of what one observer feared: the spread of cynicism and "political cunning" into the domestic sphere and private life. "But is this political cunning to be carried into social life, and to prevail between the most intimate friends? If so, all sincerity is to be banished from the world, and it is to become one universal masquerade, for the characters of dissimulation and hypocrisy."[37] Contemporaries connected the superficiality of acquisition with the duplicity of such socially ambitious Londoners. "Vice is concealed under fair disguises, dignified by genteel appellations, and dressed out in specious colors, in the very garb of virtue."[38] This vision of London as the scene of mass disguise, of "seemingness" in the employ of evil aspirations, was frequently expressed in these years. "As for the metropolis," James Fordyce warned in 1776, "what is it else but the general mart of all that can propagate admiration of an outside, or, if you will, one entire and enormous scene of enchantment, where fashion, opulence, and ostentation, are incessantly practicing their witchcraft?"[39] London was universally regarded as the center "where all the corruption and futility of these times are concentrated." This case provided a living tableau of the sordid and dangerous reality behind the smiling, cozy face of London's West End squares. Contemporaries undoubtedly also saw in this debacle a larger instance of what Fordyce described as the war between the sexes. "The greater part of either sex study to prey on one another. The world, in too many instances, is a theatre of war between men and women. Every stratagem is tried, and every advantage taken, on the side of both."[40] Men and women, it was said, succumbed to vice and crime, not out of need or desire, but because Fashion required it. "Alas! in me no want, no passion's sway, / Can palliate guilt; 'twas Fashion led the way," lamented one fictional fallen wife.[41] It was the very desirability of the life of fashion, the seductiveness of its conspicuous consumption, that made the case so interesting and yet generated such anxiety among newspaper readers. In this world loyalty was often an undervalued commodity, friendship a cover for fraud, and love a compact between thieves.

FORGING A SELF

Daniel Perreau and Margaret Rudd were said to have first met at a masquerade, where, a commentator noted, "the knave and the man of probity, the fool and the philosopher, join willing hands, and in dear festivity lose every moral, every civil distinction." This experience was often taken as an epitome of the confusion and anarchy that was disclosed by the case. Journals were full of laments about this situation. "The world is now nothing but a masquerade," one contributor wrote in 1773, "wherein every one wears, not the dress which suits her character, but the most pleasing to her fancy, and under which she thinks she shall be best concealed." The extraordinary fashions worn to pleasure gardens like Vauxhall, Ranelagh, and the newly opened Pantheon were meant to draw attention and to inspire desire. These locations were intended to be places of enchantment. The self was on display—not the true self, but the imagined, fantasized, artfully contrived self. Social relations became little more than playacting, with pleasure the only pursuit. The frequent complaints about the immorality of the age scarcely dented the enthusiasm for adventure. For every person who condemned the pointlessness and waste of the Pantheon, hundreds of others saw it as the height of splendor and hastened to join the throng seeking admission.[42] Many historians have discussed the emblematic quality of disguise and the masquerade, both as social practice and as symbol, in the social world of eighteenth-century London. With the growing publication of books teaching aspiring members of the ton how to walk, curtsey, and dress, with the increasing possibility of appearing more or other than what one was, came the "frightening possibility that nothing stood behind decorum. No gold standard guaranteed inflated or deflated currency; no original preexisted the copy; no durable skeleton shored up the frail anatomy."[43] The maid might well be mistaken for her mistress.

This anxiety about the false decorousness of eighteenth-century society helps explain the notoriety that the Rudd-Perreau case achieved. As it unfolded, the affair became more, not less, "spectacular"; the spectacle of riches sought and lost, of meteoric rise and fall, of uncertain innocence and incredible cunning, played to the packed house of a spellbound public. And yet, unlike a theatrical play, where one could willingly suspend disbelief for its duration, this was "real life," though no less engaging than any Drury Lane production.

Perhaps "authenticity" and "sincerity" became highly valued attributes in this period because people sought some assurance of stability in this world of pretense. "Looks had to speak true, and a new physiognomy was needed to tell the honest face and the heartfelt look."[44] Yet the make-believe world of fashion also held out promises, especially for people who wished to rise quickly. For the world of fashion was in tension with the world of birth and fixed hierarchy. The latter claimed a static and stable character, while the former not only exposed a dynamic principle but revealed the shifting composition of the upper classes. Fashion depended upon consumption, upon display and leisure. It required wealth, but it converted wealth into taste. If it announced exclusion, it also offered a principle of mobility, a means to translate money into elegance. Fashion encompassed a wide social segment of those who clung precariously to their status or who aspired to gain entry to the select world. After his trial, one commentator, looking for the seeds of perdition that had brought Daniel to the fatal tree, found it in his early love of expensive clothing. While still at school, a mother of another pupil, a reputed demi-rep of elegance, convinced him that his first step in advancement must be sartorial. In response, he discarded his old tailor "to make room for the tailor of Sir Francis Blake Delaval." From then on, there was no going back.[45] Thus fashion offered at one and the same time the distinction of manner that the elite sought to maintain and the parody of that distinction, the reduction of it to crude drives and values. Much of the discussion of fashion as an ideal was ambivalent at best, more often critical and mocking. But these were futile gestures in the face of fashion's power, as testified to by the deference accorded to the participants, the amount of space they won in the papers, the allure of dress and manner. Fashion was an alternate way of establishing precedence. It offered a shortcut for the socially ambitious to leap ahead, especially those with shady claims to birth and inadequate income. Fashion was part of a gamble. When, during their 1771 trip to Paris "to get [trading] intelligence," Daniel remonstrated with Mrs. Rudd about her extravagance, she replied "that if they did not keep up an intercourse with, and display their hospitality to people of a certain rank ... it would be fruitless to think of reaping any advantage from their journey."[46] If the gamble succeeded, one became a part of a world that possessed power, status, and influence. If not, ruin and loss of reputation followed; one became another example of how fleeting, insubstantial, and fantastical were its promises. Contemporaries realized this superficiality and saw how directly it applied to the frustrated hopes and desires of Mrs. Rudd and the brothers Perreau. "Believe me, my dear," wrote one author on the case, "it is the ton to confine the view merely to the surface. A handsome house, and a full purse, are the only credentials required with the first families in the kingdom."[47] As always, these dreams gained substance in the material expression of the Daniel Perreau household and person, with their carriage and new residence, fine furniture and elegant dress.

To many, Mrs. Rudd epitomized the deceitful social climber. Fascinating and beguiling, full of extravagant habits and claims to high birth and respectability, what seemed to lie behind her outer appearance was a calculating mind ready to sacrifice the innocent to the gratification of her selfish desires. Certainly that is how Daniel characterized her in his "Narrative"; he claimed she was able to have accomplished his ruin through "the most wicked and treacherous Artifice, under a Mask of the tenderest and most faithful Friendship, worn by a Woman."[48] To many others as well she appeared the embodiment of diseased fashion, the female figure of decadent habits who threatened to subvert the masculine virtues that produced national strength. She seemed like the masked "specter" of speculative society—fantastical, imaginative, and inconstant.

At the height of the controversy surrounding her role in the crime, a correspondent sketched an image of an unnamed woman who could be none other than Mrs. Rudd. It was often from the other sex, he remarked, that a man could expect ruin. Normally, men preferred a "modest woman" to one who had "lost her inestimable Virgin Treasure." But "amidst the crowd of licentious females, I have found one species her equal, if not her superior, in artfully administering the Circean Dose." This woman combined "a most engaging person" with "the most insinuating manners and address." "A genteel education was given her by indulgent parents who little thought they were fostering a siren, fatally to attract the attention of unguarded youth." She "gleaned" a knowledge of the genteel world from "the men of fashion" with whom she associated. "Her own sense had sufficiently secured her from all low, vulgar prejudices, and without the disgusting boldness of a prostitute, she has acquired the easy freedom of a courtesan, which gains upon the young and gay, ten times more than the stupid bashfulness of some modest woman." When seen in public, she was "elegance itself," and "no mark of infamy" could be seen in her features. She had a false but persuasive way of arguing, so that no admirer could resist her. "A man rises from her bed with that exaltation of spirits, from having possessed so sensible and so fair a creature, that he cannot persuade himself he has been doing wrong." She had every quality to make herself "an enchanted mistress."[49]

This aspect of the female adventurer, the woman out to better herself by using—and abusing—men, was especially remarked upon in 1775, the year of the case. That December, an anonymous correspondent wrote to the *Town and Country Magazine:* "Every year seems to be peculiarly marked with some events that particularly distinguish it from the rest. This seems to be marked by beauty and impeached innocence. A Butterfield, a Rudd and a K—n have stamped 1775 with indelible signs of female power, wit, and fortitude." The same month, an anonymous writer, signing his letter to the *London Chronicle* "A profound Admirer of the Fair Sex," also noted, "This seems to be the Age of Woman."[50] Perhaps by placing Mrs. Rudd's portrayal with those of Miss Jane Butterfield and the Duchess of Kingston, and by adding that of another daring woman whose fate was reported on and read about as the case emerged, Queen Caroline Matilda of Denmark, we will get a clearer idea of the unease such women inspired.

THE YEAR OF THE WOMAN: MRS. RUDD, THE QUEEN OF DENMARK, THE DUCHESS OF KINGSTON, AND MISS BUTTERFIELD

The story of the bigamous Duchess of Kingston created one of the great scandals of the later eighteenth century. As Miss Chudleigh, the impecunious orphaned daughter of a Cornish military officer, she had shocked and delighted society by her appearance as Iphegenia at Ranelagh, in a dress that was diaphanous to the waist and scanty thereafter. Like Mrs. Rudd, she was said to have acquired her many talents through a boarding school education, "dancing, music and French, in which she was a great proficient." Although she was the subject of gossip and censure, she "seemed a salamander, insensible in the midst of flames ... upon the point of being pronounced a most accomplished coquette." After a brief marriage to the younger son of the Earl of Bristol (which both agreed to put quietly behind them), she formed a liaison with the Duke of Kingston. Wishing to marry the duke, she destroyed the register of her previous marriage and proceeded to take a second husband. Only on the duke's death was the fraud detected and the now dowager duchess summoned home from Italy, where she was visiting the Pope.[51] The whole nation was preoccupied with the prospect of her bigamy trial before the House of Lords. One of the most flamboyant of the women of the world, she flaunted her success and therefore her immorality, rather than displaying a tactful silence.

Stories about the Duchess of Kingston were repeated with mingled delight and horror. On leaving Rome, it was said, she had persuaded her banker, a Mr. Jenkins, to refund some money she had left with him, by waiting, with a brace of pistols, "on the steps of the door, and declar[ing] her determination there to remain until he returned, were it for a week, a month or a year."

The duchess got her money, for, as the *Newgate Calendar* put it, "the duchess possessed that gift of utterance for which ladies of spirit are sometimes so eminent." This facility served her well in her sparring with Samuel Foote, the playwright, who proposed featuring her, as Lady Kitty Crocodile, in his new play, *A Trip to Calais*. Foote, angered by having had the performance of the play canceled through the intercession of the duchess's friend, the Lord Chamberlain, made their correspondence public and claimed center stage of public gossip. Many feared Foote's pen, but the duchess proved she could retaliate in kind. She had her agent prosecute him on a sodomy charge, which, although not sustained, may well have contributed to his death in 1777.[52]

As Mrs. Rudd sat in prison, the duchess awaited trial before the House of Lords. The two women inevitably invited comparison. "The Trial of Mrs. Rudd," quipped the *St. James's Chronicle*, "is put off till next Sessions, that the Fate of two Female Adventurers may be determined as near the same Time as possible; whatever Disparity there may be between the Ladies in Rank and Condition, it is doubtful to which of the two the Pardon for Art and Address ought to be given."[53] Both women seemed hypocrites. Each had employed her sexual wiles to take advantage of easily deluded men. Yet they had the audacity to appear before the public proclaiming their virtue and demanding justice in a legal proceeding.

Mrs. Rudd's supposed career excited comparison with that of other extraordinary women. Hannah More reported that Foote, a shrewd observer of social ranks and conditions, had said "that the Empress of Russia, the Duchess of Kingston, and Mrs. Rudd, are the three most extraordinary women in Europe."[54] A fourth, Queen Caroline Matilda of Denmark, sister of George III and adulterous wife of the Danish king, died in May 1775. She had had a difficult life. Caroline had married Christian VII on November 8, 1766. The young king, being infatuated with a court follower, Count von Holtke, had little time for his new queen. She also faced the open animosity of the dowager queen. Alone in a strange country, tied to a weak man, she began to assume a wider responsibility for the country's governance. She was aided by the court physician, John Struensee, who became her lover. He rose to become the chief minister of the government and an active reformer. Antagonized, the nobility, together with the dowager, used Struensee's adultery as a pretext for a coup that swept him to the gallows. Caroline's life was only saved through the resolute actions of the British envoy, Robert Murray Keith. Threatened with war if they did not let the now divorced queen leave the country, the Danes gave way. Reluctant to let her return to England, since Queen Charlotte disapproved of her scandalous behavior in Denmark, George III sent her to a castle in Germany, where she died of fever at age twenty-four.[55] In death she became the sympathetic figure she had never been in life. By July, newspaper articles and pamphlets vindicating her conduct and exonerating her crimes appeared in the English press. She was described in Britain as a martyr, "sacrificed in the first bloom of life, she was sent an inexperienced victim to a court the most despicably dissolute and debauched in Europe." Her taste for dressing in masculine garb, for hunting and horseback riding, were glossed over; instead the eulogy of a correspondent to the *London Chronicle* noted that she "managed the horse with uncommon address and spirit." Her main concern, he claimed, was her children; "the feelings of the Sovereign were absorbed in those of the Mother; and if she wept the day when she quitted the island of Zealand, it was because she was then bereft of those dear objects of her maternal fondness." In presenting this panegyric to her memory, its author gave the public yet another transgressive woman, though of the highest rank, to contemplate. Like the Duchess of Kingston, the queen was publicly mannish and over-bold, and, like Mrs. Rudd, she claimed that love explained her crimes but insisted that her grieving heart remained with, and was always entwined around, the fate of her children.[56]

The last of the year's "sensations" was Miss Jane Butterfield, who was charged with poisoning her lover and keeper, William Scawen. Like the Rudd-Perreau affair, the Butterfield case also produced a series of pamphlets,[57] though in this case all were favorable to her and sought her acquittal. Their authors roundly chastised Sanxay, the druggist who had convinced Scawen that he was being poisoned by Butterfield, for his criminal incompetence and for being the tool of others interested in inheriting Scawen's wealth themselves. "If an innocent person is liable to suffer such hardships as these," they argued, "without redress, the boasted equity of our laws is a mere phantom."[58] Yet the pamphleteers never entirely resolved the major issue of the case; it was clear that Scawen had died of poisoning, but had he killed himself, or was Butterfield responsible, and if she was, had it been an accident or deliberate? Unable to come up with a conclusive answer, they fell back on the argument from character: Butterfield could not have murdered Scawen, a man with whom she had lived so intimately for so many years, because she was not that sort of person, because, despite minor lapses, she was a virtuous woman and not a courtesan. Varying stories were told of her early life. One account claimed that she was seduced and abandoned by a brewer and then took up with a "young gentleman of the army," with whom she lived for a period. Others argued that it was Scawen himself who had seduced Butterfield when she was only fourteen. All agreed that, despite these irregularities, she proved her irreproachable character by her garb. She dressed "not to allure as a shewy kept-mistress, but as a representative of an engaging careful wife." "Butterfield was not a vicious wanton:—perhaps few were ever born with sentiments so nearly allied to honor and virtue."[59] Scawen had lived with her in apparent amity, and for more than a decade he had introduced her into his family and she passed as his wife. In 1774 he had gone so far as to make a will leaving her his chief beneficiary to "a legacy of £20,000." A year later he fell ill; despite her constant nursing, he became sicker still and died in great agony. Miss Butterfield was charged with murder, and some speculated that she, enamored of a new lover and desirous of both lucre and freedom, had ended her relationship with Scawen by feeding him arsenic gruel. The story was sensational and widely reported just as Mrs. Rudd awaited the court's decision about her crown witness status. Before Butterfield came to trial, an anonymous pamphlet appeared that found similarities in the three cases.

> There are at this time three criminal prosecutions carrying on against three females of different ranks in life; to what end are they carried on? Is it for justice sake that the prosecutors of the Duchess of Kingston pursue her, or for the sin of bigamy? or is it her fortune, they have in view?—does the aged and avaricious baronet prosecute Mrs. Rudd for justice sake, or to destroy the woman's claim on the effects in his possession? Has Jemmy Scawen [William Scawen's heir] no fears about him, that if Miss Butterfield gets acquitted, that the Lord Chancellor will make him refund, and place Miss Butterfield, on the same ground she stood, before the alteration of Mr. Scawen's will?

Butterfield was tried at Guilford, but as "the proofs against her were weak and ill-supported," she was acquitted, "to the satisfaction of the court." "The prisoner behaved, throughout the whole trial," one magazine reported, "with the utmost propriety, and with that appearance of decent fortitude which is known generally to accompany innocence." [60]

Many other comparisons were made between the cases: the Robin Hood debating society thought the Rudd case raised as many complex legal problems as the Scawen case raised medical ones; the *St. James's Chronicle* retorted that "the Story of Miss Butterfield has so frightened a great many old Keepers, that many of them have turned off their Handmaids, and others think they have sufficiently secured themselves by burning their Wills; but Mrs. Rudd laughs at that Precaution, and can teach the Miss Butterfields how to secure the Legacy, though the Will is destroyed."[61] Butterfield's acquittal in August seemed to augur a similar verdict in Rudd's case. "The Success of Miss Butterfield has given great Spirits to more than one Lady whose Conduct has been examined by the Grand Jury; and it is hoped that the Politeness of these Times will secure the Fair Sex from the Severity of a Petty Jury."[62] But the Butterfield story, despite the horrors of Scawen's slow death, remained less enthralling than the Rudd case. Unlike Kingston and Rudd, Butterfield was always spoken for by her advisors and friends, and her voice was never raised in her own self-defense. Perhaps innocence, albeit tarnished, had fewer attractions for the reading public than revelations of fashionable vice.

In this "Year of the Woman," to paraphrase a bit, the difficulties of all three women were said to have arisen from the same cause, "love or attachment to the male sex." However, while both Mrs. Rudd and the duchess were described as women "of spirit, sense, and intrigue," or of distinguished "charms, sense, and repartee," that is, as assertive, self-seeking, and strong women, Miss Butterfield's piteous tale "justly merited the compassion she excited in every breast," since her misfortune, unlike theirs, "appears to have been owing to the operations of craft and avarice upon the weakness of a dying man." The duchess and Mrs. Rudd were often described as having powerful and willful minds; Miss Butterfield, though a kept woman, was properly shy and retiring. Seeming to realize the idealized picture of the relation between lover and demi-rep, Miss Butterfield's life could be exculpated, if not celebrated. In contrast, both Mrs. Rudd and the duchess, by refusing to be simply love objects and by insistently and to some extent successfully being subjects, makers of their own lives and destiny, were much more disturbing. At a time when England's military might and valor, England's manhood, was being severely tested by rebellious American colonists, it was an evil omen that her womenfolk were so bold. One correspondent suggested that it would be well for the nation if Mrs. Rudd, like the Chevalier D'Eon, could change her sex and become a man.[63] After such a transformation she could "assert the honour and dignity of the Mother-country, by taking such vigorous measures as will force the stiff-necked rebellious Yankies to bow submissively to her supreme authority."[64]

FASHION VERSUS PRUDENCE: APING THE *BEAU MONDE*

The reading public alternated in its attitude toward the case, expressing at one moment dismay or outrage at the conduct of the participants, while at the next giving voice to undisguised curiosity about their possessions and behavior. There was little sense of conflict between these emotions. For many, the forgery went well beyond the notes that the luckless Robert Perreau tried to pass off. These were just the inevitable result of the larger and previous forgeries, those of the character and visages of the protagonists themselves. In the faces of the Perreaus and Mrs. Rudd, contemporaries could see that the countenance of such forgery was both handsome and fatal. In this light, the case served a useful purpose, could provide a living exemplum, a "beacon to that large class of people in this metropolis, who like [the Perreaus] despising the government of their own reason, as well as the line of their circumstances, permit themselves to be swallowed up in the too general vortex of dissipation." "Let their sad Example, therefore, teach others to well know themselves, as well as their Duty to God and their Neighbours"; to "drink deep, or taste not of the Pierian Spring"; to "cast away Ambition"; to "be just and fear not"; to avoid "the Way that seemeth right, the Ends whereof are, alas! the ways of Death!"[65] Just as it was said that the Americans were attempting to subvert a stable social hierarchy by bringing "one man ... from behind the counter, to be a member of a sovereign Congress; ... [and] another from a barber to be a colonel," the Perreaus and Mrs. Rudd were driven to crime, for it was a well-known maxim that "the idle and the vain unhesitatingly prefer guilty affluence to insulted industry,"[66] glitter to solid worth.

Barbara Stafford has written of the painstaking process whereby eighteenth-century social theorists attempted to construct a "depth psychology" in an effort to "ferret out imitation, that is, to uncover faces pretending to be sincere, or like the original, but which, at bottom were false."[67] This new social tool, this Diogenes lantern, was vital, not only in facilitating ordinary household relations of social interchange, but even more for the multiplicity of vital credit relationships that rested, in the last analysis, largely on trust. If people were not what they seemed, if the worlds of reality and appearances were not roughly congruent, then one had no way of reckoning who was honest and who criminal, whom to trust and whom to doubt. The Rudd-Perreau case seemed to exemplify and heighten such anxieties. "Plausibility is, at the same time, worn as a cloak, and he who has a design on your purse, your life, or your country, will assume all the appearances of cordial friendship and unpolluted honour. I believe it is well known, that the graces, the agreeable qualities ... and the appearance of the most amiable virtues, were possessed in perfection by a Perreau, a Dodd, a Donellan and a Delamotte."[68]

The desire for acceptance into the *beau monde* had inexorably led to crime, and crime of a particularly frightening sort. The case raised the possibility that there were criminals not only in those nurseries of vice, the low dives and narrow turnings of the urban poor, but also in the spacious and well-appointed houses lining the West End's great squares. With Jeremiah-like invective, the *Bath Journal* warned of a coming deluge of crime, spawned by a too-ardent desire for tonish friends and possessions. Many, it noted, felt pity and astonishment at the fate of the Perreau brothers, but few looked to the causes of their plight. If "thousands in this metropolis, who, under the ridiculous pursuit of what is called the bon ton, are trampling upon all the laws of subordination and common sense," is it surprising that crimes like forgery occurred? For has not "fashion [become] the substitute for prudence? And is not the predominant feature of that Fashion to provoke and indulge the appetites at the expense of almost every virtue? No wonder then our calendars swell every session with unhappy criminals."[69]

Many of the themes rehearsed in the case arose as well in the sensation and controversy surrounding the publication of Lord Chesterfield's *Letters*. A major commercial success, the letters became popular reading for those most engaged in observing the Rudd-Perreau episode. Although praised for their form as models of politeness and elegance, they were more widely condemned for their lack of morality and their feared influence. According to his critics, Chesterfield held up the pursuit of fashion, wealth, and worldly acceptance as the highest goal. He not only applauded ambition and recommended emulation, they noted, but encouraged unprincipled, cynical conduct. He encouraged "the semblance more than the substance of virtue; artificial manners, polite address." One such critic, William Crawford, offered an apocalyptic vision of the triumph of Chesterfieldianism. "The laws would be deprived of their salutary power, the tenderest, the dearest ties of humanity would be violated, dissoluteness of morals would usurp the place of decency and good manners, and the British Empire, the glory among nations, would be shaken to its very center." For many contemporaries, the Perreau-Rudd affair seemed like a forerunner of such a general conflagration, a harbinger of implosive societal breakdown.[70]

Six

PRIVATE CREDIT AND PUBLIC CONFIDENCE

BOTH THE PERREAUS, IN their accounts of Mrs. Rudd, and Mrs. Rudd in defense of her own reputation, made her pretensions the most frequently debated issue. For many, the forgery of the bonds had receded before the scandal of her seeming forgery of birth and character. But this case cannot be understood without reference to another set of concerns arising from the peculiar financial circumstances of the 1770s. If fashion and ambition describe two strands of this complicated affair, economic context illuminates a third. The use of paper instruments as the mainstay of the system of credit was widely believed to have been responsible for the flourishing state of the English economy in the second half of the eighteenth century. However, a severe financial crisis in 1772 renewed fears about the vulnerability of these credit arrangements, and, in the aftermath of this collapse, forgery was viewed in the most alarming terms. The crash of that year was, according to T. S. Ashton, "one of the fiercest financial storms of the century." The *Scot's Magazine* characterized the crisis as the worst "since the famous South-sea bubble in 1720." Credit had never received "a severer shock, nor a total failure of it been more generally dreaded." "Like a plague, it threatened destruction far and wide, and its baneful influence hath been felt from one extremity of the island to the other."[1]

As the Perreaus, sitting in prison under sentence of death, struggled to shift responsibility for the crime onto Mrs. Rudd, their difficulties were compounded by the charges she leveled against them. Although their defenders made much of the absence of a motive for their involvement in the scheme, she suggested a compelling reason, one which, if proved, would cast the brothers in the worst possible light. She accused them of having participated in the speculative frenzy leading up to the great crash and of engaging in precisely those dishonest practices that many believed were responsible for the desperate plight of the nation. These revelations weighed heavily with a public struggling to make sense of so obscure an affair.

Mrs. Rudd's accounts of the Perreaus' financial dealings were convincing and disturbing, for she named names, offered addresses, gave sums. Especially persuasive was her recounting of their various stock transactions. She said she had paid £1300 to cover Daniel's losses soon after they came together, later saying the money was given to Messrs. Graft and Blackburne, merchants in Scot's-Yard. This sum, she wrote, was cleared at the very time his certificate of bankruptcy was signed, so he could not have aided her *and* settled his own accounts as he had claimed. Rather, "by her generosity alone" was he enabled "to appear in May with eclat in the Alley." The following March she paid a further £800, which he owed to Portis, a broker. In the autumn of 1771 she supplied Daniel with £1400 to pay Messrs. Keble and Sadleir, insurance brokers, to insure against the risk of war. This money was lost, since no war broke out. She reimbursed Daniel's sisters, Susan and Esther Perreau, £800 that he had borrowed and lost in other transactions. In April 1772 he came to her again for £500 to pay Messrs. Gemmells of the City. In this case he apologized to her because earlier she had given him money to cover this debt. Later that summer she gave him £400 for a broker, Mr. Greenfield, and £150 more to pay Mr. Sapertas.[2]

Daniel's were not the only dealings in the Alley that were revealed. Various anonymous letters to the press told of Robert's stock gambles: the £1500 raised from Dr. Brooke's Ayr bonds, for example, which went to Mr. Vaughan, a gold and silver laceman, to settle a note Robert had given him. Another letter told of Frankland's draft on his bank being "paid in four £1000 bank notes, one of which has been traced to Mr. Sanxey, tea-man and druggist, in the Strand, and was paid ... in part for losses in the Alley by Perreau to him."[3] In an anonymous correspondence, although one that bears every mark of having come from Mrs. Rudd's hand, the writer revealed that Robert had "paid lately differences in the Alley, to the amount of several thousands, and carried seven hundred pounds with him when imprisoned." Robert was also accused of having lost his wife's fortune as well as £500 destined for his son, of which he was trustee. Even before Daniel's return from the West Indies, Robert, it was said, had become involved with "a junto of stock jobbers," at whose head stood John Huske, late member from Maldon.[4]

The Perreau trial took place against a backdrop of extraordinary financial uncertainties in the 1770s. It both revealed the shape of financial credit in these years—its foundation in acquaintance and reputation—and threatened to expose its more disturbing underside. The financial crisis of 1772 left the public shocked, angry, and suspicious. Many innocent people suffered from the frenzied and often unscrupulous speculation that led to the collapse, and there was a bitter outcry against those held responsible. To contemporaries, the disclosure of the Perreaus' activities both confirmed their worst fears about the vulnerability of private credit and reminded them of the dangers of stock-jobbing. It raised troubling questions about who the brothers really were and whether Robert in particular deserved his reputation as an honest and honorable man.

CREDIT, CHARACTER, AND RISK

A great deal of the commercial activity of eighteenth-century England was based on paper instruments. There was too little specie to meet demand, and much of it was defective. Although banking had developed rapidly since mid-century, the majority of paper in circulation still consisted of personal notes of hand. The system was well developed, with established rules for the creation and negotiation of such instruments. Shopkeepers and customers alike presented notes that were little more than individual promises to pay. Their worth depended entirely upon the reputation of the person presenting them and the value attached to the signatures that appeared on them. Indeed, a note gained credibility as it circulated, because each transaction represented a new endorsement of its worth. Still, it was risky to take a note; you relied upon the word of the person presenting it. More often than not you had no more than the appearance and reputation of the person negotiating the note to go by when making an assessment of its authenticity.[5] In 1750 an English merchant, John Badcock, responded to an inquiry about the creditworthiness of a London acquaintance from a Dutch correspondent. "I have taken all opportunity," he replied, "to inquire about the Person you spoke to me about. In general he is reputed a Man of Good Character and Credit ... It is reconed he had about four or five Thousand Pounds to begin with, and about 3 or 4 with his Wife, has no Children, keeps a Chariot, and has lately hired a Country House." "But it is almost impossible here," Badcock conceded, "to know for Certain what the true Circumstances of any Man is."[6] A person's greatest security came from dealing within a tight circle of family and friends, but even here there was risk. The circulation of paper required a high degree of confidence that mere paper represented something of value.

Trust and familiarity were features of borrowing on paper instruments and of accepting notes. Money was raised through networks of personal relations and by informal agreements. Reputation counted above every other consideration. Everything depended upon rumor, belief, and an evaluation of the person asking the loan. The Perreau case well illustrates the nature of eighteenth-century borrowing. The brothers were careful to borrow within their circle of acquaintance, from clients, neighbors, and friends, from people who were familiar with Robert's credit and character. They approached these people privately. They even expected a bank like Drummonds, one of the principal houses of the metropolis, to accept their dubious story. Had it not been for the suspicion aroused by the handwriting, they may well have succeeded, as they had earlier with another city banker. Robert approached Henry Drummond because the two men had long known each other, both socially and professionally. Drummond knew something of Robert's circumstances, had encountered the apothecary in the homes of people of the first rank, and had heard him praised there.

Thomas Frankland was a patient of Robert's, as well as a social acquaintance. The admiral was typical of many London money men who had a good deal of capital and who were looking for a profitable opportunity for investment. The alternative—refusing to enter into such transactions—doomed one to cling to unproductive assets or watch opportunities for profit pass by. Frankland was no ingenue in financial matters; his sharp dealings were well known to the public. Yet he was happy to oblige Robert Perreau. The papers marveled, after the fact, that "so knowing a man in money matters as the knight is said to be" would loan so large a sum "upon any man's hand, without seeing the person that was to pay it when due." Frankland, however, explained that he had been Robert's patient for some fifteen years. He had "always looked upon him as an honest man, and I thought he was incapable of ever deceiving me at all." Frankland's uncle had thought so highly of him that he always referred to him as "honest Perreau."[7] No doubt Frankland had another advantage in mind as well; he was familiar enough with the family to be aware of the sudden improvement of their fortunes. He had heard hints which attributed this splendid rise to the mysterious influence at work on behalf of the wife of Daniel Perreau. Frankland saw an opportunity for a favorable investment that might pay a social as well as a fiscal dividend.

The bonds that the brothers offered as security for these loans seemed to bear out the rumors swirling around the Perreaus. The bond, a legal instrument drawn up by a scrivener, pledged one person's support in an effort to raise money for another. It involved no immediate transfer of funds; rather it aided efforts to secure a loan from a third party. With the right name on it, and presented by a creditworthy person, it offered access to vast sums of money. Bonds might be drawn up for six months or a year, but it was not unusual for them "to run for much longer periods." Much lending, especially among individuals, took place on this basis. It was a favor one might extend to a relation or friend, the sense of relationship deepening the sense of obligation on both sides.[8] A bond could be presented, as it was in this case, ostensibly by an agent for the signatory, supported by a story that he did not wish publicity but rather chose to remain anonymous for some reason, perhaps in aid of a "natural" daughter, or because he did not want his financial needs or activities known. Robert Clive, "conqueror of Bengal," used many such agents and ruses in his attempts to gain control of the East India Company, and subterfuges of this sort were not uncommon.[9] Still, the hazardous manner in which the loans in this case were made inspired one writer to say, "I never yet met with such improbable credulity, and such ignorance of the laws relative to securities, as hath appeared in this matter, and from some men of sense, very conversant in money transactions."[10]

For much of the century private credit attracted less attention than public credit, as politicians and economic thinkers hotly debated the threat of national bankruptcy. By the 1760s, however, this situation had changed as the intensification of these credit transactions among individuals became clearer.[11] Most writers conceded that credit and its chief form, paper, had become essential to the nation's prosperity. It was useful in tapping unused stocks of wealth. Substituting paper for gold and silver, wrote Adam Smith, enabled the country "to convert a great part of this dead stock into active and productive stock." Paper credit was the vehicle for increased circulation, which in turn multiplied "the materials, tools, and maintenance" available to a society.[12]

"A quick and constant circulation of credit," John Campbell argued in 1774, "produces, and, which is more, supports industry with better, and even greater effect than money." Seen in this light, credit could even be called a promoter of virtue. Sustaining a good name required "an unremitting assiduity and application" in the individual. For when a person staked his credit, not only his fortune, but even his "honour" was at risk. "Thus credit," Campbell contended, "should make people cautious and attentive, and encourage good habits in the whole nation."[13]

The trouble was that credit could also encourage extravagance and even duplicity. As the volume of paper in circulation threatened to become a flood, and growing numbers found themselves drawn into complicated credit relations, some authors issued a warning of the dangers to the country. "It is certain," wrote one contributor to the *Gentleman's Magazine,* "that, in a commercial country, like ours, private CREDIT is of great advantage, when kept within the bounds of moderation." The credit system, he was convinced, had reached a critical point. The temptation to create new instruments, with no security behind them, was so great that it had become a kind of legalized fraud. So many were caught up in taking advantage of this situation that no one dared to condemn it. The line between forgery and normal business practice with respect to paper transactions was often hard to draw. "Pretended" bills passed as real; "it gives the holder a speedy opportunity of reinvesting his money in goods, making a superior interest, and taking advantage of any favorable conjunctures." But it was, this author warned, "an evil of the first magnitude," no more than an encouragement to "perpetual forgeries."[14] When even reputable businessmen engaged in transactions of such a fictional nature, less moral or prudent people were induced to behave even less responsibly. A few marks on paper, one observer noted, gave "it whatever value the credulity and greediness of men will allow it." "Great imaginary riches" were created by "bold and enterprizing men, who trade on paper credit beyond their real capital to an amount that is incredible."[15] If seemingly honest dealers were exposed as unworthy of the trust bestowed on them, if reputations could not be relied upon, then the wealth so ostentatiously displayed in London might well prove to be an illusion.

Such a conclusion appeared obvious to Richard Price, the nonconformist minister and moral author, who was particularly suspicious of paper instruments and the dangers they presented to society. "Paper," he wrote, "owing its currency to opinion, has only a local and imaginary value." It could stand no shock; "it is destroyed by the approach of danger; or even the suspicion of danger." He went on to list characteristic threats to the confidence upon which its circulation depended; "the destruction of a few books at the Bank; an improvement in the art of forgery; the landing of a body of French troops on our coast; insurrections threatening a revolution in Government." Almost anything that might create a panic, however groundless, would "annihilate" belief in the value of paper and leave the country with no adequate "medium of traffic." The collapse of confidence would strike individuals first, but its inevitable effect would be to bring down the entire system of credit. Rich as England appeared, Price feared that this wealth was built upon a shifting base.[16]

It was to meet such criticism, and even to defend stock-jobbing, that Isaac de Pinto, a Dutch-Portuguese Jew familiar with Anglo-Dutch finance, wrote *An Essay on Circulation and Credit.* Surprisingly, or perhaps not so surprisingly, for the interconnections in this case abound, de Pinto was also the Amsterdam correspondent of Joseph Salvadore, Mrs. Rudd's erstwhile lover. De Pinto argued that England's strength was her national debt; England could use foreign capital to support commercial expansion. Easy credit, he explained, by promoting the flow of funds into the markets, created wealth and fostered enterprise. The funds aided circulation; loans multiplied the wealth of the country.[17] While de Pinto represented the most enthusiastic endorsement of the financial system, even his translator and editor expressed a more cautious, and a more typical, viewpoint. Writing under the name of his relation, Rev. Baggs, Philip Francis (the man now believed by most historians to have been the elusive Junius) feared that stock speculation ruined people and could do the same to the nation. "Great sums," he added in a footnote to de Pinto, "easily gained, are squandered in an extravagance which not only brings distress along with it, but disables the mind from returning to habits of economy and active industry." The most recent episodes of speculative frenzy demonstrated how, far from advancing circulation, such activity could destroy the elements that made circulation possible. While "credit is more than a creature of the mind," Francis opined hopefully, "and has always had a real existence, ...

like any other resource, it may be destroyed by an injudicious exertion. Like the precious metal, whose place it supplies, credit may be extended ad infinitum, but as they both lose in solidity what they gain in surface, a breath of air is sufficient to blow the golden leaf away."[18]

GAMBLING IN THE ALLEY

To most observers, the disease to which the paper economy was most prone was speculation. When contemporaries discussed the dangers of speculation, they had one particular setting, the stock market, and one figure, the "stock-jobber," in mind. Perhaps no group was so reviled in this period. Few charges were as likely to damage the reputation of a gentleman as that he gambled on the Exchange. There had been several attempts to legislate against the practice, although with little success. Many respectable people owned stocks, but, it was believed, only a particular group speculated in them. In her commonplace book, *Thraliana,* Mrs. Thrale reflected on this sort of gambling: "Oh what a Curse upon Commerce is this modern Spirit of *Speculation* as 'tis called! but lest it should one Day become an unintelligible Phrase, I will here give a Page or two to explain it. By Speculation is meant Trading upon Conjecture, buying large Quantities of any Commodity [or stock] when cheap, in hopes it may soon become dearer."[19] Commercial speculation suggested moral failure; financial failure solidified and deepened the moral fault. One who played in the Alley had no patience for building up a hard-earned competence. He followed no regular occupation or profession. Instead, he pursued illusions and phantoms, trying to take advantage of every rumor that might send stocks up or down. Or worse, such men might instigate rumors in order to benefit from the ensuing panic. For example, in 1774, "the Lord Mayor received a counterfeit letter as from the Admiralty, informing his lordship, that there was a pressing necessity for manning a large fleet, and desiring his opinion officially on the speediest method of raising men to man it. The letter had a temporary effect upon the stocks, for which purpose it was calculated. They fell considerably."[20] Such rumormongers were not only a danger to themselves; they also damaged the financial stability of the country. Using the press to their own advantage, they profited through the creation of forged news.[21] Most commentators not only saw them as extremely irresponsible but charged them with squandering other people's money in their selfish search for easy, unearned wealth.

The subject of the stock gamble produced considerable moralizing in the press and pulpit and on the stage. Even Mrs. Rudd criticized the pernicious practice, noting that it arose from one of England's great merits.

> The iniquitous Art of stock-jobbing has sprung, like a great many other Abuses, out of the best of Blessings, Liberty, the benign Influence of which the English Nation, to its immortal Honour be it recorded, is ever studious to extend to Foreigners ... From the free Liberty ... to buy into, or sell out of, our public Funds, the diabolical Art of Stock-Jobbing took its Rise, and is now arrived at its Meridian of Iniquity.—Of this Corp were the C(olonel Kinder) and Messrs. P(erreau).[22]

No one defended it. In the aftermath of the Perreau case, one correspondent expressed his wonder

> that the sober part among persons of distinction, who see and lament the fatal effects of gambling in the Alley, and the polite clubs at the West End of town among the nobility as well as the gentry, and the first merchants of this Kingdom, do not use their endeavours to stop that evil. Such and so general are the fatal effects of this vice, that not only nine-tenths of those who have been esteemed persons of opulence, are almost reduc'd to the state of beggars; but it must shortly bring on fatal consequences to the nation at home and disgrace among our neighbors abroad.[23]

The topics of speculation and financial ruin not only filled the periodical and daily press; they found their way onto the stage in the early 1770s. Two plays in particular took the bankruptcy of Alexander Fordyce, to be discussed later in this chapter, as the occasion for a treatment of financial speculation, Samuel Foote's *The Bankrupt* and George Colman's *The Man of Business*. *The Bankrupt* was a familiar comedy that contented itself with lampooning those who gambled in the Alley. Colman's *The Man of Business* was more ominous and moralizing in its treatment of the danger represented by this kind of gaming. Significantly for the fate of the Perreaus, it appeared in 1774. Though it contained comic elements and concluded with the requisite redemptive ending, the story was grim and alarming. The plot centered on a young man,

Beverley, who possessed the standard character flaws; he too readily indulged his desires in the company of rakes and schemers. He, of course, was not himself an evil character, but one with too little principle, and therefore was unable to resist the lures held out to him or to see through the promises and pretensions of those who made them. He failed to attend to business and began to gamble on the Exchange. Beverley played heavily in India stocks, and their fall left him on the verge of ruin. His true friend reprimanded him for participating in such "infamous gambling." He told Beverley that he was not entitled to pity, "you, who have so grossly abused the mutual confidence between man and man, and betrayed the important trust reposed in you— What? a broker, a banker, Mr. Beverley, not only squandering his own fortune, but playing with the property of others!—the property of unconscious persons silently melting away, as if by forgery, under his hands, without their own prodigality!" This connection between stock speculation and forgery was not accidental; forgery, as we have seen, was the emblematic crime of the period; within its trope it contained concerns about finance, character, and duplicity. And the crime was the central metaphor of this drama. Beverley was chastised by his friend for a lack of candor, for paying too little attention to his own character and moral principle. Just as his fortune was built on sand, so was his identity. And both were swept away by rapid changes in fortune. In a final blistering indictment, Beverley was rebuked:

> Not content with one species of enormity, but industriously multiplying your ruin, and combining in yourself the double vices of a man of business, and a man of pleasure! Gambling the whole morning in the Alley, and sitting down at night to quinze and hazard at St. James's; by turns, making yourself prey to the rooks and sharks at one end of the town, and the bulls and bears at the other! Formerly a young spendthrift was contented with one species of prodigality—but it was reserved for you and your precious associates to compound this new medley of folly, this olio of vice and extravagance, at once including dissoluteness of an abandoned debauchee, the chicanery of a pettyfogger, and the dirty tricking of a fraudulent stock-jobbing broker.[24]

Beverley, like so many young men of the period, believed that huge sums of money were to be made in and from England's new imperium. He was to learn at his own cost that empire came at a price.

At the end of the Seven Years' War, the British found themselves masters of a world empire of colossal proportions. As important as the acquisition of territory, however, was the confidence that the victory engendered among her citizenry. Britain was to be the new Rome and all things were possible for Englishmen. Abroad, in the East and West Indies, men were making impressive fortunes:

> A[n East India] Company servant was said to be able to get "20 or 25 per cent by a trade in which he runs no risque and has no trouble, merely for producing to his banyan [Indian trading partner] permits or dustucks" ... When the young [English] man pointed out that "he had not a capital of his own for such a business," he was told that "it was not material"; he had "only to execute and deliver his interest bond or bonds to him from time to time." The master contributed nothing to the partnership beyond putting his signature to various pieces of paper.[25]

Not only were many personal fortunes made in India; they could be made at home by dealing in the stock of the East India Company. During much of the first half of the eighteenth century, stock in the corporation had been one of the most stable and secure forms of investment. This changed in the wake of Clive's victories. But Clive's and the company's success was also its undoing. On the one hand, speculators were drawn to its stock because of the promise of a vast increase in the company's wealth. Clive helped to foster these expectations with the enthusiastic reports he sent back to England, especially after his return to India in 1766. The stock began to rise, attracting those ready to gamble on how high it might climb. The stock's movements were also influenced by a second factor, the intense struggle that went on for over a decade for control of the company. This conflict led prominent investors to buy up stock in hopes of influencing the outcome of elections of the directors of the company and led, in Lucy Sutherland's phrase, to "the introduction of Asiatic wealth into the electoral activities of the Company." It also produced extravagant promises and the demand among restless investors for hefty dividends. Eventually these demands would lead to growing government intervention in the company, but in the short run they made the stock highly unstable.[26] The result was growing speculative frenzy in connection with East India Company stock. The intense struggle between Clive and Laurence Sulivan for control of the company exacerbated the situation, leaving the leadership unable to stop the jobbers. On the contrary, the tactics of each side played into the hands of the designing and desperate. Clive himself may have used his inside information to benefit from this rise. Stock prices climbed steadily from 164 in April 1766 to a peak of 273 in 1767. But this rise "came to an abrupt end" in 1769, when news arrived from India of political and financial uncertainties. The stock fell back to 239, and those who had engaged in the political contests were particularly exposed to losses. This surprising setback caused many to think about the connection between the fate of England and her Eastern empire: "The alarming and unparallel fall of India stock, has afforded matter of serious reflection to every well wisher to his country. The interests of that company are now so interwoven with those of the nation, that whatever materially affects the one, must necessarily make a deep impression on the other."[27]

The war's end led not only to frenzied speculation in East India Company stock but to over-investment in large-scale capital ventures. In Scotland, both the Forth and Clyde and the Monkland canals were begun before 1770, as was the building of Edinburgh's New Town. These ventures were largely financed by the expansion of private banks all through Britain, which loaned these corporations the start-up funds. Between 1769 and 1772, thirteen new banking houses were founded in London alone. Immortalized in *The Wealth of Nations*, Douglas, Heron and Company, or, as it was more commonly known, the Ayr Bank, founded in 1769, was one of the main Scottish agents to fund these expansions. Created to promote "the trade, manufactures, and agriculture" of Scotland, it followed a vigorous policy of pursuing clients, extending easy credit as a way of expanding its note circulation. By issuing bonds, granting loans greater than its gold reserves, and discounting its "paper" to the Bank of England, this bank both created credit and made it more likely that the entire system would become more vulnerable to a crisis of confidence.[28]

A number of separate events combined in the first years of the 1770s to explode this credit bubble. In part this collapse was due to bad harvests: in Bengal in 1769–1770, and in Scotland in 1770–1771. Also contributing to the boom of the late 1760s and early 1770s was the "too generally prevalent ... spirit of over-trading": in Scotland with the overexpansion of the linen industry at the very time when the crisis in the Americas created gluts in that market, in India with the overdrawing by East India Company servants of specie almost five times as great as the official sum allotted for such demands. In the wake of these strains and disasters, and entangling many individuals and companies on the course that would lead to fraud, forgery, and the near-collapse of international banking and finance, was the trouble over the Falkland Islands in 1770.[29]

The Spanish seized the Falkland Islands in 1770 and expelled an English garrison. The rumor of war "obtained considerably in the nation." The insult to British honor produced loud calls for action, especially among those who had been excluded from power by the King. The new ministry of Lord North proceeded with care, in part because of British naval weakness, but also from a desire to avoid a needless conflict. While the rhetoric in Parliament sounded a war tocsin, the government conducted secret negotiations. The French played a crucial role in these efforts, acting as a conduit for communications and, in their reluctance to be drawn into a wider conflict, offering a check to Spanish ambitions. Finally a compromise was worked out whereby the Spanish returned possession of the islands to the British while refusing to acknowledge England's right to them.[30]

As often happened in such cases, rumors of war produced a flurry of speculation on the stock exchange. Stocks rose and fell on each new report of the chances for peace or war; the affair "occasioned stocks greatly to fluctuate." Although by early 1771 there were indications that a peaceful resolution might be found, in March a fresh war scare caused stocks to fall. As so often happened in the Alley, "the matter some how got wind." One journal hastened to "pacify the doubts of many of your readers, who may have very large concerns in the alley, there is not the most distant probability of any rupture at present between the courts of Great Britain and Madrid." However, whatever the journals said, a great many people had speculated on the possibility of war. Sir Philip Francis bet and lost £500 in such Falklands speculation.[31] As we have seen, the Perreaus, too, bet and lost on the outcome of the conflict. For Joseph Salvadore, the Falklands debacle was to prove his final undoing.

By the late 1760s, Salvadore was in serious financial trouble. He had experienced reverses in the Portuguese trade after the Lisbon earthquake, and the decline of the Dutch East India Company adversely affected him as well. Although he continued to advise Charles Jenkinson in shaping policy under Bute and Grenville, and he played a role in the English East India Company, supporting Clive in his successful effort to return to Bengal in 1764, by 1768 he was writing to friends discussing his embarrassed finances, and about this time he withdrew from involvement in the diamond trade. In 1771 he transferred his last block of East India stock.[32] Perhaps in a desperate effort to repair his fortunes, Salvadore became involved in a conspiracy to secure political information that would help him benefit from the movement of stocks, a conspiracy that involved buying secret intelligence about the likelihood of a Falklands war. Bathelemy Tort, secretary to the French ambassador to England, the Count de Guines, assured Salvadore that with the aid of inside information obtained from the ambassador, large sums could be won gambling on an outbreak of fighting. Contacting him through Salvadore's former mistress, a Belgian woman named the Countess of Moriencourt (who may have been Mrs. Rudd, or at least may have known her), Tort persuaded Salvadore to invest £8500 in the scheme. The Count de Guines would later claim that Tort, along with several English ministers, was entirely responsible for the mistaken investments. "The speculations of the English bankers at these periods, were not founded on the true objects of these political questions; but solely on the assurance Tort gave them in my name." So the bankers decided "to job for war," and this decision brought on their losses.[33] Not only did Salvadore lose money on this scheme, but his reputation was severely damaged as well. The Perreaus gambled, too, and the £1300 they lost would eventually lead to the forgeries and the gallows.

While Salvadore and the Perreaus were attempting to corner the information market and to acquire early, inside intelligence in order to realize a financial coup, Sir George Colebrooke was engaged in an even larger and more audacious venture. In many ways Colebrooke's activities brought together the various strands of the international speculation. A banker, director, and, in 1769, chairman of the East India Company, Colebrooke was often abusively referred to in the press of this period as the "little stockjobbing baronet." Addicted to gambling in "futures," to speculating in the wholesale commodity markets, he had unsuccessfully attempted to corner the world supply of hemp before he turned his attention to establishing a similar monopoly in alum. In 1771 and 1772, Colebrooke and his confederates controlled nearly two-thirds of the world's stock of this mineral. Even before June 1772, when the firm of Neale, James, Fordyce and Downe, with whom Colebrooke had large sums invested, stopped payment, it was clear that Colebrooke's scheme was in serious trouble; with Fordyce's flight, Colebrooke was forced to give up the venture, at an estimated loss of £100,000. With the wisdom of hindsight,

Mrs. Thrale gave the endeavor the following epitaph: "So Sir George Cole-brooke purchased prodigious Quantities of Alum, intending to dispose of it when scarce at his own Price ... while the People enraged with Sir George Colebrooke's rapacious and monopolizing spirit, entered into Combinations to obtain Alum & Hemp some other way, or do without; till the *Speculator* was left to contemplate his unsold Commodity, fretting his Health away in Ignominy & Distress."[34]

THE MACARONI GAMBLER

No episode exposed the dangers of the expanding world of private credit so forcefully as the collapse of the banking house of Neale, James, Fordyce, and Downe, largely as a result of the frauds practiced by Alexander Fordyce. Called "The Macaroni Gambler" on account of his lavish spending on lux-urious clothes and his flutters on the stock market, he was a remarkable member of an extraordinary family. Bred a hosier, he soon found this career too limiting. He went to London and joined a bank, where he soon displayed great skill and industry. After he was taken on as a partner in the firm, he gambled heavily in stocks and prospered in particular from the sharp rise in East India stock in 1764–1765. For a time Fordyce appeared to be the most successful of a generation of bankers and dealers who had bounded into the highest level of society on the basis of fantastic wealth. He purchased a large estate and squandered an immense sum in a losing effort to secure a seat in Parliament. An aristocratic marriage in 1770 seemed to cap his ascent. How-ever, the Falkland Islands scare "gave a most sensible shock to his finances," and Fordyce was soon scrambling to cover his failed speculations. Although he tried to manipulate India stock in 1771–1772 so that it would fall, it did not begin its decline until September. In the meantime, he made use of his bank's reserves to cover his Falkland losses. When his partners challenged him, he threatened them, but he also showed them a vast number of bank-notes (which he had borrowed, unbeknownst to them, for a few hours) that the bank still possessed. "Such are the effects of gaming in Change-Alley," one magazine moralized, "a vice more fatal to commerce in such a trading na-tion, than all the sharping at Newmarket."[35] When Fordyce's efforts to stave off disclosure collapsed, he fled to France on June 9, 1772, starting a chain of bank failures that looked, for a while, like the beginning of an international collapse.

The duplicity of Alexander Fordyce overshadowed all other scandals of the early 1770s. The failure of his bank and the subsequent crash of at least twenty other firms as an immediate consequence, which Lucy Sutherland describes as "the biggest international credit crisis which Europe had yet seen," filled the letters of the period. Mrs. Carter, the scholarly translator of Epictetus, writing to her friend Mrs. Montagu, lamented the tide of troubles caused by Fordyce: "What a terrible ruin has Fordyce and the other gamblers in the alley, brought upon numbers of unhappy innocent people! and how dreadful have been the consequences, particularly in those families where some have been driven to the horrors of self murder." Horace Walpole, writing to his friend Horace Mann, commented that "one rascally and extravagant banker had brought Britannia, Queen of the Indies, to the precipice of bankruptcy! It is very true, and Fordyce is the name of the caitiff." Most eloquent perhaps was the report of the disaster in the June edition of the *Gentleman's Magazine*:

> It is beyond the power of words to describe the general consternation of the metropolis at this instant. No event for 50 years past has been remembered to have given so fatal a blow both to trade and public credit. An universal bankruptcy was expected, the stoppage of almost every banker's house in London was looked for. The whole city was in an uproar; many of the first families in tears. This melancholy scene began with a rumor that one of the greatest bankers in London had stopped, which afterwards proved true. A report at the same time was propagated that an immediate stop of the greatest must take place.[36]

Fordyce's bank losses ran to hundreds of thousands of pounds, while Walpole estimated the total loss at 4 million. Fordyce's behavior and its effects led to much moralizing in the following years. His career was seen as emblematic of all that people feared about the effects of new wealth and paper credit upon society. Later, commenting on the ruin Fordyce brought on both his family and the nation, his sister-in-law noted both the fairy-tale quality of his rise and residence and the nature of the ambitions that led to both its acquisition and its loss. "The magnificence and style" of his establishment, she said, "raised an expectation of beholding something more resembling the magical splendour described in the Arabian Nights' Entertainment, than the real elegance of an English gentleman's mansion." Characterizing the qualities that led to his rise and fall, she described her relation as a man who, "disdaining the thought of mediocrity, without any moderation in his vast desires, aspired to be the richest commoner in Britain."[37] Fordyce's rise, but especially his ruinous fall, may even have produced a harsher attitude toward "sharpers" and forgers and thus had an indirect effect on the Perreau case.

The Ayr Bank, which had largely dealt with Fordyce in an effort to capture much of the paper circulation of Scotland, collapsed as a consequence of the general conflagration. By mid-June the nationwide panic had spread as many respectable bankers found themselves hard-pressed for funds. "A general consternation took place, and occasioned such a run upon the bankers in general, that every one trembled for the event." "The nabob Richard Smith was said to have saved the Drummonds by depositing £150000 in notes," and many members of Parliament were "hard hit." It was a dangerous time to be a debtor or to have too much of one's wealth tied up in notes. The number of bankruptcies rose from 398 in 1772 to 623 in 1773.[38]

James Boswell hastened to join his voice to those lamenting what they took to be a fatal alteration of society produced by speculative frenzy. To the old sources of woe—war, famine, and pestilence—a new one had been added, mass bankruptcy. Not only did the new financial system destabilize the traditional orders of society, but people were now tied to each other in ways that spread the effects of mismanagement or fraud in ever wider circles. In 1772 Scotland had been shaken "by a kind of commercial earthquake, while, like a company connected by an electrical wire, the people in every corner of the country have almost instantaneously received the same shock." Not all bankers were to blame, but some had imposed upon others, pretending to have "the appearance of strength without the reality." The difficulty was telling the real from the fraudulent. Boswell, like many other authors, cautioned against condemning the entire system. Bankers were useful in making a reservoir of credit from "small shallow and useless rivulets," which prevented funds from lying idle and supplied neighbors with "plentiful draughts." In his pamphlet he sought to help people to "distinguish between good and evil." He particularly warned against "upstarts," who were "adventurers in the article of money and credit; owing either to extravagance, negligence, or the desire of being precipitantly rich." Mrs. Thrale's brief history of Fordyce's career reiterated this swashbuckling image and reinforced Boswell's warning: "Fordyce began the World an Adventurer; & had at one Time as I have heard those who knew it—say: amassed by this *Gaming* method of Commerce called *Speculation*—more than three Hundred Thousand Pounds, as he amassed it however only to trade in the Alley, it all went at once, and left him ... [at] the mercy of Fortune." Thus, at his examination before the Bankruptcy Commission, when asked "in what manner he had lost the sum of seventy-eight thousand pounds, which appeared to be deficient," all that Fordyce could or would respond was, "That, when his misfortunes came upon him, the raising the money by drawing and redrawing had swallowed up that enormous sum."[39] Others were less forgiving; a popular ballad of the day concluded with the stanza, "Should I live and grow rich as at present I'm poor / No banker on earth e'er shall handle my store / Since bankers turn bankrupts pray take my advice / Trust not to their honour not even F(ordyce)."[40]

The 1770s saw an important shift in the nature of financial crises, away from distress caused by dealings among public corporations and toward crises arising from private arrangements. The financial crisis of 1772 was pivotal. Crises after this date spread more widely, producing more bankruptcies, entangling people who might not have been touched by earlier periods of distress. This change was a direct result of the expansion in both the size of transactions and the numbers of those making use of private credit instruments such as bills of exchange and book credit between tradesmen. "Because of the business community's heavy dependence on credit instruments, the stability of which was largely maintained by confidence, because those instruments were easy to create, and finally, because growth encouraged risk taking and speculation, genuine expansion found itself periodically beset by a debility in private finance that bordered on complete paralysis."[41] Thus the collapse of Fordyce's bank, in the wake of the widespread losses following East India stock speculations, produced a crisis of confidence that rippled throughout Britain. People found themselves pressed for money and called in debts owed to them. When some could not pay, this weakened the ability of others to meet demands upon themselves. Every debtor might be suspected of insolvency or duplicity.

The 1772 crisis demonstrated the vulnerability of the system to misbehavior or fraud, as people issued more notes than they could cover. The means to expand and seize new economic opportunities became a snare that could destroy one's business and trap one in debt. Even prudent people could find themselves overextended or suddenly lacking funds because they had accepted the unsupported paper of another. Daniel, when he was negotiating for the purchase of the Harley Street house, asked his lawyer, Joseph Hickey, for a £1500 loan, offering him only a note of hand as security. Hickey's son later admitted that had his father "entertained the most distant suspicion of his client's real situation at the time of the above transaction and while he remained so seriously his debtor, he would have been in dreadful alarm." At such moments businessmen discovered that what they believed was true wealth was all imaginary. The realization of danger could be terrible; it often led to a somber assessment of the entire financial system. "Gambling, irresponsibility, extortion, usury, avarice, and excessive ambition," one historian has written, "were all seen as intimately and inevitably connected to the extensive and intensive use of credit. In short, a new amorality was perceived as being part and parcel of the credit economy." These reflections were also produced by reports of forgery. Samuel Orton, a "much respected" businessman, explained that he had been forced to commit the crime from a desire "to keep up my credit." The Ordinary of Newgate took the occasion of Orton's execution in 1767 to suggest that his life was "a melancholy memento to those inconsiderate people of easy circumstances, who not satisfied with competence and content, are continually aiming at more, and suffer an openness of spirit to end in prodigality." Such warnings did little to restore confidence in the system of credit. An instance of forgery or a severe economic downturn taught similar lessons. Trust gave way to mistrust when glittering reality was exposed as illusory. "We are here in a very melancholy situation," David Hume wrote from Scotland in 1772, "continual bankruptcy, universal loss of credit, and endless suspicions."[42]

AFTER THE CRASH

This chain of failures and bankruptcies was finally halted in England by the willingness of the Bank of England to extend credit to many (though not all) merchants and financiers, and in Scotland by the partners of the Ayr Bank raising money in London, using their vast landed estates as collateral. "It is said that £750,000 worth of landed property had to be sold" to repay the bank's creditors.[43] However, the economic storm was far from over. By mid-1772 the East India Company was once again in serious trouble. Unable to declare a dividend in September of that year, Sir George Colebrooke, its chairman, announced "that the Company was negotiating with the Government for power to raise a loan." The price of stock fell precipitously. From June 1772 to January 1773, East India stock fell from 224 to 159. By June it would reach a low of 142. This company malaise, combined with the involvement of a large foreign investor, the house of Clifford, in the great alum disaster, brought many of the great Dutch financial houses into the widening circle of ruin. Cliffords was caught up in both the alum disaster and the East India decline and had no way of meeting the claims upon it. Some said it failed with debts of £700,000. Rumors spread through Amsterdam as they had in London. "Credit had completely disappeared, the discounting houses closed their doors, and the market awaited apprehensively the news that Cliffords were unable to meet their obligations."[44] The collapse of Cliffords further damaged the already impaired fortunes of Joseph Salvadore.

Faced with an impasse and without funds to continue, the East India Company was forced to apply to Lord North, "and he (perhaps glad to grasp the glorious object) took public ground, and demanded a state of our affairs to be laid before Parliament."[45] A cartoonist illustrated that moment, with Colebrooke and Clive kneeling at North's feet, imploring his assistance and offering large bribes, while a Bute-like Scottish figure in the background attempts to slay a blindfolded Justice. In looking back on the commercial crisis of the year, the *Annual Register* remarked that the failures "were of so alarming a nature, and so extensive in their influence, as to threaten a mortal blow to all public and private credit throughout Europe." These failures "were the effect of an artificial credit, and of great speculative dealings in trade, as well as in the public funds of different countries." The losses to individuals might have been as much as £10 million sterling.[46]

For many, including the policy-makers of the Bank of England, this perilous state of affairs was blamed on the self-serving actions of the Scots and the Jews. In his letter to Mann, Walpole noted that since Fordyce was a "Scotchman, and as the Scots have given provocation even to the Bank of England by circulating vast quantities of their own bank's notes, all the clamour against that country is revived, and the war is carried very far, at least in the newspapers." The *Morning Chronicle* of June 30 had charged that the Scots bought "English gold with notes discounted by the bank [of England] and afterwards (carried) on a gold trade with Dutch Jews to the diminution of the coin of this kingdom and the immediate disadvantage of the discounters of Scotch notes." The *Gazetteer* of July 3 argued that "the great shock lately given to public credit by some bankruptcies in this city (and which might have been attended with the most melancholic consequences to this kingdom, but for the prudence of the Bank Directors) is not to be attributed solely to the extravagance or excessive gaming of Mr. F[ordyce], but to the extreme and imprudential stretch of the *Scottish nation,* by issuing notes that infinitely surpassed their means or power of satisfying." Even Colebrooke in his memoirs dates his eventual fall from his alliance with Scottish interests: "I detached myself as much as I decently could from my old connextions, and lived together with these new friends, who, being all Scotch, gave insensibly a turn to my bind in favour of their nation—a circumstance I lived afterwards to repent of."[47] In this crisis the Bank of England refused to accept doubtful paper, it was said, with the intention of breaking those Jewish houses most engaged in the speculative efforts. The bank had acted quite rightly, the press thought, in refusing to discount Scottish bills or to help those who had Jewish-Dutch connections.[48]

Not surprisingly, the economic distress of these years saw a renewed public outburst of anti-Jewish sentiment. The bitter comments linked rich and poor Jews together as engaged in shadowy practices—swindling, fraud, and theft. "A correspondent," the *London Magazine* reported, "insists that the Jews never showed more wicked ingenuity than at present." Jews, he insisted, often appeared at bankruptcies to prove debts against tradesmen whose notes they had discounted. Able to elude the laws, they lived like wasps and drones, on the honey stored up by the industrious. "Jew bail, Jew evidence, Jew creditors in commissions, Jew brokers have reigned so long with impunity and success, that the practices of these devilish arts will shortly prove the ruin of trade and commerce, by stripping the fair merchants of their property, and destroying all confidence between man and man." Such views were long-lived; perhaps it was such sentiments that, on September 30, 1779, led the Coachmakers Hall debating society to debate the following question, "Would not a tax on Jews be a very proper measure in the present urgency of affairs?"[49] Many periodicals complained that robberies were being carried out by Jewish gangs, who were encouraged by Jewish pawnbrokers.

The intensity of anti-Jewish and anti-Scots sentiment was, in part, a consequence of the relative impunity of some of those most responsible for the disaster. The chief perpetrators, the Fordyces and Colebrookes, were neither criminally punished nor financially ruined. Robert Perreau's jobbing partner, John Huske, it was true, died in hiding in Paris in 1773, after apparently defrauding Charles Townsend of many thousands of pounds. He was rumored to have gone there to set up a banker's shop with two other men. On the other hand, although clearly guilty, Alexander Fordyce had returned to

England, declared personal bankruptcy, and by December 1772 agreed with the bank's creditors to be responsible for repaying them only four shillings on the pound. Though he ostensibly had lost all of his money, and his life was threatened by the mob outside his examination room, by 1778 Mrs. Thrale asserted that, because "they ... were luckily *Scotch* People," he and his wife "had a Pension settled upon them on which they now live, and face the World with a Degree of Confidence which no other Country could pro- duce."[50] By 1780 he was confident enough of his rehabilitation to run, though unsuccessfully, for Parliament.

Colebrooke's affairs were more protracted and complex. When the pre- cipitous slide in the East India Company stock began, some of the directors, especially Colebrooke, were accused of "selling out their own holdings in good time while keeping the true state of things from the public ... " Burke spoke of Colebrooke as "under imputations all of which he cannot remove and without any natural resources (further than some kind of resolution) to carry him through a labyrinth of difficulties." Though he got a short reprieve in his banking business when the Bank of England accepted his bills after the Fordyce debacle, the next March his banking house stopped payment, although he assured his creditors they would all be paid in full. However, less than six weeks later, it was reported that only seven shillings on the pound would be paid immediately, and the rest over a period of two and a half years. The very day this announcement was made, Lord North introduced a peti- tion from some of the metropolis's most eminent bankers requesting that a bill be passed making the estates of failed bankers liable to seizure and bankers' appropriation of funds felonious.[51] Colebrooke had settled £80,000 on his wife, which could not be touched by his creditors, but despite this, in 1776 he again stopped payment and by 1777 had fled to France to avoid cred- itors. In 1778 Mrs. Thrale noted that he was now living in Boulogne "on his Creditors' Allowance of £300 a Year," while that very year the East India Company voted him an annuity of £200 per annum.[52]

THE PERREAUS, THE ALLEY, AND THE WAGES OF GREED

Now we are in a position to understand the gravity of Mrs. Rudd's evidence about the financial operations of the Perreaus. They were, she charged, in- volved in each of the phases of the speculative economy of the early 1770s. She first became aware of these transactions when Daniel borrowed money from her to settle his debts. She learned more about them during a trip to Paris in March 1771. There she met Colonel Kendal and learned of his influence over her "husband." Kendal, she later charged, had been born in Ireland, and had been in the "French service" since his youth. Upon his return to England, he was employed by the French embassy, for whom he carried out undisclosed "business." On the basis of this connection, Kendal was "esteemed" as an oracle by "a considerable junto of stock-jobbers," among them Daniel Perreau. When the government gained some hint of his activities, Kendal was forced to flee to France. There he was rewarded for his services and became a familiar figure "at the tables of several persons of fashion in France." Kendal soon enticed Daniel into joining him in a scheme that promised to make something of the information to which the colonel had access.[53]

Kendal, Mrs. Rudd reported, had earned her instant mistrust. "The fact is," she later wrote, "I perceived from his conversation and account of himself, that he was a consummate hypocrite; and I saw a designing plausibility in all his behaviour to Mr. Perreau, whom he influenced at pleasure." The colonel played upon Daniel's "foibles," his "excessive vanity," and "an unhappy passion for speculating in the alley." So foolish was Daniel, she explained, that he agreed to sustain any losses they incurred but would give Robert and the colonel a third of any profits. Daniel, one author suggested, conveniently served as a puppet for those more experienced in the game. "In the course of his gay pursuits, and his plans for ways and means, he got connected with some people in the alley, who perceiving that nothing more was necessary to give him the air of a gentleman, than being dressed as such, played him off with very tolerable advantage both to him and themselves." Daniel was an affectionate man, Mrs. Rudd asserted, until Kendal mastered him. "Whenever Change Alley business was on foot," she wrote, "his brother or the colonel engrossed his attention, [and] he became captious, inconsiderate, and unprincipled."[54]

The scheme in which Kendal and Perreau participated may have been related to that which involved Salvadore and Tort in a gamble on the likelihood of war over the Falkland Islands. Since Mrs. Rudd had, for some time, been Salvadore's mistress and had, more recently, become Daniel's lover, she may have been a link between the two plans to speculate on the possibility of conflict, especially if, as the Countess of Moriencourt, she had acted as an agent for the Jewish financier. It is possible that she passed on the information to the Perreaus and they seized the opportunity to gamble on the Exchange. Or they may simply have developed their plans in imitation of Salvadore. At any rate, according to Mrs. Rudd, they solicited the cooperation of Joseph Jacques, a man with connections in the French embassy in London. Robert Perreau told Jacques that for £300 they might both secure from the secretary to the Spanish embassy a political secret "from which they might both derive a considerable advantage." Jacques advanced the money to Perreau but later asked for it back after his wife heard about the transaction.[55]

The authorities must have gotten wind of the plot, for by June 1771 a Bow Street agent and his assistant, at the direction of Sir John Fielding, were following Jacques. Over the next several months the agent returned a regular report of Jacques's contacts. In addition to maintaining friendships with a King's messenger and a Treasury messenger, Jacques often visited the French ambassador's residence. Jacques was a busy man, attending various coffeehouses, frequenting the resorts of seamen, and consulting with a man in a "chariot." One day the Bow Street agent was able to follow the carriage to Pall Mall court, where he identified its occupant as "Dr. Perreau." Since the address was Daniel's, it is more likely he was the person to whom the agent referred. Jacques and Daniel were frequently observed together, and Perreau's servant several times carried messages between them. There was something furtive about all these meetings; one report talked of a "boy in black" who lounged around the street as if keeping watch for the men. Daniel's use of his brother's carriage, and his visits to the "Doctor's House," support the suspicion that Robert was involved in whatever scheme was afoot.[56]

These reports led the government to monitor Daniel Perreau's mail. One intercepted letter was addressed to a Colonel Kendall at Count de Chatelet's in Paris. Chatelet had preceded Guines as French ambassador and was known for his anti-British feeling. Walpole believed that "he drew the Spaniards into the attack of Falkland's Island."[57] In this letter Perreau wrote that Sir George Rodney had informed the ministers that "further disputes" with Spain were likely, that he was prepared to "be hostile," and that he had sent three ships "to intercept a rich Spanish ship." It was widely known that Rodney was in desperate financial shape as a result of heavy gambling losses. Facing ruin, he had leapt at the offer of a West Indian posting and the prospect of a Spanish war as a way of settling his debts. He was a bold sailor known to take action on his own initiative, and some in England may have been ready to gamble on him provoking a war.[58] Daniel Perreau was one of these. His "cabinet friend," he confided in the letter, was "out of town," which limited his ability to "get particulars from that authority I used to do." But he knew a courier had been sent to Madrid with new English demands of the Spanish. "It is, however, a great secret, and people do not seem so much alarmed in the City as I might expect." The ministers, he wrote confidently, expect "some disagreeable event." "You see," he added in haste, "how important it is to get a certain account of the answer that will come from Spain. I verily think it will be a very serious affair. For God's sake turn heaven and earth to come at the Spanish answer in time to let me know before it comes to Prince Maserano, and we shall do great things; and don't spare the expense of a courier with very great secrets."[59]

As none of this bustle led to anything, the Perreaus lost their gamble "to capture the market." This experience, however, did not deter the brothers from further attempts to secure "political information" that might enable them to recoup their fortunes. In the autumn of 1773, Mrs. Rudd noted, since little remained of her fortune, Daniel went off to Paris again, claiming he was going to meet two gentlemen with whom he hoped to go into business. Upon his return he claimed to be independent of her fortune and on the way to making his own. Despite all his reverses, she trusted he would repair their situation. "Every one who knows any thing of 'Change-Alley, knows that numbers have, and actually do, make fortunes out of it." She expressed no surprise at the sums he now produced or the increased scale of their establishment.[60] "From this time particularly," she later wrote, "I firmly believed that Messrs. Perreau were in possession of the good political information they told me they were; Robert received his from Lady F(rances) B(urgoyne) who made a point to serve him; and for that purpose asked Lord G(uilfor)d and Lord N(ort)h questions; also that he had advises from Sir George V(andepu)t, who got it from his friend Lord R(ichmon)d, and lastly, from a director of the East India Company." Daniel also claimed to have information from Mr. O— of D—s—t and from a gentleman belonging to the Treasury. Col. K(endal) provided the foreign intelligence, and it came from the House of P(on)tus and C(a)nut at Amsterdam or the Hague. The *Gazetteer* summarized these arrangements: "The Colonel being to procure the intelligence, Mr. Robert Perreau to manage the Alley; Mr. Daniel Perreau to find money, and Mrs. Rudd to pay the piper." For, by Mrs. Rudd's telling, it was her money that subsidized the many schemes. The goal was "to leave the Alley at their mercy," to make a financial killing worthy of Clive.[61]

By the end of 1773 the connection with Salvadore was of less and less use to the brothers or Mrs. Rudd. His fortune was in shambles. He wrote in desperation to Clive in July 1773, asking him for a loan of £5000, apparently with no success. "The times are such," he told Clive, "there is no credit."[62] He had no information for the brothers, and he could no longer be tapped for funds by Mrs. Rudd. He lingered on in London for several years, though his reputation suffered a further blow when his name became associated with Mrs. Rudd's. He became a target of anti-Semitic sarcasm, as the case made clear that he had been duped by her impostures to the extent of thousands of pounds.

At this critical juncture, at least according to Mrs. Rudd, the brothers made use of another of her connections. One day when Daniel happened to be occupied with his stock advisor, Mrs. Rudd received a letter from her Uncle Stewart containing a note from James Adair. When the consultant heard the name Adair, he remarked that Adair's son, the counselor, "knew everything relative to India matters," and that Perreau might secure information through him that would assist in making money from the fluctuations in East India stock. This same man also mentioned that William Adair had "great knowledge in these matters." Daniel, Mrs. Rudd alleged, was soon freely using this claim to a connection with the Adairs to foster the impression that here was the source of his privileged knowledge of stock movements. Daniel even originated the ruse, charged Mrs. Rudd, that had the servants deliver the forged letters and announce the imaginary visitors so as to impress guests. It was, she implied, but a short step from creating the illusion of friendship to using Adair's name to raise money. At a later date she provided details of Robert's transactions with Rev. Crane of Westminster, from whom he borrowed £3000. Robert went to Crane with a story that Adair, "his best friend," had advised him "to do business in the stocks," saying that here was a favorable opportunity. Adair, Robert told Crane, confessed that he was short of funds, but he gave Perreau permission to use his name to raise the sum. Crane, believing this account, went into the City and sold stock to oblige the Perreaus. Robert, Mrs. Rudd revealed, deposited £1000 of the money with a broker named St. Leu.[63]

These charges, at least so far as the public was concerned, depended upon the word of Mrs. Rudd and were, therefore, suspect. In retrospect at least, she presented herself as used by the brothers. "While my money administered to the Perreaus' wants, and supported their adventures in the Alley," she wrote bitterly, "I was the very best of women; after that was exhausted, and it suited their schemes to use the credit of those they called my connections, I was quite a divinity." Then, when all was exposed, they turned on her, and represented her as a vile deceiver.[64] The truth cannot be known for sure. Several authors suggested that Daniel knew the source of her money and took up with her because he expected to make use of her influence over Salvadore. A few claimed that he was himself involved in several plots to extort money from the old man.[65] Certainly her "connections," both the supposed aristocratic links and the less respectable tie to Salvadore, made her an attractive prospect for the ambitious Daniel. She may have dangled these advantages before him; she may even have encouraged him in his exploitation of the Adair name. Or the brothers may simply have, as she suggested, made use of her knowledge and sexual favors to advance their own plans.

In the wake of the Perreau trials, evidence surfaced that Robert had had a longer career in the Alley than he cared to admit. One paper reported that his attorney paid him £500 during his confinement, for differences "that turned up in his favor upon the settlement of his last speculations." It also said that some months before they were taken up Robert had applied to "an eminent perfumer" to borrow £5000 on a bond he said was from Adair. The tradesman said he would lend the money if his attorney could see the document executed. Robert at first set a time to fulfill this condition but returned to say that a friend in the country had supplied the money and so he no longer needed the loan. The implication was that Robert had avoided a transaction that would certainly have exposed the forgery. Several papers told of Robert's applying to Dr. Manningham with such a bond, but they said the doctor had told him that he had been imposed upon.[66] These reports produced a reply from Manningham, who said that Robert had applied to him for money and that he would have readily lent him two or three hundred pounds. But since Robert had asked for two or three thousand, Manningham had replied that he did not have so much to lend. Robert had asked if perhaps his brother or some friend might have that much, saying the security was a bond from Adair. Manningham confessed he had never seen the bond, though now he wished he had, as he "might have discovered to Mr. Perreau his deluded infatuation, and been the happy means of preventing the fatal issue."[67]

These stories placed the debate over Robert's "innocent lies" in a different context. A number of correspondents to the papers found it hard to believe that Robert's behavior was consistent with the portrait of deceived innocence that he drew of himself. Robert's actions in getting a bond and offering instructions for its drawing up implied to one correspondent that he had more knowledge of and responsibility for the crime than he had confessed. Would anyone offer the kind of stories to the Drummonds that he had if he had not had an "undeniable knowledge" of some scheme? "Is it consistent with any principle of rationality, that a man would advance such horrid falsities; without being privy to the transaction, and about to be benefitted by its successful issue?"[68] Robert's conduct in these few encounters was examined minutely. Everyone debated whether these lies were such as anyone might use as a matter of convenience, or whether they indicated some fundamental duplicity in his social conduct.

The effect of the repetition of these charges, as the Perreaus understood, was to endanger their position. They had produced plenty of evidence of Mrs. Rudd's fantasies and duplicitous dealings, but they had not established the motive that inspired her to play the brothers for her victims. They could show no obvious gain for her. She, on the other hand, provided them with a motive that not only cast them in a sinister light, given the times, but also made them appear less gentlemanly in their treatment of her. If Mrs. Rudd's fantasies spoke of the hope of rising through hidden birth and noble connections, the brothers' dreams were just as ambitious and fantastical.

In the aftermath of the stock market crash of 1772, some voiced the hope that the disaster had awakened people to the dangers of overspeculation. One magazine, noting the scale of the financial disruption, hoped that "people now begin to perceive the difference between actual riches and nominal wealth." If so, the suffering would "prove an advantage to the public."[69] Another correspondent thought that times of distress offered an occasion for "general reformation and repentance." "The present thunder-clap must be of infinite service, by abridging the confidence of men of every occupation; for to use the prevailing phrase at 'Change *we don't know whom we trust*." He argued that most of the vices and follies of the age arose from the extension of credit. If people had to live on real money, "the masquerades, theaters and pantheon would be less thronged." The "silly macaronis" had too much money while tradesmen verged on, or fell into, bankruptcy.[70] David Hume also thought that the crash might have long-term, positive consequences: "On the whole, I believe, that the Check given to our exorbitant and ill grounded Credit will prove of Advantage in the long run, as it will reduce people to more solid and less sanguine Projects, and at the same time introduce Frugality among the Merchants and Manufacturers."[71] These optimists did not understand that the crash had raised more serious, and more unsettling, problems. First, there was a great deal of anger at those who had made so much money so quickly, with such disastrous national consequences, and who remained at liberty, largely unpunished. And although it seemed that the newly acquired empire was coming apart at the seams, with India and America in turmoil and revolt, the crash revealed the extent to which failure in one sector of the empire's economy could have almost incalculable repercussions on national and international markets.

Finally, it made ordinary English men and women sensitive to, and deeply uneasy about, the fictitious quality of paper credit. They were acutely aware that economic growth required unquestioned trust, but that unquestioned trust at the same time was very dangerous. This is why contemporaries found the Perreau case so interesting. "The late forgeries of the above Perreaus," the *Gazetteer* offered in its first comment on the case, "seem the most remarkable of the kind that ever appeared in this country, or perhaps in the whole world: all other forgeries were commonly a grand stroke at raising money and running away with it, but these adventurers appear to have forged one bond to pay off another, and raised it at last to something like a regular branch of trade." The author wondered where all this drawing and redrawing would lead, concluding that it was "therefore probable, that the whole of their hopes were founded on the uncertain event of the death of one of the gentlemen, whose name they used ... or a fortunate hit in the Alley."[72] Such "trade" in forged instruments was not so very different in motive or result from "ordinary" trade in paper or the "ordinary" practices of monopolists or bankers. Gambling on good fortune or death connected the great world of stocks with the lesser sphere of forgery. While the Perreaus hoped that the outcome of their gamble would be either a windfall or the demise of William Adair, they neglected the possibility that neither might occur, or rather that the death in question might be their own.

The Perreaus' fate recalled for some the lessons of 1772. As one magazine concluded, while sound merchants profited by selling real goods, "the stock of a speculator is in his own brain." "The whole faculties of a speculator are bent upon contriving schemes to get money into his hands from every quarter, from rich and poor, from friends and strangers." No one was spared. Recent experience had exposed "the artful stratagems" employed to get funds "to support adventures in 'Change Alley." What resulted from this mad pursuit? "The gain is generally consumed in riot, in the support of a house, table, and equipage, which he has not a title to."[73] In the end, ruin, dishonor, and even death might conclude the chase. The story of the unfortunate Perreaus, a sort of Gothic romance gone awry, seemed a parable of the times.

Seven

DEBATING THE LAW

WHEN MRS. RUDD WAS detained after the trial of Daniel Perreau, she was
sent back to Newgate and told to await her own impending trial. This act
transformed what had been a scandal into a major legal controversy. Before
the case was over, it would raise serious questions about the law and bring the
procedures of justice itself into dispute. In the charged political climate of
the 1770s, the press and the public were sensitive to the conduct of the executive and the courts. The complex, ongoing struggle between the Crown
and the supporters of the radical MP John Wilkes over executive power and
privilege, as well as conflict between American colonists and the government
over many of the same issues, formed the backdrop for such apprehensions.
People were particularly concerned with what was believed to be the abuse
of the courts in intimidating subjects and depriving them of their legal pro-
tections. It may seem strange that such constitutional questions became central to the case of the Perreaus and Mrs. Rudd, but the decision of the authorities and judges rendered this inevitable. Once again, the press served as
the forum within which these issues were argued. Once again, the papers received a steady stream of letters, some of great length and technical sophis-
tication, contending over such issues as the proper role of magistrates and
the obligation of the authorities to respect promises, even those made to
criminals. Overshadowing all these debates was a concern with the operation of secret influence working to bias the course of justice.

As already noted, the grant of crown witness protection had an important place in the prosecutorial strategy adopted by eighteenth-century English justice. In order to secure convictions, a grant was made to an accomplice, who then testified against her or his confederates. In return, the practice, never explicitly spelled out, was for the witness to escape prosecution. Now, for the first time, the judges had stripped a crown witness of this protection. It is difficult to know who was responsible for the decision. The Perreaus, since their trials, had been hard at work on their cause. Daniel was rumored to have sent a copy of his case to the Lord Chancellor with a request that he look over the evidence and consider their melancholy situation.[1] They also had powerful allies. Within days of their conviction, petitions were presented to the King from "many persons of rank and reputation." While it was also said that "His Majesty has refused to listen to any solicitations in favor of the unfortunate Perreaus," rumors continued to circulate that important people were making every effort on their behalf.[2] These reports gained substance when the King agreed that the sentence against the brothers should not be carried out "till after the trial of Mrs. Rudd." The signatures of the Duke of Buccleuch, the Duke and Duchess of Ancaster, and "seventeen others of the nobility and people of the first fashion" on a petition addressed to the Queen secured this favor.[3] If the attempt to affix the crime on Mrs. Rudd had not worked at the brothers' trial, the Perreaus' supporters now hoped that taking away her protection and bringing her to trial might gain a royal pardon for one or both of the brothers.

Not everyone who supported her disqualification as a crown witness belonged to the Perreau camp. Many felt that Mrs. Rudd was a disreputable figure who had made a mockery of justice. If they did not necessarily believe in the innocence of the brothers, they did feel that she had lied about her role in the crime. There was a general feeling that further investigation was required to get to the bottom of the business. Yet, granting these considerations, it remained a serious step for the authorities to remand her for trial. Her counsel refused to acquiesce quietly to this maneuver. On June 14, almost two weeks after the Perreaus' sentencing, a writ of habeas corpus was granted to bring Mrs. Rudd to King's Bench, where she could "either be discharged or recommitted." In essence, her lawyers questioned the legality of the decision to prosecute her after she had been made a crown witness. "The propriety or impropriety," one paper noted, "of her being admitted evidence for the crown (in the late transaction with the Perreaus) by magistrates of Bow-street, is imagined will be fully determined at the same time."[4] It was, in fact, to be almost six months before she stood trial before a jury and pleaded for her life. In the interval, the public watched and participated in a debate that mingled deeply personal feelings and judgments with grand constitutional questions.

Mrs. Rudd charged that this strange turn of events was the result of a conspiracy against her. She portrayed the Perreaus and their allies, men like Dagge and Frankland, as her chief enemies, and asserted that influential politicians were helping them. In June she complained of the combination of "all the fallacies of a fine dress'd tale, and the power, perjury, and bribery which has been exerted to destroy my character, and take away my life." She would later accuse a "city patriot" of orchestrating the effort to prosecute her, saying that he used the voice of "Mr. W[ilkes]" to press the argument that she was not a proper witness.[5] One paper reported gossip that seemed to bear out her accusations. She was to be tried, it asserted, on four charges "on purpose to search to the bottom of this complicated scene of villainy." This strategy, the paper claimed, was the product of the intervention "of a certain personage."[6] To the Perreau supporters these mysterious interventions seemed the actions of beneficent forces, but to others they spoke of a darker conspiracy to subvert the law and exercise influence "behind the curtain."[7]

FIELDING ON THE DEFENSIVE

In committing Mrs. Rudd to prison at the conclusion of Daniel Perreau's trial in June, the judges offered a series of disparaging remarks upon the conduct of the Bow Street magistrates. While Justice Burland took the lead, he clearly expressed a view shared by his colleagues, Justices Aston and Hotham. The judges took the view that the magistrates had so mishandled the committal process that an extraordinary intervention on their part was required to save the cause of justice. Angered by this rebuke, Sir John Fielding, within days of the trial, took the equally unusual step of expressing his displeasure with the decision of the Old Bailey bench. Speaking on behalf of his fellow magistrates, he declared that the Bow Street magistracy "were surprised and hurt to hear that a learned judge had expressed himself dissatisfied at their having admitted Mrs. Rudd to bail." This censure "had occasioned a variety of very insulting reflections to be thrown upon them."[8] Fielding was particularly incensed at the harsh treatment he had received in the press. His pride had been deeply wounded. It was an ominous prelude to the heated legal arguments that followed.

In the first few days after the discovery of the crime, the papers had praised Fielding for his handling of the case. By the time of the Perreau trials, though, many felt that the magistrate had been played for the fool. He had made the crucial decision to accept Mrs. Rudd as a witness. He had, by implication, allowed himself to be swayed by the adroit performance of a woman with a seductive voice. A number of letters to the press pursued this provocative line. "Tis it," one asked, "the Bow-street custom, after an accomplice has lodged an information, to admit as an evidence the principal taken in consequence of the information, and to leave the informant to the rigor of the law?"[9] Another author took a more insulting line. If the magistrates, he mocked, "crowing upon their own dunghill in Bow-st," normally provided an "innocent amusement," their justification in swearing Mrs. Rudd "was the most singular instance of stupidity and knight-errantry ever displayed in this kingdom." "What a pity," he concluded, "that out of the three learned sages on this bench, the wisest of them should be totally blind, and the other two should never have been able to see the length of their nose."[10]

Even those who defended his actions accepted that Fielding had been misled. "This she-devil," one apostrophized, "had the cunning and address, by a fictitious tale, so to impose upon the most knowing and useful magistrate in the kingdom, as to admit her an evidence for the Crown."[11] Another pointed out that the witness rule was not perfect; "there is no doubt but that the good intentions of the legislature, in this as in other things, may be done away by the artful and designing."[12] Others took a stronger line. "Sir John Fielding," one author argued, "was censurable in admitting [Mrs. Rudd] an evidence for the Crown." If the justices had simply looked at the evidence of Robert's conduct, they were bound to realize that no sane person, if he were guilty, would have behaved as he did. "Instead of prosecuting the principals and the accomplices in gradation according to their respective degrees of apparent guilt, they have wilfully, with their eyes wide open, let the principals slip through their hand, in defiance of common sense."[13] One pamphlet writer argued that Fielding's mistaken decision had influenced the course of Robert's trial. The Bench, under the spell cast by Mrs. Rudd's beauty, intelligence, and emotional appeal, had created the impression that she "could not possibly be the principal actor in this iniquitous business; for who could have dreamt that the principal would be admitted as an evidence?" He asserted that because Mrs. Rudd could no longer be touched once the award had been made, the jury decided to make an example of Robert.[14]

Fielding and his colleagues were stung by these accusations. The magistrates hastened to write to Baron Burland to know the nature of the judges' displeasure. The judge at first responded that while he would be glad to meet them as gentlemen, he could not discuss with them anything that had come before him "in his judicial capacity." Fielding replied to Burland with a letter that "clearly and politely stated the whole cause of their uneasiness, and grief at the illiberal and unjust calumny which prejudiced some men's minds against them." The baron wrote back that Mr. Edward Reynolds, a clerk at the Old Bailey, had told the judges that Mrs. Rudd had been admitted evidence in the face of clear proof that she was the principal in the case. Based upon this account, which Fielding characterized as "gross misrepresentation," the judges, Burland said, had delivered their rebuke to the magistrates.[15]

In response to this information, Fielding summoned Reynolds to explain what had happened, accusing him of having injured the public by his irresponsible charges, which "had instilled prejudices into the minds of the judges." The magistrates were officers of the public, and he lamented "that superior Magistrates should imbibe a false opinion of their conduct, which was ever open to the observation and the correction of the Public." Since Reynolds had, by his remarks, degraded the police, causing "a public injury," it was essential that he appear before the magistrates "and do a public justice." On June 28 Reynolds presented himself at Bow Street, denied misrepresenting the conduct of the magistrates, and blamed the newspapers for spreading erroneous stories. "On the gentleman's declaring his innocence, Sir John [Fielding] made an apology to him," in his turn. Fielding concluded his comments on the affair with a spirited defense of his office. "He sat there," he announced, "as a magistrate to do public justice, animated with just sentiments; that he was rewarded by the bounty of his Sovereign, and the testimony of his own mind; that he was conscious he never injured the meanest subject, neither was he ever influenced by persons of the highest rank to deviate from the principles of justice."[16] This altercation was only a taste of the debate that would eventually involve the twelve chief judges of England in a review of the conduct of the case. But it demonstrated that the contest could spread acrimony, division, and recrimination within the system of justice and cast doubt upon the conduct of some of its most respected figures.

In depriving Mrs. Rudd of her status as a crown witness, the authorities provoked a legal crisis. Although the practice had prevailed for decades, it had a dubious sanction, and as this case made clear, the rules governing the grant were anything but clear. As a result of Mrs. Rudd's appeal, the judges now faced the task of determining its legality and applicability.

The crown witness system had arisen as an answer to the inadequacy of English policing, especially when the authorities found themselves confronted by the challenge of breaking a criminal conspiracy. Largely unable to conduct a detailed investigation of a crime, their best hope for securing a conviction lay in enlisting the assistance of one of the confederates. An offer of immunity from prosecution was held out to one party if he or she would testify against the other participants in the crime. This offer was so enticing, especially at a time when so many offenses were capital, that it often created a rivalry among criminals to turn evidence and thus escape prosecution. The competition to impeach one's allies made some uneasy; it put a premium upon betrayal and upon telling whatever tale was required in order to escape the consequences of a crime. Although often accepting such evidence, juries sometimes bridled at a prosecution based solely on the word of a witness who had the most powerful of motives for lying. Still, the necessity for some such offer, however distasteful the award, was widely recognized by those in power.[17]

One consequence of this procedure was that it elevated the importance of pretrial process. The investigating magistrate had considerable power in deciding whom to admit as a crown witness. This official felt most acutely the urgency of discovering the full extent of the crime and detaining all the suspects before they could flee. He had to make a snap judgment, often on the basis of imperfect information, about who would provide the fullest disclosure as well as make the best witness at the subsequent trial. The justice might well try to take into account such matters as relative guilt and mitigating factors such as sex or age, but his overriding concern was with solving the crime. In a strict legal sense, the magistrate had no power to enforce this award. The grant had no statutory sanction; it had arisen for reasons of expediency and proved itself through long use. It was a matter of custom rather than law that the authorities at later stages in the judicial process honor the initial promise. In becoming a crown witness an offender did not receive a pardon, only the promise that he or she would not be prosecuted for any of the crimes under investigation. The only compulsion behind this commitment lay in the widespread realization that criminals would not volunteer information if they did not believe the grant would be honored.[18]

The procedure had few critics before the case of the Perreaus and Mrs. Rudd revealed latent tensions and the unspoken consensus that supported its operation broke down. The prosecution of Mrs. Rudd provoked "the great case treating the status of the crown witness."[19] A number of authors expressed uneasiness with the discretion placed in the hands of the magistrates. The judges, in particular, questioned whether this activity infringed on their own power. They saw themselves as the guardians of justice; they exercised a wide and largely unchallenged authority over the criminal trial. Yet in the case of crown witnesses they found themselves constrained by the decisions of inferior agents. The Rudd case permitted the explosion of long-simmering judicial discontent at this situation. The judges, however, also realized that a weakening of magisterial authority threatened to deliver a devastating blow to practical policing.

Given the importance of the question, it was appropriate that it first fell to Chief Justice Mansfield to consider the arguments, which he did during the hearing granted under the writ of habeas corpus. Mansfield was the commanding legal figure of his day; his decisions in a succession of major cases transformed the common law's relationship to commercial activity. Yet his judicial activity was oftentimes overshadowed by his political responsibilities. He had considerable influence with the King. Conservative by instinct, he abhorred the forces of disorder. An upholder of the judge's authority in libel cases against the claims of the jury, he was a firm advocate of coercion of the American colonies in order to reestablish the supremacy of Parliament.[20]

Mansfield was a powerful and feared figure, an imposing if unloved judge. His strength lay in his ability to organize an argument whose relentless logic convinced his listeners. "His eloquence was peculiar; rather subtle and insinuating, than forcible and overpowering." "His cold reserve and sharpness, too," Boswell wrote of one encounter in 1773, "were still too much for me. It was like being cut with a very, very cold instrument." "Lord Mansfield," he confided in his journal, "has uncommon power. He chills the most generous blood." These qualities shaped his judicial activity. He had a well-deserved reputation for being one of the more severe judges when it came to dealing with crime. He was also an unstinting enemy of forgery. He saw the offense as a major threat to the commercial life of the country and invariably turned back efforts to secure pardons for those convicted of the crime. Swift and certain punishment in such cases, "for the sake of example," was his goal.[21]

The contest that came on in July between Mansfield and Mrs. Rudd involved important legal questions, but it had a personal dimension as well. Hundreds came to the court to see the confrontation between the "piercing eyes" for which the chief justice was known and the "dark piercing" eyes of Mrs. Rudd.[22] "All the avenues leading ... [to the court] were crowded early in the morning, in expectation of seeing" her. Her lawyer opened with an appeal for mercy in her case. Her health, he said, was bad; "she was troubled with fits; and if she was continued in prison she probably would not be alive at the Sessions." One reporter, however, noting the elegance of her black sack, remarked that she "seemed to be no way impaired or dejected by confinement." The judge apparently shared this view, for after a desultory hour spent in argument, Mrs. Rudd was remanded to her cell until the next day. When she returned, the court was so packed, "more crowded than ever known in the memory of the oldest man living," "that it was with great difficulty the barristers got admittance to their allocated situations." Her demeanor during her ordeal once again was the focus of attention; "she had a smelling bottle in her hand, which she often applied to her nose; and when she retired, she made a very low curtsey to the Court, but did not appear in the least dismayed."[23]

The shifting arguments put forth by the prosecution and the defense revealed just how confusing was the legal status of the crown witness procedure. The former opened with a statement that "denied the authority of the magistrates to offer her protection." James Wallace, for the prosecution, argued that "he knew of no statute which gave the magistrates power to promise protection, and that the irregularity of their proceeding was no cure for her guilt." Here was a claim that went to the very heart of the practice.[24] Mrs. Rudd's counsel, Thomas Davenport, rehearsed the proceedings that had led to her being made a crown witness in March and attempted to show that she had done all that was expected of her. She had, he claimed, faithfully answered all questions addressed to her, appeared before the grand jury, and attended the trial of the brothers, ready to appear as witness in their case. She had acted throughout in good faith, depending upon the promises made to her by the magistrates.[25]

Lord Mansfield intervened decisively at this point. From the first he had adopted a line that could only result in Mrs. Rudd being brought to trial. His determination to achieve this outcome was apparent in every word he spoke. He narrowed the argument, turning it away from the general question of the power of the magistrates to grant crown witness status and toward the issue of whether Mrs. Rudd had acted in good faith. If the proceedings bore out the claims of her counsel, he admitted, she would be entitled to bail. But he denied Davenport's contention that once she had been bound over to appear she became just like any other witness who was called to testify at a trial. This argument, he added, went too far in ignoring the circumstances and conditions that had led to the grant. An accused person was made a crown witness if he or she confessed to a crime and swore to reveal all he or she knew about its commission. Everything depended upon Mrs. Rudd's performance of these conditions. At this point Mansfield pointed to a central ambiguity in what she had told the justices.[26] Mansfield suggested either she was a guilty person who had earned a protection or she was innocent of the offense and therefore entitled to no protection. If the tale she told the justices was true, of being forced by Daniel to sign the bond at knife point, then she was innocent. Thus she was not eligible to plead the protection of a confessed accomplice. She now stood in court, he added significantly, like any other person, innocent, but "still liable to be prosecuted for any undiscovered offense." Mansfield concluded the day's deliberations by calling for the submission of the official proceedings in the case, "observing, that the whole case would on a great measure depend on those transactions."[27]

When the hearing resumed the following day, the affidavits of the Bow Street magistrates were read. The justices claimed that they had admitted her as a witness on condition that she reveal all she knew, not only about the bond immediately under discussion but also about all other related crimes. The prosecution spoke next, proposing three grounds for depriving Mrs. Rudd of her protection. They argued that forgery did not come under the acts of William III and Anne that offered encouragement to accomplices to betray each other. However, their remaining arguments showed how attentively they had listened to Mansfield's presentation. They eagerly seized upon "Lord Mansfield's suggestions." Following his hints, they contended that by her own account she was guilty of no crime and therefore was ineligible for a status reserved for confessed offenders. Finally, the prosecution pointed out that she had not fulfilled the terms of the grant that required her to volunteer everything she knew about the conspiracy.[28]

Davenport responded that he would not deal in legal disquisitions but was content to point out that this protection had never been withdrawn except in cases where an attempt had been made to "evade or defeat public justice." Mrs. Rudd, he argued, had been entitled to protection when it was first granted, and she legally had a right to expect its performance in this court. She had told her story at Bow Street under the expectation that she would not be prosecuted, and everyone there had treated her as if the grant were correct. It would be unfair to deprive her of it at this late date. History and common justice were on her side. A promise had been made and accepted, he concluded, and her detention since the Perreau trial was an act "against the good faith which was held out to her."[29]

The issue between the prosecution and the defense rested on a question of faith. The prosecutors argued that Mrs. Rudd had not lived up to her pledge to tell all she knew. They drew upon the public outrage felt at a woman whom many were now convinced was at best an inveterate liar, at worst a masterful, immoral, and disturbingly powerful deceiver. Her counsel replied that much of the evidence to prove such a charge was inadmissible. She had done her utmost, he argued, to live up to her responsibility as a crown witness. She could not be held accountable for errors made by the magistrates in questioning her. They had not asked her about the other forgeries. All that remained, Davenport concluded, was for the court to uphold the law's reputation for fairness by honoring the pledge given her.

Despite the great legal complexity of the case, Mansfield did not hesitate to attack the central issues. In his many years on the Bench, he had never been "accused of judicial timidity." His usual style was to rehearse the legal arguments in detail and then to call upon common sense in proposing his solution. But his "common sense" always led one way, and he seldom gave ground before his critics. Mansfield treated the common law as fluid and flexible, especially in the hands of a skilled judge guided by the dictates of reason. Although he accepted that usage carried some weight, he also believed that "usage against clear principles and authorities of Law never weighs." His opponents accused him of being high-handed and autocratic. They warned that he was using notions of equity to undermine the safeguards against executive power contained in the common law. Junius charged that he "made it the study and practice of his life to undermine and alter the whole system of jurisprudence in the Court of King's Bench." The Wilkites refused to accept his pretense of calm and disinterested justice. They scented a conspiracy to increase the power of government under the cloak of judicial authority. The debate over Mrs. Rudd's grant of crown witness status overlapped with this longer-running controversy. Her defenders warned that the dispute involved a great constitutional principle. If the judges could—by legal sophistry, as they saw it—overturn at will a grant that extended a protection to a subject, then no faith could be placed in a government promise and all English liberties were in doubt. Thus, while Mansfield attempted to narrow the terms of the dispute, treating it as a question about the terms of a contract, other voices insisted on considering its political implications.[30]

Mansfield spoke for nearly an hour, "with his usual precision." He pursued his familiar strategy of clearing the ground and then setting forth his own conclusions. The practice of admitting evidences, he began, "had been much abused from its primitive intentions." He proceeded to summarize the various ways in which an accused person could become a crown witness. The thrust of his argument was that the practice had no secure foundation or even settled rules. Taking the word of accomplices was an imperfect procedure fraught with hazards. Dispersing power among too many parties compounded the problem. In an attempt to remedy what he saw as procedural laxness, Mansfield proposed a strong model of judicial regulation of decision-making in criminal cases. "A justice," Mansfield argued, "has no authority to select whom he pleases to pardon or prosecute, and the prosecutor himself has even less power or rather pretense to select than the Justice of the Peace." The justices had overstepped their authority in offering the witness what amounted to a promise of pardon. Only the judge could make such a recommendation, and this only after considering the conduct of the witness at the trial. Mansfield's conclusion was not a good description of existing practice, which permitted a wide range of people to exercise influence over the course of justice. It was instead a bold statement of the judge's claims to exercise a decisive review over every phase of the criminal process.[31]

Having determined the limits of magisterial authority in such cases and asserted the right, indeed the obligation, of judges to evaluate the performance of witnesses, Mansfield proceeded to offer specific criticisms of the conduct of the Bow Street magistrates with respect to Mrs. Rudd. The evidence of the hearing, he argued, pointed up their failure. Their treatment of her was entirely inconsistent. When she first appeared before them, she took the entire guilt for the forgery upon herself, which made her the principal in the commission of the crime. Later she proclaimed herself innocent, saying she acted only at knife point. In neither case was she an accomplice to the crime. In declining to keep her in custody, the justices admitted as much. Still, Mansfield would have been inclined to recognize the grant if Mrs. Rudd had observed the terms of the contract. She had not done so. "It did not therefore at present appear," he noted, "that there was that candid conduct, that regular and invariable adherence to truth on the part of the prisoner, which were circumstance indispensably necessary to render her an object of favour with the court." Proof of her deceit lay in the charge under which she now labored: she stood accused of forging a bond dated three months before the one for which Robert Perreau had been convicted. Here was clear evidence that she had not made a full disclosure. "Her information," he concluded, "is therefore false, and the conditions offered to her by the Justices not complied with." Upon these considerations, he decided that he could not grant her bail and instead would leave her to stand trial at the next sessions.[32]

The impact of this decision on the case was extraordinary. The most influential legal mind of his day had, in effect, declared that Mrs. Rudd was a liar. In the recital of the evidence, he had invoked testimony that created a strong presumption of Robert Perreau's innocence. He cautioned that nothing she had said in her "confession" could be used against her. Yet everything he said in his judgment was bound to work to her disadvantage. The judicial authorities were trying to correct what they had come to see as an error at an earlier stage in the legal process. They could not disguise, however, that this action was heavily influenced by the revelations that had surfaced about Mrs. Rudd's past. Mrs. Rudd was returned to Newgate to await trial. One paper reported that the decision undermined her stoicism; it "so affected her that she shed tears."[33]

THE JUDGES DECIDE

Mansfield's decision resolved the appeal against her detention, but it did not settle the question of the legality of depriving her of crown witness status. Her counsel continued to protest against her being tried, even as her trial began on the morning of September 15. Once again public anticipation of this event was unparalleled. Reports circulated in the press that a guinea and a half had been given for admittance to the court galleries, and that "one of the Sheriffs lost a sleeve of his gown going into the Sessions-house." "The public Avidity to hear [the case] was manifested by a very early attendance. Several persons were in the Galleries before seven o'clock, and by half past eight they were crouded by very genteel company." Yet again Mrs. Rudd's clothes and conduct were minutely dissected by the papers.[34] In her dress and deportment, Mrs. Rudd never disappointed her audience.

Amid all the turmoil and noise of the courtroom, the three judges who sat at the Old Bailey that day were asked to rule on the propriety of her being brought to trial. In one of the seminal moments of the case, Justice Gould dissented from the opinion of his colleagues and, by implication, rejected the arguments advanced by Mansfield. A judge of Common Pleas since 1763, Gould was more known for "the soundness of his law than by the power of his oratory." Son of a barrister and grandson of a judge of King's Bench, he had had a long legal career by 1775. Although possessing a quiet disposition, he was capable of acting with great firmness. His decision in this instance proved of immense importance. He denied that what had happened in King's Bench should influence "this court." Their task was to look with a fresh and unbiased mind at the arguments advanced by the prosecution and the defense. Since statute offered no clear answer to the question they faced, they had to look elsewhere for guidance. For Gould this meant turning to customary practice. "It has been the practice of almost a century," he offered, "to permit justices of the peace to admit persons, guilty of capital offenses, to convict their accomplices, under the promise of pardon, which has always been faithfully and punctually observed." This grant had become crucial to the operation of justice in the country. It would, he implied, be folly to overturn so important an instrument of justice.[35]

Gould was equally decisive when it came to considering the merits of the case before them. He was persuaded, he said, to adopt his own course in the present instance because no testimony had been offered to prove that Mrs. Rudd had lied. The court, he argued, could only move to disallow her pardon by making an assumption that was not theirs to make, that she was guilty of a crime to which she had not confessed. The record of the case, which was all they had before them, permitted no such deduction, and it would be unfair to make one at this point. The prosecution, he pointed out, had not been able to discover one instance wherein a person had been tried for failing to make a complete and total confession. Such a grant had been overturned only when the witness had deliberately lied, and even then the person was convicted of perjury, not of the offense to which he confessed. Common practice alone, Gould concluded, should guide them as they decided the issue before them. He even challenged the prosecution claim that Mrs. Rudd was on trial for a crime different from the one for which the Bow Street magistrates made her a crown witness. The various forgeries, he said, all formed part of the same offense. It was impossible to ignore what had gone before. Gould's statement had a stunning impact upon the deliberations. He had, in effect, accepted virtually every part of the defense argument.[36]

Gould's break with his colleagues, and his support for the defense position in open court, represented a strategic victory for Mrs. Rudd. Had their ranks remained unbroken, the judges might well have exercised considerable influence on the deliberations of the jury. Now, even though it was a solitary dissent, the defense gained a measure of legitimacy. The case would have to be referred to the twelve judges—the body that ruled on disputed legal issues—to settle the point of law. The trial would be further delayed until all the judges had had a chance to discuss the difficulties among themselves. The deliberations would also keep the issue of fairness before the court. In addition, custom was that when the judges were divided on a question of interpretation, the Crown pardoned the offender in the event of conviction.

Justice Ashurst and Baron Hotham, in their statements, did their best to repair the damage. Each focused on the argument, offered by Mansfield, that Mrs. Rudd had not honored the terms of the grant. She was supposed "to relate all the facts that came within her knowledge. She had not done this." "In my opinion," Ashurst announced, "if she has failed in the conditions annexed to the implied pardon, she has of course by that act forfeited any claim or title to it." Hotham added that a court had to have the power to refuse such an award if the judges discovered in the course of the trial that the disclosures had been less than full or, even worse, outright lies. "They are bound," he proposed, "in honour on both sides, or on neither."[37]

The judges met on November 7, and their decision was announced at the beginning of her trial on December 8. All of the arguments were rehearsed one more time. "It being judged a point of great weight and importance in the criminal law," Justice Aston announced at the outset, "fit to be fully considered and finally settled, how far, under what circumstances, and in what manner, an accomplice, received as a witness, ought to be intitled to favour and mercy." Nine of the eleven judges (later joined by Lord Chief Justice de Grey), he reported, agreed that she should stand trial. Gould alone dissented.

Speaking for the majority, Aston explained that an accomplice who fully confessed all his guilt and who, upon being made a crown witness, "acted a fair and ingenuous part," "ought not to be prosecuted for his own guilt so disclosed by him, nor perhaps for any other offense of the same kind, which he may accidently, without any bad design, have omitted to confess." But no offender had the right to plead this grant against an indictment, "for it is merely an equitable claim to the mercy of the Crown." The gift made by the magistrate, Aston asserted, cannot "control the authority of the Court of Gaol Delivery." Furthermore, "the Magistrates' express or implied promise of an indemnity" could only be called upon if "certain conditions ... have been performed." The judges at the trial, in making their assessment, had to consider the entire history of the case and the conduct of the witness. In the present case, Aston said, the judges had read her information and determined, to their own satisfaction, that she had not confessed to any crime. Therefore the question of her guilt or innocence was still undecided and it was up to a jury to settle the issue.[38]

Throughout these complicated and tedious deliberations the judges wrestled with competing claims and legal issues. Seldom had they been asked to rule on a practice that had become central to the operation of English law enforcement. They approached the question with varying degrees of hesitation. Guided by the firm hand of Mansfield, the majority expressed its discontent with what appeared an infringement on their powers and privileges by the magistracy. But always before them, and acting as an additional spur, was the figure of Mrs. Rudd and the story of her conduct. Even as they announced that nothing arising out of their deliberations, nor anything that she might have said in any previous setting, should be taken into account or allowed to influence her trial, they conceded how much they had been influenced by precisely these statements. While they tried to discover the general principles that might guide them through this procedural thicket, their words revealed that it was the untrustworthiness of the woman before them that goaded them into considering this difficult subject.[39]

LETTERS AND THE LAW

The newspapers gave full coverage to these judicial deliberations. They also offered space to the heated controversy among correspondents over the wisdom and justice of putting Mrs. Rudd on trial. This debate mirrored the confusion among legal authorities about the nature and terms of the crown witness process. However, the dispute soon took up other, more fundamental, questions about justice, equity, the rights of subjects, and the power of government. Letters written about the case touched on a host of issues, from the proper role of judge and jury in capital cases to an examination of the operation of pardon. What they reveal is the case's multifaceted appeal. In part, the public fascination with the episode arose from the story's melodramatic elements. Both Mrs. Rudd and the Perreaus seemed like figures from a Gothic novel: victimized, entrapped, imprisoned. However, it would be wrong to think that the romance of its characters entirely explained the public's concern with the legal issues raised by the case. Like the Wilkes affair, this case, though rooted in the particularities of person and place, provoked discussions of larger, unexpected questions. When interest seemed to be flagging, some new dimension would appear, always figured through the main actors, yet drawing upon sources of anxiety that were independent of the Perreaus or Mrs. Rudd.

In the period between the end of the Perreaus' trial and the trial of Mrs. Rudd, at least one hundred letters and seventeen correspondences were published that dealt with the case. Not only does this represent a substantial number of letters for the period, but they tended to be much longer than usual, longer even than those dealing with the war in America.[40] They offered serious and detailed reflections on the law, in sharp contrast to the invective and sordid gossip that marked the letters between April and June. Clearly the authors felt that, beyond the lives of the accused, general principles were at stake. The correspondence provides a glimpse at the rich variety of beliefs about English justice that circulated in London in the late eighteenth century. They show us contemporaries thinking about such issues as policing, the death penalty, and the operation of influence upon judicial decision-making. The letters demonstrate that the English public not only took an interest in legal matters but believed that it had a right to participate in discussions touching the law.

Perhaps the best example of such a letter was one published in defense of Robert Perreau in the *Public Advertiser* on August 21, 1775. This essay (for it was more than four thousand words long and stretched over most of the first two pages of the issue) covered a remarkable range of issues in a dense and technical plea on his behalf. The author began by complaining of the failure to grant "persons, charged with capital Offences, Counsel at their Trials."

The fate of the accused, as a result, depended far too much on the actions of the judge, who, in his final summation, exercised an undue influence over the outcome. "In the Arrangement of, and commenting upon, the various Circumstances of Evidence in a long and intricate Trial, an artful Judge imperceptibly worms his Opinion into the Breasts of the Jury." In a pointed reference to Aston's charge to the jury, the correspondent wrote of "how truly melancholy must be the Condition of that Man who standing at the Bar anxious for the Acquittal of his Country" could only watch while "his Judge by sarcastic Observations" destroyed "the Whole of his Defence." Calling upon the authority of Blackstone, the author argued that it was unjust to have the fate of the accused rest upon the "Whim and Caprice" of a judge.[41]

The man who signed himself "Lex Terrae" next proceeded to criticize the jury verdict as flawed, since Robert had been convicted of uttering the bond, but the prosecution had failed to prove, in the words of the charge, that he did so "with intention to defraud." This error clearly offered grounds, the author argued, for setting aside the sentence. He hoped that the authorities would not be such slaves to custom and precedent that they failed to right an obvious procedural error. Perhaps aware that his legal arguments were unlikely to carry the day, "Lex Terrae" shifted the focus in the letter's concluding paragraphs. He was in no doubt where justice lay in this case. Robert Perreau was "so long a Stranger to the real Character of Mrs. Rudd" that he fell "a sacrifice" to her schemes. Their respective characters made the choice of outcomes easy. If all else failed, there was, finally, an appeal to the mercy of the King. Displaying his "Wilkite" sympathies, he could not fail to note that this pardoning power had been sometimes abused to let "hardened Characters" loose upon the world. Here, he contended, was an opportunity to right the balance. "In the present Case, Ten Thousand Circumstances, which speak stronger than personal Interest, all combine together in their Supplications to the Throne, for the Gracious Pardon of *Robert Perreau*."[42]

The most intense debate, however, centered on the question of whether Mrs. Rudd should face trial. Mansfield's pronouncements failed to overawe these correspondents. If anything, given his unpopular political standing, his intervention only sharpened the dispute and brought new participants into the fray. His role in this case attracted criticism not only for his attack on the ability of justices to offer crown witness status but also for what was perceived as his challenge to jury independence. In London especially, the center of Wilkite agitation, criticism of dictation from the Bench struck a responsive chord among the public. The charges made in the *North Briton* against Mansfield in particular could not but echo seven years later in the minds of citizens reading about the deliberations concerning Mrs. Rudd. "The judge," the journal contended, in setting forth a view sharply at odds with Mansfield's, "has little more to do than to superintend the trial, and to preserve inviolate the *forms* of justice." Yet, how differently he behaved: "Who confounds, controuls and browbeats a jury? Who changes, garbles and packs a jury?" What was one to make of a judge who "is perpetually talking of supporting the measures of the government, that is the prerogative of the Crown, but never once of supporting the privileges of the people?" Mansfield acted, the paper charged, "as if the sole duty of a judge were to assist the *great* in opposing the *little,* and not to protect the *little* against the oppressions of the *great.*"[43] Thus his strident role in the Rudd case, whatever its legal merits, had the effect of raising concerns about the dangerous extension of judicial discretion at the cost of the subject's liberties.

Occasionally the criticism directed at Mansfield could be highly inflammatory. One author complained that his decision partook of the spirit of Judge Jeffries and the Inquisition. Surely, "Amator Justitiae" wrote, mercy was an integral part of English justice, and if "sacrificed to a base spirit of revenge" it would be compared "throughout the world" with the bloody deeds of that notorious hanging judge in the dark days following the Monmouth Rebellion. Furthermore, if Mrs. Rudd were put on trial, after giving incriminating evidence against herself, justice would be stained "with the foulest blot that ever disgraced the history of this country ... it would be availing ourselves of a method of obtaining proof not less cruel and far more treacherous than the tortures used by that detestable court the Inquisition." The specter of that Scot, Jeffries, was raised both by Wilkite lawyers and letter writers to drive home the polemic against the Scottish Lord Mansfield. They all took shelter behind the notion that "common law was precedent," using it as a shield against what was seen as the autocratic style of these non-English judges. Most seemed convinced that "law was opposed to [Mansfield's view of] equity, and [that] the equitable authority of the judge needed to be contained to prevent its undermining the law itself."[44]

Not everyone took so negative a view of the judges' decision. "People are much divided in opinion," observed one paper, "respecting Mrs. Rudd's recommitment."[45] Faced with the great difficulties of this case, one correspondent felt the judges were warranted in adopting an unusual course of

with this evidence, Fielding made the right decision.[58] Another author reminded his readers that "had she been the wedded wife of Daniel Perreau, the law should, I am told, of itself have supposed her to have acted by compulsion," and so held him responsible for the crime. Yet she had lived with him and been accepted as his wife. It seemed unfair, not to say ungentlemanly, to ignore her true situation.[59]

As the controversy neared its climax in December, the debate centered on whether Mrs. Rudd was the kind of woman who deserved the generosity that the law traditionally displayed toward women. She continued to present herself as the self-sacrificing wife and mother, the weak and defenseless female, who had a legitimate claim upon the sympathy of the court. While the tide of judicial as well as public opinion seemed to be running against her by the summer of 1775, the assumptions about gender that conditioned eighteenth-century justice continued to work in her favor.[60]

JUSTICE ON TRIAL

The many letters to the papers demonstrated the lively interest the public took in the operation of justice. Correspondents felt free to pass judgment on the conduct of the courts. English justice, most authors argued, had no rivals; it was "justly admired and respected." It displayed a tenderness for the lives of the subject, if not in its punishment, then in the attention to legal process. Trial by jury was the "noblest and best Invention" the world had seen for "discriminating the Innocent from the Guilty."[61] Yet the operation of the law in the Perreau-Rudd case told a different tale. No institution of justice or legal actor emerged from the case with his reputation unstained. Lawyers such as Henry Dagge and John Bailey appeared to transgress the normal limits on the actions of counsel on behalf of clients. In several instances, the papers or one of the parties hinted that they had engaged in efforts to suborn justice. The magistrates at Bow Street stood accused of mishandling the initial investigation, and as a result an innocent person might suffer death. Letters to the press expressed discontent with the judges' highhanded intervention in putting Mrs. Rudd on trial. At her trial in December the hard-hitting tactics of Mrs. Rudd's lawyers would inspire general outrage. Peculiar evidentiary rules seemed to exclude witnesses whom everyone believed were vital to clearing up the business. Jury verdicts were repeatedly questioned. Throughout the case charges of bias and secret influence poisoned the atmosphere. There was plenty of evidence that Mrs. Rudd had skillfully exploited the legal prejudice in favor of women, while the Perreaus had made full use of patronage and connection to secure favorable judicial decisions. There was little to celebrate about English justice on this occasion. The public seemed dissatisfied with the workings of the courts, the behavior of individuals, and the actions of the press.

It is necessary here to remark upon the obvious. This case assumed the proportions it did because a murky transaction was brought to the light of day in a court of law. Its questions were shaped by legal process and lent urgency by the haunting shape of the gallows. When the normal processes of the law failed to satisfy both the public and those in authority, these processes became a matter of dispute. Criminal trials normally do not attract notice, especially when those on trial are the poor, illiterate, or unrespectable. But a sensational trial focuses attention on the legal process and can expose the flaws and weaknesses in the operation of justice. Contradictions in that process become amplified by divisions in the society. The outcome of this protracted case left everyone dissatisfied. The law was supposed to get at the truth and serve justice. It also existed to maintain the moral integrity of a society. All too obviously, in this case, these goals seemed to recede as the disputes intensified.

Eight

WRITING HER LIFE:
MRS. RUDD'S LIFE STORIES

WHY WRITE

MRS. RUDD WROTE THE first version of her life, her "Case," just after her arrest in February. After the brothers' trial and her remand to Newgate she wrote another version, published this time as a pamphlet, "Facts." Her pen had not been idle in the interval. Indeed, she wrote with frantic energy from the opening days of the case until its close in January of the following year. The volume and vociferousness of her writing are the most singular features of the entire peculiar episode. While the occasional opponent suggested that she might not have been the author of her "Case," by the time "Facts" appeared, no such charge was made. Although many found her writings puzzling, by that time everyone accepted them as hers. Even Admiral Frankland and Mrs. Robert Perreau, who both had reason to hate and wish her ill, never made this charge. And she continued to write, penning not only these two versions of her life and times, but after a decade's silence another set of darker and more embattled self-portrayals.[1]

Ridicule and exposure, far from silencing her, only goaded her to produce more strident efforts. One cannot escape the feeling that she loved the attention. Her writing had a kind of inspired spontaneity about it. It often seemed makeshift and overwritten, always verging on the preposterous. She offered different poses within the same text and employed several different voices. The contradictions in the content and style of her stories never seemed to bother her. Neither in print nor in a court of law did she falter in the face of considerable opposition. She was never at a loss for words. She held to her stories with a determination that often confounded her contemporaries. There was something outrageous about her claims to innocence and the veil she attempted to throw over her past life. Such actions invited scorn. Caught out in lies, trapped in her own exaggerations, her inconsistencies in full view, she seemed almost a parody of the artful deceiver described by the Perreaus. Yet her activity sustained their basic argument, that she was manipulative, imaginative, and false.

It is not clear why she wrote so much. Rarely, if ever, had a woman involved in a criminal case turned to print to vindicate her conduct before the actual trial. Her motives for writing are as complex as the stories she told. She spoke in cryptic terms of a conspiracy on her life and of rumors meant to impugn her character. After her initial arrest, some of her writing was designed to correct statements she claimed had been misreported. Any other woman would have issued such a statement under the name of her attorney or some male relative, or just ignored the mistaken comments. That is what Jane Butterfield did with such success. But Mrs. Rudd could not remain quiet. She seemed compelled to write, even though this activity served as additional proof to some that she had not only the ability but the motive and character to forge the bonds on Adair. Unlike Butterfield, Rudd adopted the same tactics as the Duchess of Kingston. In her conflict with the playwright Samuel Foote, Kingston also published denunciatory letters in the daily press, adopting a masculine and biting tone, as befitted an aristocrat in conflict with a mere player. Like Kingston, Rudd may have felt that attack was the best defense, that total rout was all her enemies deserved, that a strong and assertive style was the final proof of her claims to exalted lineage. Her noble birth, she seemed to feel, justified her demand for respect. It gave her the power to scorn the insulting words of her inferiors. "How falsely my enemies represented me," she wrote, because "envious of my superior goodness."[2] She had a lofty disdain for those merely jealous of her quality. She did not doubt her own worth, however much others did.[3] Her exalted birth remained a focus in all her many tales about herself.

Or she may just have been unable to stop. For Mrs. Rudd seemed to love to offer descriptions of herself. She had an amazing physical presence, an ability to convince people of her sincerity, and an astounding confidence in the power of her written self-descriptions to influence how she was viewed. Her fanciful stories and volubility were an undeniable part of her success in society. She poured forth an unending stream of such portraits, each seeking to outdo the last in its representation of her nobility and virtue. Perhaps this passion was simply an echo of the way she had presented herself in fashionable London circles for the preceding decade. The somewhat clumsy written performances should not lead one to underestimate her success as a lively and engaging hostess. That previous success may have inspired her to attempt to duplicate it in the new medium. If so, her charm did not survive the translation. She, however, did not notice the failure. She continued to believe that the correct verbal formula would lead the public to see her as she saw herself. Once she was understood, she was convinced, she would be vindicated. Whatever the reasons for the writings, they served to attract, perplex and fascinate the reading public and to fix the case in the popular mind.

How did Mrs. Rudd justify first writing to the papers with her "Case" and then publishing her "Facts"? How, ten years later, did she explain her final efforts? In some ways the early stories were masterful. In terms of proprieties, the sort of narrative she needed to create to vindicate herself had not only to explain away her obvious involvement in the forgeries but also to do so in a manner that would draw sympathy and not blame to herself. She could not appear as an adventuress, albeit one innocent of this particular crime. Nor could she display a willingness to shop her husband and his brother to save her life; this would have reinforced her image as a heartless conniver. Despite these difficult demands, within two weeks of her arrest, she had published the first part of her explanation, her vindication of herself and her life. In its very first sentence she explained both how she came to be in such a terrible situation and why she had used the press to clear her name.

> The conspiracy formed against my life by Messrs. Perreau, the detainer of all my wearing apparel, and every other part of my property; that is to say, jewels, plate, china, household linen, and furniture, whereby I am left totally destitute, with three children, of even the common necessaries of life; will, I hope, be considered by the world a just cause for my laying before them the following narrative of facts, which nothing less than the injuries I have sustained could extort from me.

It was necessary for Mrs. Rudd to explain this public notice, for direct appeals to the public by women were almost unheard of. One of her great early accomplishments, then, was realizing how she could turn this unusual appeal into a potent weapon, and understanding what a powerful potential ally the press could become if she addressed the newspaper audience directly and kept her case firmly in the public eye.[4]

Both her supporters and detractors commented on this stance. Her friends advised her "to publish her case directly, and submit her cause to the impartial public, who are ever ready to espouse justice and oppressed innocence." When she decided to suppress the second part of her story until after the brothers' trials, "Unknowing and Unknown," only one of the host of letter writers who anonymously commented on the case, applauded this action. "Indeed if ill-rewarded, unsuspecting, and too generous actions, can claim worldly protection or prepossession in your favour, there you certainly stand forth first claimant in an impartial publick's eye."[5] Although some newspaper correspondents represented her as the sinister and deceitful manipulator of innocent people, making the Adair forgeries seem no more than a part of a larger pattern and the Perreaus only two of many victims, she claimed that *she* was the only victim of misplaced trust.

> I do, and ever must, with the keenest anguish lament my credulity and misfortune in having confided the most inestimable blessings in life, honour and fortune, to a man, who, in return for such exalted generosity and faith, the purest, most unbounded affection, has with unparalleled villainy and black ingratitude, combined against my life; plotted to bring me to an ignominious death, in a mode and for reasons which humanity must shudder at; and what one would imagine the most hardened villain could not have been bad enough to put into practice; defamed me and his children; reduced us to absolute beggary and irreparable misery.[6]

Yet even at this early date, Mrs. Rudd could not resist complicating her own narrative. While insisting that her appeal to the public was the only avenue still open to a friendless, innocent woman, she also adopted a more masculine tone and response, admitting that her "public vindication (though it exposed Mr. Perreau) was in justice a duty I owed myself, circumstanced as I was with character, and everything valuable in life at stake." Her recourse to the press then, and through the press to the sanction of the impartial public, was, even by her own words, doubly motivated, moved both by necessity and by pride.[7]

A number of themes appeared repeatedly in her publications. Most prominent among these was the discussion she offered of her "two families." One family consisted of the aristocratic connections she claimed for herself, which played the largest role in constituting her own identity. The other was the family she had created with Daniel and their three children, but that also included the other Perreaus. There was a tension between these two systems of connection, and this showed in the different tone she adopted when writing in the persona of offended *grande dame* or injured wife and mother.

Although Mrs. Rudd was later to say that she had been misquoted, one of the earliest personal details reported in the press was her claim to be the "daughter of one of the first Noblemen of Scotland." In contrast, Dr. Brooke, as we have already noted, thought that Mrs. Rudd was "either a ward, or a natural daughter of Mr. [William] Adair's." For Mrs. Rudd, and for many of her contemporaries, it was vitally important to establish the "truth" of her family of origin. If her lineage and breeding could be established, her birth could become vital, though indirect, evidence for or against her. Both Rudd and her opponents based many of their statements about her role in the case and her veracity on who she was, what sort of family she came from, and what color blood flowed in her veins. English society relied on knowing who (in the sense of what kind of person) someone was in deciding whether they were or could have been guilty of a crime. By the time the papers published her letters she had denied ever saying that she was the daughter of a Scottish nobleman. She now claimed to be "the daughter of an untitled man of fashion in the real and true signification of the word." She was "infinitely too proud even to wish myself descended from any other family than that which I have the honour to derive my birth from, being convinced there are very few so noble—none more so."[8] In time she cleared up this confusion by explaining that it was through her mother that she owed her relation to several aristocratic Scottish families, and thus noble blood did flow in her veins.

Neither Mrs. Rudd nor her contemporaries believed that the fact of lineage alone was sufficient to command respect. Instead, they thought that noble birth and the education that followed from it could develop and highlight certain qualities and characteristics most often associated with being wellborn. These included a certain nonchalance, a depth of feeling, and casual rightness of demeanor. These were the qualities that Mrs. Rudd claimed her Scottish relations saw and valued in her. "Their esteem," she noted, "arose from a knowledge of the excellencies of my heart and disposition, and, what they were pleased to term, the amiableness of my manners."[9] Similarly, her supporters argued that "the woman of birth and education is visible in her deportment and conversation," while her critics insisted on knowing "*who was* your father, and to desire you openly to aver what family you are of." It may be that some of her detractors sought to expose her lies in this instance, and so cast doubt on her general credibility. But there seemed to be more at stake, both for her and for them. Both she and they seemed to agree that if she was indeed of noble extraction, if her blood and lineage were what she claimed, then that fact alone would make her guilt less likely. True aristocrats, the feeling seemed to be, might commit crimes in hot blood, but not through cold cunning. Even when letter writers like "Honour and Justice" argued that "virtue needs no ancestry," they quickly added that "the unhappy Mrs. P[erreau] is a lady of respectable family and connections."[10]

In one sense her claims to birth and breeding simply acknowledged one of the central facts of eighteenth-century life, that family was the crucial factor in one's identity. How one got on in the world depended chiefly upon family, and for no one as much as for a woman. Mrs. Rudd, from the first, used her claim of high connection as a way of gaining recognition. Much of her conversation was taken up with displaying an intimate knowledge of the aristocracy, based, she said, on personal familiarity. Although her claims to exalted relations may have helped her as she sought to move in fashionable circles, it was not simply a pose for her; she believed that noble blood flowed in her veins and that she deserved respect, wealth, and happiness.

Whatever the truth of Rudd's original family, equally mysterious and contradictory were the reports of her life and circumstances as a married woman. Here, too, Mrs. Rudd's story clashed with those her critics offered. She never denied that she had been and might still be married to Valentine Rudd, but she downplayed that relation. In her "Case," she both passed over this marriage and justified her adulterous relationship with Perreau with the mere phrase, "there was then a reason why it was impossible for us [her and Daniel] to be married."[11] In doing so she portrayed herself as a woman more sinned against than sinning, a victim more of external fortune than of internal vice. Later, she elaborated. Rudd, she noted, was both brutal and insane, and her

honor as well as her safety demanded that she leave him. It was "in the beginning of March 1769," she claimed, that she and Rudd "finally separated."
Little more than a year later, according to her narrative, she began her "acquaintance" with Daniel Perreau.[12]

Her detractors, of course, told different stories of this marriage and its dis-
solution. They depicted Rudd as a young man far from home, ensnared by
an ambitious, lower-class Irish girl, eager to "extend her Travels" and through
marriage to "constitute her[self] a Gentlewoman." When, they claimed, she
had wrung all the advantage she could from him, she tossed him aside, leaving him to debtor's prison and dishonor. They also told a wide variety of stories about the period between her parting with Rudd and her meeting with
Perreau. This, they maintained, was of several years' duration, a much longer
period than Mrs. Rudd acknowledged. Mrs. Rudd herself protested that these
rumors were all based on misapprehensions. In order to escape Rudd's obsessive and violent jealousy, she said she had borrowed, and lived under the
name of, Mrs. Gore. The real Mrs. Gore, she later contended, was the woman
with the busy social and sexual life; she herself, Margaret Caroline Rudd,
merely took the blame for her friend's escapades. It was in this unsettled time,
after fleeing from Rudd, that an unnamed friend died, leaving her £16,000
"in consideration of the unmerited ill treatment I had received from Mr.
Rudd."[13]

Despite the fact of her previous marriage, she firmly maintained that she
had "never lived with, nor was the *mistress* of, any man. My connexion with
Mr. Perreau can never be considered but as that of being his wife."[14] When
she met Daniel, she was drawn to him for the most honorable of reasons.
"He appeared everything a rational, virtuous, and delicate woman would
wish." "Our union," she wrote, as if describing a wedding day, "took place
the 20th of May 1770." She felt for Daniel "the purest, the most unbounded
affection." "[I] confided my FAME, my FORTUNE, and HAPPINESS to Mr. Perreau."[15] This union, she had hoped, was to be the basis for a new and better
life, not only for herself, but for Daniel and their as-yet-unborn children. It
is in her descriptions of this "made" family, which in reality consisted of her
paramour and his relations, as well as their own illegitimate offspring, that
Mrs. Rudd's familial narratives become most elaborate and confused.

Even as she wrestled with these issues, one point remained constant, that
of her fortune and how it was used. From the very beginning, money played
an important part in this almost-marriage. In her first account, Mrs. Rudd

explained that over the years she had lived with Daniel Perreau, she had at one time or another given him £13,000, which he had lost in the stock market. Included were the £800 she had sent to the Perreau sisters as well as the £3500 used to cover "the intire expences of house-keeping, family and personal expences of all sorts for near four years." She would not have brought this all up, she noted, but for the plot on her life; when she united herself with Daniel and confided her "honour, person and fortune" to him, she was moved by the "delicate, powerful sense I felt of the duty I owed him as his wife (for as such I ever considered myself and acted) and the unbounded confidence I had in his mutual love and honour."[16] Daniel's charge that she had been destitute when he met her seemed to rankle Rudd. She countered that far from her having been poor, it was she who helped him out of debt and then, later, sustained his extravagances. This question of money loomed large in all subsequent disputes between the parties, and it was never entirely settled. Much was at stake. Daniel, for his part, wanted to show that he was never in need, that he was attracted to her in part by her pitiful state. The clear implication was that she had come to him as his mistress, with all that that implied about her moral standing. Mrs. Rudd, in far more grandiose terms, portrayed her wealth as an indicator of her social standing and argued that she had come to Daniel as more than an equal. The possession of money made her association with Daniel more honorable. Since both Daniel and Mrs. Rudd had past histories to live down—he as a debtor and she as a courtesan—the question of money touched closely on issues central to the case. Money also figured in the question of motivation and responsibility—which of the parties stood most in need of money and which was more disreputable in handling it.

Even in her first account, which concentrated more on the idyllic conditions of their early years together, Mrs. Rudd's financial wherewithal played a central part in her account of their relations. "From the moment we lived together I considered myself in every sense his wife and practiced the virtues and duties of one in the fullest sense" and so was pleased, rather than unhappy, to give him large sums of money. The "inferiority of [his] fortune gave me pleasure; as it afforded me an opportunity of proving the disinterestedness of my attachment, and the supreme felicity of obliging him by a delicate, well-timed generosity." Not only was she their main financial provider, but she also "managed [the] family with genteel frugality; attempted no parade nor finery beyond the reach of [her] finances; and paid all tradespeople within [her] department punctually." Despite his shady associates and gambling on the Alley, Rudd maintained she remained devoted to Daniel, willing to serve him in all ways, as long as he remained true to her and to their marriage.[17]

Although money was central to both accounts, the stories were rather differently inflected. The first telling was mainly concerned with establishing Mrs. Rudd's financial generosity, not only to Daniel but to the entire Perreau family. This account highlighted Daniel's fiscal and moral irresponsibility; in addition to the money she had given him, Daniel had spent the monies entrusted him by a Mr. O, funds meant to provide an annuity for O's retired mistress. Mrs. Rudd also replaced these. All in all, she said, he had made presents to his friend and contact, Col. Kinder, "and all and every part of his own family . . . which transactions, presents and expences was paid for with and from my money."[18]

Beyond cataloguing Daniel's faults, this first account ended with a strong denunciation of Mrs. Robert Perreau and the whole Perreau family. Mrs. Rudd clearly felt vulnerable in relation to the Perreaus. In her retelling of their relations, she jumped quickly from a sentimental description of how she sacrificed time and money on their behalf to sharp anger at their slights and insults to her. She expressed resentment at their suggestion that as respectable people they had kept her at a distance. They had been less particular, she pointed out, when the family depended on her money and pinned their hopes on her relations. In fact, Mrs. Rudd argued, "the daughter of a man of fashion, nobly descended and as nobly allied as I am, could be no degrading alliance to any family: to so private a one as this it was certainly a very great honour." When she felt slighted by the Perreaus, she appealed to her own connections, so superior to theirs, as proof of her status and worth. In a remarkable letter, John Stewart, Mrs. Rudd's uncle, using rhetoric and style curiously reminiscent of hers, also attacked both the background and pretensions of Mrs. Robert Perreau. "I suppose she derived those high sentiments from the noble descent of a West Indian parson's daughter, and the elegant education given her under the care and direction of the late Mrs. Perreaus, Milliner, in Tavistock-street." "Such little gentry," he remarked with disdain, "are a pest to superior society, and a burlesque on the name of gentlewoman."[19] Here we see one important function of Mrs. Rudd's putative family of origin. In her debate with the Perreaus, she could present her financial and social association with that family as a proper condescension, and a more than generous forbearance. Thus, in letters sent to the Perreau sisters in Wales, Mrs. Rudd not only discussed her many efforts to promote the careers of the brothers but made clear that their good fortune came as a result of her quality and birth. "For my part," she concluded one letter, "you must know, that I am highly proud of the matter, and bless fate that I was born a little gentlewoman, and that nature and education inspired me with a due sense of the blessings of an illustrious descent (as his Majesty was pleased to term mine), and ambition to claim advantage from it."[20]

Another theme broached in this first account that was repeated in the subsequent version was Mrs. Rudd's many attempts to create a "real" family with Daniel, not only through gifts of money but more importantly by becoming the mother of his three children. Her frequent mention of her children served to remind her readers that she had not been merely "kept" by Daniel. She was a mother, and the children were proof of the bond that had existed between Daniel and herself. They were living evidence of how hard she had worked to maintain that bond until the Perreaus' fatal betrayal. While she had remained true to their family, sacrificing her fortune and the glittering sphere to which she was born to throw in her lot with theirs, the Perreaus sought to undo all she had worked for through selfish cowardice and an unmanly repudiation of the family she had made.

Her second narrative, written after the Perreaus' trials, necessitated, she claimed, by "the strong prejudice the public seems to have conceived against me, from the Perreaus' defence," answered some of their charges, elaborated on some of her previous statements, and attempted to implicate others in the conspiracy on her life. Explaining her mysterious letter-writing, for example, Mrs. Rudd cited Daniel's "prying curiosity," his insistence on reading all correspondence from her family and her responses to them, which she said obliged her to write "frequently when Mr. Perreau was absent, for, had I wrote in his presence, I should not have had peace until he read the letters." In this second version of the case, Col. Kinder emerged as the evil genius responsible for Daniel's downfall. Kinder, who, according to Rudd, originally came to London as the pander and general factotum to the libertine Earl of Barrymore, found in Daniel a pigeon ripe for plucking.

When Mrs. Rudd, a prudent wife, stopped Daniel from loaning Kinder a large sum to purchase stocks, he, from that day forth, "bore [her] a secret enmity and revenge for being the cause of this disappointment to him." It was also Kinder who, according to Mrs. Rudd, was responsible for Daniel's lavish expenditures; "I can't avoid saying, that I am convinced his pernicious counsels, and sinister designs, induced and urged Mr. Perreau to commit many indiscretions and extravagancies." The last time the colonel returned to France, Daniel had presented him with £100 and a new post-chaise as marks of his esteem.[21]

If Kinder had been the secret influence behind the Perreaus' dissipation and gambling, then Henry Dagge, Robert Perreau's lawyer and friend, emerged together with Robert and his wife as the band of evil forces behind the plot to implicate Mrs. Rudd in the crime. Induced by the brothers, Mrs. Rudd offered her jewels and a weakly contrived story to Dagge, who, Robert assured her, would act as their intermediary with all possible complainants. From then on, according to Mrs. Rudd's account, the case unraveled, with Robert and Mrs. Perreau plotting with Dagge against Daniel and herself. At this point Mrs. Rudd had urged Daniel, for their safety, to consult with "some solicitor or council of reputation and abilities, who would give us a judicious impartial opinion." Daniel, however, deaf to her words and blind to her tears, would not "suffer [her] to see nor speak to any lawyer except Mr. Dagge." Although Daniel trusted both Robert and Dagge, Mrs. Rudd's suspicions of the latter continued to grow. "Though I could not divine what Mr. Dagge was about, or what he meant ... I naturally inferred, there must be something sinister and unfair." These suspicions, however, were raised only by her apprehension for Daniel's safety, for "the conspiracy against me, or a thought of any thing prejudicial to me, never entered my imagination." She never explicitly accused Dagge of being the author of the scheme to shift the blame for the forgeries to her, but her comments clearly implied as much.

Neither Robert nor Daniel was freed of complicity in this cowardly expedient. Toward Daniel especially, Mrs. Rudd reserved her most scathing familial rebukes: "The father of my three inoffending, lovely infants, whose helpless innocence alone ought to have engaged him, for their sakes, to have held their mother's life, character, and property sacred, that in her fond maternal care, and tender affection, they might have a protector, guide and support in life." Describing her conduct on the morning before their arrest, while she, at least, still thought they were imminently to flee to France, Rudd noted that her heart was riven by the coming separation from her children. "I dreaded to hear the voices of my children should they wake, and should they leave their nursery, and be brought to me as was customary every morning at breakfast; their smiling innocence would have disarmed me of all resolution, and I could the sooner [have] faced death itself, had that been the alternative, than torn myself from them."[22] Daniel, on the other hand, chose to return to his own family and to betray theirs by siding with his brother before the justices.

Even after she and Robert had been arrested by the Bow Street magistrates, Mrs. Rudd said that she had resolved, if possible, to say nothing to involve Robert in the crime; this she was prepared to do "out of mere humanity to him and his family; that it was a tender point, and that I should at least feel a solid good, by rendering good for evil." However, when Robert publicly revealed her irregular union with Daniel, thereby unmaking the family she had worked so hard to create, she was freed from this impulse. "I could have forgiven any thing on earth sooner than this shameful injury, and I believe every one present saw it [as] a piece of wicked cruelty." From then on, Rudd was on her own, fighting against the Perreaus for the lives and futures of her children and herself. From then on, for the next five months until her trial, Mrs. Rudd consistently presented herself as "an unhappy and distressed mother," "the persecuted mother of three distressed babes." At this point her grand family narratives, the claims to nobility or refined gentility gave way to the reiterated portrayal of an innocent though defamed mother, to the basic, universal evocation of attenuated though heroically maintained family life.[23]

"THE AMIABLE WEAKNESS OF WOMEN"

In offering up her portrait as the good wife and mother, Mrs. Rudd aligned herself with popular images of femininity, of female virtue founded on tenderness. Weakness, nobility, and true womanliness were frequently presented as inextricably tied; Harley, the sentimental hero of Mackenzie's *Man of Feeling*, commending his own sympathetic tenderness, noted, "I am as weak as a woman." This conflation of femininity and weakness was not confined to the novel but was often articulated in public conversation and dispute. Debating the propriety of the Salic law, several female participants argued that women rulers suffered under fearful innate disabilities: "Declining all female pretensions to imperial sway," these female orators mentioned the "natural softness and sensibility of [female] minds ... [of the] trembling tenderness and sympathetic pity of [their] sex." It was natural for women, they held, to feel deeply, to love strongly, and to pity completely. Mrs. Rudd also subscribed to, or at least employed, these views of female character. As she herself noted, she "was not the first woman of character who ... suffered the tenderest of all sentiments to subdue her reason and to lull her prudence."[24]

From first to last Mrs. Rudd presented herself as the epitome of the sentimental heroine. As with other female heroines, her very excellencies seemed to lead to distress; her very virtue "invites its own punishment." Repeatedly, she described herself in terms of the familiar family drama as a naive, innocent, and trusting woman played upon by deep, designing men. Her high regard for Daniel and respect for Robert misled her about their characters. She had in full, she said in one account, "the weakness of a woman." "Possibly had I possessed less sentiment, I should have acted with ... more rectitude." Her refined sensibility was precisely what marked her out as an unusual woman, extraordinary in her capacity for feeling and self-sacrifice. In her life she had only tried to do what was right. She had devoted herself to fulfilling wifely duties. And although she refused to acknowledge it as coming from her pen, it is small wonder that the reading public could think that the "Pathetic Elegy," published within a month of the arrests, was a genuine expression of her deepest feelings. This piece, addressed to Daniel, began with the following verse, "Unhappy partner of my widow'd breast, / Once its dear pilot thro' life's stormy sea, / Tho' with unnumbered wrongs thou'st broke its rest, / In spite of vengeance, still it beats for thee."[25]

The elegy suggested its putative author to be a woman of sensibility and delicacy. A letter by John Stewart, also addressed to Daniel Perreau and published in April 1775, portrayed Mrs. Rudd as a gentle and loving female, betrayed by her natural protector. As his wife "in the sight of God," her mind was under Daniel's sway, under "the *same ascendancy* as if the priest had joined your hands." Stewart's letter also evoked another literary theme, that of the female orphan raised by the kindly guardian who educated and nurtured his beautiful charge but ultimately failed to protect her from deception by evil men. Stewart's description of the young Margaret Rudd could easily have been spoken by the loving guardian in Frances Burney's *Evelina,* the Rev. Mr. Villars, about Evelina's mother, Caroline Evelyn: "I was the guardian of her youth ... I ever loved her as such, and she was all the fondest one could wish; sensible, an elegant, accomplished mind, filled with every female virtue; beautiful, well bred, and to use the poet's words 'of gentle manners,' and a soul sincere."[26]

Mrs. Rudd's recounting of her story, and especially the account of her generosity to both Daniel and Robert, further underlined her tender and benevolent femininity. At every opportunity she freely offered her property to these loved ones, without thought of future recompense. Even in prison, betrayed by these very men, she sacrificed herself for their comfort. Well before their trials, she highlighted her great womanly loving kindness by comparing herself in this regard with the other Mrs. Perreau, Robert's wife:

> I believe her capable of any thing, when she discovers so unfeeling, so shocking a disposition, as never to visit her husband since he was removed to Newgate; and suffered him, in that miserable place, to *want a bed;* a matrass spread on the floor was all the bed he and his brother had between them, until I heard (from a lady Daniel wrote to) of their dreadful situation; upon which I contrived to send him a decent bed, with bedstead and furniture to it, enjoining the lady to say *she gave it,* and was obliged to send a pair of sheets belonging to one of my poor infants, who has but another pair left for its own bed; nor am I ashamed to confess, that to enable myself to purchase this accommodation for D. P. I was necessitated to part with *one gown* out of the only *two* I am mistress of.[27]

Even in her benevolence, she kept her giving secret, preferring the brothers not to know that she was their benefactor.[28] But she could not, would not spare Robert's wife. Why, Rudd asked, was she suspected of complicity in the forgery when it was just as likely that Mrs. Robert Perreau would have known of her husband's business affairs? "Has she since her husband's commitment shown even a decent sorrow? has she not gone out as much as usual; sees company at home, and keeps two footmen to attend her; employs a great part of her time in getting scurrilous letters wrote abusing Mrs. Rudd." In fact, one of her supporters, "XY," in a letter ostensibly addressed to Dr. Brooke, argued that it was "Mrs. R. Perreau [who] strongly urged you to prosecute D. Perreau with rigour ... to induce you to think that [her husband] is totally innocent."[29]

Mrs. Rudd's self-descriptions not only rested on her claims to come from a certain type of background but also entailed the corollary that this background endowed her with an acute sensibility, a feeling heart, and a sensitive soul. First, she attempted to show that she possessed a sympathetic and delicate character, which established her claim to be both upper-class and morally worthy. Simply by her display of feeling she offered conclusive proof that she could not have committed the crime. She sought to demonstrate these qualities time and again in her writings, modeled as they were upon the conventions of contemporary popular fiction. She was the higher being, preyed upon by crude and malicious men, who took advantage of her finer feelings. Remarking on her many gifts to Daniel, for example, she noted that "the *manner,* more than the gift, confers the obligation—My feelings on this point have ever been so refined, that while he preserved *even the shadow* of decorum in his frequent calls for money, I studied to know his wants, to relieve them *unasked,* and thereby spare his and my own sensibility the pain of discussing so unpleasing a topic." Second, she asserted that her readers, if they too possessed such sentiments, must acknowledge her innocence. She drew a self-portrait in the strongest sentimental terms, no doubt believing that her prose would win her allies, just as the figures in popular novels compelled their readers' tears. "The inexpressible anguish of such a situation is more easily conceived than expressed," she wrote, "indeed no language could give an adequate idea of my feelings; let those who possess nice sensibilities, a genteel mind, and feeling heart, judge of, and pity me."[30] "Possessed of sensibilities too refined for my own peace," she said in another letter, "and sentiments more adapted to the superiority of my birth than situation, I feel with double poignancy every misfortune to which the peculiar severity of my fate has reduced me."[31] In her portrayal of herself as a female Harley, she hoped to convince the reading public that she was simply the innocent woman of feeling whose qualities rendered her vulnerable to the Perreaus' mischievous schemes.

In many ways, Mrs. Rudd perfectly "fit" this picture of the sentimental heroine. Although mystery surrounded her birth, she seemed somehow innately possessed of an elevated refinement of taste and elegance of manner. Her clothes and demeanor were impeccable, her conversation easy and innocent, her language lofty and well crafted. James Boswell was surprised by her modest appearance when he met her months later. She was, he confided to his wife, "rather a little woman, delicately made, not at all a beauty, but with a pleasing appearance and much younger than I imagined ... her language was choice and fluent and her voice melodious." In this interview Rudd confided to Boswell that though "she had formerly deluded herself with hopes of enjoying happiness, [s]he was now satisfied with insensibility," the latter word suggesting that her problems were consequences of an overly receptive nature.[32] Here, too, Rudd fit the model of trembling sensitivity, the woman who sought insensibility, for her nerves were too close to the skin. The language of all her writing testified to the state of her sensations. It was the "extreme shock my mind has recently suffered" that prevented her from immediately refuting the Perreaus' calumnies; her health, impaired by the "state of afflicting events" that had occurred since she lived with Perreau, "tortured and kept me in a state of distressing agitation"; she was "almost distracted" by the thought of Daniel's perfidy toward her. A Rousseauan heroine, Rudd shed copious tears: after being told of Daniel's designs to find a wealthy wife, "deprived of the power of utterance," she "could only thank [her] kind advisor with tears"; telling Daniel of Robert's proposal that she forge Adair's name, "the unaffected tears and emotion with which I delivered the speech" temporarily deflected his insistence. The actions of her body mirrored the emotions of her heart; finally told of the other forgeries, Rudd reported that she "wrung [her] hands in agony, and fell on [her] knees to beseech the Almighty to take [her] from such a scene of piercing wretchedness" and end her life.[33] All she now asked for, she assured her readers, was that pity to which any innocent *"woman of feeling"* was entitled, and the justice that any innocent "well-bred woman of fashion" might claim.[34]

This sentimental narrative of femininity was not without its dangers, however. While the tender heroine, the woman of delicate sensibility, could be a devoted partner and matchless mother, a model of faithful attentiveness and care, the same qualities could cause her to fall into error and make her vulnerable to corruption. While the sensitive man could eschew the opinion of the world and remain, like Sir Charles Grandison, the sentimental hero of Samuel Richardson's eponymous novel, unspotted and pure, such a claim was much less likely to be well received from the woman of sentiment. Sensibility had its critics as well as converts in eighteenth-century society, and the revelations about Mrs. Rudd's life and conduct fell in with the conventional concern about the dangers of feelings ungrounded in Christian morality. Excessive cultivation of feelings was seen by some to be shallow and insincere; "there are not wanting instances of refined sentimentalists, who are contented with talking of virtues they never practice." Furthermore, sentimentalism might be a cover for more dangerous practices, which, by using the jargon, accents, and gestures of sentiment, were designed to deceive the unwary and defile the innocent. Women of sentiment were particularly open to this charge. One might note the other female characters to whom Mrs. Rudd was disparagingly compared. Like that infamous woman of Naples, Selini, who "persuaded no less than five hundred persons that she was a virgin, and always began her courtship with a piteous account of the delicacy of her temper, which would not permit her to cohabit with her husband, whom she abhorred," Mrs. Rudd was accused of using sensibility both to entrap the Perreaus and to fool Fielding. Like Mother Eve or Millwood, Mrs. Rudd was charged with employing her femininity to enrich herself and ruin her associates. As compelling as the reading public found the sentimental heroine when they opened the pages of their favorite novel, they were suspicious of such a figure in "real life." Readers undoubtedly found the sort of escape offered by sentimental tales delightful and emotionally gratifying, but their charm was enhanced by their unreality; in the mundane world, such attributes could be easily shammed, donned like masquerade clothes, to fool and confuse. At best, Mrs. Rudd might be a wild, unlikely character like Arabella, the sentimental heroine of Charlotte Lennox's *Female Quixote*; at worst, and much more likely, she might be a siren, singing a siren's song, only to batten on the flesh of her victims.[35]

"A CROW QUILL PEN DANGEROUS AS THE SWORD": MRS. RUDD'S BAD LANGUAGE

Mrs. Rudd's spirited replies to her critics could not have won her the sympathy of many newspaper or even novel readers. She had shown that "a crow quill pen" was as "dangerous as the sword," one poetic satire charged.[36] "Nor is it the low-lifed sarcasms of anonymous reptiles," she replied to another attack, "which can depreciate my conduct, or induce me to desist from doing what reason and humanity suggests; the approbation of my own heart and conscience will always be a sufficient consolation for doing good, however the world may mistake or judge me for it."[37] While novels allowed their female protagonists a proper pride, Mrs. Rudd's masculine sarcasm went well beyond the bounds even of literary propriety. Outside the novel, on encountering a woman discussing her sensibility in so strident a manner, most contemporaries must have felt that either crime, madness, or desertion had already occurred or were soon to follow.[38]

If Mrs. Rudd displayed what might even be termed an excessive sympathy and femininity for which she was derided and criticized, she was neither a timid nor a passive woman. Her pride and self-respect demanded a certain deference and civility. When, after their arrest, she was confronted by the brothers, who burst into her room, demanding to speak with her, she rebuked them both "in so resolute and forcible a manner that they turned upon their heels and retired." Here, too, there were literary parallels. Like Mrs. Rudd, Ellena di Rosalba, the heroine of Radcliffe's *The Italian,* claimed that it was the "pride of conscious worth [that] revived her courage," that she was governed by "a just regard for her own dignity." A woman proud of her resoluteness and "manly" determination,[39] Rudd used, or perhaps overused, the language of self-approbation to explain her "unfeminine" determination.

Mrs. Rudd combined this strength of character with strength of mind. She was a well-read woman who used what she had learned to shape and tell her story. When James Boswell interviewed her in 1776, he noted with interest the books she had about her: a copy of a court calendar, Duncan's *Logic,* Watt's *Logic, Johnsoniana,* Pope's *Essay on Man* as well as his *Essay on Criticism,* and "a very good novel against the practice of some men in gaining the affections of young ladies only for conquest, as they soon neglect them."[40] This catalogue displayed both her intelligence and its quality. If sentimental novels with their simple moral conclusions played a significant role in shaping her thought, so did works of logic. As important were the books that offered collections of clever quotes and witty comments from Johnson, Garrick, and Samuel Foote, in which one found both gossip and the extravagant use of satire to humble one's opponents. The books on logic offered more than simple guidance in argument. They proposed that logic was a science especially suited to the challenges of modern life. Duncan advised that since we live in a various world, the reader should develop "powers and faculties" for dealing with these difficulties. One was "happy or miserable in proportion as we know how to frame a right judgment of things, and shape our actions agreeably to the circumstances in which we are placed." Watt offered a more moral, less practical, view of logic. "Think seriously with yourself," he advised, "how many follies and sorrows you had escaped, and how much guilt and misery you had prevented, if from your early years you had but taken due pains to judge aright concerning persons, times and things."[41] Such books were more than merely ornamental; Rudd used her readings to give her writing an almost masculine, certainly a well-bred, persuasiveness. In letters bearing her name she cited not only classical works, like Milton's *Paradise Lost* and Shakespeare's *The Merchant of Venice,* but also contemporary popular works, like Anstey's *Bath Guide.*[42] Several of the anonymous letters in her behalf relied on the same sort of cultural authority and may well have been written, either wholly or in part, by her. They begin or end with verses, from Shakespeare, Young, or Mason's *Elfrida;* one even quotes from Sir William Draper's letters on the quality of compassion.[43] Like the argument from origins, the argument from intellectual attainment was meant to demonstrate to the public that Rudd was a woman of substance whose life was deeper and more meaningful than her bon tonish exterior might suggest.

This was not the only use made of her reading, however. The praise she bestowed upon Junius at the conclusion of one of her pamphlets may suggest another significant model. Junius's anonymous letters, which Mrs. Rudd praised for their "happier and more beautiful energy,"[44] mingled principled criticism with personal attacks. Mrs. Rudd clearly had other models to draw upon, but she seems on many occasions to have been striving for the same kind of effect as Junius. Even if she had not been influenced by the style, she certainly was aware of his tactics in conducting a campaign of letters and pamphlets. Like him, she never sought to answer her opponents' charges directly; rather she dismissed them out of hand. A case in point revolved around the famous Stewart letter. Full of affection for Mrs. Rudd and violent in its portrait of all the Perreaus, perhaps it overshot its mark. The prose alone hinted at a too-close relationship with her. By the end of May, several letters had charged that there was no John Stewart, that the letter signed with that name had come from her pen, that he was just another figment of Mrs. Rudd's imagination. Mrs. Rudd responded with a letter under her own name—a remarkable performance, even by her own standards. She replied to her critics that even if her uncle had not written the letter, such an issue lay only between herself and him, while the important point was that the letter contained a true account of the case. "I really apprehend," she wrote, "that we were both, and each of us at liberty to do that which we might think proper, without becoming reprehensible or accountable to any one for it; nor can I see, if a thousand letters had been wrote, while they contained strict truth, that it authorises people to be impertinent to me, much less am I obliged to give reasons why and wherefore things are or are not." This pose, its tone of imperious truth teller borrowed perhaps from Junius, ran through all her work. This defense of herself, this self-description as the beleaguered but undaunted person of transparent honesty, subtly underlay many of her written defenses. "I never," she wrote, "imposed a fallacious story on the public; I rest my defence on stubborn facts, and plain-told truths." She had no doubt that these facts and truths would triumph over the lies being told about her. She returned time and again to the power of the forces arrayed against her, but she never expressed despair or foreboding. She only asked "the impartial part of mankind not to condemn me unheard, or suffer their minds to be warpt by prejudice, by a specious story, supported by an interested, numerous party."[45]

As we have seen, the public response to her letters and writings was as multiplicitous as her own confessed motives. Much of this response was articulated in terms of her literary style, as though a judgment about her writing skill could be translated into one about her innocence or guilt. While her supporters considered her style "strongly marked with humanity, and every period closes with heart-felt tender sensation," even some of those who accused her of falseness could note that her "Volumes in Folio" were "elegantly written." Most detractors, however, criticized her writing, satirizing its heat and vehemence. Commenting on her self-attributed "unadorned Truths and conscious INNOCENCE," "Plain Truth" questioned these virtues, "which she so emphatically in Capitals asserts."[46] "Lycurgus" also criticized her style, adding that he thought "a less impetuous (I might add *abusive*) language would not lose her the countenance of those who would wish to be her friends." "Justice," however, went much further, asserting that "a thorough knowledge of the *vulgar tongue* is all the education [she had] ever received." Other critics merely lambasted "her letters, ridiculous as they are," or said they "bespoke a total Ignorance of her own Language."[47]

Mrs. Rudd and her friends responded in kind. Although she insisted that she would not "condescend to answer anonymous letters," she did note the "vulgarism of the stile, the palpable actual lies and ignorant insolence" they contained. Her supporters went even further, accusing her critics' writings of being "a compound of falsity and low-lif'd abuse; with an *affectation* of being very smart, you are very stupid, glaringly ignorant and vulgar." She seemed to relish trading blows with her opponents, but the venomous prose of her resentment clashed with the language of her sentimental pose. Although she presented herself as an innocent and loving woman in a world full of enemies, her abusive language seemed out of touch with her self-portrayal. She had told the Perreaus that Robert Adair had plotted to cut her off from William Adair's bounty. Valentine Rudd pursued her relentlessly. Frankland sought her death; Wilkes colluded in the scheme. Henry Dagge and Col. Kinder joined together to betray her to the authorities. And, above all, the Perreaus, despite all she had done for them, now defamed her and offered her as a sacrifice to cover their own iniquity. Even the meekest creature, she seemed to say, must rise up against such treatment. A fierce anger bubbled just below the surface and often erupted into the many stories she told of her life and trials. "The wickedness and infamy of my accusers' deeds, and their whole treatment of, and behavior to me, will best speak my innocence and their guilt."[48]

It was this combination of styles, using elements of both the pathetic and the combative, swinging between images of insulted innocence and resolute defiance and retribution, that so enraged and fascinated contemporaries. She tended to overwrite, to swing between lofty portrayals of herself and her motives and savage, belittling indictments of her enemies. At one moment she expressed concern about her children; at others she showed more anxiety about her property, which she listed in great detail. She often employed the clichés of sentimental writing when describing her feelings, but resorted to biting sarcasm to characterize her opponents. She claimed that her only concern was to present truth and facts, certain as she was that they would "ever prevail over falsehood and fabricated scandal."[49] Excess was the rule in everything she wrote, whether it was in the length, the detail, the violence of her language in describing her foes, or the pathos with which she represented her own situation and injured sensibility.

There is no evidence that Mrs. Rudd's writings won her supporters. If anything, her prose was more likely to inspire satire. The inconsistencies in the stories she paraded before her readers should have been as damning as her handwriting on the forged notes. Her writing activities actually supported the Perreaus' characterization of her as a spinner of tales, fabricating relationships where none existed and acting out her fantasies. There was also something disconcerting and annoying about the insistent way she turned to the press. Most troubling of all, the tenacity and combativeness of her pen suggested to many readers the work of a "masculine" mind rather than the silent suffering they expected of a good woman.

MRS. RUDD OR MRS. STEWART: THE BELLE WIDOWS

Mrs. Rudd turned to print in 1775–1776 to present a potent if not very consistent self-portrait and thereby both defend her character and save her life. Over a decade later she once again used print in an effort to justify herself and rescue her fortunes. There are differences but also striking similarities between the writings of these two periods. Her later pieces, *Mrs. Stewart's Case* (1788) and *The Belle Widows* (1789), revealed her as an older, more desperate woman who still hoped that her "quality" would be recognized, that she would be properly rewarded for her outstanding personality and character traits, and that she would secure admission to the world of elegance, wealth, and taste to which she had always claimed a right.

It is likely that *Mrs. Stewart's Case* and *The Belle Widows* were written during Mrs. Rudd's incarceration for debt in 1787. As she explained, in 1785 she "voluntarily relinquished a dependence, which, consistent with my better feelings, I could no longer retain. Impoverished as this resignation left me, yet obliged to support that decent appearance of circumstances, without which neither reputation nor respect can be maintained, I necessarily became embarrassed, and contracted unavoidable debts."[50] Adopting her mother's maiden name, Stewart, to stress the affinity, she wrote to her high-born relations, the Moiras, Galloways, and Rawdons, appealing for their assistance and for a pension. They sent some money, and did so on two subsequent occasions. However, her hopes for a permanent allowance were soon frustrated. In this, her own celebrity, or notoriety, worked against her. Recalling in many ways the case of Richard Savage, a friend of Dr. Johnson's who claimed aristocratic parentage and financial support, Mrs. Rudd's demands on her "families" were first met and then rejected. Like Savage, Rudd perhaps hoped to embarrass or blackmail her relations into support; like Savage, Rudd learned that such assistance was at best temporary.[51] Although Lord Rawdon, a purported relation, at some point had given credence to Mrs. Rudd's claim to be a family member, at least insofar as to aid her with several sums of money, once she was confined to prison for debt, her "relations" washed their hands of her. Neither he nor Lord Galloway responded to her appeals. Her creditors had released her so that she might carry on her appeals, but she had not succeeded. She warned her family that she would appeal to the public if they did not respond to her just claims for aid. Her pamphlet, *Mrs. Stewart's Case,* was the fulfillment of this promise.

Her response to what she considered familial abandonment was to sally forth one more time to assert her rights and defend her reputation. She published her case in terms reminiscent of her campaign a decade earlier. In her pamphlet she spoke of her disinclination as a private person to put herself before the public. As she had fourteen years before, she also described herself in terms of birth, family, and misfortune. She once again pointed to her descent from Scottish kings, authenticated by the keeper of the Lyon Office of Scotland. However, adversity, she claimed, had always stalked her.

From my being an only surviving child, and an orphan, I am consequently without the advantage of parental or fraternal relative; yet
having cousins and alliances whose opulence gives ample power of
munificence, from those I might reasonably expect to benefit; and that
people high in rank, and proud of ancestors, would at least respect
their own birth in one their kinswoman. But vain is the folly of hoping that the ties of affinity can engage, or the plea of misfortune avail,
where callous posterity reigns; where the sense of humanity is stifled
by sordidness; and the pampered insolence of superior fortune leads
the possessors to conceive, that they may neglect the obligations of
propriety, and the duties of kindred.

She complained that, despite her acquittal, gossip and hard language continued to slander her.

Her account was full of the familiar details. She blasted Rawdon and her
relations as hypocrites who did not live up to the standards of their class.
"My sex protects your Lordship from personal chastisement," she hissed. As
a defenseless woman, she must appeal to "public judgment" for help. "Every
liberal indulgence [is to be hoped for] from a generous and enlightened publick, to whose judgment I presume to appeal." If no one called Rawdon to
account, no character would be safe from calumny, she asserted. Rawdon
had become the sinister figure behind a campaign to leave her in misery. Like
the other villains who had plotted her downfall, "Lord Rawdon was not
merely unfriendly but actively malevolent." In a postscript she wrote bitterly
of what she called the efforts made to prejudice the public against her. Long
after the fact, she continued to protest against a familiar reading of her case:
"That my trial produced nothing but a full confirmation of their exclusive
guilt, and my entire innocence, the execution of their sentence is the best
proof. To arraign the purity of the proofs, is, I believe, an impeachment of
individual integrity and legal rectitude, exceeding, in outrage to JURIES, and
insult to the legislature, whatever has hitherto been offered to this country,
or tolerated by Englishmen." Flattering the reading public, English humanity, and the jury system, she explained her parlous circumstances as the effects
of that "VULGAR PREJUDICE first excited against me by sanguinary conspiracy
and fraudful artifice." Like her earlier attacks on the incompetence of Frankland's writing, she adopted the same criticism in response to negative comments of her pamphlet: of one of these, Mrs. Rudd noted that "his Lordship
seems indebted to the *exalted sentiments* and *clerk-like* qualities of his porter

or groom."[52] Rudd's combative style, with its superior disdain and proud claims to connection and family, seemed even more strident and assertive than her earlier efforts. One major change between this version of her life and the earlier stories was the absence of any mention of her children or husband. No longer relying on the appeal of sentimental motherhood, being unattached and unallied to any family of her own making, her only remaining resource could be the putative family of which, from the beginning, she claimed to be a proud offspring. She was a woman alone, with only her honor and sense of self to sustain her.

Unlike her earlier epistolary attempts, however, this piece met with uniform hostility and denunciation in the press. One particularly virulent letter, addressed to her and signed "Justice," concluded with the following castigation: "Retire Madam, into perpetual obscurity; suffer not your vanity to delude you into an opinion, that your literary talents are deserving the notice of the Public, or that though the mildness of the law has secured you immunity, mankind are in the least mistaken with respect to the true nature of your character." The pamphlet's only positive review, probably written by Rudd herself, was found pasted into Sir William Musgrave's copy of *Mrs. Stewart's Case*. This clipping described the pamphlet as "perhaps one of the most spirited, and at the same time the most elegant and temperate compositions that has appeared since the days of Junius ... This may be regarded as a puff for the book;—be it so; it is however different from other puffs in one respect—it is *literally true*." Neither Musgrave nor the public at large agreed with the anonymous reviewer.[53] Whatever her cachet or fascination more than a decade before, by the late 1780s Mrs. Rudd and English society both had changed. At the most superficial level, Mrs. Rudd was no longer "interesting," no longer young or notorious. The accusations of the aging demi-rep did not win the admiration or evoke the compassion that the woes of the younger woman had. At a deeper level, she had lost the public's sympathy for other reasons; perhaps the plea of "female weakness" no longer mitigated her profligate past and unsavory associations, perhaps the absence of offspring or the public's memory of what happened to the man she had called "husband" weakened her claim on public pity. The bluster of *Mrs. Stewart's Case*, with its proud demands for support and its "smiles of defying contempt"[54] could easily be dismissed as exhibiting a deranged and malicious intellect, an unwomanly and unfeeling harshness.

This may be why her next effort was a novel, a comedy of sorts of the life of the *beau monde*. This work, originally called *Vulgar Prejudice*, appeared anonymously in 1789 as *The Belle Widows*.[55] Though as a piece of art it is a total failure, it is of great interest insofar as it gives us one last glimpse of how Mrs. Rudd would have liked her life to have developed, what she thought her talents merited, and what reward (albeit in a kinder world of fiction) such talents should have received.

This is a story of two "belle widows," unfortunate in their first marriages, who find happiness and public recognition in their second. While the bulk of *The Belle Widows* is about the courtships and marriage of the first widow, Margaretta Tempest, there is reason to think that the original novel, perhaps more closely autobiographical than the rewritten work, centered on the life and trials of the second, Augusta DeCourville. The name of the latter heroine is reminiscent of some of the French pseudonyms that Mrs. Rudd was alleged to have taken—the Countess Moriencourt, Caroline de Grosberg, Madame De la Rochette or MalFaisons. Mrs. DeCourville is described as a woman who has suffered (although we never learn how or for what reason) but who is proud and cannot bear insult. This, the author notes, is a "great but dangerous disposition." Mrs. DeCourville treats all calumny with profound resentment and revenge, but she holds all confidences sacred, thinks the best of people, and is often imposed on. Her distinction, according to the author, consists of her physical beauty and mental vigor. She is courageous under trial but conquered by kindness. She combines a manly reason with feminine perfection. Like Mrs. Rudd, she has had her faith in aristocratic honor shaken, although she still thinks family pride proper and important. In short, she is, like Mrs. Rudd, the *Victim of Prejudice*.[56]

The second and only surviving version of the story revolves around Margaretta Tempest. Enough similarities remain between the two characters and their author to make an investigation worthwhile. A scion of an ancient family, having married a first husband through "juvenile thoughtlessness," as much to get to London as anything else, Margaretta soon realizes that she has made a terrible mistake. Not only does she not love Mr. Tempest, but he soon reveals his true nature and brutally mistreats her. Her delicate and indignant mind rebels at such treatment and they agree to part. Tempest goes abroad, and after a while Margaretta receives word that he has died. Although she has no certain proof of his demise, and there is a passing reference to the possibility that he may still be alive, Mrs. Tempest presents herself as a widow, for as a separated wife she has been treated with envy and scorn by society. In the Tempest marriage we read only too closely the version of her own marriage that Mrs. Rudd wished to present. Furthermore, Mrs. Tempest, like Mrs. Rudd, is by no means without faults, but they are amiable ones, for she is described as a rather gay widow. Indulging in follies rather than vices, Margaretta is a bit of a flirt and a coquette. Despite these vagaries of character, she unites in her person two usually disparate qualities—the splendid and the amiable. In addition, all her male admirers remark on her powers of observation and the charms of her conversation.[57] As in Boswell's account of Rudd's varied chat, ranging from family gossip to philosophy, Tempest combines mental with physical attraction.

The novel is filled with clothes, parties, and masquerades. Like the many press accounts of the clothes and headdresses of the Perreaus and Mrs. Rudd, the clothing and hairstyles of the novel's protagonists are described in lavish and extravagant detail. Verisimilitude and interest lie, we are told, in the details. And along with the accoutrements and pleasures of fashionable life, the novel is filled with real, famous people, only thinly disguised. Presented as the Nabob General Sumpter, "the renowned conqueror of *rupees*," Robert Lord Clive makes his first appearance in the novel in "a glaring equipage, caparisoned and fine enough for the Grand Mogul himself."[58] Lady Almeira Carpenter, a notorious women of the ton, appears as Lady Almeira Freely, and John Wilkes, MP, newspaper polemicist, and political agitator appears as Mr. Jesuit, a man whose "brilliant talents, patriotism, and above all, his sapient spirit—unclogged by the aukward diffidence which often impedes the aggrandizement of less *wise* folk—had raised him from the obscurity of a brandy-vault to senatorial dignity, and a pension. While *in office* he had realized, through the medium of honest *Will* and *Dick,* an estate sufficient for qualification."[59] In the reference to Wilkes, we recall the ambiguous press whispers of a soured relationship between Wilkes and Rudd, or at least an acquaintanceship in that peculiar Wilkite world of political opposition, personal debt, and sexual license.[60] True to its subtitle, the novel firmly identifies itself and its protagonists with London's bon ton, with her charmed and charming inner circle.

Several novelistic moments practically jump off the page when one knows the life and history of its author. In a conversation between Sir Edmund Stafford and the charming Margaretta, the latter gives an extended and malicious description of jumped-up middle-class people, emboldened by an increase in fortune, who live as and pretend to be upper crust. While Sir Edmund describes these folk as "courtlings," Margaretta uses the term "mushroom quality," a variation of the description used by John Stewart in his open letter to the Perreaus. After declaring her undying love for Belmour, she finds herself wooed by Stafford; she is pleased rather than annoyed, for she thinks it entirely possible to love two men at once. Odd, above all, is the discussion of the contingency of human affairs and how all things are governed by fortune: the author, in a philosophic afterword, remarks, "We are continually taught to see upon what very *luck,* what mere breath of *contingency,* depends our fate—And how ignorantly absurd, how every way presumptuous, are those judgments which ascribe to the merit or demerit of the individual, that or that fortune!—where accident alone govern!"[61]

These comments, however, seem almost incidental to the main outlines of the story. At its end, both belle widows are rewarded in a fantastical surfeit of happy endings. Although Rudd said this was not a romance, its denouement is more unreal than even that of *Sir Charles Grandison*. Both women, both belle widows, win peerless husbands, cash, and cachet. Margaretta marries Belmour, whose fiancée conveniently dies and leaves him her fortune; Augusta marries Sir Edmund, heir to an earl, and the present earl, his uncle, gives her, for her sole use, a wedding gift of £50,000. Despised as widows, the two young women are wooed and flattered by all when they become wealthy, powerful, and beloved wives. Disappointed in life, writing in debtors' prison, aging and a pariah, Mrs. Rudd imagined herself twice-blessed, receiving a doubly appropriate reward for a life of bad luck and fruitless effort.

TELLING TALES: MRS. RUDD'S SELF-REPRESENTATIONS

"Her story," wrote one early critic, "appears extremely contradictory and evasive." As though these words were not condemnatory enough, he went on to present Mrs. Rudd as an embodiment of corruption and of a shrill and self-promoting, deceptive depravity. "Vice," he concluded, "when retired to the shade of shame and sorrow, should be pitied; but when she boldly steps forth, expecting our support and approbation, let her be detested and punished." These sentiments were what one might have expected. More surprising was their failure to silence her or close her access to the press. While the second of these factors can perhaps be explained by the hunger of the dailies of the 1770s for scandalous news, Rudd's perseverance and apparent confidence in her ability to vindicate her life and behavior are more mysterious. Perhaps she completely believed what she wrote in a letter to the Perreau sisters: "I am neither afraid nor ashamed of anything I do, say, or write."[62] In any case, she continued her relentless campaign to clear her name and win her rightful place in society by all the means she had available.

Her opponents never found a way to check her energy or counter her use of vitriolic invective. The courtesan posing as a virtuous woman was a staple in the plays of the period. Her fantasy of noble connections and honest wealth could be seen as a symptom of a diseased and debauched female imagination. Portraying her as a pretender to virtue and sentiment, however, as one who merely employed the appearance of "fairness" for her own sinister purpose, did not disarm her. Indeed, her adversaries had few terms available to describe what was so compelling about her performance. Yes, she was both sentimental heroine and pretender to aristocratic birth, but her stridency, her vindictiveness, combined with her mastery of detail, all fell outside the normal conventions for representing gender. Her detractors criticized her writing, satirizing its heat and vehemence. Nonetheless, they could not diminish its power or cool its ardor.

From what Mrs. Rudd wrote one can quickly grasp the most important elements in her self-representation. First, there was birth and high relations. Then there were her own qualities, her fine sensibility, her loyalty to husband and children. Then there was her situation in the world, attacked by a host of enemies who sought to deprive her of reputation as well as life. Mrs. Rudd tirelessly offered a portrait of herself whose chief elements were beauty, elegance, birth, sensibility, and, above all, aristocratic refinement. The steady stream of these portrayals suggested less a self-conscious and cynical manipulation of the press than the continuous efforts of a woman who believed everything that she wrote, whether the belief preceded or followed from the writing. One author, writing after the events of 1775–1776, assumed that his or her readers knew "what Mrs. R's publications have spoke her to be; but self representation and facts are frequently very opposite things." Representations and facts, however, were not such "opposite things" in this case. The question with Mrs. Rudd was never simply one of the truth or falsehood of what she asserted, for in many ways she seemed to have no sense of balance or control in, or over, her writing. She wrote passionately, often repeating facts or expressing opinions that could only injure her case. In an age when imitation and acting were both admired and feared, she presented a challenge. She embodied at one and the same time the most obvious lying and yet an unnerving sense that she believed in the truth of her own performance. This excess, combined with the early appeals to sentiment, perhaps defined her initial ability to fascinate. Her performance did not exactly win confidence or belief, but it possessed a power that few could resist. She won a grudging acquiescence, even from the worldly who never accepted her sincerity. "Her story," one author wrote, "when told in her own words, was not a little romantic." By the end, however, in the 1780s, the public seemed wearied and unconcerned about the fate of a self-involved creator of tales who demanded more attention than she deserved. Her ability to compel interest had finally worn out.[63]

Nine

MRS. RUDD ON TRIAL

By DECEMBER 1775, MANY were impatient for Mrs. Rudd's trial. The public had endured nearly nine months of controversy concerning the case. It had listened time and again to the rehearsal of the same facts and opinions. Irritation was mounting. The Perreau defenders complained of the repeated delays. Mrs. Rudd's trial had been put off several times for the judges to decide the legal claims in her case and to give her time to prepare her defense. One letter expressed annoyance at the "doubts, opinions, and scruples, among these sages, on a point of law which I expected to find by [this] time made clear to every attorney's clerk." The legal questions had been raised and settled by Lord Mansfield; nothing new had surfaced in all the subsequent deliberations. The continued debate argued "a shameful inattention, or incapacity somewhere."[1]

Few people could have expected new revelations at her trial. The issue had become more tactical. It was now a question of fairness for the brothers, perhaps of saving their lives. If the justices at Bow Street had made a mistake, as many correspondents as well as a majority of the judges argued, here was an opportunity to set it right. Putting Mrs. Rudd on trial restored balance to the proceedings. The Perreau supporters looked not for answers but for a conviction, which was required if they were to plead for a pardon for one or both of the brothers. Although the King and his ministers had refused to commit themselves on this point, the assumption was universal that pleas for mercy would be heard. Her conviction seemed within reach. The judges, in their well-publicized deliberations, appeared to give the jury the lead. Mrs. Rudd entered the court at a considerable disadvantage.

This case had already produced one memorable trial. Robert's trial had shown what a skillful defense could do. The impressions still echoed powerfully six months later. His counsel had presented a carefully crafted story; the evidence supporting it was strong and consistent. Robert's own person, the calm dignity he had displayed in reading his statement, and the long list of impressive character witnesses he had called all operated to create a solemn and coherent portrait of a man betrayed by his innocence. The general decorum that marked the trial seemed to second this impression. Only the jury's failure to be persuaded marred the performance.

Mrs. Rudd's trial was to be memorable, too, even surpassing the effect of the earlier one, though it was the antithesis—the word is almost not strong enough—to Robert's orderly affair. Unlike Robert, Rudd faced no restrained prosecution. Her opponents were determined to convict her. Her counsel responded in kind, encouraged no doubt by her own adversarial instincts. Rudd's prosecutors employed witnesses with the keenest and most obvious interest in securing a guilty verdict. Mrs. Rudd's lawyers badgered, browbeat, and finally humiliated every one of them. Charges of gross impropriety and misconduct flew around the courtroom, touching both prosecution and defense. By the end of the trial the judicial process was in a shambles, reputations had been blasted, and the much-vaunted English jury was made to look capricious. It may have appeared to many, on the eve of the trial, impossible for the case to do more damage to society's self-image and confidence. They were wrong. The debacle that followed was, if possible, worse than anything that had preceded it. As with so many other aspects of this case, the spectacle was as unseemly as it was riveting.

Rudd's trial opened on December 8, 1775. Once again it attracted a large crowd. "The avidity of the public to hear this trial was such, that the galleries were crowded soon after daylight." Additional constables had to be placed at the doors to keep people from forcing their way in. The elite of London society was in attendance. The courtroom became so hot that some ladies had to leave because they were in danger of fainting. The Lord Mayor, judges, and aldermen assembled a little before the hour. At nine she was brought in and charged, on four indictments, with forgery. A chair was provided for her use if she felt like sitting. Mrs. Rudd appeared "neatly dressed in second-mourning." The papers were uniformly impressed by her style and performance. "[D]ressed in black, in the same taste of decent elegance which distinguished her when she was brought up before," she "displayed the most astonishing composure ever seen on a similar occasion." The effect upon the audience, even on those doubtful of her character, was profound. "The general deportment of Mrs. Rudd, in so awful and trying a situation, so far raised the admiration of all present, that every spectator became interested in her cause."[2] One witness, seated near her at the bar, thought that she "looked pale," but "such was her address, that no one could have discovered in her manner the least consciousness" of evil.[3] Rumors had circulated as early as July that she had "written every part of her own defense, which she intends to speak at her approaching trial."[4] The public had become familiar enough with her literary output that few could doubt the report. Everyone expected a remarkable trial.

Shortly before the trial, a portrait etching of Mrs. Rudd appeared. This was based on a portrait painted by Daniel Dodd, who was also to paint this trial. We do not know the circumstances under which she and Dodd met, or who first suggested the portrait. Nor do we know how Sibelius, a Dutch engraver whom Sir Joseph Bankes frequently employed to produce flower etchings, came to transform the portrait into an etching. Dodd exhibited the portrait at the Free Society of Artists showing in 1776, but it seems to have disappeared and perhaps been destroyed. The etching survives, though, and it portrays Mrs. Rudd as she must have most wanted to be presented. She looks confident but innocent, dressed in restrained but exquisite manner, and it is tempting to suppose that this portrait, like so many of her addresses to the public, was her attempt to convince the world at large of her guiltlessness.

The trial lasted from nine in the morning until almost eight in the evening.[5] The prosecution, conducted by William Lucas, Henry Howarth, and Murphy, presented a less than persuasive case; the defense, shared between Serjeant Davy, Thomas Davenport, and Cowper, was alternately hectoring and humorous. The trial fell into three distinct acts, almost like a stage play. First the presiding judge, Aston, addressed Mrs. Rudd, telling her why she was on trial and informing her of the opinion of the twelve judges. Then the prosecution presented its witnesses and laid out its case. Although the testimony of Mrs. Robert Perreau and Admiral Frankland figured prominently, a number of minor actors appeared as well. In this part of the presentation Mrs. Rudd's counsel worked hardest, both directly to discredit the opposing evidence and indirectly to lay the groundwork for a further attack on the character and sincerity of the prosecutors. In the midst of this examination there suddenly appeared the revelation of an attempt by the accused and one of her lawyers to suborn a witness. Finally, her much anticipated defense proved an anticlimax. Overall, the trial was full of dark hints and sly innuendo, false starts and testimony that led nowhere. Witnesses became confused and angry. The jury must have had a difficult time making sense of the proceedings. The judge had little success bringing order out of the tumult.

In reply to the reading of her indictment, Mrs. Rudd "cheerfully acquiesced in the opinion of the judges," pleaded not guilty, and declared that "she would be tried by God and her country."[6] Of the four indictments, it was clear to everyone in the courtroom that her fate rested on the outcome of the charge that she had signed the name of William Adair to a bond used as collateral for securing a loan from Sir Thomas Frankland. She faced this charge because the offense predated the events to which she had testified in March. But the form of the accusation presented the prosecution with peculiar difficulties. To repeat a point made earlier, it was far easier to prove the uttering of a forged instrument than to prove the actual forgery. Both charges relied upon circumstantial evidence for their proof; the act of uttering necessarily involved a witness, however, while the composition of the note usually took place in secret. Suspicious behavior in the former case was taken as proof of guilty knowledge. Proving that someone had been responsible for penning a forged note was a much more difficult task. The prosecution in this instance operated under the additional liability of having to avoid using any evidence that referred to the crimes of which the brothers had been convicted. This limitation meant that it had to draw its proof from a period for which there were fewer witnesses. These combined burdens would have been hard to overcome under the best of circumstances.

HENRIETTA PERREAU ON THE STAND

Mrs. Robert Perreau was called as the prosecution's first witness. The logic of such a move seems clear. She was the only witness from within the household who might have status enough to offer convincing proof of Mrs. Rudd's suspicious behavior. Perhaps the prosecution hoped that the evident contrast in character and moral standing between her and Mrs. Rudd would work against the accused. The Perreau forces may have expected that sympathy for her and her husband would operate upon a jury conscious that the only hope for Robert lay in Mrs. Rudd's conviction. They no doubt believed that Henrietta's suffering and her gentility had earned her respectful treatment. If so, they were to be disappointed.

Henrietta inspired deep hostility in Mrs. Rudd. The latter's anger had mounted steadily since the first disclosure of the crime. Mrs. Rudd, sensitive to every slight, was alert to the comparisons being drawn between the two women, to her decided disadvantage. "I could forgive an *injury,*" she wrote in her "Case," "but not an intended insult." Where once they had lived on terms of intimacy, and Mrs. Rudd had "esteemed and loved her," now Henrietta denied the relationship and propagated "detestable and indelicate untruths" about her. Mrs. Rudd claimed to detect her hand behind many of the schemes concocted to her disadvantage. She exhibited "a species of mean depravity which exceedingly surprizes me."[7] Mrs. Rudd continued to complain that the press was fooled by Henrietta's "art," and that it was her task to expose the truth. "I shall only observe," she wrote in May, "that destitute herself of sentiment and the amiable virtues which result from a feeling heart, her little mind prompts her to revile and misrepresent me, because heaven has indued me with both."[8] In June, now confined and awaiting trial, Rudd railed against the injustice of the invidious comparisons. "Have not I three destitute, helpless children!" she thundered. "Is her situation to be lamented more than mine?" She had "the luck of being a wife," "otherwise she has an equal right to be suspected as me; nay, more if *probabilities* were attended to." "Wherein consists her merit?"[9] For Mrs. Rudd, Henrietta's treatment summarized all the injustice, all the disappointment, she felt at her sudden fall from fortune. The trial now brought them face to face.

No sooner was Henrietta called than the defense challenged her status, arguing that she was disqualified because she had an interest in the outcome of the case. English procedure was strict on this point; a witness was disqualified if an interest, usually understood as economic, could be demonstrated. In this instance the challenge was novel, but like other aspects of the defense strategy, it had already been rehearsed in the papers. "Now the law," wrote one of Rudd's defenders, "very wisely rejects the testimony of the wife, where the life of the husband is concerned, knowing the insuperable motives which will induce her at all events to preserve it, and that it is to be supposed her affection will overcome every obstacle, if his safety and life may be preserved thereby." Other correspondents asked why Henrietta was testifying against Mrs. Rudd when she might as well have appeared at Daniel's trial. Her appearance now was unseemly. The fact that her testimony had not been previously used suggested to Rudd's advocates that some new sinister motive was at work. "Do not these considerations," one correspondent complained, "suggest to every one the idea that her accusation is merely an afterthought, a scheme fabricated against Mrs. Rudd?"[10] Another letter, quite likely from Rudd, said that Mrs. Robert Perreau's testimony would make a mockery of justice. It begged the public to divest itself of prejudice and to look "upon this unfortunate woman [Rudd herself] with an eye of pity and compassion." "I am persuaded much has been said in prejudice of Mrs. Rudd, with a view to exculpate the Perreaus." The author appealed to "an English jury" for help, calling upon it to "perceive the spirit of rancour and malevolence" that was responsible for "this shameful prosecution."[11]

Serjeant Davy began his examination on this question of qualification by asking Mrs. Perreau if she hoped for her husband's pardon. At first avoiding a direct answer, she finally admitted that she supposed Mrs. Rudd's conviction would operate in her husband's favor. Cowper followed with a long discussion of how the very suspicion of interest should invalidate a witness's testimony. He pointed to a civil case where Mansfield had disqualified a witness who had simply imagined that he might have a stake in the outcome. Lucas, for the prosecution, protested that the acceptance of such an argument would cripple all criminal prosecutions, since it could be objected that a witness expecting a reward or the restoration of goods should be disqualified. Justice Aston ruled against the objection; Mrs. Perreau could testify. She might, he pointed out, hope for a pardon, but the conviction of Mrs. Rudd did not guarantee it, nor would her acquittal necessarily rule it out. However, Baron Burland conceded more to the defense when he admitted that Henrietta's interest in Robert's fate might "possibly lessen the credit of her testimony with the jury."[12] The defense must have been satisfied with this ruling. The objection set the tone for the trial; the defense would exploit every opportunity to cast doubt upon the integrity or reliability of a prosecution witness. It would spare no one's feelings; it would respect neither person nor social standing.[13]

Mrs. Perreau, once she began her testimony, offered a detailed account of the events relating to one of Frankland's bonds. She told of seeing Mrs. Rudd give her husband a bond for £5300, signed by William Adair, on December

24, 1775. Carefully examined on the details she offered, Henrietta claimed to remember not only the amount but also the names that appeared on the bond. When pressed to explain why she looked at it with such care, she replied that, "having never seen a bond, she was curious to know the nature and form of one," and so she had studied it well. Henrietta then described the eagerness with which Mrs. Rudd waited for Robert's return. Once she received Frankland's draft, she hastened off, saying that Adair would want to know the outcome of the transaction. The next day, Christmas Day, Daniel and Mrs. Rudd dined at Golden Square, along with some Welsh friends of the Perreaus', a Mrs. Williamson and a clergyman, Mr. Barker. Later that evening, Mrs. Rudd, Robert, and Daniel discussed how to make up the full £4000 in order to settle with Mr. Collins for the Harley Street house. Since Daniel denied having the funds on hand, Robert lent him the balance. These details were meant to establish the authority of Henrietta's memory. They became instead the target of a searching cross-examination.[14]

William Davy, who now undertook to question Mrs. Perreau, was an experienced counsel, some said "a master of the art," whose first major case, coincidentally, had been an unsuccessful defense of a forger in 1753. He had played a role in a number of celebrated cases, as a prosecutor of Elizabeth Canning and as a defender of the slave James Somerset. He had even been known to turn his humor against the formidable Mansfield.[15] Perhaps spurred on by Mrs. Rudd, he offered a full display of his skills in what at times seemed a ruthless attack upon the prosecution witnesses. He adopted a rough, confrontational, and often mocking tone to unsettle or anger them. Such a tactic was still unusual enough that it attracted hostile comment, but in this instance it proved effective. "Her counsellors," a witness recalled, "managed her defense with uncommon exertion and skill." Davy pressed Henrietta about how she could have overheard the brothers and Mrs. Rudd when she was entertaining guests. She replied that they were intimate friends and so she did not feel constrained to prevent them from hearing the discussion. She conceded that "they might have heard what passed." When asked why they were not in court, she said Mrs. Williamson was in the West Indies, while Mr. Barker had returned to Wales. Davy greeted this response with sarcasm, opining that "he believed it was not the wish of the witness that they should be present in Court." Her evidence was further undercut when another witness proved that Daniel had a balance of £600 in his account on the day when, as Henrietta testified, he was supposed to have borrowed £20 from Robert. This revelation, intended to cast doubt on the precision of her memory, was described in one paper "as a very *striking* circumstance."[16]

This cross-examination, according to one paper, "was so extremely abrupt, that she burst into tears and was near fainting." She had to be handed smelling salts and water in order to continue. One letter later claimed that she indeed had "fainted twice from his behavior only." She had to be "carried out of court in a state of insensibility," a witness remembered, and had not been able to return for a quarter of an hour. "The whole court was ready to cry shame" for the "hardness to a woman" that Davy displayed, through his "abrupt and cruel" language and manner. Another correspondent, writing after the trial, believed that "her weakness was her strength; for when the learned serjeant, with more humour than humanity, by a gross imputation, shocked and overpowered her spirits, the generous hearts of the audience liberally sympathized with her, and gave more credit to the genuine tears of affronted virtue, than to the callous jests of practiced ribaldry." This last claim was wishful thinking. Even this writer had to admit that the jury seemed less than fully convinced by her performance.[17] Having had so many months to prepare the defense, knowing in such detail the evidence that would appear against the defendant, Mrs. Rudd's counsel proved resourceful in calling into question the motives as well as the memories of the key prosecution witnesses.

FRANKLAND VERSUS RUDD

The prosecution fared little better when the plaintiff in the case, Sir Thomas Frankland, was called to give his evidence. The admiral's fate was doubly ironic; perhaps no one else's reputation was so injured by being swept up in this affair, and yet, given his deep antipathy to her, no one so lent himself to Mrs. Rudd's cause. Although the papers usually referred to him with the respect due one of his service and title, the reports often contained an undercurrent of mockery. Frankland had entered the navy in 1731 and had become an admiral in 1770. Despite his continued appearance on the flag list, he did not have active command after 1756. Originally from Yorkshire, his fortunes were profoundly influenced by imperial events. His father had been a governor of Fort William in Bengal, and he himself had married a daughter of the governor of South Carolina. An agent for the sale of captured ships in the West Indies, in 1760 he was caught up in a nasty struggle with the Treasury over a claim for £40,000 left from the sale of prizes. In 1766 a compromise led him to pay £30,000 by way of settlement. He had been elected an MP for Thirsk and was associated with the Rockingham group, but he was widely understood to put profit before political conviction. Tight-fisted, thin-skinned, and ill-tempered, Frankland made a far from ideal witness.[18]

It did not help his cause that he and Mrs. Rudd had a well-publicized history of confrontation. No one could imagine that he would be fair to the accused. Mrs. Rudd had made Frankland a particular target of her anger and abuse from the first letters she wrote to the papers. She struck out at him even before he became her formal prosecutor in the wake of the June trials. These attacks drove him into such a fury that he seemed increasingly to resemble Rudd's caricature of him. He was both suspicious and gullible. In some respects Rudd and Frankland were well matched, each possessing an inexhaustible passion to secure property and reputation, each capable of a relentless pursuit of those who had crossed or opposed her or him.

Frankland earned her ire as a result of his haste to secure his money after the first discovery of the crime. The Perreaus, advised by Dagge, still hoped that by satisfying their outstanding creditors they might forestall prosecution. They made a deal with Frankland that he could have the house in Harley Street along with all the goods it contained. Many of the possessions in the house belonged to Mrs. Rudd, including clothing and jewels, as well as furniture. She was not about to acquiesce quietly in Frankland's seizure of them. "I presume he thinks my poverty secures him from the power of the law," she wrote in early April. "I will not only have my right from him, but expose his whole behaviour to me upon this occasion."[19] In May she published a list of those goods she claimed to have bought with her own money and warned anyone buying them that she would prosecute to recover them. She portrayed the admiral as a scoundrel who had left her and her children destitute and nearly naked, consigning her to prison and them to the workhouse. One correspondent reported that she had written to him, informing him of his illegal measures in taking "her jewels, plate, furniture, wearing apparel, and other effects." She also severely reprimanded him for spreading "false and wicked scandals of her."[20] The drama of Mrs. Rudd's possessions, and the battle with the avaricious admiral, provided some of the most comic moments of the case.

Frankland elicited some of Mrs. Rudd's most astounding performances. In May, in a stinging letter written in the midst of this contest, she told him that she had "so thorough a contempt for you, and for your character, that I should deem you beneath my notice, were I not informed you take advantage of my silence." She demanded that he reveal the promises he had made to Robert in order to secure the surrender of her and Daniel's goods. He had, she charged, vowed not to prosecute the brothers, and then, once he had been reimbursed, had pressed Brooke to proceed against Daniel. "Your whole conduct on the occasion is dishonourable," she pronounced, "particularly towards me; detaining my wearing apparel, which was no part of the assignment, is an act of savage brutality, if not actual dishonesty." "MAMMON is your God!" she thundered with mounting passion. "To gratify your insatiable avarice, you illegally possessed yourself of, and now detain Daniel Perreau's property and mine, and was for sending our children to the workhouse, at the time you took possession of (at least) twelve thousand pounds worth of our effects." "This action alone," she continued, "shows the complexion of your heart: Such barbarity is surely a disgrace to human nature. Your conduct is a scandal to your rank, and the very name of gentleman."[21]

Extreme as was the language of this charge, she had not finished with her indictment of Frankland's character. The violence of her prose increased as the letter went on. His efforts to make her appear in a bad light were but feeble attempts to distract the public from his own reprehensible behavior. "You should reflect, Sir Thomas, when you take impertinent freedoms with my name, that you are speaking of a person greatly your superior; one who has the mind, as well as the manners, of a gentlewoman, and would think it a worse misfortune and reproach than any she has yet experienced, to resemble you in either." "Had you existed in Shakespeare's days, his character of Shylock might have been much heightened. The Jew would have the money, or the man's life; but you, a Christian, are not contented without having both." She cursed him for her children's sake, and she exposed him as the ally of Henrietta in spreading vicious lies about her. But Mrs. Rudd refused to be cowed by the injustices she faced. "I should be the wretch you represent me, or as mean as yourself, were I intimidated by such discourse. No, Sir, to your confusion and disappointment I shall stay here to render justice,—and give the lie to your scandal and that of my enemies."[22]

Mrs. Rudd's letters might have had less impact had Frankland not acted in ways that tended to render him ridiculous and culpable in the eyes of the press. The widespread rumor that he had refused to sign a petition on behalf of the brothers contributed to the picture of him as mean-spirited and vindictive.[23] In his eagerness to secure jewels in the possession of Daniel and

Mrs. Rudd, he ignored the claim of Mr. Belliard, a jeweler in Pall Mall, to a diamond ring worth £2000. After Frankland refused to return it, Belliard hired Joseph Hickey to take the case. When the lawyer visited him, the admiral repulsed the request, saying Belliard's right to it was not "worth two pence." Outraged at Frankland's lack of civility, Hickey replied that he would take him to court to demonstrate that he was "as ignorant as unjust." When this hearing took place, not a single witness appeared to support Frankland's cause, while several people, including both the Perreaus and Mrs. Rudd, supported the jeweler's claim. The court shared Hickey's indignation; it not only ordered Frankland to surrender the ring but made him pay £200 in court costs as well.[24]

Frankland became embroiled in another dispute over property in July, when a sheriff's officer served an execution against Daniel's goods for a debt of £1500 owed to an upholsterer who had furnished the Harley Street house on the eve of the crime's discovery. The admiral had already seized the furnishings on the basis of the bill of sale signed by Daniel. The man Sir Thomas had stationed in the house to protect his claim tried to hold the door against the execution. The sheriff's officer was forced to enter the house through the upper story. When Frankland appealed to Bow Street for help, the magistrates refused to "meddle." On July 20 the various demands on the household effects were withdrawn since Daniel, as a convicted felon, forfeited all his goods and lands to the sheriffs of London and Middlesex. One of the high sheriffs went to the house to assert this claim. A letter soon appeared justifying the conduct of the authorities and proving that they had a legal title superior to that of Frankland. Even as it acknowledged their right, the author expressed the hope that the sheriffs would make a careful inquiry into the goods that belonged to Mrs. Rudd and see that justice was done to her. They should not, it concluded, "suffer Sir Thomas to continue a fruitless dispute to make her more wretched and miserable."[25]

From the first, Mrs. Rudd fostered the idea that Frankland's only interest in the case was in seizing her property. At every opportunity she portrayed him as a greedy man who would gladly sacrifice her life if it would gain him a few pounds. No sin could be blacker in the mind of the sentimental philosopher. At the time of her appearance in King's Bench, Mrs. Rudd accused Frankland of hoping for her death in prison, so that he might be secure in his illegal possession of her goods. She also charged that he had intimidated a pawnbroker who offered to stand bail for her by warning him that he could lose £20,000 by the action.[26] One letter signed "A Foe of Oppression and Cruelty," but almost certainly from her pen, warned Frankland that "the eyes of the whole kingdom are now upon you." "What man, Sir, possessed of common sensations, or in whose bosom dwells an atom of humanity, can behold a noble mind struggling with the grievous pressure of accumulated sorrows, and deny the tear of pity, or the fostering hand of succor?" Mrs. Rudd needed a foil for her self-portrait as the woman of sensibility imperiled by the machinations of an unfeeling villain. Frankland met this need. His antics, his exaggerated charges and blustering conduct, served to arouse sympathy for her cause and vindicate her characterization of her enemies.[27]

Frankland's efforts to expose her character were constantly misfiring. In yet another instance of the drawn-out contest between the two, Frankland brought a charge against Mrs. Rudd's first counsel, Bailey, "for a conspiracy." The grand jury declared it an unwarranted charge.[28] In late September, Frankland or an ally exposed what he assumed was perfect proof not only of her fraudulent identity but also of her penchant for forgery. Within the Perreau circle, Mrs. Rudd had displayed a pedigree, signed by Robert Boswell and dated January 16, 1773, as evidence of her claim to noble connections. Her critics now pronounced this legal document a forgery.

> Can a woman whose mean birth is now well known and ascertained; who obtained the great seal of a kingdom, or counterfeited such seal, under inconceivably false pretenses, to keep her royal pedigree, and her hereditary connections with the first personage of the land; who exhibited these preconcerted instruments of fraud and imposture, to Robert Perreau, his wife and family, with intent to command and fix their implicit belief in her high birth and pretentions.—Can, I say, such a woman be entitled to one single atom of credit, in any case whatsoever?[29]

It was difficult for her foes to avoid gloating. The pedigree seemed to afford crushing proof of her duplicity. Not only did this evidence lend support to the story of how she deceived the Perreaus by calculated proofs, but the fact that these documents were forged showed her familiarity with the crime.

Mrs. Rudd never doubted that Frankland was behind this charge. "If there was not a moral certainty that the original of the above letter was holograph of Sir Thomas, the illiterate manner in which it is wrote, and the barbarous inhumanity of the intention, were sufficient to sink it below contempt." Not content with satirizing his style, she produced her own counter-coup. She published a letter from James Cummyng, Keeper of the Lyon Records, an office whose authority was recognized throughout Europe, which confirmed the pedigree as genuine. "They were so scrupulously exact in her case," Mrs. Rudd announced triumphantly, "as to be satisfied of the identity of the character she assumed before any thing was done, which was ascertained by such of her relations as I had access to know, who are all persons of fashion and fortune."[30] Not content with this victory, a letter soon followed, signed "An Admirer of Literary Merit," almost certainly from her pen, with a scathing satire of Frankland's prose style. "What a pity is it, Mr. Printer, that men of real genius should let their talents lie hid in a napkin, and not employ them for the advantage of mankind!" Only the accident of this case had permitted the world to learn of his "prodigious abilities and immense erudition." The letter concluded with the hope that they would see more such performances from the admiral.[31]

With a backdrop of so much previous controversy, the examination of Frankland followed the well-trod path. He had little to say that advanced the prosecution case; he had not proved a compelling witness in the trial of Robert Perreau. All he attested to was that Robert had brought him a particular bond on a certain date. The defense cross-examination was far longer and more searching. Davenport proceeded to bait him, in that "species of wit which sometimes prevails at the bar." Frankland proved both truculent and evasive from the first. He seemed eager to distance himself from any knowledge of Mrs. Rudd or acquaintance with her, despite all the evidence in the papers to the contrary. When asked if he had taken possession of her clothes at Harley Street, he said sulkily that he had not known they were hers. He admitted he had the jewels, valued at £2800, as well, even though the "poor jeweller is not paid to this hour." Davenport immediately pressed him about why he kept them as his own if he knew the jeweler was unpaid. Under the pressure of this examination about her clothes and jewels, he became increasingly confused and angry and was made to look absurd, as he denied having any knowledge that they belonged to the woman who had not been a party to the sale. "By whom did you suppose the gowns and petticoats and other women's apparel were worn," Davenport challenged, "by the two Perreaus, or by whom?" "They might go in masquerade," the admiral feebly responded. Finally he conceded that he was at law with Mrs. Rudd over the right to these various items. One paper reported that "in his cross examination he afforded no small diversion respecting the seizing of the jewels, wearing apparel, &c. of Mrs. Rudd, which he had taken under a bill of sale from Robert and Daniel Perreau. Mr. Davenport kept him to the stake for some time, to the satisfaction of the whole court." At last, after half an hour of such stuff, the counsel was stopped by Baron Burland, who told him that he had made his point.[32]

Frankland's ordeal, however, was far from over. Even more unsettling for the prosecution, the admiral was forced to admit that since he was in Yorkshire at the time the bond was presented, it was a letter from Robert Perreau that advised him that "such a bond was to come." This confession, far from fixing the crime on Mrs. Rudd, suggested that Robert had been more active in arranging the transaction than his defenders had allowed. Frankland compounded the damage when, in his rush to disavow all familiarity with Mrs. Rudd, he insisted that he had only dealt with Robert and had made the loan solely on the basis of Robert's reputation. He disclaimed any knowledge of Robert's dealing in stocks. Upon further examination, however, he conceded that in perusing papers found in the Harley Street house, he had discovered a list of Daniel's transactions in East India stock "amounting to £460,000 with a large sum for interest." Now the weakness of the prosecution case, as a result of their being deprived of the Drummonds' evidence, was apparent to all in the courtroom. Nothing could be presented of Mrs. Rudd's confession to offset the impression of Robert's industry in negotiating the bonds and the evidence of Daniel's heavy stock dealings.[33]

Before he finished, Frankland offered one more peculiar twist to the trial. He grudgingly acknowledged that he had gone in search of information about Mrs. Rudd, asking for her under different names. "Then I ask you," Mrs. Rudd's counsel demanded of Frankland, "whether you have prosecuted this woman as and believed her to be a Mrs. Potter or Mrs. Porter at Hackney?" "I know nothing at all about that," Frankland replied; "I don't know that she is, but I believe she is." He seemed extraordinarily reluctant to admit that he had carried out such investigations, although Davenport pressed him hard on this point. He must have known that his collection of rumors and a list of names scarcely amounted to evidence of duplicity. The papers were puzzled by this line of questioning; "the use apparently intended to be made of this part of the cross examination [by the defense] was never carried into effect." Clearly, however, it was pursued in order to suggest once again that she was being persecuted by a vain and petulant man who was so desirous of her ruin that he was ready to believe any wild accusation. His evasive responses under Davenport's pressure further injured his credibility.[34]

This approach must have involved a gamble. The evidence might well have been damaging to her cause if it had been presented in a different fashion. Hints about Mrs. Rudd's facility with assuming disguises and taking on novel identities had been widely circulated since the first days of the case. She admitted to passing as Mrs. Gore in order to escape her husband's vindictive jealousy. Several correspondents charged that she had pretended to be different people in order to defraud Salvadore. Something of the allure and mystery of the case surely appeared in this line of speculation. The defense had no interest in settling the issue. No doubt Davenport dropped the subject once he had gained his twin objectives of casting Frankland in a bad light and associating the charges with the admiral's revengeful imagination.

That much more might have been said on the question became clear in the aftermath of her trial, when several works appeared offering fresh revelations about her earlier history. The most widely reviewed was "She Is and She Is Not," which claimed to be the story of Miss Caroline de Grosberg, alias Mrs. Potter. Here were two of the names raised by Davenport in his interrogation of Frankland. Lest the point be missed, the pamphlet was also dedicated to "Mrs. M—t C— R-dd." In his satiric address to her, the anonymous author commented that the "several questions ... put to [Frankland]" during her trial "plainly give countenance to the insinuation" that the two women were really one, and that the woman who posed as a French countess while in the employ of the Earl of Lauderdale was the same woman who, as Margaret Caroline Rudd, convinced the Perreaus of her exalted Scottish connections. The earl reported that during her two-week stay as a governess to his family in 1764, "her conversation [was] so ridiculous and extravagant ... and the accounts she gave of herself ... were so contradictory and absurd, sometimes calling herself this great person, and at other times by another great name," that he felt compelled to fire her. The essay concluded with the reflection that "there are many other concurring circumstances which mark the two characters, and create a most striking resemblance between them. For instance, ... they both appear to be excellent *pen-women,* quick at *invention,* full of ... and *intrigue, boasters of high descent,* pretenders to *fine feelings,* and the nicest sense of *honour.*" De Grosberg had disappeared before the truth could be discovered.[35]

The account was a slight one, confused and incredible, but in the aftermath of the Perreau-Rudd episode, it gained considerable attention. The two major reviews of the day accepted the charge. The *Critical Review* thought the case proved; "she seems to be a perfect adept in all the mazes of artifice and intrigue." "In the narrative here given," the *Monthly Review* asserted, "we behold a female adventurer, so nearly resembling the famous Mrs. Rudd, that we cannot help concluding with the Author of this account, that C. de G., Mrs. P. and M.C.R. are only different names, used at different times, by one and the same woman." The dexterous duplicity of de Grosberg, the reviewer noted, "would be really astonishing, had we not seen such extraordinary instances of what a genius of this kind is capable of achieving."[36] It is difficult to credit half the varied performances attributed to Mrs. Rudd at this time. Still, Frankland and many others believed there was a sordid history to be revealed that might influence the outcome of her trial. Sadly for the Perreaus, there was too little evidence to substantiate the rumors, and the admiral proved inept in his introduction of the suspicions.

A SINISTER CHARGE

If the trial to this point seemed both scandalous and obscure, what with the severe treatment of Henrietta Perreau and the dark hints offered by Frankland, what followed threatened to turn it into farce, albeit with a sinister twist. The prosecution called as a witness Christian Hart, a poor woman of Scottish descent who had been a servant to Mrs. Rudd for a brief period in 1770–1771. In a pamphlet published after the trial, Mrs. Hart offered a history of their relationship that sounded even more like a fairy tale than the de Grosberg story. Hart came, she said, from a family that had supported the cause of the Pretender. Her father had died at Carlisle, and her mother had tended wounded rebels. Mrs. Hart claimed she came to work for Mrs. Rudd because she thought her a natural daughter of the Pretender. She spoke of her love for the woman; "she was the best mistress I ever lived with." She described how she helped Mrs. Rudd in several attempts to draw men into her net, before she finally succeeded with Daniel Perreau. Mrs. Hart offered a vivid picture of the tensions within the household, of how her mistress got rid of several unfriendly servants and replaced them with people more pliant to her cause. She told of Mrs. Rudd living at great expense and wearing splendid dress that would "even tempt his holiness to sin." Despite its brevity, Mrs. Hart portrayed their connection as deep and affectionate.[37]

Mrs. Hart implied that it was only natural for her, when she heard of the troubles afflicting her former mistress, to seek out Mrs. Rudd and offer her help. She presented a portrait of Mrs. Rudd's confinement strikingly different from that which the accused had put forth. Far from being the despondent and desperately ill prisoner of her own sentimental tale, Mrs. Rudd was the busy contriver of her own defense, according to Hart. The former servant reported she had found her deep in conversation with her attorney, John Bailey. When she offered Mrs. Rudd a guinea to assist her in prison, the latter replied that she had no need of money. On the contrary, Mrs. Hart testified, she promised her £200 if she would assist in a particular errand. Mrs. Rudd then asked whether Hart had a house where someone could visit unseen. Mrs. Hart, thinking that she sought a refuge for herself, hastened to assure her that "if you ever expect to get out of this place, come to my house, and I will never part with you till I get you to Ireland or Scotland." Mrs. Rudd quickly made clear that she had something else in mind. She proposed that Hart go to Justice Wright with a story that Mrs. Perreau and Frankland had met at her house. Mrs. Hart refused the task, saying she was reluctant to lie and fearful of authority. "I told her, though I loved her as my life, I was afraid to meddle with such rich people, and I never was before a justice in all my life." Mrs. Rudd persisted. Hart was a simple woman who had a difficult time explaining what it was that she was desired to do. But the paper presented in court, in Mrs. Rudd's handwriting, offered damning evidence of a conspiracy to commit perjury. The letter instructed Hart to say that Mrs. Robert Perreau met Mr. Williamson (who had since departed for India) at her house, and that they spent a good deal of time with a pile of papers, some of which she heard referred to as bonds, and that they mentioned the name Adair as well. She was also to swear that in June Mrs. Perreau asked to use the room to meet Frankland and that she overheard him promise Henrietta money if she would testify against Mrs. Rudd. Further, she was to say that Frankland vowed that "he would hang Mrs. Rudd, if it cost him all his fortune."[38]

According to Mrs. Hart, when she left Mrs. Rudd she vowed to herself to have nothing more to do with the affair. On returning home, however, her husband, angry at her for having been away so long, forced her to show him the paper and tell him the full story. Annoyed by what he heard, he ordered her to report the proposed scheme to the justices. John Hart, a journeyman, supported his wife's version of events. Mrs. Rudd had sent for Mrs. Hart, he testified, on the pretext of leaving her children with her. When his wife returned home after the second visit, she was "all on a tremble" and holding some papers in her hand. He demanded to know where the children were. "She said there were no children." Later that night, Hart continued, Bailey came to him in a great sweat, asking for the return of the papers. Hart replied that he had given them to the justices three hours earlier. Bailey then requested that Hart send his wife to Mrs. Rudd. "She shall not go out of my door," Hart responded. "I would sooner break both her legs."[39]

The suggestion of a conspiracy involving Mrs. Rudd was as damaging as any testimony to appear at her trial. Just how seriously her defense counsel regarded it became clear in the ingenious interpretation they proposed. Serjeant Davy attempted to give the story a different cast; he asked Mrs. Hart if the paper did not represent "an offer that you made to this Mrs. Rudd, and asked to have what you said you would swear taken down in writing." The defense called Bailey to support their version of events. Bailey said Mrs. Hart came to Mrs. Rudd's cell in July. When she sent a note up requesting admittance, Mrs. Rudd laughed, saying she had nothing to do with such a person. Later, Mrs. Rudd reported to him that Mrs. Hart had told her "a very strange incredible story." "I said, I could not think there was any probability in such a scheme." He was present, the next day, when the woman returned. She seemed "a good-natured poor ignorant creature." He then described how he looked on as Mrs. Rudd wrote down the tale contained in the paper the court had heard. "She wrote," Bailey swore, "nothing but what Christian Hart told her." Once she had finished, Mrs. Rudd gave her a copy and retained the original, which Bailey now presented to the court. Upon cross-examination Bailey insisted that this statement *was* the original. He admitted the visit to Hart but said that the man was so angry that he could not make sense of what he said. "I doubted very much," he concluded, "that she had so much friendship to Mrs. Rudd as she professed: I thought rather she was a person sent with an intent to hurt her." Two days later he consulted with Davenport about the paper, describing it then as a "strange improbable romance." They both agreed at that time that there was nothing in it.[40]

Appearances were certainly against Bailey and Mrs. Rudd. Mrs. Hart strenuously denied that the paper she carried away was a copy. The court, in looking at the two documents, suggested that the paper presented by Bailey was not an exact copy, but "a paper wrote from recollection." John and Christian Hart came across as honest if rough witnesses. On the other hand, it came down to the word of Bailey, supported to some extent by the prestige of the other defense counsel, against the humble couple. The spirited cross-examination, which included several questions from jurors, did little to resolve the controversy. One newspaper called Mrs. Hart's evidence incoherent, while another wanted to pass over it in silence as the work of a vulgar woman. The reviews were divided in their judgment, one calling Hart's pamphlet "a frivolous personal altercation, unworthy the attention of the public." The *Monthly Review,* on the other hand, found the work "written in a vulgar, but, perhaps, honest strain," and applauded its "well-founded aversion towards Mrs. R." Hart's work included the rueful reflection that "all who knows you, are infatuated by your spells and love you; and all who love you, you bring to destruction as fast as possible."[41]

There seemed no way to get to the bottom of the business. One newspaper, in justifying its omission of that portion of the trial, concluded that it "neither went to prove or disprove the forgery or publication, and could only be adduced as a collateral, circumstantial evidence of the confirmed baseness and turpitude of one or other of the parties."[42] The judge appeared embarrassed by the whole episode. In his summation, he noted that the evidence of Hart and Bailey was contradictory. He did not doubt that "if the truth could be attained, it would go a great way in establishing or overthrowing every thing that has been sworn here today." "It certainly gave the conduct of that side who were in the wrong a very bad appearance." But since there was nothing more to say, he instructed the jury to pay careful attention to the remaining evidence.[43]

UNSATISFACTORY CONCLUSIONS

Mrs. Rudd's own statement to the court was, in every way, typical of her: short, full of anger and self righteousness, yet sentimental. As with most of her case, no one doubted that she had written it herself. Indeed, her conduct during the trial surpassed expectations. Rather than sit quietly by while her lawyers managed her defense, she was constantly offering them advice. "During the trial she wrote near fifty notes to her counsel."[44] Much of their strategy bore the marks of her authorship. Reading now from the paper she had composed during the trial, she dismissed the value of the evidence against her on the grounds that the witnesses were biased or untrustworthy. She complained of the broken promise made to her. She repeated the view that Mrs. Robert Perreau was an interested witness, that Frankland "behaved in a way sufficiently disgraceful to himself," while Daniel's servant John Moody, by his own testimony, was "a very bad man." She called Mrs. Hart "a most infamous character," and she asked if anyone could believe that she would entrust her life to so absurd a creature. Her case was simple: "I have lost my property; I have suffered a dreadful imprisonment: and now my life is to be taken away to save the Perreaus." She reminded the jury that "it was in [her] direct and cheerful compliance with the law" that she fell victim to "the cruel confinement she had suffered." She concluded with a direct appeal to the jury, saying she thought they "were honest men" and that "she trusted she was safe in their hands."[45]

After so many hours of drama and contention, the trial sputtered to a conclusion. In some ways this was a surprising result, for this portion of the proceedings was most under the control of the defense. It was at this point that Robert's team had done such a successful job of presenting the evidence that implicated Mrs. Rudd. Her counsel had mounted an effective if brutal assault on the prosecution witnesses. Now they seemed to lose focus. Perhaps they had less material to work with; perhaps there was little agreement over how to proceed. Normally the last witnesses in such a case would speak to the character of the accused. On this occasion, far from aiding her cause, the fragmentary testimony only added to the suspicions surrounding her past.

The names of a great number of people were called, but only three appeared. Two people sought to rescue Mrs. Rudd's reputation from the sordid accusations concerning the source of her "fortune." Mary Nightingale testified that she had seen Mrs. Rudd receive £4000 in March 1770 and £3700 in April 1771 from a trustee. The effect of this testimony was immediately undercut when Nightingale refused to reveal the names of the persons concerned. Another person could only add that the money did not come from Salvadore. Characteristically, the third witness was a broker, called not to defend Mrs. Rudd but to attack Robert Perreau. He was asked if he knew of Robert's "dealing in the stocks." He denied even knowing Perreau. "The officers of the court again called on the witnesses, as set down in the briefs of the counsel." None appeared. Cowper then suggested to his client that she rest her case.[46] Many people, after the trial, commented on how unsatisfactory her defense had been. Some wondered at the fact that so many names had been called when so few appeared. Several correspondents condemned her effort to defame the reputation of a man sentenced to death. A pamphlet published after the executions wondered why the woman she summoned had not been more closely interrogated. "It is remarkable that the counsel for the prosecution, with all their abilities and chicane, could extort no satisfaction with regard to several interesting particulars."[47]

No doubt Justice Aston spoke with conviction when, as he began his summation, he described it as "a very tedious trial." He asked the jurors to consider carefully whether the evidence offered satisfied them that the accused was guilty of either the forgery or the utterance. That the bond was forged was proved; that Mrs. Rudd had forged it "rested only upon presumption." While he mentioned that Mrs. Perreau had a hope that a conviction might aid her husband, he added that the testimony of Cassidy and Frankland lent support to her testimony. The judge went on to make the usual point in forgery trials, that if a person was possessed of a forged note, the accused must show how she or he came to have it. "The prisoner," he noted with some severity, "has produced no evidence of any kind whatsoever, but what observations she made herself on the characters of the persons who have appeared against her." The jurors should bear this in mind as they deliberated. "If any doubt should arise," he cautioned them, "relative to the credit of one part of the evidence, or the sufficiency of the other," he recommended that they "lean to the side of *mercy*."[48]

Aston took an hour and twenty minutes in summing up the evidence. The jury took no more than half an hour to reach a verdict. Throughout the trial the jury had displayed a characteristic independence. One juryman, in particular, when a witness mumbled, told the court that the jury had heard nothing that had been said. When another spoke too quietly and the judge offered to summarize the testimony, the juror responded that he "thought we were seated here to collect the viva voce evidence of the witness, and not to have it explained to us by any third person whatever." This juror also interrupted Aston's summation, setting him "right in an essential point, ... clearly proving the equivocation of a material witness, and which would otherwise have been left in full force against the prisoner."[49] "As the jury returned," one witness remembered, "the prisoner fixed her fascinating eyes upon the jury-box, when the conduct of the foreman, a well known gay auctioneer, did not escape observation; for by a smile, which he significantly glanced towards her, many anticipated the verdict." "According to the evidence before us," he proclaimed "in a solemn fashion," the jury found her "not guilty." This extraordinary verdict was greeted with "the loudest and most extravagant plaudits ever heard," "the loudest Applauses on this Acquittal, almost ever known in a Court of Justice." She was then acquitted on the three other charges against her as no evidence was offered. "She appeared," one correspondent wrote, "confounded with joy at her discharge."[50]

Not surprisingly, both the papers and the public were divided in their reactions to this verdict. As both the *Middlesex Journal* and *Morning Chronicle* announced,

> This custom of clapping and shouting upon the acquittal of a prisoner at Sessions of gaol delivery, although it strongly shows the humanity of the English, is a token not only of our want of decency on the most solemn of all possible occasions, but of our catching at the shadow instead of the substance, and expressing satisfaction where we should at least hesitate and consider for a moment, whether the event, though it appears to be a momentary triumph over law, may not in effect prove a dreadful sacrifice of morality.[51]

Once again the *Morning Post* was the most enthusiastic in its celebration of the decision. It was "impossible," the paper concluded, "to do justice to the candour of the judges and the unbiased integrity of the true English jury, who thus conscientiously decided the fate of this poor woman." The conduct of the jurors, said the *Post,* displayed the genius of the constitution. The jurymen, it asserted, "came into court, impress'd with a proper sense of their own importance, and consequently with a view not to be biassed by the authoritative nod of a judge, or the chicane of the counsel." They chose to hear and interpret the evidence for themselves. They looked upon the judges "as their assistants, to set them right if any point of law arose, and then to leave them to the free exercise of their own opinion on it." Future juries could not do better than to follow the example set at this trial. "Upon the whole," the paper remarked, "we never remember a trial that gave us so high an opinion of this excellent part of the British constitution." In this paean to English justice one can almost hear the echoes of "Rudd and Liberty" joining similar compliments to other jury decisions, to Wilkes and Junius.[52]

Much of the press commentary was more sober. "Plain Truth," in a card to the *Public Advertiser,* argued, "Those who indecently and unjustly huzzaed and triumphed on the Acquittal of the said Fair *Innocent,* may take Shame on themselves, for bringing Scandal on a most respectable and supreme *Court* of Justice, and Disgrace to the Nation in general; thereby confirming certain Foreigners in their declared Idea of the Inhabitants of this blessed Island, being the *Savages of Europe.*"[53] One correspondent sought to explain the acquittal by suggesting that the jury "were glad of an opportunity of *rejecting* the evidence of Mrs. Perreau, in opposition to the opinion of the twelve judges, which was far from being well received out doors."[54] Several contributors pointed to the peculiar wording of the verdict as scarcely constituting a ringing endorsement of her innocence. "According to the evidence before us," the jury had said, implying that it was legal nicety that secured her freedom. There were very few instances, in the eighteenth century, of a jury going to such lengths to circumscribe the meaning of a decision. Later reports drew a picture of a deeply divided jury. "Justice and Humanity" appealed to an article in the previous *London Packet* that five of the twelve jurors were for finding Mrs. Rudd guilty. In the light of this division, he asked, "what will those *Worthies* say for themselves, who so shamefully huzzaed on *such* Acquittal, and drew the Fair *Innocent* all over the Town in a triumphant Chariot."[55] A case and verdict that some interpreted as a vindication of the oppressed against the conspiracies of the strong, others saw as a moral scandal and a terrible wrong.

The public had come to this trial expecting to enjoy a highly unusual spectacle. They were curious to see the woman at the epicenter of this ongoing controversy. Her beauty and talent had been much praised. Her relentless energy and tenacious will inspired wonder if not respect. She did not disappoint. Her sober but rich dress set off her features. Her evident self-possession and busy scribbling suggested an intelligence every bit as acute as had been rumored. But this was not simply a tableau upon which one meditated; it was a drama that aroused powerful sentiments. Thus the proceedings produced more conflicting feelings. The courtroom cheers that greeted her acquittal represented a spontaneous eruption, an expression of released tension and pleasure that this attractive woman had escaped her peril. A little reflection soon altered the mood. If Robert's trial had seen the careful projection of a pleasing portrait of an "honest" and industrious gentleman, Mrs. Rudd's trial presented a disturbing reflection of a mixed character. Her hand was revealed everywhere in shaping both the style and content of her defense. It largely consisted of an unstinting attack upon her prosecutors, which instead of answering any charges against her, resorted to crude satire and savage character assassination to humble her accusers. She might well have been guilty of an attempt to corrupt justice. And as in so many of her performances, her extravagance tended to draw attention to her exaggeration and deception, where a discreet silence would more clearly have been to her advantage. Her trial, and we mean not only the outcome, satisfied no one except the accused herself. She read it as vindication; everyone else saw it as a bungled job or a terrible betrayal of justice.

Ten

"IF INNOCENTS SHOULD SUFFER"

THE OUTCOME OF MRS. RUDD's trial was a blow for the Perreaus. The brothers had staked everything on her conviction, and they had had every reason to expect a different result. Once again, a jury of their fellow citizens had dealt them an unexpected reverse. The public seemed no more satisfied with the verdict than the brothers. The trial did not put to rest lingering doubts about the justice of the proceedings; on the contrary, it only heightened a sense of frustration and indignation as the fundamental questions remained unresolved. "The case of the Perreaus affords matter capable of almost infinite discussion," wrote one newspaper on the eve of the scheduled execution, "and a variety of arguments, to specious and ingenious men."[1] Ironically, Mrs. Rudd's acquittal served to increase the feeling that she had gotten away with the crime. Still worse, it appeared that her sinister triumph would be crowned when the brothers perished at Tyburn.

The drama, however, had not played itself out. In some respects its most powerful scenes were yet to come. The month following Mrs. Rudd's trial produced agitation and activity that surpassed even that of the preceding March. The story dominated the news; people could talk of little else than the fate of the brothers. Should they hang; would they hang? Bets were taken on the likelihood of various results. The Perreaus were not without hope. Their friends and allies still had much they could do for them; a jury verdict in a capital case was never the last word. Only a minority of the condemned actually suffered on the gallows. The rest were pardoned, most on condition that they be transported abroad. Pardon was "a fundamental element in the administration of the criminal law." A capital verdict was often the signal for launching a campaign of letters and petitions requesting mercy for the condemned. In most cases this effort consisted of a letter from a parent or employer, and a petition from a local cleric or prominent landowner, followed by the signatures of friends and neighbors. The addresses usually mentioned factors intended to incline the authorities in favor of ameliorating the sentence, such as general reputation, age, previous good behavior, the influence of a supporter. These campaigns were frantic, as interested parties urgently solicited the assistance of the neighborhood. Everyone looked to the King and his chief ministers as they awaited the result of their deliberations.[2]

If appeal to the Crown was normal in capital cases, the pardon effort for the Perreaus was anything but usual. Mrs. Rudd's flamboyant conduct in the aftermath of her trial, seemingly flouting opinion, raised an outcry that something had to be done to remedy a course of justice that had gone badly awry. The Perreaus' supporters sought to capitalize on this sentiment by mounting an unparalleled effort to secure a pardon for Robert. They called upon the influential intervention of a long list of aristocrats, and they combined this initiative with a public petitioning campaign. As ever, the press played a significant role in amplifying the effect of this activity. The papers seized upon every theatrical gesture, every rumor or report, helping to build an irresistible sense of the drama of the moment. Their correspondence columns overflowed with debates about every aspect of the case. Some letters rehearsed yet again all the evidence, pressing for a reinterpretation of some crucial act. Others criticized the jury decisions or explained why a pardon was necessary. Like the debates on other aspects of the legal process, these letters mingled high-minded appeals with vicious attacks upon one or the other of the parties. Once again, and against all expectation, Mrs. Rudd participated in this overheated controversy.

Overshadowing all of this tempest and spurring on the debate was the specter of the gallows at Tyburn. Several hanging days had passed since the Perreaus' conviction. Each one, with its handful of victims, reminded Londoners of what awaited the brothers. The Perreaus stood at the climax of eighteenth-century justice, poised between the mercy of the King and the public spectacle at the fatal tree. Certain rituals and calculated gestures governed these deliberations. Each was reported to a public relatively unembarrassed about discussing the details. The reports contained in equal measure pious reflection, sentimental anguish, and grim fascination. The imminent prospect of death, made more acute for the respectable classes by the brothers' social status, had seldom excited such passions.

MRS. RUDD AND THE WICKED EARL

When Mrs. Rudd departed the court, acquitted by her jury, many of the newspapers reported that she went, in his carriage, to a house taken for her by her great and good friend, the "wicked" Earl Lyttelton. She was also seen, according to several accounts, in his chariot on the way to the theater. Within days she was said to have departed for the most fashionable of retreats, Bath. It is not known whether Mrs. Rudd had become Lyttelton's mistress; as with Rudd herself, stories about the earl, based on his well-deserved reputation, circulated in exaggerated and embellished form. Lyttelton would not have been the first noble with whom she had been associated. Various pamphlets recounted a checkered history, joining her name with those of Lord Deloraine, the Marquis of Granby, and even the Duke of Cumberland.[3] However, with Lyttelton, her career was connected with that of a man who was not only a well-known rake and profligate aristocrat but was intimately and visibly involved in national politics and moral issues of weight. Like Rudd, Lyttelton seemed larger than life, wickeder than more mundane individuals. "He has," an American visitor wrote, "an indisputable Title to all the vices which disgrace and degrade the human Species. Effeminacy and Debauchery have marked him for their own, and infamy has stamped her indelible Print on his Brow."[4] He gained in notoriety when compared, as he always was, with his father, the "good" earl, the friend of Pope and a poet himself. Perhaps it was inevitable that their names would be associated; despite their different ranks, Mrs. Rudd and Lyttelton appeared to the public as kindred spirits.

Whatever his other qualities, no one denied that Lyttelton had a first-class brain and enormous personal charisma.

> That he has oratorical skills cannot be disputed. Nature has been very bountiful to him in bestowing on him such mental talents, as could not fail shining, with the education he has received: His voice was har-

monious, his person tall and genteel, and his action graceful. Add to these qualifications he had a tenacious memory and was possessed of that happy effrontery which secures a man from the shafts of raillery, or the confusion of an abrupt or unexpected replication.[5]

Having spent much of his youth in dissipation, he was soon deeply in debt. He took the classic escape of the impoverished aristocratic scapegrace; in 1772 he married an older, slightly vulgar, monied woman, Mrs. Peach, the widow of a governor of Calcutta. Once possessed of her fortune, he dashed off to Paris with a barmaid. Characterized, while still a young man, as someone "whose ambition will bear no control," Lyttelton's brief stint in the House of Commons bore witness to the "dazzling facility of his eloquence." His speeches, according to one witness, were "fluent, nervous, manly and argumentative ... his stile irresistibly captivating." By 1775 he was a frequent speaker in the Lords and a privy councillor, supporting the North government in firm measures against the colonies. Lyttelton's linguistic facility and overheated rhetoric, like Mrs. Rudd's, both attracted admiration and created suspicion and dislike. His involvement in politics did not curtail his activities as one of the most notorious of the bon ton. He was not only one of the main organizers of the Regatta in the spring of 1775, but also the leading light of a club, the Savoir Vivre, dedicated to drinking, gambling, and high living.[6]

There was another cause in which Lyttelton's involvement was conspicuous, and that was in the proceedings against the Duchess of Kingston. Less than a week after Mrs. Rudd's trial, the committee charged with considering the duchess's case, a committee that included both the infamous libertine Lord Sandwich (popularly known as Jemmy Twitcher, after the duplicitous character in Gay's *Beggars' Opera*), and his protegé Lord Lyttelton, decided that she would be tried in regular court in Westminster Hall, rather than in the Lords. The spectacle of Lyttelton condemning Kingston (he was reported to say that since the duchess could not pretend to chastity or modesty, there was no room for compassion) for moral faults must have seemed as ludicrous as Sandwich's upbraiding of Wilkes for his pornographic *Letter on Woman*. Such disingenuous conduct on the part of someone whose behavior repelled even this tolerant age earned frequent condemnation. "Lord Lyttelton," Walpole wrote to his friend Mann, thought that "he has talents for secretary of state, and that want of principles is no impediment." He "was apt," Walpole said on another occasion, "to go point blank into all extremes without any parenthesis or decency; nor even boggled at contradicting his own words."[7]

Lyttelton's life, mingling as it did notorious vices and notable talents, among them an ability to sway people with his rhetoric, stood as a fitting parallel to that of Mrs. Rudd. Word that they had taken up with each other spread quickly through the polite circles of London. Mrs. Delany, in a letter to Mrs. Port, reported: "They say Lord Lyttelton is so charmed with the cleverness of Mrs. Rudd (adores a mind so like his own) that they say he has adopted her as his mistress—and what mischief may not *two* such *heads* and *two* such *hearts* do? It is frightful to think of. That human creatures could be so depraved!"[8] Mrs. Rudd was not unaware of the damage that these reports, linking her to a man whose talents and weaknesses were so like her own, did to her reputation. Asked about the relationship by James Boswell, she denied even knowing the earl; "'though one who has been a good deal at publick places knows most people of distinction by sight I really do not know Lord Lyttelton by sight." "Besides," she continued, "Lord Lyttelton is not a person with whom one could form a connection as he is quite a profligate."[9] She also wrote to the papers, seeking to portray the accusations as one more attempt by her enemies "to stab the reputation of a fellow creature." "The notorious falsehood," she protested, "that the fact asserted in this paragraph is the present talk of the town, is a weak and pitiful attempt to impose it upon the public."[10]

Her protests were unavailing, and the rumors of her conduct had a profound impact upon public perception of the Perreaus as they awaited execution. Instead of accepting her victory in discreet silence, she had the effrontery to parade her wantonness before the public. Despite her narrow escape from the gallows, she displayed no trace of repentance. She could not have made a more significant contribution to the Perreau cause. She seemed to vindicate the most damning description of her character. Even if the reports were exaggerated, they were universally believed. In part as a result of this escapade, the attacks on her reached a new level of intensity. Here was "a woman who is a scandal to her sex."[11] One correspondent declared that he knew no better symptom of the degeneracy of the times than the defenses offered "of a profligate prostitute," and this in papers read in families. He mocked the call to draw a veil over her life before 1770, "because probably there is no one action of that life which will bear the light." He was appalled that one of her defenders had "the assurance to call an open, avowed life of adultery, by the soft term of the weakness of a woman!" It was disgraceful, this author concluded, to treat the crime as if it were a minor failing and more disturbing that a paper would publish such an idea.[12]

In these diatribes Mrs. Rudd appeared as a powerful and sinister figure. She had "not only deceived justices, jurymen, judges &c. but also endeavours to pervert the wisdom and justice of a privy council; and to withhold the mercy of a benevolent sovereign, the best of Kings." "How great," one author wrote, "will be her exultation should she succeed in her diabolical attempt." Those who defended the convictions of the brothers had been "infatuated and hood-winked by the potent charms of the triumphant Circe," a woman whose duplicity had been demonstrated when she said in a recent letter that she had "never been the mistress of any man." The Perreaus had been convicted because of the prejudice she had created against them. "So artfully horrid were her tales, that men ran from house to house inveighing against inhuman villains, and expatiating on the enormity of their crimes before they had been heard."[13] In this finished portrait of Mrs. Rudd, she appeared as one who had plotted for the brothers' destruction from the outset. Every turn in the case testified to her fiendish cleverness. "O how her diabolical spirit will exult," one letter concluded, "if she can sport with human reason, and compel the wisest to become her instruments to shed the blood of innocence."[14] "If innocents should suffer," read another letter, "while guilt triumphs, who would not grieve?"[15]

PLEADING FOR THE PERREAUS

The papers were almost unanimous in their rejection of Mrs. Rudd's acquittal. They interpreted it as the product of a technicality, the result of confusion on the part of the jurors. The world remained convinced, went one letter, that she was "mistress of the art of deceit to an inconceivable degree." Another wrote,

> I believe every one is well satisfied that she was the contriver and executor
> of the forgeries; and provided there was no other foundation for mercy, I
> should think that of itself, joined with Mrs. R's state of safety (arising
> from such a series of good fortune, which can only be equalled by the fa-
> tality that in the whole course of this unfortunate business has attended
> R. P.) would induce your majesty to extend your clemency to him.

While her trial had not resulted in her conviction, everything that transpired during it substantiated the charge that she had deceived the brothers. "Whatever the perversions, insinuations, and insolence of counsel may effect," expressed one dismayed correspondent, "whatever peculiarities the forms of law may require, or however carefully jurymen should be not to attend to any thing but what should immediately appear before them," yet nothing had come out at the trial that pointed to the guilt of the brothers. Far from the outcome of her trial convincing people of her innocence, it had "operated in an adverse direction."[16]

Not content to trust entirely to this general mood, Perreau supporters flooded the papers with arguments on Robert's behalf. The most eloquent case for pardon came in a series of letters addressed to the Earl of Suffolk, a secretary of state. The author denied that the acquittal of Mrs. Rudd now made inevitable the brothers' execution. The original respite of their sentences had been granted because of a powerful suspicion that they had been duped by her. All the evidence offered at their trials, from her confession to the Drummonds to the stratagems practiced to make the brothers believe in her connections, "created, and certainly justified, a general opinion that they were deluded men." Her trial had done nothing to remove these doubts. On the contrary, the proofs presented there, although not strong enough to bring home the crime to her, reinforced the belief in her involvement. She escaped conviction because none of the testimony offered at Robert's trial could be presented at hers. Although it was, no doubt, proper to exclude this evidence when her life was at stake, the Crown, in determining the fate of the brothers, would be remiss in not considering its meaning. "If it be asked, why the evidence, which I have described as so strong, failed of its effect to convict Mrs. Rudd, I answer, that the question bears no relation to the present argument: the object of which is, not to establish the certainty of her guilt, but to prove the probability of the Perreaus' innocence." The jury, this writer argued, went as far as it could when it added to the words "not guilty," the qualifying phrase, "from the evidence that had appeared to us."[17]

The author went on to argue that "her uniform success in all her schemes, and many almost incredible have been undertaken and executed by her, best proves her consummate skill in the deepest arts of deception.—Without attending to common popular tales which may, or may not be, the invention of the day, I have heard, well attested, so many instances of her victorious artifice, as justly rank her in the highest class of imposters." Nor were these "barren conquests." The fact that she advanced Daniel large sums of money was "supported by authority which cannot be denied." In a dramatic reversal of the story Daniel had first told of his relationship to Mrs. Rudd, the brothers' supporters were now eager to accept her own claims about possessing "a fortune." They quoted Nightingale, who had testified on Mrs. Rudd's behalf, that she had £4000 in 1770 and £3700 in 1771 from her gentleman. No wonder Daniel had come to believe that she "was really a most intimate favorite of Mr. Adair." The distribution of these sums was calculated to strengthen the hold she had on their minds. "The splendour of [the] Harley-street house," their defender argued, "the extravagant richness of her clothes, and the great value of her jewels found there, prove that her relish for finery and pomp was not inferior to her financial skill in supplying the means; or, what is equally the duty of a good financier, keeping up a good figure and credit."[18]

The author of these letters to the *Morning Post* drew together many of the stories circulating about Mrs. Rudd's past. Her real career, he charged, had begun seven or eight years earlier when she gained admission to James Adair on the basis of a letter from a friend in Ireland. He was moved by her affecting tale of financial distress and domestic unhappiness. He did what he could to help her. But she soon broke from the constraints of her immediate situation and aimed for a "larger sphere." "Numberless were her adventures, and incredible was her success." This writer claimed to know personally a number of men who had been deceived by her and who had paid dearly for their pleasure. Soaring ever higher, she finally secured the gift she celebrated, £16,000. After this "various career," however, "she directed her policy to a more established and plausible situation." She secured a connection with Daniel Perreau and renewed her acquaintance with James Adair by announcing that she had married into the Perreau family. In turn, she played upon her connection to the respectable family in Soho Square to entrench herself in the regard of the Perreaus. "Every particle of this she swelled, she magnified, into intimacy and friendship, besides the invention of numberless particulars that never existed." Daniel was attached to her by a passion that was blind, while Robert accepted the evidence of what he saw, their splendid establishment.[19]

As these letters drew to a close, the author contrasted the characters of the accused. While Mrs. Rudd displayed in every aspect of her behavior that artifice and deceit were her central attributes, Robert had never, before the forgery, revealed any inclination or ability to dissemble. How absurd then that he stood accused of having so mastered such an art that he could convincingly play an innocent victim before the Drummonds and William Adair. It was not conceivable, their defender went on, "that from the tenor of such a life such a violent transition should at once be made, into such consummate and sagacious guilt." One would have to imagine him insane to tell a lie that could easily be disproved and then agree to a course of action that must expose the falsehood. The only alternative, this correspondent argued, was to see Robert's act as an innocent lie founded upon the total confidence he had in Mrs. Rudd's connection. Unfortunately for him, "a little misrepresentation of an incidental circumstance," had been "magnified by the prudes into an odious, horrid, and monstrous falsehood."[20]

The themes of the "little" lie and Robert's innocence echoed through the many letters published in the month before the execution. Robert, these correspondents agreed, was guilty of no more than "a good-natured action in going on an errand for Mrs. Rudd."[21] The Drummonds, despite carefully observing his behavior, could detect no evidence of guilt. "Where was there any sign of the so much talked of force of a guilty conscience? What no shuffling evasion! no confusion! not a stammer nor a blush!" His confidence, this author charged, only left him, as it would any innocent person, when he discovered that he had been imposed upon and stood confused, alike concerned that his life was in danger and his reputation suspect.[22] It made no more sense, in the words of one paper, "to hang a porter for going of an errand to the banker's as execute Robert Perreau, whose folly in going of an errand for Mrs. Rudd, and his telling a lie to oblige her, seem to constitute the whole of his crime."[23] The story told by Robert to the end of his life and the consistency with which he maintained it troubled those who read it. His solemn declarations, his calling upon God to be his witness, his appeal to the plight of his wife and children, all reinforced the anxiety of many people that an innocent person would suffer an unjust penalty. He became a popular cause, "the unhappy deluded tool of others," "acted upon by the most premeditated, artful, wickedness that can be devised."[24] He was made to seem a martyr. Letter after letter invoked the efforts "of a miserable wife, almost heart-broken, and her helpless children, who may soon become orphans."[25] The *Public Advertiser*, after publishing letters from Henrietta and Susannah Perreau, returned to the difference between "the goodness of their hearts" when "set in contrast to the other." The latter was "elegant and artful," while the two Perreau women were "truly, the most esteemable and amiable characters, the plain and simple."[26]

As the campaign neared its climax, Daniel sought to assist the efforts made on his brother's behalf by sending a letter to the secretary of state, pleading that only he, deceived as he was by his affection for her, should suffer for having introduced Mrs. Rudd into his family. Although he denied any complicity in the crime, he nonetheless announced that he was ready to suffer death. Robert had never, he swore, used for his own purposes the money raised by the bonds.[27] In a further attempt to strengthen the case, Henry Dagge made public a letter he said James Adair had received from Mrs. Rudd on March 10, 1775. In this letter she entreated him to interfere with William Adair to stop the discovery of the crime. She declared that Robert was innocent, even as she presented herself as a dupe of others as well. Adair had replied that he refused to have anything else to do with her. The correspondence appeared now through the decision of Mrs. Robert Perreau to release it to the press. Thus Mrs. Rudd's own words seemed to reinforce the pleas for Robert's pardon.[28]

THE THEATER OF MERCY

The prerogative of mercy was one of the highest attributes of monarchy. The law, Blackstone said, attributed to kings not only the powers and means necessary to govern, "but like wise certain attributes of a great and transcendent nature." Chief among these was the power to pardon. "Holding a court of equity in his own breast," the monarch could "soften the rigour of the general law." This act cast monarchy in a favorable light, showing the King engaged in works of "compassion." "To him therefore the people look up as the fountain of nothing but bounty and grace." The "acts of goodness" endeared "the sovereign to his subjects," and contributed "more than any thing to root in their hearts" affection and loyalty.[29] Here was a power that belonged exclusively to the monarch. It was a prerogative that called for great circumspection and care in its exercise. "The power of suspending the laws," William Paley wrote, "is a privilege of too high a nature to be committed to many hands, or to those of any inferior officer in the state."[30] The law required some such authority, a final court of appeal, where injustice could be corrected and the claims of humanity recognized.

Letters in support of Robert Perreau lauded, as was the custom, the glory of this royal attribute. Here was a "God-like" power, "the highest human tribunal, the throne of justice in mercy." The propriety of the Crown's intervention in cases of great merit or extraordinary doubt was universally accepted. The overwhelming consensus held that Robert was a deserving object of royal favor. Correspondents called upon the King to use "those powers which God and the Constitution have placed in your hands" for the "protection of innocents."[31] "It is generally believed," one paper reported in June, "that Robert Perreau's universal good character previous to the transaction for which he has been tried, together with the great interest of his friends, will operate so powerfully in his favour with the greatest personage in this country, as to save his life."[32] Within three weeks of the Perreau trials, the Robin Hood Society, a useful barometer of popular opinion, raised the question of "whether the two Perreaus were not proper objects of Royal clemency?" "A great majority [voted] in favour of the prisoners."[33]

By December the Perreaus were engaged in an elaborate campaign to sway the course of justice. Both the scale of the effort and the extensive use made of the papers to try to influence the Crown were unprecedented. Petitions flowed in calling for mercy on Robert's behalf. Several merchants submitted one in which they expressed doubts about his knowledge of the crime. No part of the money, they noted, had been applied to his use. In another petition seventy-eight bankers and merchants of London argued that even if Robert had been rash, the world knew whose hand had written the bonds. Their call mentioned with especial tenderness the fate of his blameless wife. A request from an economic group whose commercial interests were particularly threatened by forgery might be expected to carry weight. A third proposal, to present a petition from "several physicians, surgeons, and apothecaries of the greatest eminence in their profession," was also started.[34] These efforts met, one paper noted, "with the wishes and prayers of all worthy and good people." A correspondent writing in French conducted a one-man struggle through the press to persuade the King to act. "Never was the greater interest made to save the life of a criminal than has been for that of Mr. Robert Perreau." So impressive was the campaign that it was widely expected that it would meet with success.[35]

This effort on behalf of the Perreaus drew strength from the growing criticism in the 1770s of the frequency with which English justice imposed the death penalty. Although there had been isolated complaint against the capital code throughout the century, the publication of Beccaria's *On Crimes and Punishments* in an English edition in 1767 inaugurated a period of steadily mounting condemnation of the criminal law. "It is so replete with good sense," wrote a reviewer of the work, "sound reasoning, and universal philanthropy, that we doubt not but it will, in time, make a proper impression on the minds of those who have it [in] their power to amend, or repeal, the irrational and inhumane laws that were made in the times of ignorance, superstition, and barbarity."[36] Beccaria's principles were endorsed by Blackstone in his *Commentaries on the Laws of England,* and William Eden's *Principles of Penal Law,* published in 1771, elaborated on this criticism. Robert Perreau's attorney, Henry Dagge, contributed to this reassessment with his three-volume *Considerations on Criminal Law.* This flurry of works suggests mounting uneasiness with the law, especially among the professional and intellectual elite of the capital. The same sentimental language that played so large a part in how the defendants in this case presented themselves was also employed to call into question the existence of the capital code.

Several correspondents to the papers picked up the themes of this criticism, expecting their readers to be familiar with the arguments of Beccaria and Blackstone. In one letter, not explicitly addressing the Perreau case but clearly commenting on it, "Anti-Draco" argued against the infliction of death for "theft of any kind, unaccompanied by force or violence." Pleading for a legislative review of such punishments, he charged that its wholesale use "had rendered our criminal law the most cruel and defective now existing in any civilized country under heaven." Although a growing variety of causes excited "humane outrage" against the law, the approaching death of a genteel person focused particular attention upon the gallows. With increasing frequency, respectable people were ready to support appeals to the throne for mercy. They mingled together the pleas of policy and humanity in charged protests against the "blood-thirsty" laws.[37]

As the date for the brothers' execution neared, friends arranged for Mrs. Robert Perreau to stage a dramatic appeal for pardon. Already cherished by the public as the true embodiment of the maternal and domestic values to which Mrs. Rudd pretended possession, Henrietta was thought to have a particular claim upon the Crown's attention. With her three children, she attended upon the King and Queen as they were on their way to the Chapel Royal. All were dressed in deep mourning. Her petition on behalf of her husband was "graciously received." Mrs. Perreau, overcome by emotion, fainted. The papers were filled with pathetic accounts of how the youngest child looked intently at her mother's face, giving expression to the grief she found there. "It was a picture of distress which, surpasses imagination, and which made a visible impression on the minds of those few who were present." "A scene so distressing," one paper added, "never appeared within the Chamber of St. James." A week later she repeated the scene when she presented another petition to the Queen, provoking similar comment in the press.[38] Her petition spoke in piteous terms of the sad plight of her husband and of the miserable condition of his family. She would, she said, no longer speak of his innocence, but appeal on behalf of "her misery." She looked upon clemency as "the peculiar virtue of the King." "Justice has never been so rigorous in this country," she wrote, "as not to hear the cries of humanity." She also waited on the Countess of Egremont and Lady Weymouth, ladies of Her Majesty's bedchamber, with petitions, which they immediately carried to the Queen. The Perreaus placed great hope in this appeal to the Queen; the press believed that it had succeeded in winning her over to the cause of saving Robert's life. Few could imagine how this plea from one virtuous wife and mother to another could fail.[39]

MRS. RUDD RESPONDS

For much of the five weeks between Mrs. Rudd's trial and the January date for the brothers' execution, the frantic activity to secure mercy for Robert preoccupied the press and public. The papers were filled with sympathetic portraits of Robert and his family, as well as moving descriptions of the carefully staged appeals for royal favor. The Perreaus and their defenders clearly counted on the near unanimous voice of the public to sway the monarch's conscience. In mounting this effort, however, they failed to account for the actions of Margaret Caroline Rudd. No doubt they expected that, after her narrow escape, she would quietly retire from the scene. Her reputed liaison with Lyttelton had been a godsend, reinforcing the character they had sought to give her over the preceding six months. She had nothing to gain by drawing further attention to herself.

But the campaign to pardon Robert, with its scathing caricature of her character, provoked her to yet another defense of her reputation. In January word suddenly reached the papers that she had been in communication with Lord Weymouth. An enigmatic account appeared in the *Morning Chronicle* that "a celebrated coadjutrix in their affairs" had written to the secretary of state that if he doubted the guilt of the brothers, he should "ask such and such particulars as she pointed out, of such and such gentlemen." Weymouth, the paper asserted, made the inquiries and received satisfaction.[40] The contents of this letter were revealed in a long pamphlet she soon issued, a publication, addressed to the lord, as vigorous and indignant as any she authored. It was, perhaps, her most successful work. She denied any desire to see Robert executed; she did not, she said, oppose the endeavors made to save him. But she was driven to write because "the advocates of this unhappy man take such unjustifiable methods to gain their point, as ought for the sake of common justice, to be exposed." She also resented, she announced in a confusing display of loyalty, the abandonment of Daniel to the gallows by those who labored so hard for Robert's pardon.[41]

Her pamphlet began in her usual fashion, with a condemnation of the efforts to make respectable the deeds "of the most abandoned men." She would, she assured her readers, present the simple truth. The productions of "delusive falsehood," she warned, were only to be feared "because they have assumed a guise of all other the most becoming, that of amiable compassion and soft-eyed humanity." Her task was to detect the "imposters" and to protect "the generality" from "deception." The Perreau partisans, she charged, chose to malign the reputation of a woman since they could not prove the virtue of the brothers. She sought to clear her reputation, to expose their stratagems and undo the effect of their lies. All the appeals for mercy, she announced, sought to hide the "secret transactions" of the brothers from "the public eye." In this "whitewashing," Robert was presented as "no stock-jobber," and one who had enjoyed none of the proceeds of the forgeries. She promised to expose these deceptions. Although she claimed to be able to "trace Robert Perreau's alley transactions, and recite several instances of his indigence for many years previous thereto," she limited herself to a discussion of his dealings in the period since her connection with Daniel. Once again she offered facts—names, dates, and sums—in dizzying succession. She said that she had summoned men to her trial who could have confirmed these assertions, but she had not called them, the court "intimating that there was no occasion for farther evidence." She fell in with the suggestions in hopes that it would operate in the Perreaus' favor. The ugliness of their accusations now spurred her to reverse her decision.[42]

In a further demonstration of her tenacious opposition to the Perreaus' charges, she published the full text of a two-page letter from Daniel to Weymouth in which he cleared his brother of any involvement in the crime. She did so in order to refute it point by point. He made "a mockery of religion," she charged, by offering up such a story "in the very hour of death." She ridiculed the efforts to explain away Robert's "innocent lie." On the contrary, she demonstrated, he had offered a succession of lies. He had spoken falsely to Drummond about buying a house in Suffolk and about the title deeds being in the country. She reminded her readers of the care Robert had taken to have Wilson antedate the bond he presented to Drummond in order to cover the story he had told at their first meeting. When pressed whether he had seen Adair, he not only replied yes but told of his being a good friend and having money deposited with him. More relentlessly than the prosecution at his June trial, Mrs. Rudd proceeded to point up the central inconsistencies in the characterization of Robert's actions.[43]

To drive home her argument, she offered a little lecture on the evils of stock-jobbing. She concluded this sermon with one more round of chastisement of Frankland, Moody, and Col. Kendal for having the temerity to testify against her. Kendal was a notorious fellow who commanded only an "Irish brigade" and had been raised in the Alley. Moody had told a tale "whose fable of the Crows quills has been so frequently buzzed into the public Ear" that she would not "deafen" her readers by "a tiresome repetition." But her most savage satire was reserved for her investigation of the various ways in which they sought to represent her. "In short," she announced, "so compliant are her adversaries to any argument that can bend to their purpose, that, in some places, she possesses powers even beyond the refinement of exquisite art; and in others, they invest her with an understanding, below the dignity of an idiot." She mocked her accusers for making use of "the obsolete doctrine of enchantment," for calling her "a sorceress." She charged them with turning her into a character out of a novel. They presented her as "possessed of that artifice to project, or temerity to enterprise schemes beyond the conception of stock-brokers, or, by an extraordinary superiority of talent, could infatuate men, the very spirit of whose profession existed by chicane."[44]

Finally, she returned to the legal context of the case, not only the question of her standing in the court, but of her status in the eyes of the world. Had she been Daniel's legal wife, she argued once again, everyone would have supposed that she acted "under the coercion, and influence of her husband." But, in fact, she and Daniel had lived together as, and had been assumed by society to be, husband and wife. She treated him as her "protector" and "obeyed him with the same duty." So, she now maintained, even granting that she had "actually signed those bonds," should she not be assumed to have acted from the same motives of "affection" that would be used to explain the actions of a legal wife? Here was the only conclusion that would explain her conduct at the moment when the crime was first discovered. "From the delicate texture of her feelings, she might have been seduced by such an influence; a sublimity of soul, added to a refinement of sentiment, roused the same passion that would actuate the legal wife, the legitimate mother—to declare with the voice of nature, 'I only am guilty.'" It took the shocking discovery of Robert and Daniel's plan to betray her to alter these sentiments. Then she felt free to unravel their misdeeds. Yet the world, far from sympathizing with her desperate situation, had been persuaded by their allies to malign her. Her innocence had become obscured by their pretended guiltlessness. Fortunately she could appeal to the decisions of two English juries, one of which had found them guilty, the other which had determined her innocent.[45]

Her passionate phrases seemed to allow no room for consciousness of irony. In this latest performance, Mrs. Rudd satirized those who sketched her as possessed of extraordinary talent and power. Yet by the force and peculiar extravagance of her writing, in addition to the simple fact of its existence, she justified in the eyes of many these very fears. To what extent it influenced the King's final deliberations we cannot know; that it had an impact that worked against Robert's appeal seems clear. He, at any rate, acknowledged the damage she did to his cause, when, upon hearing word of her letter to Weymouth, he altered the story he told Villette. In contrast to his former claim never to have played the market, he now swore "that he had been in the Alley, but not with the money obtained on the forgeries." In one more demonstration of her tenacity as a controversialist, she not only reported Robert's response, but proceeded, in closely packed sentences, to confute it by offering yet more evidence drawn from his stock transactions.[46] Even at the end the brothers sadly misjudged the abilities of the woman with whom they had engaged.

FINAL DELIBERATIONS

As the date for the execution drew near, all eyes turned to the King. People speculated on what the Privy Council would recommend. Large bets were placed on the outcome. "The custom of gambling on matters of life and death," one paper lamented, "was never more shockingly conspicuous than in the case of the Perreaus, immense sums having been *done* (as it is phrased) and large bets having been made at several Coffeehouses on the fate of the unhappy Brothers."[47] The papers competed fiercely for any scrap of information. "Some even say," one correspondent noted, "that because the principal hath escaped, the others must suffer if *only* because it is necessary *some* example should be made out of the parties engaged in such capital frauds."[48] But no one knew for sure which side would triumph in this evenly balanced contest. Public opinion was firmly on the side of mercy, as were a number of influential aristocratic members of the government. But several important legal figures supported the sentence, for the safety of the country. It was hard to predict what the monarch would do. George III was not easily moved by popular feeling. He took a serious approach to the duties of his office. At the time the King was preoccupied with the rebellion in the colonies, where he was pursuing a policy of firmness in support of the established order. The council had spent considerable time deliberating on the disposition of troops for America. Yet it now set aside valuable hours for a debate over the outcome of the Perreau appeal.

Part of the problem for the King was the fact that this decision did not take place in isolation. George III was widely unpopular in 1775. "The bulk of the people in every city, town, and village," reported John Wesley after a tour through the country, "do not so much aim at the ministry ... but at the King himself. ... They heartily despise his Majesty, and hate him with a perfect hatred."[49] Although most letters on behalf of the Perreaus were respectful in their address to the Crown, in many there was a harsher undercurrent. Typical was the scarcely veiled warning in one that the King needed to pardon Robert "lest further fatal acts be committed, to the Scandal of all Law and Justice, and to the Disgrace of the Royal Mercy and Humanity."[50] Such warnings were not likely to move George III from what he took as his duty, but he could not simply ignore such an outpouring of sentiment. At a time when the pageantry of justice was understood to play an important role in the maintenance of order, the King had to be concerned about the impact of his conduct. He needed to be sensitive to appearances, to the lessons that would be learned from his action.

In part the issue boiled down to a contest between feeling and a proper understanding of the nation's interest. Sentiment was all on the side of Robert Perreau. On the day of the execution the *Public Advertiser,* the paper that had taken a leading part in Robert's cause, spoke openly of its hope that the King would pardon him at the last moment. The author of the passage said he had taken the lead in efforts to secure royal mercy. The public, he wrote, had been greatly affected, "which is now manifest in the opinion of many from the great number of the most respectable nobility and gentry, who have signed their names to the petitions presented." The prime inspiration for this labor was "one of the most deserving women, the wife of the unfortunate Robert." It was impossible to imagine that a man like Robert, facing death, would continue to protest his innocence if it were not true. "Shall we," he concluded, "then hesitate to believe a man, whose whole life (if those who knew him may be credited) has been one continued scene of virtuous actions. The conclusion that naturally follows is that Robert Perreau is innocent; and shall an innocent man suffer? Forbid it honour; forbid it justice; forbid it all those feelings that do honour to humanity."[51]

Such moving appeals touched many, yet some resisted the conclusion they sought to promote. A column in one paper noted that every reader of "sensibility" was likely to be affected by the sentimental descriptions of Mrs. Perreau. Her case was "truly a pitiable one." But there could be no hope of pardon. "They stand convicted," the author observed, "of a crime of the most enormous magnitude in a commercial country. His Majesty has perhaps more feeling than any of his subjects, but the public welfare must ever be preserved by a good father of his people." It would be "impolitic" to extend "his mercy to criminals fully convicted of forgery." "The unhappy lady," he concluded, "is sincerely wished every possible comfort, but it is unfortunately impossible this comfort should any where now be found for her, but in the purity of her own actions and in the innocence of her children."[52]

Just as pressing was another concern: How would it appear if two well-off individuals received special consideration from the King? This debate had raged since the brothers' conviction the preceding June. Supporters of the Perreaus contended that their social status created a greater entitlement to pardon. The language they used to describe their worth echoed with the claims of class. Men, one correspondent wrote, "who have enjoyed a liberal education, who have kept the most respectable company, and whose characters have been hitherto unexceptionable, much more deserve our pity than the hardened wretch whose life has been a continued series of crimes."[53] The end of punishment had already been secured. "Their sudden fall from prosperity, their suffering the miseries of a dungeon for above seven months, and their names, character, and family being the sport of unfeeling crowds," such afflictions weighed more heavily on genteel persons. The further indignity of the gallows would only serve to undo the good the example of their fate offered to the fashionable and ambitious.[54]

Not everyone agreed. "Men," argued "Common Sense," "favoured by Nature with the Means of getting acquainted with the best Families, and of establishing themselves so as to bid Defiance to the World," lacked the essential requisites for pardon. They had not committed their crimes driven by necessity or pressed by poverty, but were moved by greed and ambition. Such malefactors, he argued, were not "entitled to Exemption from the Punishment sanctified by Law, and inflicted (without Reflection) on all who are not fortunate in their Connections as the Persons in Question."[55] "T. R." admitted the force of this argument. In the minds of many, Robert's former affluence and connections were a handicap, since "the uncandid and illiberal will impute the influence of justice to the interposition of rank and court interest." Only the monarch's "superiority of mind," his "determination to be guided by those feelings which have ever evinced a noble and tender soul," could be counted on to overcome such popular prejudice.[56]

The brothers' fate, one writer opined, "had excited a laudable ground of compassion in those bosoms who are not destitute of humanity." Still, their sentence exhibited "a forcible picture of the justice of our laws, which knows no distinction of persons in crimes which attack the very vitals of a commercial state." The public, the *Craftsman* argued, should focus on the moral of their story; "the sufferings of two men, torn from surrounding luxuries, and the comforts of agreeable connections, in the very meridian of life, will be a deterring example to all those who are embarked on the wide sea of expensive folly and dissipation."[57] There were those in power whose primary thought was less to untangle the issues of guilt and innocence than to present the most compelling image of a justice that punished rich and poor alike and that served as a sermon on the dangers of luxury. For them the execution was "ordered for the public good in terrorem to others." The brothers' deaths formed a "sacrifice" to the honor of these principles.[58]

These arguments about economic interest and the appearance of justice were aired again at a Privy Council meeting that sat for three hours. Among those present were the Lord Chancellor, Lords North, Suffolk, Germain, Barrington, Denbigh, Falmouth, and Lyttelton, and the Bishop of London. The Earl of Denbigh was especially inclined to mercy. According to one report, the King displayed considerable uneasiness about the guilt of Robert Perreau. A "distinguished Law Officer" who had worked hard to get to the bottom of the affair pointed out "that some of [Mrs. Rudd's] forgeries have been discovered, of which it appears highly improbable the unfortunate sufferer could be unacquainted."[59] Most other accounts emphasized the importance of the commercial aspect of the question. A law lord,

> who has much the ear of the Privy Council, spoke for near half an hour on the late report of the two unfortunate brothers. His Lordship's argument, which was very forcible, were upon the absolute necessity of supporting, in all cases whatsoever, the paper faith of this country. It is said a Great Personage walked about during the whole time, seemingly much agitated, but at last submitted to the majority of his Council.

Lord George Germain was said to have seconded the opinion.[60] "If they were pardoned," one paper reported in summarizing the position that triumphed, "in consequence of the mere influence of powerful application, no pretense could be made against extending Royal Mercy to any forger who had a man of fashion to espouse his case. This, it was feared, would operate as a powerful stimulus to the dissipated younger sons of nobility, to adopt the Perreau's method of raising money." If twenty committed this offense, not one could be executed, "with so strong a precedent in their favor."[61] Another paper said that the Duke of Newcastle applied to the King on Robert's behalf, saying that he had never requested a favor before. The King responded, however, "that the affair in question was of such fatal tendency in a trading country, it precluded all clemency."[62] In private correspondence with Lord Weymouth, the monarch took a stronger line, suggesting that he was persuaded of Robert's guilt. "There cannot be," he wrote on January 15, "the smallest doubt of the justice of the sentence found against Robert Perreau; therefore the enclosed petition will not induce me to mitigate the sentence."[63]

EXECUTION DAY

There was to be no pardon for the Perreaus. Nor was there to be a revelation that would at long last clear up the deep mystery that still seemed to surround the case. Instead, the Perreaus' impressive performance at their execution, especially their last protests of innocence, carried great weight with the public. One correspondent wrote that "he was at a loss which most to admire, whether the serene composure of the unhappy sufferers, or the evidence of the compassionate feelings of the persons present; every eye dropped a tear; and even the gaoler, accustomed as he is to such scenes, could not forbear joining in the general effusion of sorrow and pity." Several noblemen attended the execution; it was said that Lord S— was so overcome by the behavior of the brothers that he fled from the scene before the execution.[64] The brothers were dignified and self-possessed throughout the final proceedings. No word or gesture escaped from either of them that might indicate a weakening of their resolve. They acted in unison. One correspondent marveled at "these men" who had "never separated their interest or in the least accused each other."[65] Their clasped hands at the moment of death offered final testimony to the solidarity they had maintained throughout their ordeal. It fused their identities once and for all in the popular imagination.[66]

After hanging for the usual time, the seven bodies were cut down and given to friends (except those of the coiners, which were drawn and quartered). The bodies of Daniel and Robert Perreau were placed in different shells and, as befitted their status, conveyed in a hearse and four to the home of Robert in Golden Square. One who viewed them there said the resemblance between the brothers was even stronger in death than in life. Robert had, with characteristic thoroughness, settled the funeral arrangements with Mr. Flack, an undertaker in the Strand. He had resolved his family affairs, in the words of one account, with "a composure becoming a philosopher and Christian."[67] The family may have hoped to escape attention in their mourning, but public curiosity continued to attract people to the scene. As arrangements for the funeral were completed, a large but well-behaved crowd gathered at Golden Square. In an effort to secure privacy, the family arranged for an evening service, with no tolling of the bell until its conclusion. Despite these measures, they failed to escape the watchful crowd. At half past nine in the evening two hearses carried the coffins, covered in black cloth, each identified by a black nameplate, toward the church. They were followed by two mourning coaches containing Robert's two sons, along with Dr. Jackson and Vaugh Hilton, both brothers-in-law of the family. The Perreaus drew together once again in their sorrow. They were careful to display all the tokens of their respectability and status in death as they had in life.[68]

The procession moved without lights, accompanied by a large throng. By the time they reached the church of St. Martin's-in-the-Field, the crowd was so large and rude that the mourners had trouble gaining entrance. One spectator even snatched a hatband from a mourner, although it was recovered before the perpetrator escaped. The papers said that people were drawn in hopes of seeing the unfortunate youths who had accompanied their father's body. It was only with great difficulty that the curious were prevented from following the coffins into the crypt. The brothers were buried in the family vault. It was an honor granted them by the vestry of the parish, for that privilege "would not surely be granted to notorious and real criminals." It was one more indication that the public had not supported the authorities' decision. In a gesture further intended to inspire sympathy for the Perreaus, the coffins of four of Robert's deceased children were laid over his. After the church wardens drove the crowd away, the mourners were conducted to the vestry, where they were refreshed with wine. Ironically, both church wardens had been on the jury that convicted Robert, and one had been the foreman.[69]

In death the brothers achieved a kind of success that had eluded them in the courts. Respectable society provided them a posthumous restoration to its ranks. Their behavior at their execution, despite their refusal to acknowledge their crime, earned universal praise. The Perreaus, one paper reported, "behaved on this dreadful occasion agreeable to the advantage of their education, with decency, contrition and resignation." "Nothing could surpass," concluded another, "the manly and decent behaviour of the two unfortunate Perreaus yesterday. When they got out of the mourning coach, and stood in the cart to be tied to the fatal tree, they displayed such Christian resignation and true fortitude, that few persons in their unhappy station could possess." The language of such praise was conventional, but it nonetheless completed the rehabilitation of Robert Perreau, which had begun with the campaign to secure him a pardon. "If tranquil resignation, settled composure, and a becoming fearfulness of approaching death," a third paper added, "are characteristical of Christian innocence, there can scarce remain a doubt but the ill-fated brothers Perreau, were really so. Never was, surely, at that awful moment, a more solemn display of even welcoming mortality, than they demonstrated ... They appeared truly sensible of their most momentous change; and seemed to look with brightened hopes beyond it."[70]

For many, the Perreaus' final statements, when combined with their fate, were decisive. Or perhaps this was simply what all desired. A correspondent wrote to the *Gazetteer* that there no longer remained a shadow of a doubt about Robert's innocence; he died due to "the black arts of an unprincipled woman." One could, he confidently asserted, trust the solemn declaration of a man on the threshold of death, who recognized that there was no longer any hope of pardon. His perseverance in protesting his innocence to the end deserved credit. "It cannot reasonably be presumed a man would, in so solemn a manner as the unfortunate sufferer has, call the Supreme Being as a witness to the contents of a paper, unless they were (as he himself declared at the time) strictly true."[71] Another paper pronounced that since it was the crime and not the punishment that dishonored, Robert had not been made ignominious by his death. By his "noble and exemplary" death he had "amply atoned for all the folly and wickedness he was guilty of from too great confidence in, and affection for, his equally deluded and deceived twin brother."[72]

TROUBLING QUESTIONS

Despite the repeated expressions of hope that the brothers' deaths had, however tragically, revealed the truth about the case, the evidence offered by the newspapers was unsatisfying. On the contrary, mistakes and misinformation continued to fill the papers. Reports rapidly circulated that Mrs. Robert Perreau was near death and that her eldest son was ill as well. Most papers, immediately after news of the execution, told of the Queen bestowing a grant of £100 per annum on Henrietta. Others said that a subscription had been set in motion to provide for the family. These tales were as quickly followed by published denials of their truth. "The report of Mrs. Perreau being dead, or of her and her eldest Son attempting to destroy themselves, is, like many other Reports concerning that unfortunate Family, without the least Foundation."[73] Letters appeared demanding that the participants provide information, that the Drummonds confirm that they had proof of Robert's guilt, that Frankland report what he found in tracing the money, that Mrs. Rudd, now that she could not be touched, tell all she knew.[74] The mood of suspicion and doubt lingered.

Villette, the Ordinary of Newgate, quickly published his account of the last moments of the brothers. But so skeptical had the public become at every rumor connected with the case that letters demanded proof that his statement was true and came from his pen. Finally, Villette issued an affidavit confirming the accuracy of what he had written; David Cassidy, Robert's assistant, and Samuel Harman swore to its veracity.[75] Many papers rushed into print with an "authentic list" of the forgeries, in hopes that it would provide a true picture of the extent of the frauds. Immediately, letters appeared challenging the list's accuracy. One correspondent denied that a bond offered to an upholsterer had been signed with Adair's name. Robert, the letter claimed, had tendered his own note of hand and repaid it with interest as soon as it was due.[76] The list had also mentioned a bond for £1000 sent to a Reverend Barker, a Carmarthen clergyman, who, it was said, had been paying his respects to their sister Esther. According to one report the bond was returned; the transaction occasioned a split between her and Barker. An angry letter followed this story, "authorized by Esther Perreau," saying that all these tales were untrue. Rev. Barker, she noted, was a married man with several children. Such rumors appeared to be part of a scheme to defame the memories of her poor brothers. "This hitherto mysterious labyrinth of iniquity," the correspondent concluded, "planned by some lame ducks and sons of Moses, and patronized by some Right Hon. Scoundrels, in order to reimburse themselves, for screening a female prostitute, shall very soon be open to public vengeance."[77]

Several magazines hastened to defend the course of justice. "To the honour of this country it may be said," the *Weekly Magazine and Edinburgh Amusement* editorialized, "that it is not friends, it is not power, it is not interest that can save a criminal from condign punishment; and whilst humanity drops the tear of pity for their shameful exit, wisdom and good policy must respect that authority, which has done such manly justice to so excellent a constitution." But many people were not satisfied. Angry outbursts followed, as the public revealed how irritable the outcome had left it. Some blamed the King for the debacle. Several authors renewed discussion of the pardons given to the Kennedy brothers in a case of murder, whereas "an innocent, though unfortunate man" was denied mercy. "Clemency," this writer concluded, "is one of the greatest virtues that can adorn a throne, but when improperly shewn, never fails to excite our indignation."[78] A correspondent writing to the *Gazetteer* complained of the many letters written about the conduct of "the Juries who tried the unfortunate brothers." At least they had the excuse of having to cope with "so intricate a story in a very small space of time." The King could offer no such apology for his decision. Months elapsed between the brothers' conviction and execution. "Public opinion became much divided; very many of all ranks grew dissatisfied." The King gave in to those about him; "he washed his hands, ... like Pilate of old." The brothers died.[79] One correspondent hastened to answer this charge that the King was, in effect, guilty of murdering an innocent man. "It would be," he wrote, "more the part of a dutiful subject to suppose that his Majesty would not have done this without the fullest and most uncontrovertible proofs of his guilt, particularly as such powerful interest was employed to save him."[80] A third letter handled the critics still more brusquely. Disappointed in their efforts to secure a pardon, the Perreau forces vented "their spleen upon a gracious King, whom this nation ought to adore equally for his justice and humanity."[81]

If many were persuaded by their manner of dying that Robert at least was innocent, ambiguity and bitter contention continued to obscure the case. Amid the flood of letters that proclaimed Robert's martyrdom, several correspondents dissented. "How frequently, alas," one writer noted, "is it the case, that the worst offenders persist in their innocence even at the fatal tree?" This was scarcely proof that they were not guilty. Robert had had powerful motives for lying even at the end of his life. He had, after all, changed his story several times to accommodate unpleasant revelations; the various parties to the episode continued to issue conflicting tales. "Does not the contradiction they contain preclude even the least belief of either?"[82] Another angry letter disparaged attempts to dismiss the "little" lies Robert had told. Did they not reveal that he fell "victim, even by his own confession, to the propagation of deceit and falsehood"?[83] Most unsettling were the continued rumors of Robert's involvement in the Alley. They undercut basic elements in the defense argument, that he did not need money and that he was an honest, hardworking man, content with his station in life. Even commentators dissatisfied with Mrs. Rudd's *Letter to Weymouth* were forced to acknowledge the effectiveness of her case. She had revealed the inconsistencies in Robert's final statement. "That declaration is here," one review concluded, "indeed, plainly shown to have been evasive and unsatisfactory." Her letter was hard upon Robert but showed that he "richly deserved" to share the fate of his brother.[84]

Still, reviewers were impatient with her continued protests. "But as to the author's attempt to present the innocence of the woman," a commentator on the *Letter* added, "it is not less evasive and unsatisfactory." Perhaps her letter, he concluded, would have gained more credit for the humanity of its author if it had been published after rather than before the execution of the brothers.[85] One correspondent admonished Mrs. Rudd to refrain from such publications; she should make no "further endeavour to provoke the vengeance of Heaven and Earth, but to atone for her many capital offences, and the terrible consequences of them, by honestly, publicly, and amply confessing and repenting them." "In the opinion of the virtuous Romans," he concluded, "no one would undertake to defend a confessed prostituted adultress, and perjured forger, than such abandoned lawyers as they very properly termed the Devil's advocates."[86] The *Public Advertiser* complained of reports condemning the brothers when they were no longer alive to answer the charges. People, the author wrote, should show more respect for a last statement delivered at the most solemn moment imaginable.[87]

Slowly the papers lapsed into silence, most announcing that this was the only course they could, with honor, follow. The trials were over, the *Morning Chronicle* editorialized, "but the minds of mankind are not easy; and as rational conviction and legal convictions are essentially distinct, we cannot so far sacrifice our own sensations to the rigid punctilios of law, as to admit her acquittal as an indisputable proof of her innocence." The paper would not disclose private opinions, and in its public capacity it would refuse "insertion to any articles tending to extenuate the supposed criminality of Mrs. Rudd at the expense of the memories of two men, who, were they guilty to the fullest extent of possible criminality, have suffered as much as the law, in its wisdom, deems an adequate punishment."[88] "We have," announced one reviewer of a book on the case, "more than once expressed our disapprobation of obtruding upon the public any further account of Mrs. Rudd; and the present narrative, however authentic it may be, is not sufficiently interesting to justify this repeated insult to our patience."[89] Silence was not so easily secured, however, and the paper found it difficult to abide by its own promise. In February it published a letter announcing a pamphlet that would reveal "the falsity and incredible viciousness of the dying declaration of these men" and would devote the profits to the care of Mrs. Rudd's "innocent infants." Another letter followed that called its editor, Woodfall, to account, questioning the propriety of aiding children who were the "issue of prostitution and adultery." Mrs. Rudd responded in fury, defending, in particular, her own children. The editor, weary of the controversy, declared that he would publish nothing more related to the Perreaus.[90]

In this unsatisfactory manner, at least at the level of public discussion, the case came to an end. It was a pained silence that descended. Nothing had been resolved. "Since the execution of the Perreaus," wrote the *Gentleman's Magazine*, "the people appear to be as much divided in their opinions about the guilt or innocence of Robert Perreau as about the American cause." Appearances were against him, and they could not credit his dying declaration unless they imagined him to be acting under the "influence of some fatal necessity." To do that, the author concluded, would require one to suspend belief in free will. "The question is perplexing; but it is yet in the power of one person to solve the difficulty; and it is hoped that before she leaves the world she will for the satisfaction of the public and the salvation of her own soul, leave a faithful relation of all her transactions with Robert Perreau." The magazine was willing to leave her connection with Daniel veiled, "for the sake of her innocent children."[91]

Mrs. Rudd never obliged these many requests to tell all she knew. She had already said many things, all of which she claimed were true. A jury had not been ready to convict her, but the public had by 1776 come to believe she was guilty of the crime. Even as the press condemned her to silence, it continued to express the hope that she would speak the words that would heal the wound opened by the case.

Eleven

LOOKING BACK

In proportion as the minds of men become debauched and enervated, they are open to delusions of every kind. Human nature perhaps could never form a greater contrast than betwixt the *old Roman republic* and the modern dealers in beads and catgut, who disgrace the same ground . . .

I think our infatuation falls little short of the Papists, when we can in good earnest believe the wealth and power of a great nation to be truly and substantially exprest and represented *by scraps of paper,* which are so far from being property, that they may signify nothing truly, but imposture on one hand, and credulity on the other; they may be annihilated by an opinion, a report, a dream, . . . the small *bubble of Ayr,* that Caledonian *frog,* swelling to ape the English *ox,* has thrown it into violent agitation. . . So that when we see a wise and philosophical nation hugging phantoms for realities, running mad in schemes of refinement, taste, pleasure, wealth, power and greatness, by the sole aid of this civil *hocus pocus;* when we contemplate paper gold, and paper land, paper fleets, armies and revenues; a paper government, and a *supreme paper legislature;* we are apt to regard the Fairy Tales, the Travels of Gulliver and the Arabian Nights Entertainments as grave relations, and historical facts. We are really the true Enchanted Island. I begin to suspect the Thames before my eyes to be no better than a theatrical river, made of paper or tinsel; and I have frequently my doubts, from the strong propensity I find to paper, whether I am myself of any better materials. We have carried the paper manufactory to a great height, indeed, when our very houses are not only lined but built with paper. We have had our gold, silver and iron ages of the poets; the present, to mark its frivolity, is the *paper age.*

REGULUS,
London Magazine, September 1776

THE EXECUTION OF THE Perreaus left the public stunned and subdued. In the theater of the day imposture was treated comically; duplicitous characters defeated themselves, and truth was revealed in the end. Although the Perreau-Rudd case inspired a great deal of humorous comment as it unfolded, suddenly, against expectation, it ended at the gallows. It remained unclear whether the brothers' deaths represented justice to criminals, the price paid for extraordinary folly, or the murder of two innocent men.

This uncertainty made it difficult to settle on a genre within which to narrate events. The case did not fit the conventions of the standard criminal biography with its tale of downward descent into crime and last-minute repentance on the gallows. Contemporaries speculated on the best mode in which to relate the story. It was compared to a theatrical performance: "The whole conduct of these persons is such a farce as was perhaps never represented on the stage of any of our theatres." Most commonly, however, it was viewed as a "romance." The author of *The Authentic Anecdotes of the Life and Transactions of Mrs. Margaret Rudd,* for example, began his account by noting that "the contents of the following narrative may appear romantic." The anonymous *Observations on the Trial of Mr. Robert Perreau* also employed this trope. Citing Henry Drummond, it said that "Mr. Perreau's imagination seemed Quixote-like to be stuffed with *fanciful conceits.*" The lives of the brothers, a third reported, "may be considered as a dream." Explaining his notion, the author continued: "There is no doubt but the reader has perused *The History of the Seven Champions of Christendom, The Arabian Nights* entertainments and *The History of the Great Man Mountain* recorded by Swift of facetious memory; and if he reads their accounts, he must acknowledge that they are only trifles when compared with the history of the celebrated Mrs. Rudd and the Messrs. Perreau."[1] An essential element of this story lay in its make-believe quality, its fairy-tale-gone-tragically-wrong tone. Everyone involved seemed to be engaging in pretense, pretending either, like Mrs. Rudd, to be of noble lineage and family or, like the brothers, to be successful brokers and men of wealth. Romance, however, proved an unsatisfactory choice once the brothers had died on the gallows. Before long, and retrospectively, a consensus slowly emerged that would eventually blossom into unshakable conviction. It reshaped the story, simplifying the characterization of the protagonists and painting a stronger moral conclusion. The process involved selective remembering and forgetting. The new tale, a morality play, offered a form of consolation and brought closure to the episode by substituting a familiar figure, the "dangerous woman," for the more deeply troubling uncertainty about identity that had marked the experience of the case between March 1775 and January 1776.

REMEMBERING

The process of revision began almost immediately. Two Americans accorded the brothers' execution special notice in their journals. The former governor of Massachusetts, Thomas Hutchinson, remarked on encountering the people returning from Tyburn. He repeated the main outlines of the case: Daniel was a merchant and "great dealer in the Alley" who lived with a woman named Rudd; Robert was "said to have had as fair a character as any man, and to have been greatly beloved by all his acquaintance in business." Although there was no evidence against Robert of the forgery, he had attempted to pass the forged bond and told several lies to the Drummonds. "Everybody agrees that Mrs. Rudd ought to have been hanged, as being the most guilty; but the Jury had not evidence before them to convict her."[2] The other American, Curwen, who had followed the case since his arrival, noted that the two "unfortunate Brothers" had suffered while "the most guilty person, and who, in the public judgment, was the Original cause of the scene of Villainy," Mrs. Rudd, was "by an unaccountable train of crafty measures acquitted; and now lives in triumph in her wickedness."[3] These men, who saw themselves as in some sense victims of a misunderstanding and trapped by an inexorable march toward war, perhaps found in the fate of the Perreaus a history with which they identified. Hutchinson in particular, reviled by the Massachusetts radicals, accused of the wrongdoing that had precipitated the violence, might see in Robert's death the image of his own history. The "triumph" of Mrs. Rudd appeared to both men as a way to explain what was wrong with their world, a world that encompassed both the villains in America and the dangerous inattention of the imperial authorities in London.

Whatever the extent to which their special circumstances predisposed them to this reading of the event, Hutchinson and Curwen were not alone. Anne Pellet wrote to her friend Mrs. Elizabeth Shackleton in Lincolnshire in July 1775: "All conversation is I think turn'd wholly on the infamous Mrs. Rudd and her two accomplices." Mrs. Shackleton employed a different tone when she noted in her diary "the sufferings of the Perreau brothers at the hands of 'that infamous vile woman Margaret Caroline Rudd.'"[4] This explosion of anger and invective against

Mrs. Rudd became the typical way of talking about the case. Within months the complexity of the Perreau-Rudd case, which had thrown the public and justice into such confusion between March and January, receded from view, to be replaced by a simpler tale of male credulity and female duplicity. With the passage of time the brothers assumed a one-dimensional existence. Guilty or not, they came to be seen as the pawns of a more skilled and compelling figure. The success of these productions can be measured by the frequency with which Mrs. Rudd's name was repeated in succeeding decades and the long survival of this interpretation of the case.[5] While Robert Perreau passed into memory as the "innocent" Perreau, Mrs. Rudd achieved a more dubious distinction. She was called the "celebrated" or the "infamous" or, as often, the "fascinating" Mrs. Rudd. The specter of Mrs. Rudd rose out of this case to become its most memorable aspect. She stood for sexual license, unbridled passion, and at the same time cynical control and selfish manipulation. Above all, she appeared as the master of lies and deception. The fact of her escape, despite public conviction that she was a liar, consolidated a portrait of her as a consummate villain. Too late to do the Perreaus any good, people came to accept their claims as to her character, powers, and achievements. Despite her pleas that a jury had vindicated her behavior, most people believed exactly the opposite. She was the whore who exploited men and turned male institutions upside down.

As was often the case in eighteenth-century London, a flurry of theatrical and poetic productions sought to capitalize on the notoriety of the trial. Mrs. Rudd figured in a number of poetic satires that attacked the morals of the age, works that singled out the image of the duplicitous and licentious whore as the embodiment of evil. These works contributed to the legend growing up around her name. Each sought to outdo the other in mounting invective against the figure of Mrs. Rudd. Samuel Foote altered his play *The Cozeners* to include a parody of Mrs. Rudd. A still more savage portrait appeared in an opportunistic imitation of William Combe's popular *Diaboliad*, called *The Diabo-Lady*. Mrs. Rudd figured prominently among a number of candidates to become the wife of the devil.

> First appeared and to conviction swore,
> Her smallest crime was that of being Whore;
> Adultery she added to her plan,
> Defying equally both God and man;
> In forgery and perjury owned such art,
> She palmed the Gold, while others paid the smart.[6]

The devil theme was continued in a broadsheet published after the brothers' execution. "The London Tragedy" represented Mrs. Rudd in bed, either being cheered on or instructed by the Devil himself. In another scurrilous poem, "A Particular Account of the Dreadful and Shocking Apparition of the two Unfortunate Perreaus," the ghosts of the brothers, "who all appeared like flames of fire in her Bedchamber," came back to counsel repentance, "while Mrs. R— was in the Arms of a certain noble Lord well known for her Favorite." The final accusation was delivered by the ghost of Mrs. Robert Perreau (the author accepting the widespread, though erroneous, reports that she had died of grief in the wake of the executions): "Thou infidel of a woman, stop thy wicked and diabolical proceedings; though wickedness you seem to take a pride in."[7]

At one and the same time Mrs. Rudd provoked an anger, fear, and fascination that sometimes found expression in ribald humor. In the years following 1775, Mrs. Rudd's name was invoked at particular moments; in one example, a newspaper, satirizing the conduct of an aristocrat who had criticized the Americans, compared him to Mrs. Rudd boasting "of her delicate feelings."[8] In writing of the adventures of a young woman, a paper suggested that perhaps Mrs. Rudd was teaching "her to make her fortune," adding that the woman would soon "write a good bold hand."[9] One magazine told a tale that seemed to confirm the suspicion that "cuckoldom still rages in this metropolis." In a case that showed the clergy also had trouble keeping "their wives in proper order," the wife of Rev. Jenkins stood revealed as one who had conducted numerous intrigues around town. She was detected at a residence in Berwick Street, Soho, where she had taken the name of Mrs. Rudd.[10] Mrs. Rudd's reputation was not limited to Britain. In the heated exchanges over Warren Hastings's policies in India, one participant claimed that a defense of the Rohilla War had been "unworthy of Mrs. Rudd."[11] Mrs. Rudd occupied a secure place, for a generation or more, in the popular imagination as representative of both a dangerous and ludicrous form of female power.

What these expressions reveal is how quickly a particular interpretation of the episode impressed itself on the public psyche. This combination of elements was not extraordinary; it was the staple of previous "panics" in which sexual and political unrest were figured through the image of a woman. But seldom had a series of real-life events enacted this scenario so vividly and with such "fatal" consequences. There was something beyond simple moralizing that became associated with her name. Instead of being discreetly forgotten, her name was invoked with special intensity and vehemence. She embodied, it seemed, transgression and the threat that it would be successful. If the Perreaus surrendered to temptation, it was nonetheless Mrs. Rudd who seduced them with her glamour and her lies. They appeared strikingly passive and deluded, whereas she was in control. The enduring portrait of Mrs. Rudd was of the triumphant woman, whose schemes had all been realized, at the moment of her greatest victory, standing before the gallows on which were suspended the bodies of the Perreaus.

FORGETTING

The trouble with this portrayal is that it ill-accords with the various representations of her during the unfolding of the case and clashes with the conviction that her escape from punishment had as much to do with luck and prejudice as it did her skill. She owed her life to the mismanagement of the case by the authorities and the favor the law, in certain instances, showed to women. Some of her performances were masterful, but many were little short of burlesque. More often than not her written productions seemed outlandish. The public was more startled when one of her claims proved true than by the discovery of her falsehood. Measured by what she lost through this episode, her reputation and her "family," the outcome was a calamity for her.

If success in putting across a particular representation is what we look for in this case, then the palm goes to Robert Perreau. He lost his life but emerged from the catastrophe as "honest" Perreau, his reputation redeemed by what came to seem a form of martyrdom. His performances at his trial and at the gallows, and to a lesser extent those of his brother, won the applause of spectators and the press. No doubt his death encouraged people to forget the ambiguities, not to mention the shadier aspects, of his conduct. It seemed unfeeling to dwell on his indiscretions after he had paid the ultimate price for his behavior. Yet it was also true that Robert had much that he did not want the public to know. Over the course of the case considerable evidence surfaced of his involvement in unscrupulous financial deals. More might have been disclosed. None of this seemed to matter to those who now convinced themselves of Robert's integrity. It had become an article of faith, a justification for the intensity with which they mourned his fall.

This forgetting extended to the relationship between the crime and the society from which it sprang. During the period from March to January commentators sought to explain the case in terms of tendencies they observed at work in their society. The conduct of the Perreaus and Mrs. Rudd seemed all too characteristic of a certain class in London. The attention devoted to the case at a moment of acute imperial crisis in the life of the nation was offered as one more symptom of the whimsical fancy that had conquered the country. The terms for analyzing this condition had been well established by 1775. In 1771, the *London Magazine* complained of the effects of wealth upon the nation. The vast expansion in the size of England's Oriental empire had enabled new men to acquire "sudden and immense fortunes," so that they exceeded the ancient nobility in "luxury and extravagance." This alteration had produced a spirit of emulation that spread to every rank and created "a general lust of dissipation." "In fact, what with the enormous sums rapaciously accumulated in the East Indies, what with the disproportional gains of commissaries and contractors, the peculations of ministers and the frauds of stockjobbers, riches universally engrosses the minds of men." The nation was possessed by the passion for riches and display.[12] Wealth was the great corruptor of the nation, and the pursuit of fashion the clearest sign of this dangerous obsession. The public as a consequence lost its moral bearings, confused illusion for substance, and lost its sense of balance.

The specifics of the Perreau-Rudd case seemed to capture the essence of this indictment of the nation. As the preoccupation with this case intensified, forgery tended to become a metaphor for describing what was wrong with society. In passing worthless bonds the Perreaus and Mrs. Rudd presented themselves as persons of quality and presented paper as objects of value. Was it surprising that imposture and forgery should go together? Were the two in fact not inevitably connected, both consequences of the desire to be other than what one was and to have more than one had? This is why some members of the reading public considered the Perreaus to be nothing more than "Swindlers in High-life," and why Mrs. Rudd's costume and Newgate furnishings were criticized as unseemly, as "an insult [to] the Justice of their country, either by adorning a Prison as an elegant Assembly-Room, or their Persons as if going to a Ball." Things should seem what they were; a trial dress and a prison cell should be plain and unadorned. If high life was so corrupt, so permeated by "seeming," what could be expected of the rest of society, especially at a period when many felt that the "Dignity and Authority" of English justice had been "so abused and insulted as to require the most strict and severe Discipline to restore her again to due Respect and Authority"? It was "decency only, not an affected parade" that was most appropriate, not only for Mrs. Rudd, but for England in such perilous times.[13]

Discovery of forgery spread doubt everywhere. Newspaper editors, driven by the need to sell papers, faced the choice of either accepting news as genuine only to find it false, or rejecting news as forgery only to find it correct. When, following the Perreau trials, most of the London papers published a letter, ostensibly from Mrs. Rudd to Daniel's sisters in Wales, they had to justify its inclusion despite lingering doubts about its authorship. The *Morning Chronicle* attempted to make a game of the problem.

> We sincerely believe it genuine; if, however, there should exist some among *the public at large* (to use the favorite phrase of a learned Advocate) men of a different opinion, and a Bill of Indictment should be found against us by a Grand Jury of our Readers, we frankly confess we have nothing to plead in our favor but the hackneyed Old-Bailey defense.—*We are as innocent of* FORGERY *as children yet unborn;* and we solemnly protest *we do not utter it,* KNOWING IT TO BE FORGED.

News, like bonds, was increasingly necessary for the sort of life urban, commercial London had to offer, but like other paper instruments, at the end of the day its authority rested upon faith, and this case revealed how precarious such a foundation might be.[14] When the speculative schemes of Mrs. Rudd and the Perreaus exploded, there was no institution left untouched—not the press, not the authorities, not even the King.

"Juridicus" made scathing use of the Perreau case in its aftermath. Comparing the crime of private forgery with that of public or government deceit, the author concluded that the former was but a "trifling sin." "What is the Guilt," he asked, "of private Robbery to that which reaches a whole Kingdom, and by which Millions are injured and oppressed? Sir, the forging of Acts of Parliament is a crime of the greatest Magnitude, and which I will venture to call High Treason to the People." This passage of false laws, made possible by the use of "Bribes, Places and Pensions," had not only "robbed the Kingdom of its Money" but "abridged it of its freedom." The men responsible for making laws that did not flow from or represent the will of the people, "Juridicus" claimed, were forgers of the gravest sort, "a Kind of licensed Felons, who escape Justice, as numerous Bandetti often do, when there is no Force or Power strong enough to bring them to Justice."[15] Thus, from reflections on the interesting and scandalous case of forgery, from contemplating the motives and ends of its participants, contemporaries saw larger and potentially more serious threats. Questions of class and gender, law and journalism, and even of government itself, were raised in its wake.

Forgery seemed rampant in 1775; the crime was emblematic of the kind of nation Britain had become, a country so wrapped up in dreams of quick wealth and the pursuit of fleeting fashions that it could not distinguish illusion from reality, the wicked from the moral. It was a "true Enchanted Island," as the *London Magazine* lamented in September 1776; the situation would have been hilarious except that the consequences were so serious. A nation lost its colonies; two men perished on the gallows. No one in authority seemed able to halt the slide into disaster. Magistrates had been accused of making the wrong decision; perhaps they were biased or had been manipulated by sinister influences. Justice appeared chimerical, the laws bloodthirsty. Nagging doubts and troubling uncertainties reinforced the sense that appearances could not be trusted and that fatal results flowed from such confusion. These were the reflections that occurred to people as they wrestled with the question of the guilt of the Perreau brothers and Mrs. Rudd.

While the outcome of the case remained in doubt, the contest between Mrs. Rudd and the Perreaus played into deeper sources of unease associated with questions of empire, fashion, and paper credit. We have exploited this tension to explore the fault lines that ran through eighteenth-century London society. But as we have tried to suggest in these few pages, the significance of the case did not suddenly end with the execution of the brothers. Rather a reinterpretation of the entire episode was soon under way. This revision of the tale was not just a matter of simplification. It also involved a censoring of the story so that the ambiguities, many of which cast an unflattering light upon English culture, were left out. Even more significant, its most important voice, that of Mrs. Rudd, was silenced, as she had never been during the actual unfolding of the events. Mrs. Rudd ceased to speak for herself; instead she became a symbol of the ills that were attributed to her society—a diseased fashion, an insidious immorality, a sinister corruption. In this way, the more diffuse worries about the effects of luxury and extravagance were reorganized along gender lines. The dangerous figure appeared to be the woman of will, ambition, and skill. The solution was to reinforce the sense of woman's proper sphere and to reprove more fiercely women who departed from that path. In a small way, then, this episode contributed to the transition that took place in the later 1770s and gained strength in the 1780s, a movement characterized by earnestness, seriousness, and religious revival. Energy was directed into efforts to reform the nation and the world, to advance the reformation of manners and abolish the slave trade. This movement mingled evangelical themes with renewed appreciation for institutions such as the monarchy and the law. It insisted upon greater moral rectitude in private as well as public life. It imposed a stricter censorship upon the press and the stage. The Perreau-Rudd case convulsed a society at a precarious moment, when wild swings in the nation's fortunes, from victory to civil war, boom to bust, had produced doubt, uncertainty, and a sense of loss of moral direction. The folly and excess it exposed spurred on those advocates of moral reform and social conservatism who sought to promote a national revival. In retrospect, at least, the public was no longer in doubt about the identities of the participants in this strange and unsettling affair.[16]

EPILOGUE

After flooding the daily newspapers for almost a year, the story of the famous forgery and its protagonists faded from public view. Whether or not justice had been done, the price had been paid, the Perreaus executed, Mrs. Rudd released, and the case closed. However, many of the case's main characters survived for several decades.

Admiral Frankland died in 1784, with only a brief notice in the press. In September 1809 Mrs. Henrietta Perreau died in upper Mary-le-bone Street, Fitzroy Square. In the immediate aftermath of the executions she had been reported to have attempted suicide or gone raving mad, but in fact she seems to have stayed on at the Golden Square address until 1798, when she presumably moved to the new lodgings.[1] Her son, Robert Samuel Perreau, left Westminster School in 1775 and in 1777 became a writer for the East India Company in Bengal. He was nominated by a former chairman of the company and soon to be member of the Supreme Council in Bengal. His appointment showed that, despite the scandal, the Perreau family retained influential connections. In 1808 Robert transferred to Sumatra, where he died in 1811. His aunt, Esther Perreau, died in Carmarthen in 1810.[2] Alexander Adair, the son of William, died in 1834. He had been an army agent, like his father, conducting an "extensive business." "In 1775," the *Gentleman's Magazine* noted, "his name came before the public as that which was forged in the memorable case committed by the brothers Perreau." On his death,

Alexander left several hundred thousand pounds along with an estate in Suffolk purchased by his father.[3]

What of Mrs. Rudd? We have seen how, in the late 1780s, she re-emerged briefly as a failed essayist and novel-writer; we have another glimpse of her through the eyes and pen of her last known and perhaps most famous lover, James Boswell. In 1776, when he first met her, Boswell was not yet ensconced in his "canonical" niche; like many of the other actors in this account, Boswell had come to London to make his name and fortune and had still not achieved his ambition. Throughout his life, he was drawn to the extraordinary, and fame, or infamy, was an almost irresistible temptation. It seemed fated that he and Mrs. Rudd must meet.[4]

Boswell's great genius was his ability to impress his personality onto every individual he described or discussed. Boswell's Johnson thus comes across as quite different from Thrale's or Sir John Hawkins's Johnson. Comparing himself with Homer, Boswell took immense pleasure in the public impact and influence of *his* Johnson. Repeating the comment of an "honourable and reverend friend" that Boswell had made the world of fashion "all talk Johnson," Boswell added, "Yes ... I have Johnsonised the land; and I trust they will not only talk, but think Johnson." Of course, the Johnson he was referring to was the man immortalized and preserved in his own *Life* of the man.[5] In his account of Rudd, like his life of Johnson, of paramount importance was her impact on him. We read in his journal of her ability to bewitch and amuse him, but we get more sense of the man than of the mistress. Mrs. Rudd, in these accounts, becomes Boswell's "creature," almost his creation. Even while noting that her conversation was the only woman's that Boswell ever cited, posterity reads of Mrs. Rudd through Boswell's eyes.[6] Even so, Boswell's comments on Rudd accord with how Mrs. Rudd presented herself, in both her own writings and public performances. Her qualities of mind, her verbal facility, and their shared hopes of social success are all visible in his depiction.

Before they met, Boswell confessed to Dr. Johnson that he was attracted to her "as a woman of extraordinary address and insinuation." At their first meeting he recorded his feelings of surprise and anxiety and his fear of bewitchment. His interest in her was "induced by the fame of her talents, address, and irresistible power of fascination." Later, Boswell reported that Johnson exclaimed, "I envy him his acquaintance with Mrs. Rudd."[7]

Even before she returned to her apartments, where Boswell sat waiting for her, he noted a "sort of palpitation at my heart," and he terrified himself with thoughts of resident murderers or ghosts. When he heard her on the stairs he "was all impatience and trepidation." Boswell narrowly detailed her imperfections, but, on the whole, he was so pleased with her that he "could believe her power to be quite what we have read." He told her that she was reckoned "quite a sorceress, possessed of enchantment." She did not contradict him, but replied that she could not enchant anyone. He wrote of the power of her eyes and voice, which made no direct assault but worked unseen to capture a soul. She combined those elements he always found exciting—notoriety and the danger of sexual transgression.[8]

Why did Mrs. Rudd encourage Boswell's attentions? Even Boswell wondered. Concluding a remarkable letter to his wife, telling her of this first interview with Rudd, he speculated: "I wondered what she thought of me. I imagined I was very agreeable, and it pleased me much that she never asked my name, or any thing at all about me, which shewed perfect good breeding. I would not for a good deal have missed this scene." While it is undoubtedly the case that Boswell could be charming, in 1776 Mrs. Rudd required more than agreeableness in a male. She confessed to Boswell at their first meeting that she would not marry again "unless it was a man of rank and fortune that could bear her up."[9] While a man of Lyttelton's stature might offer her entry into polite society and supply short-term financial assistance, Boswell was in no position to do either. Married and at least publicly faithful to his dear Margaret, Boswell had neither the will nor the means to keep Mrs. Rudd in any style at all. Yet she agreed to see him twice, in April and May 1776, and renewed and deepened the friendship in 1785.

One possibility for her encouragement is that Boswell was related to and stood on good terms with several of the great families of Scotland, families with whom Rudd too claimed affinity. Though she may not have known, and did not ask his name at that first meeting, his card informed her of his acquaintance with Robert Macqueen, later Lord Braxfield, a man of importance in the North. At their first meeting she spoke to Boswell easily and to the point about their mutual acquaintance—Lord and Lady Gower, the Galloways, and Lord Rawdon. She told him "she liked Scotland and would perhaps visit it again, and would go to the house of Mr. Stewart of Phisgil to which she had many invitations." Together they searched their family lineage and found they were distantly cousins. It is possible that through Boswell Mrs. Rudd hoped to find support, both fiscal and social, from those wellborn members of the family she claimed as her own.[10]

On August 8, 1785, Boswell received a note from Mrs. Rudd sending her compliments and asking him to call on her. He went and found her "as well as ever and ... exceedingly agreeable." By the mid-1780s Boswell was a person of wide repute, and now Rudd asked him for a recommendation to Dundas so that he in turn might introduce her to the Lord Chancellor. She hoped that the latter would make "a man do her justice with whom she had lived six years." She also begged that Boswell not forget her. When Boswell returned (we never learn whether he, in fact, managed the recommendation to Dundas) he confessed to being tantalized by but in no position to keep her. Whether Rudd still hoped for something else from this relationship, or whether, no longer young, she merely wished for some companionship, we cannot know. At forty Mrs. Rudd was clearly on the wane.[11] To Boswell, however, she still seemed desirable and enticing. By November 1785 he mentioned his "cravings" and a visit to her. By February 1786 he had become a regular caller; a day seldom passed without his seeing her. Once, he woke in great distress when he dreamed that Dr. Munro had told him that his long-suffering wife's cough was serious. But when he told Mrs. Rudd the dream, implying a guilty conscience about his behavior, she told him it "imported all was well at home." Boswell seemed content with that answer and amazed at her perspicacity. He was less easy after Mrs. Rudd expressed anger at an unexpected late-night visit to her. He was shocked to find his enchantress angry, and he departed with a conviction that he must break with her. But the next day when he returned and found "a gentler reception," he was reconciled with her. He promised to dine with her and did so on March 4. It was an engaging evening filled with "much agreeable conversation" on topics from Rousseau to current politics.[12]

Boswell attempted "to charm" Mrs. Rudd, and she responded with "a romantic letter." In this period Boswell wrote of her as kind and understanding. She soothed him. He could not help thinking of her as he danced with a "pleasing girl." Boswell wrote in a kind of ecstasy of her: "So good, so generous, was she. Elegantly dressed; satin *couleur de rose;* her hair in perfect taste—not to be discomposed."[13] Even in her middle age, her attention to dress and her ability to charm seemed unabated.

Yet he was aware that his association with Mrs. Rudd might "sink him."[14] Although he projected on to her the power of the witch to enchant and manipulate, the greater fear that haunted him was his concern with popular approval. Thus, he wrote to a friend, asking him to keep the details of the "*ten-*

dresse" quiet. "There is no harm in talking of it with levity as I do at large. But no *particulars*."[15] He used code names to refer to her, calling her "Down-patrick" on one occasion, and "Neck or nothing" on another. When he spoke to his friends the Stuarts about her, Mrs. Stuart responded that "a woman who thought as she did might retire with a lover to a desert island without remorse, but was culpable in offending against the laws of society." Still, she could not but confess being "pleased with her extraordinary talents." Colonel Stuart was more outspoken, calling her a "w—re." "I was shocked by his hardness," wrote Boswell.[16]

On April 23, 1786, Boswell joined Mrs. Rudd, at her suggestion, on a visit to the Magdalen Hospital, an asylum for penitent prostitutes. His friend Courtenay joked to him, "to leave her there?" But the witty comment some-how worked upon Boswell, for this was his last visit with her. Perhaps what finally caused the rupture was her reflection, which deeply affected him, that she no longer went to St. Martin's to hear Dr. Harrison preach because of "who is buried there." Suddenly Boswell, chilled perhaps by the fatal memory of her former lover and his end, decided he "disliked this *low* association."[17]

He made a resolution to reform, then regretted his choice and fantasized about reversing it. When, a year later, on May 29, 1787, troubled by a dream in which his wife and Mrs. Rudd battled over him, he sought her out, he discovered she was no longer at the old address. "Two old gentlewomen, sis-ters, to one of whom the house belonged, gave me a sad account of her con-tracting debts, saying she had an estate in Ireland and one in Scotland, and being now in the Fleet prison." "They claimed much of her; were desirous to know who I was, and asked if my name was Rawdon." Boswell replied no, but that they should tell Mrs. Rudd that "Mr. Parr had called."[18] Boswell, like Mrs. Rudd, was not above using pseudonyms when it suited him. They were never to meet again, though in 1792 Boswell received an anonymous note from an unknown admirer suggesting he should undertake her biogra-phy, that only his talented pen could do her credit.[19]

Mrs. Rudd's death was reported many times. One periodical printed a no-tice that she had died in Ireland in 1779. A few years later the *Morning Post* made light of such reports. It announced that the "celebrated Mrs. Rudd," "so often killed by the newspapers," had, in November 1786, attended the "Covent Garden Theatre." In 1794 the *Carlton Magazine* said that the woman "whose adventures have so often been the subject of public curiosity" was in Newgate, where she lived wretchedly. She was living with a man on the debtor's side and seldom stirred "out of the place in which they sleep."[20] The *Times* in 1797 told of her death "a short time since in an obscure apartment near Moorfields." The *Gentleman's Magazine* in 1800 reported the death of a Mrs. Rudd in Hardingstone, Northamptonshire. "Mrs. Rudd," the announcement went, "was the person who had so narrow an escape for her life on her trial for the forgery for which the two Perreaus were hanged." She had "gained a competent living by writing for the Reviews."[21] When Valentine Rudd died in 1809, one journal remarked that he was the husband of the famous Mrs. Rudd, "who in 1775 engaged the attention of the public by shaking off from her own neck to those of the Perreaus a halter in which she was very near being caught for forging a bond." It was then reported that she had died on February 3, 1800, but that her husband had remarried on October 8, 1798. He had called himself a widower at the time he married a woman named Judith Briggs, and he proceeded to live with her in the Duchess of Marlborough's almshouse in St. Albans.[22] It seems likely that sometime between 1798 and 1800 Mrs. Rudd died, though we shall probably never know where or when.[23]

Before we leave her to fate and obscurity, however, we should consider Horace Walpole's evaluation of her public impact. On Saturday, February 26, 1791, the aged correspondent sat down in his home in Berkeley Square to write a letter to one of his favorite young ladies, Miss Mary Berry, his "angel, both inside and out," who was then in Pisa. At seventy-four, after a lifetime of letter-writing, he had honed his ability to interest friendly young women. He knew that young people longed for scandal, but at this time he regretted having none to retail: "The present season has been very unprolific, and we are forced to import French news, as we used to do fashions and *operas comiques*." How odd, he reflected, that the tattle should, perforce, be so thin, for London was usually such a nursery for gossip. London was a fertile hotbed of remarkable people, so "apt to produce Wilkes and George Gordons, and Mrs. Rudds and Horne Tookes and other phenomena wet and dry."[24] Miss Berry had been just a young girl sixteen years earlier, when the Rudd case was a cause célèbre, yet Walpole assumed, and probably rightly, that she would know all about Mrs. Rudd and understand and agree with his assessment of her as in the same league as three of the most famous, or infamous, men of the age.

ABBREVIATIONS

Following are abbreviations of the most frequently cited newspapers and magazines in the notes.

AR   *Annual Register*

CM   *Craftsman, or Say's Weekly Journal*

CR   *Critical Review*

DA   *Daily Advertiser*

DNB   *Dictionary of National Biography*

FFBJ   *Felix Farley's Bristol Journal*

Gaz   *Gazetteer and New Daily Advertiser*

GEP   *General Evening Post*

GM   *Gentleman's Magazine*

LC   *London Chronicle*

LEP   *London Evening Post*

Lloyd's   *Lloyd's Evening Post and British Chronicle*

LM   *London Magazine*

MC   *Morning Chronicle and London Advertiser*

Mdsx J   *Middlesex Journal and Evening Advertiser*

MP   *Morning Post and Daily Advertiser*

MR	*Monthly Review*
NM	*Newcastle Magazine*
OBSP	*Old Bailey Sessions Papers*
PA	*Public Advertiser*
SM	*Scot's Magazine*
St. J's	*St. James's Chronicle; or British Evening Post*
T&C	*Town & Country Magazine*
UM	*Universal Magazine*
WM	*Weekly Magazine*

NOTES

INTRODUCTION

1. *MC*, June 17, 1775. For an interesting comparison with the French cause célèbre, see Sarah Maza, *Private Lives and Public Affairs: The Causes Célèbres of Prerevolutionary France* (Berkeley: University of California Press, 1993). While in terms of the role of the press and the criticism of legal institutions the French and British cases appear strikingly similar, in other respects the episodes point up differences between the two nations. Letters to the newspapers played a much larger role in the Perreau-Rudd case, and issues of class assumed a different character. Most significantly, the British episode had no political consequences.

2. This is the first line of *The Genuine Memoirs of Messrs. Perreau* (London, 1775).

ONE. TO THE HANGING TREE

1. Samuel Curwen, *The Journal of Samuel Curwen, Loyalist,* ed. Andrew Oliver, vol. 1 (Cambridge, Mass.: Harvard University Press, 1972), p. 107.

2. *MC*, January 18, 1776.

3. Clive Emsley, *Crime and Society in England, 1750–1900* (London: Longman, 1987), p. 209; V. A. C. Gatrell, *The Hanging Tree: Execution and the English People 1770–1868* (Oxford: Oxford University Press, 1994), especially chapter 2.

4. *MC*, January 18, 1776.

5. John Villette, *A Genuine Account of the Behavior and Dying Words of Daniel and Robert Perreau* (London, 1776), pp. 10–11.

6. *MP*, January 18, 1776.

7. *MC*, January 18, 1776; *Gaz*, January 18, 1776.

8. *MP*, January 18, 1776.

9. *PA*, January 18, 1776.

10. *LC,* January 16–18, 1776; *Gaz,* January 18, 1776, January 19, 1776.

11. *MP,* January 18, 1776.

12. Villette, *Genuine Account,* pp. 10–14.

13. *LC,* January 16–18, 1776; *Gaz,* January 18, 1776, January 19, 1776.

14. *PA,* January 18, 1776.

15. Villette, *Genuine Account,* p. 12; *MC,* January 18, 1776; *Gaz,* January 18, 1776; *MP,* January 18, 1776.

16. *MC,* January 18, 1776; *PA,* January 18, 1776, January 23, 1776; *Gaz,* January 18, 1776; Villette, *Genuine Account,* pp. 8, 15, 19–21.

17. *PA,* January 23, 1776; *MP,* January 20, 1776; *MC,* January 23, 1776; Villette, *Genuine Account,* pp. 8, 15, 19–21.

18. *MC,* January 18, 1776; *PA,* January 18, 1776; *Gaz,* January 18, 1776.

TWO. ALARMING CRIMES AND UNSETTLING STORIES

1. William Addington, *An Abridgement of Penal Statutes* (London, 1775).

2. Henry Dagge, a close friend of Robert Perreau, belonged to a family of lawyers; his brothers John and James were solicitors as well. Horace Mann's brother recommended him to Horace Walpole, and the latter adopted him as his "own lawyer." He was, Walpole wrote, "in great reputation." Garrick, in 1768, wrote to his friend, Peter Fountain, that he had "always heard him Spoken of, as one of great Skill, & undoubted probity in his profession." Dagge's work, *Considerations on Criminal Law* (London, 1772), in three volumes, offered a compendium of the most up-to-date thought on the principles of punishment. Horace Walpole, *Correspondence* (New Haven: Yale University Press, 1965), 21: 365, 22: 268; *Letters of David Garrick,* edited by David Little and George Kahrl (Cambridge, Mass.: Belknap Press, 1963), 3: 989.

3. The fullest account of these transactions can be found in a pamphlet version of the trials, *The Trials of Robert and Daniel Perreau* (London, 1775).

4. *St. J's,* March 14–16, 1775.

5. Samuel Curwen, like so many recent arrivals, insisted upon attending Bow Street. He described Fielding as "a venerable elderly gentleman with hoary locks and blind (as Justice is represented to be) having a black fillet over his eyes, of a mild deportment, ready apprehension and great penetration, as his queries to the prisoners manifest" (Samuel Curwen, *The Journal of Samuel Curwen Loyalist,* edited by Andrew Oliver [Cambridge, Mass.: Harvard University Press, 1972], 1: 52). One visitor to London in 1779 expressed admiration for Fielding's management of an investigation; he "was much amused and interested with the appearance of Sir John Fielding, the singular adroitness with which he conducted the business of his office. Sir John had a bandage over his eyes, and held a little switch or rod in his hand, waving it before him as he descended from the bench. The sagacity he discovered in the questions he put to the witness, and a marked and successful attention as I conceived, not only to the words, but to the accents and tones of the speaker, supplied the advantage which is usually rendered by the eye; and his skillful arrangement of the questions leading to the detection of concealed facts, impressed me with the highest respect for his singular ability as a police magistrate." Fielding, at the time of this hearing, was still recovering from the shock of the death of his

close friend Thomas Nuthall on March 2, who collapsed after an exchange of gunfire with a robber near Hounslow Heath (Ronald Leslie-Melville, *The Life and Work of Sir John Fielding* [London: L. Williams, 1934], pp. 292–293, 296–297). See also John Styles, "Sir John Fielding and the Problem of Criminal Investigation in Eighteenth-Century England," *Transactions of the Royal Historical Society*, 5th ser., 33 (1983): 127–149.

6. *Trials of Robert*, pp. 3–6, 11–13.

7. Ibid.

8. *St. J's*, March 14–16, 1775; *CM*, March 14, 1775; *MC*, March 16, 1775; *The Correspondence of Edmund Burke*, edited by Lucy Sutherland, et al. (Cambridge: Cambridge University Press, 1960), 2: 171.

9. Hector Bolitho and Derek Peel, *The Drummonds of Charing Cross* (London: Allen & Unwin, 1967), pp. 58–68.

10. Randall McGowen, "Knowing the Hand: Forgery and the Proof of Writing in Eighteenth-Century England," *Historical Reflections/Reflexions Historiques* 24 (1998): 385–414.

11. *St. J's*, March 14–15, 1775; *MC*, March 15, 1775; *CM*, March 18, 1775; *Trials of Robert*, pp. 7, 13–16.

12. *St. J's*, March 14, 1775; *MC*, March 16, 1775; *Trials of Robert*, pp. 4–6.

13. *St. J's*, March 14–16, 1775; *Mdsx J*, March 11–14, 1775.

14. *Trials of Robert*, p. 9.

15. *MC*, March 16, 1775; *St. J's*, March 14–16, 1775; *Gaz*, June 2, 1775; *Trials of Robert*, pp. 3–6. *Mdsx J*, March 11–14, 1775, offered a fuller version of the meeting between Robert Perreau and William Adair, but it got the basic chronology of events wrong. No doubt different papers relied upon different sources to add detail to the basic story.

16. *Bath Chronicle*, September 21, 1775.

17. *MC*, March 16, 1775; *Trials of Robert*, pp. 10–13.

18. *Trials of Robert*, pp. 3–6, 11, 31–33, 54.

19. Ibid.; *Gaz*, June 2, 1775.

20. J. M. Beattie, *Crime and the Courts in England 1660–1800* (Princeton: Princeton University Press, 1986), pp. 35–41; Peter King, *Crime, Justice and Discretion in England, 1740-1820* (Oxford: Oxford University Press, 2000), chapter 2.

21. *The True and Genuine Lives and Trials of the Two Unfortunate Brothers, Robert and Daniel Perreau* (London, 1775), pp. 3–4; *MP*, March 29, 1775; Randall McGowen, "From Pillory to Gallows: The Punishment of Forgery in the Age of the Financial Revolution," *Past and Present* 165 (1999): 107–140.

22. Randall McGowen, "Forgery Discovered, or the Perils of Circulation in Eighteenth-Century England," *Angelaki* 1 (1993–1994): 113–129.

23. Add. Ms. 53808, #121, British Library, letter from James Adair to his son.

24. *OBSP*, October 19–25, 1774, pp. 467–468; *GM* 44 (1774): 592–593.

25. *St. J's*, March 14–15, 1775; *MC*, March 20, 1775.

26. *MC*, March 16, 1775; *St. J's*, March 14–16, 1775; *PA*, March 6, 1775; *MP*, March 16, 1775; *MC*, August 14, 1775; *CM*, March 18, 1775.

27. *St. J's*, March 14–16, 1775; *MC*, March 16, 1775; *CM*, March 18, 1775; *PA*, March 16, 1775.

28. *MP*, March 18, 1775; *MC*, March 16, 1775; *CM*, March 18, 1775; *Mdsx J*, March 16, 1775; *St. J's*, March 14–16, 1775.

29. *Mdsx J*, March 16, 1775.

30. For more on the rise of "circumstantial evidence," see Alexander Welsh, *Strong Representations* (Baltimore: Johns Hopkins University Press, 1992).

31. *Mdsx J*, March 16, 1775; Marcellus, *A Letter to the Earl of Suffolk* (London, 1775), p. 6.

32. John Beattie, "The Criminality of Women in Eighteenth-Century England," *Journal of Social History* 8 (1975): 80–116; Beattie, *Crime and the Courts*, p. 414; *Laws Respecting Women* (London, 1777), pp. 70–71; King, *Crime, Justice and Discretion*, pp. 196–207.

33. Theodosia, *Genuine Memoirs of the Mess. Perreau* (London, 1775), pp. 181–187; *Forgery Unmasked* (London, 1775), p. 8.

34. *Mdsx J*, March 15, 1775; *St. J's*, March 14–16, 1775; *PA*, March 16, 1775; *MP*, March 18, 1775.

35. *MP*, March 17, 1775; *Gaz*, March 17, 1775; *CM*, March 18, 1775; *St. J's*, March 16–18, 1775.

36. *Gaz*, March 18, 1775; *Mdsx J*, March 16–18, 1775; *MP*, March 18, 1775; *MC*, March 18, 1775.

37. *MP*, March 18, 1775; *St. J's*, March 18, 1775; *Trials of Robert*, pp. 16–17, 28–29.

38. Add. Ms. 53808, #121, *British Library*, letter from James Adair to his son.

39. *Mdsx J*, March 16–18, 1775.

40. *GM* 45 (1775): 149.

41. *Mdsx J*, March 16–18, 1775; *MP*, March 18, 1775, employed precisely the same language. See also *St. J's*, March 18, 1775.

42. *MP*, March 16, 1775.

43. Ibid., June 2, 1775; June 3, 1775; *GEP*, June 3, 1775. Walter Harrison reported the complaints concerning the taking of money for admission to the court. Courts were meant to be free so "that no judicial proceedings can be in a secret, clandestine manner, but that the conduct of the judges, juries and witnesses, is submitted to the eye of a judicious and impartial public, without any expense, fee or gratification whatever" (*A New and Universal History, Description and Survey of the Cities of London and Westminster* [London, 1775], p. 680).

44. Hawkins, quoted in J. M. Beattie, "Scales of Justice: Defense Counsel and the English Criminal Trial in the Eighteenth and Nineteenth Centuries," *Law and History Review* 9 (1991): 223, 227, and more generally, 221–267; Beattie, *Crime and the Courts*, pp. 340–348, 376.

45. *Trials of Robert*, pp. 13–15; *The Diary of John Baker*, edited by Philip C. Yorke (London: Hutchinson, 1931), p. 318.

46. Peter Brown, *The Chathamites* (London: Macmillan, 1967), pp. 231–262.

47. *Beattie*, "Scales of Justice," pp. 221–267; *Trials of Robert*, pp. 7–10. The trials of the Perreaus and Mrs. Rudd show defense counsel employing many of the tactics that William Garrow would perfect a decade later.

48. *MP*, June 2, 1775; *Gaz*, June 2, 1775; *PA*, June 2, 1775; *MC*, June 2, 1775.

49. *GM*, supplement (1811): 638. Cumberland described the effects of that speech on the greatest actor of the day, David Garrick: "I dined with Garrick on the very day when Robert Perreau had delivered it in court; there was a large company, and he was expatiating upon the effect of it, for he had been present; he even detailed the heads of it with considerable accuracy, and was so rapturous in his praises of it, that

he predicted confidently, though not truly, that the man who drew up that defense had saved the prisoner's life, and what would he not give to know who it was?" (*Memoirs of Richard Cumberland* [London, 1804], 205). The Perreaus had another link with the world of the theater; Henry Dagge, along with his brother James and the bookseller Leake, bought shares in Covent Garden in 1768 (*Letters of Garrick*, 2: 595).

50. *Gaz,* June 7, 1775; *MP,* June 6, 1775.
51. *Trials of Robert,* pp. 18–25.
52. Ibid., pp. 22–25.
53. *FFJ,* June 3, 1775; *MC,* June 2, 1775.
54. *Diary of John Baker,* p. 318.
55. *Trials of Robert,* pp. 26–27.
56. Ibid., pp. 17–18, 27–29.
57. Ibid., pp. 30–31.
58. Beattie, *Crime and the Courts,* pp. 350–351.
59. *Trials of Robert,* pp. 14, 33–37; *MP,* June 2, 1775; see *MC,* June 2, 1772.
60. *Diary of John Baker,* pp. 318–319. Baker secured admission to the trial through the interest of a fellow West Indian and alderman, Richard Oliver. Wilkes, the Lord Mayor, Baker reported, "never spoke once and slept during part of Aston's summing up of evidence, which lasted an hour and 42 minutes."
61. Beattie, *Crime and the Courts,* pp. 379–389, and more generally, chapter 7.
62. *Gaz,* June 2, 1775; *MC,* June 2, 1775; *MP,* June 2, 1775; *Memoirs of Richard Cumberland,* 205.
63. *PA,* June 2, 1775; *MC,* June 3, 1775, June 9, 1775; *Gaz,* June 2, 1775; *MP,* June 2, 1775; Marcellus, *Letter,* pp. 10–12.
64. *Trials of Robert,* pp. 37–38; *Gaz,* June 3, 1775; *St. J's,* June 1–3, 1775; *MC,* June 5, 1775; *MP,* June 5, 1775.
65. *Trials of Robert,* pp. 37–43; *St. J's,* June 1–3, 1775.
66. George Lillo, *The London Merchant,* edited by William McBurney (Lincoln: University of Nebraska Press, 1965). One correspondent called Mrs. Rudd "a second Millwood," one of those women who were "false as they are fair" (*PA,* January 25, 1776). See Laura Hanft Korobkin, *Criminal Conversations: Sentimentality and Nineteenth-Century Legal Stories of Adultery* (New York: Columbia University Press, 1998), for a fine exposition of the relation of the two rhetorical systems. For a useful reading of *The London Merchant,* see Stephanie Barbe Hammer, *The Sublime Crime* (Carbondale: Southern Illinois University Press, 1994), chapter 1.
67. *MP,* July 6, 1775.
68. *MC,* June 8, 1775.
69. *Gaz,* June 2, 1775; *MP,* June 2, 1775; *PA,* June 9, 1775.
70. *MC,* June 17, 1775, July 4, 1775; *Gaz,* July 4, 1775.
71. *MC,* June 8, 1775.

THREE. THE PRESS AND THE CASE

1. Solomon Lutnick, *The American Revolution and the British Press 1775–1783* (Columbia: University of Missouri Press, 1967), pp. 50–52. For a compendium of the

news of the period, see John Hampden, *An Eighteenth-Century Journal, Being a Record of the Years 1774–1776* (London: Macmillan, 1940).

2. *MC,* March 13, 1775; the identical report appeared in *LEP,* March 11–14, 1775.

3. *Mdsx J,* March 11–14, 1775; *Lloyd's,* March 11–14, 1775; *LC,* March 11–14, 1775; *St. J's,* March 11–14, 1775; *GEP,* March 14, 1775; *Gaz,* March 15, 1775; *MP,* March 14, 1775.

4. *NM* (1785): 7; William Blackstone, *Commentaries on the Laws of England* (Chicago: University of Chicago Press, 1979), 4: 151; Hannah Barker, *Newspapers, Politics, and Public Opinion in Late Eighteenth-Century England* (Oxford: Clarendon Press, 1998), pp. 1–2; Kathleen Wilson, *The Sense of the People: Politics, Culture and Imperialism in England, 1715–1785* (Cambridge: Cambridge University Press, 1998), pp. 27–44; James Boswell, *The Life of Samuel Johnson* (Oxford: Oxford University Press, 1966), p. 477; Styles, "Sir John Fielding," pp. 141–143.

5. *NM* (1785): 7; Barker, *Newspapers, Politics, and Public Opinion,* pp. 10–11; Richard Rea, *The English Press in Politics 1760–1774* (Lincoln: University of Nebraska Press, 1963), p. 169; Eckhart Hellmuth, "'The Palladium of All Other English Liberties': Reflections on the Liberty of the Press in England during the 1760s and 1770s," in *The Transformation of Political Culture: England and Germany in the Late Eighteenth Century,* edited by Eckhart Hellmuth (London: Oxford University Press, 1990), pp. 467–501. There were at least seven public debates about the value of the press during the 1770s; see Donna T. Andrew, *London Debating Societies 1776–1799* (London: London Record Society, 1994).

6. De Lolme, quoted in *NM* (1785): 6; John Sainsbury, *Disaffected Patriots: London Supporters of Revolutionary America 1769–1782* (Kingston: Queens-McGill University Press, 1987), p. 29.

7. Quoted in Jonathan Barry, "The Press and the Politics of Culture in Bristol, 1660–1775," in *Culture, Politics and Society in Britain 1660–1800,* edited by J. Black and J. Gregory (Manchester: Manchester University Press, 1991), p. 65; Barker, *Newspapers, Politics and Public Opinion,* pp. 49–53, 56, 76; Arthur Aspinall, *Politics and the Press c. 1780–1850* (London: Home & Van Thall, 1949), pp. 6–7; Ian Christie, *Myth and Reality in Late Eighteenth-Century British Politics* (London: Macmillan, 1970), pp. 311–316.

8. NM (1785): 7.

9. Wilson, *Sense of the People,* pp. 30–34; Barker, *Newspapers, Politics and Public Opinion,* pp. 25, 97, 110–111; John Money, *Experience and Identity: Birmingham and the West Midlands 1760–1800* (Montreal: McGill-Queens University Press, 1977), pp. 52–79; Barry, "Press," pp. 62–64.

10. Barker, *Newspapers, Politics and Public Opinion,* pp. 22–32, 115; Lutnick, *American Revolution,* pp. 1, 13–14, 224–225; John Brewer, *Party Ideology and Popular Politics at the Accession of George III* (Cambridge: Cambridge University Press, 1981), pp. 139–142; population statistics from G. Holmes and D. Szechi, *The Age of Oligarchy* (London: Longman, 1993), p. 345; Christie, *Myth and Reality,* pp. 324–325; Aspinall, *Politics and the Press,* pp. 16–17.

11. *NM* (1785): 61; G. A. Cranfield, *The Press and Society* (London: Longman, 1978), pp. 70–71.

12. *NM* (1785): 7, 62–63; John Brewer, "Commercialization and Politics," in N. McKendrick et al., *The Birth of Consumer Society* (London: Hutchinson, 1983), p. 257.

13. *NM* (1785): 62–63; Lucyle Werkmeister, *The London Daily Press 1772–1792* (Lincoln: University of Nebraska Press, 1963), pp. 4–7, 21; Wilfred Hindle, *The Morning Post 1772–1937* (London: Routledge, 1937), pp. 192–221; for Bate, see *Dictionary of National Biography*; and for Bate's part in the infamous "Vauxhall Affray," see Kristina Straub, *Sexual Suspects: Eighteenth-Century Players and Sexual Ideology* (Princeton: Princeton University Press, 1992), pp. 16–19.

14. Barker, *Newspapers, Politics and Public Opinion,* p. 35; C. D. Piguerit, *An Essay on the Art of Newspaper Defamation* (London, 1775), pp. 3, 8, 17, 27–28.

15. Quoted in Cranfield, *Press and Society,* p. 74.

16. Boswell, *Life of Johnson,* p. 977.

17. *Mdsx J,* March 11–14, 1775; *MC,* March 14, 1775, March 16, 1775; *Lloyd's,* March 13–15, 1775; *PA,* March 16, 1775; *St. J's,* March 14–16, 1775. These problems would complicate every effort by the papers to provide a full account of the proceedings at each of the successive trials. See *Gaz,* March 16, 1775. Curwen, a frequent visitor to the courts, often complained that the noise he encountered in English courts made it difficult to hear what was happening (*The Journal of Samuel Curwen,* p. 34). Some contemporaries would argue that faulty reporting, especially in the *Old Bailey Sessions Papers,* resulted in miscarriages of justice. In some measure, the unhappiness with the reporting of this case contributed to a reform of how the accounts were transcribed. See Simon Devereaux, "The City and the Sessions Paper: 'Public Justice' in London, 1770–1800," *Journal of British Studies* 35, no. 4 (1996): 466–503.

18. *DA,* March 15, 1775; *NM* (1785): 8; *Lloyd's,* March 15, 1775. It was only on March 20 that the *Morning Chronicle* managed to present an accurate account of what had transpired on Saturday when the case broke at Bow Street. By Thursday, nine London papers carried versions of the story; some had more than one article about the case, while others merely summarized events. By March 15, some attentive readers had a fairly full account of the affair. George Cumberland wrote to his brother Richard in Oxford with the story. He emphasized the luxury in which the brothers lived and the "method" they employed to raise large sums of money. "Their names are Perreau and one of our directors," George wrote, "is well acquainted with their family who have a small estate in St. Kitts; the apothecary bore a very excellent character and tis supposed to have been drawn in by his Brother who was lately Bankrupt." He found it extraordinary that the brothers had been at large and had not escaped. British Museum, Cumberland Papers, 1770–1778, F 1.

19. Hannah Barker, *Newspapers, Politics and English Society 1695–1855* (Harlow: Longman, 2000), pp. 101–102; Barker, *Newspapers, Politics and Public Opinion,* p. 35; Archenholz, a Prussian visitor, reported at a slightly later date that "the business" of collecting news employed a "prodigious multitude of persons." "Among these may be reckoned the paragraph writers, who go to the coffee-houses and public places to pick up anecdotes and the news of the day, which they reduce into short sentences, and are paid in proportion to their number and authenticity." M. D'Archenholz, *Picture of England* (Dublin, 1790), p. 42; more generally, Lutnick, *American Revolution,* pp. 5–9.

20. *The Diary and Letters of Thomas Hutchinson,* edited by Peter Hutchinson (London, 1883), 2: 88; *Letters of Garrick,* 3: 1011.

21. *MP,* March 13, 1775, March 25, 1775. The initial story was also reprinted as true in the *Sussex Weekly Advertiser,* March 20, 1775, and the *Leeds Mercury,* March 21, 1775.

22. *Lloyd's,* March 17–20, 1775; *Gaz,* March 27, 1775; *GEP,* April 15–18, 1775; *CM,* March 6, 1775.

23. *Gaz,* June 2, 1775, June 7, 1775; *MP,* June 6, 1775.

24. *St. J's,* March 16–18, 1775; *MP,* March 17, 1775; *Gaz,* March 17, 1775.

25. *Gaz,* March 28, 1775.

26. *MP,* May 6, 1775, May 12, 1775, May 22, 1775, July 25, 1775.

27. *Gaz,* August 5, 1775; *MC,* August 4, 1775; *PA,* August 5, 1775; *St. J's,* August 3–5, 1775.

28. Not all commentators agreed. "It has been said," one wrote in the midst of the dispute, "and perhaps justly, that Mrs. Rudd expressed very little Tenderness for her Children throughout all the former States of Sir Thomas Frankland's Persecution. To convince the Public therefore to the contrary, and regain the Good-will of her own Sex in particular ... she is now making all this Bustle about a Child who can be better taken Care of anywhere than in Newgate." *PA,* August 8, 1775; *MP,* August 14, 1775, August 18, 1775; *St. J's,* August 5, 1775.

29. *MP,* April 22, 1775, June 7, 1775, June 8, 1775.

30. Robert and Daniel's defenses appeared in *Gaz,* June 7, 10, 12, 13, 1775; Mrs. Rudd's appeared in *Gaz,* July 3, 1775. Robert and Daniel's defense appeared in the *MP,* June 6 and 16, 1775, while Mrs. Rudd's story filled that paper on July 1, 3, 4, 5, 6, 7, 10, 11, 1775.

31. *MC,* June 10, 1775; *MP,* July 14, 1775.

32. *MP,* March 23, 1775, March 24, 1775. In December the paper published a multi-part appeal to save Robert Perreau entitled "Letter to Lord Suffolk."

33. *MC,* March 30, 1775, June 10, 1775, June 12, 1775. In the immediate aftermath of Robert's trial, the paper wrote, with heavy irony, that "from every circumstance that has arisen, with respect to the P's and Mrs. R, it clearly appears, that this *virtuous, pious, all-feeling Lady,* with every *nice,* every *delicate* sensation, has been at the bottom of the *whole*" (*MC,* June 4, 1775). William Woodfall's support for the Perreaus may be explained by his connection to theatrical circles as a former actor, playwright, and critic. The character of the reporting in *The Weekly Magazine and Edinburgh Amusement* changed dramatically after the June trials. Through May it offered a full and sympathetic account of Mrs. Rudd; after that date it neglected her accounts while providing a more appealing portrait of the brothers.

34. *MC,* June 9, 1775.

35. *St. J's,* May 13–16, 1775.

36. Alvin Kernan, *Samuel Johnson and the Impact of Print* (Princeton: Princeton University Press, 1987), pp. 55–60; Sainsbury, *Disaffected Patriots,* p. 28; James Bradley, *Popular Politics and the American Revolution* (Macon, Ga.: Mercer University Press, 1986), pp. 93–103.

37. *MR* 52 (1775): 460. On printers, see H. R. Plomer, *A Dictionary of the Printers and Booksellers Who Were at Work in England 1726–1775* (Oxford: Oxford University Press, 1932); Ian Maxted, *The London Book Trades 1775–1800* (Folkestone, England: Dawson, 1977).

38. *The Female Forgery* (London, 1775); *St. J's,* April 20–22, 1775.

39. *Forgery Unmasked; MC,* April 25, 1775; *CR* 39 (1775): 432.

40. *MC*, April 29, 1775.

41. *Genuine Memoirs of the Messrs. Perreau; St. J's,* May 4–6, 1775.

42. *Trials of Robert,* p. 37. It is a testimony to how people read Daniel's "Narrative" that it appeared at the end of the pamphlet released with an authoritative version of the Perreau trials.

43. *Trials of Robert,* pp. 36–37; *PA,* June 10, 1775.

44. *PA,* June 10, 1775.

45. *Trials of Robert,* pp. 38–40; *PA,* June 10, 1775; *Gaz,* June 10, 1775; *St. J's,* June 10–12, 1775.

46. *Trials of Robert,* pp. 40–42; *St. J's,* June 10–12, 1775.

47. In 1790, a John Adair, who died at Leith, was described as a merchant of Jamaica. *Trials of Robert,* pp. 40–44; *St. J's,* June 10–12, 1775.

48. *Trials of Robert,* pp. 42–45.

49. Ibid, pp. 47–49; *MC,* June 12, 1775.

50. Ibid., pp. 59–61; *MC,* June 12, 1775.

51. *Observations on the Trial of Robert Perreau* (London, 1775), pp. 21–22; *Trials of Robert,* pp. 54–56.

52. *Trials of Robert,* pp. 56–62.

53. Ibid.

54. D'Archenholz, *Picture,* pp. 44–46.

55. Money, *Experience and Identity,* pp. 57–61; Barker, *Newspapers, Politics, and Public Opinion,* pp. 38–40; Bate had been criticized for just such a tactic. "What can excuse such violators of every tie sacred to nature," one author wrote, "as I have here set before you? And call you yourself innocent, because you have not penned them?" Piguerit, *Essay,* pp. 20–21.

56. *LM* (1773): 565–566; *AR* (1773): 147–148; *Female Artifice, or Charles James F-x Outwitted* (London, 1774), pp. 5, 12.

57. *MP,* March 29, 1775; *Mdsx J,* March 28, 1775.

58. *MC,* March 31, 1775; *PA,* March 30, 1775.

59. *MP,* March 29, 1775.

60. *MP,* March 31, 1775; *Mdsx J,* March 30–April 1, 1775; *Gaz,* April 3, 1775; *CM,* April 4–8, 1775.

61. *Gaz,* April 11, 1775; *Mdsx J,* April 8–11, 1775; *MP,* April 8, 1775, May 24, 1775.

62. The cases of Elizabeth Canning and Mary Blandy represent earlier examples of sensational crimes. See Margaret Ann Doody, "The Law, the Page, and the Body of Woman: Murder and Murderesses in the Age of Johnson," *The Age of Johnson* 1 (1987): 127–160.

63. *PA,* August 17, 1775; see also *UM* (1775): 264.

64. *CM,* April 8, 1775.

65. *St. J's,* April 8–11, 1775.

66. *St. J's,* March 25–28, July 20–22, 1775; *Mdsx J,* July 22–25, 1775.

67. *PA,* March 28, 1775; *St. J's,* March 25–28, 1775; "At a time when the American business, so very important to this nation, seems almost to be forgotten, and whilst the Perreau and Shaftesbury Punch engross all the conversation of the town" (*T&C,* April 1775, p. 205). Such moralistic commentary was a staple of all publications of the period; see Money, *Experience and Identity,* p. 73.

68. Barry, "The Press," pp. 66–67.

1. Alan Valentine, *The British Establishment 1760–1784* (Norman: University of Oklahoma Press, 1970), 2: 942.

2. Lewis Namier and John Brooke, *The House of Commons* (London: Oxford University Press, 1968), 2: 20–21; Valentine, *Establishment*, 1: 19–20; Penelope Corfield, *Power and the Professions in Britain 1780–1850* (London: Routledge, 1995), pp. 11–13.

3. Quoted in L. and J. C. Fawtier Stone, *An Open Elite?* (Oxford: Clarendon Press, 1986), p. 29; John Fielding, *A Brief Description of the Cities of London and Westminster* (London, 1776), p. xii; *Lichtenberg's Visits to England,* translated by M. Mare and W. Quarrell (Oxford: Clarendon Press, 1938), p. 79.

4. M. Dorothy George, *London Life in the Eighteenth Century* (New York: Capricorn, 1963), pp. 110–113.

5. *Mdsx J,* March 16, 1775.

6. *Boswell's London Journal 1762–1763,* edited by F. Pottle (New York: McGraw-Hill, 1950), p. 153, quoting *The Spectator;* D'Archenholz, *Picture,* pp. 76–77.

7. George Rudé, *Hanoverian London* (London: Secker & Warburg, 1971), pp. 48–63; L. D. Schwarz, *London in the Age of Industrialisation, Entrepreneurs, Labour Force and Living Conditions 1700–1850* (Cambridge: Cambridge University Press, 1992), pp. 7–10, 51–73. Of course, quite ordinary people, both middling and lower-class, also lived in the West End.

8. Hugh Phillips, *Mid-Georgian London* (London: Collins, 1964), pp. 238–239, 297–300; Rudé, *Hanoverian London,* pp. 40–46, 235–236; George Rudé, *Wilkes and Liberty* (Oxford: Oxford University Press, 1962), pp. 2–4; Fielding, *Brief Description,* pp. 12–15; and in general, Henry Wheatley, *London Past and Present,* 3 vols. (London: J. Murray, 1891).

9. Robin Gwynn, *Huguenot Heritage* (London: Routledge & Kegan Paul, 1985), pp. 22–24, 79–90.

10. Theodosia, *Genuine Memoirs of the Mess. Perreau* (London, 1775), pp. 7–28. Daniel Perreau senior was not unusual in his choices. An acquaintance of his sons, John Baker, born of a Chichester family in 1712, went out to St. Kitts in 1740 to pursue a legal career. Enriched by marriage, he served as solicitor general of the Leeward Islands from 1750 to 1752. Having secured a comfortable competence, he returned to England in 1757 to enjoy a life of leisure. *Diary of John Baker,* pp. 9–11.

11. *PA,* June 16, 1775, January 29, 1776; *MC,* January 30, 1776; Theodosia, *Genuine Memoirs,* pp. 7–28; *T&C* (1775): 300; *UM* (1775): 160. For an interesting parallel, see the history of Augustus Boyd in David Hancock, *Citizens of the World* (Cambridge: Cambridge University Press, 1995), pp. 46–48.

12. *Trials of Robert,* pp. 26–29. In talking of them to Boswell, she said that "the Perreau family (as she called it) was a little commonwealth." Boswell's "Interview with Mrs. Rudd, London, 22 April 1776," in *Boswell, The Ominous Years 1774–1776,* edited by C. Ryskamps and F. Pottle (New York: McGraw-Hill, 1963), p. 357.

13. Hector Bolitho and Derek Peel, *The Drummonds of Charing Cross* (London: Allen & Unwin, 1967), pp. 39–57, 58–64; for additional information on how family strategies worked, see Hancock, *Citizens of the World,* pp. 64–65, 139–141, and on government contracting, pp. 221–239.

14. Add. Ms. 53808, #82, #88, #90, British Library; Edmund Burke, *Correspondence of Edmund Burke,* edited by Lucy Sutherland (Cambridge: Cambridge University

Press, 1960), 2: 171, 8: 69; Ian Christie, *British "Non-Elite" MPs 1715–1820* (Oxford: Oxford University Press, 1995), pp. 92–93; Corfield, *Power*, pp. 228–229. For the count of baronets, see volume 5 (1765–1774) of G. E. Cockayne, *The Complete Baronetage of England*, 6 vols. (Exeter: W. Pollard, 1900–1909).

15. Geoffrey Holmes, *Augustan England* (London: Allen & Unwin, 1982), pp. 184–85, 191, 227; R. Campbell, *The London Tradesman* (London, 1747; reprinted New York: A. M. Kelley, 1969), pp. 63–66; William Cooke, ed., *The Table-Talk and Bon-Mots of Samuel Foote* (London: Meyers & Rogers, 1902), pp. 219–220; Richard Wendorf, *Sir Joshua Reynolds: The Painter in Society* (Cambridge, Mass.: Harvard University Press, 1998), p. 104. A directory of 1763 reported that apothecaries "may not improperly be ranked among the genteel professions" (Corfield, *Power*, p. 155).

16. Holmes, *Augustan England*, p. 227; *Free Thoughts on Apothecaries and Empirics* (London, 1773), p. 31; *Trials of Robert*, p. 32.

17. *T&C* (1776): 300; *PA*, January 29, 1776; *MC*, January 30, 1776; Villette, *Genuine Account*, pp. 7–11. For a glimpse of the family situation of Robert Perreau shortly after he set up on his own, see *Diary of John Baker*, pp. 9–11, 103–105. Baker had recently returned from St. Kitts. On November 2, 1757, he drank tea at Robert Perreau's home in Oxenden Street, and eight days later he had dinner there. It was largely a family affair, with two Mr. Perreaus, two Miss Perreaus, and two Miss Thomases, "daughters of the late Revd. Walter Thomas of St. Kitts."

18. *Memoirs of the Life of Robert Adair* (London, 1790); Valentine, *Establishment*, 1: 19–20, 191–192, 213–214, 2: 942.

19. *Memoirs of William Hickey*, edited by Alfred Spencer (London: Hurst & Blankett, 1923), 1: 1–5, 116–117, 330, 2: 236; *Correspondence of Edmund Burke*, 2: 502.

20. Theodosia, *Genuine Memoirs*, pp. 78–85.

21. R. B. Sheridan, "The Rise of a Colonial Gentry: A Case Study of Antigua, 1730–1775," *Economic History Journal* (April 1961): 342–357; Richard Dunn, *Sugar and Slaves: The Rise of the Planter Class in the English West Indies, 1624–1713* (Chapel Hill: University of North Carolina Press, 1972); Cockayne, *Baronetage*, vol. 5.

22. There was some disagreement about the reasons for the collapse of the firm; some blamed Daniel's prodigality, while others said the collapse of a corresponding bank in England ruined them. *T&C* (1775): 300; *Matrimonial Magazine* (1775): 134–135; *MC*, March 20, 1775; *Gaz*, March 17, 1775.

23. *T&C* (1776): 4. Although he was slightly younger than the Perreaus, and just a bit older than Mrs. Rudd, James Boswell, when he arrived in London in 1762, shared their passion for getting ahead. "Since I came up," he wrote in his journal, "I have begun to acquire a composed genteel character very different from a rattling uncultivated one which for some time past I have been fond of. I have discovered that we may be in some degree whatever character we choose. Besides, practice forms a man of anything. I am now happy to find myself cool, easy and serene." "The great art of living easy and happy in society," he noted at another point, "is to study proper behavior." The best means to advance this education was to be "acquainted with people of fashion in London." His ambitions were unlimited, a parliamentary career, wealth and fame. He was full of "schemes of rising in the world." He was confident that fashionable society offered the most promising avenue for an impecunious, poorly connected Scot like himself. *Boswell's London Journal 1762–1763*, pp. 47, 63, 93, 174.

24. *MC,* June 2, 1775.
25. *Trials of Robert,* pp. 33–37; *MP,* June 3, 1775.
26. *Trials of Robert,* pp. 35–37; Horace Bleackley, *Life of John Wilkes* (London: John Lane, Bodley Head, 1917), p. 323.
27. *Trials of Robert,* pp. 34–37. Biographical information from the *DNB;* Valentine, *Establishment;* Namier and Brooke, *House of Commons.*
28. *Trials of Robert,* pp. 34–35; *Mdsx J,* March 16, 1775; *The Georgian Era: Memoirs of the Most Eminent Persons* (London, 1833), 2: 464–465.
29. William Hickey, in his memoirs, remembered the compelling impression left by an encounter with Daniel Perreau. The two families had long been acquainted. Despite his own father's social success, William stood slightly in awe of the older man's establishment. Perreau had a well-furnished house and a carriage and lived at the height of fashion. Hickey supposed that his money "arose from considerable plantations in the West Indies." Hickey spoke to Daniel of going to Jamaica because he could not withstand the temptations of London life, which led him into expenses he could not sustain. In a gesture that for Hickey confirmed Daniel's status as an admirable and wealthy man, the latter gave William five guineas, under the pretense that he had forgotten to pay his father a clerk's fee for an earlier transaction. Hickey, *Memoirs,* 1: 333–334.
30. Christie offers examples of the wide variety of paths to economic and social advancement in the period. *British "Non-Elite" MPs,* pp. 26–35, 90–93.
31. On the Childs, see *DNB;* on the Hoares, see H. P. B. Hoare, *Hoare's Bank* (London: Collins, 1955); *GM* (1772): 310–311; Valentine, *Establishment,* 1: 125; 2: 589–590.
32. Cockayne, *Complete Baronetage.*
33. Her Scottish noble "connections" were the families of the Galloways and Agnews, and through marriage, the English aristocratic family of Gower. Granville Leveson-Gower, "one of the most considerable subjects in the kingdom," married as his third wife the daughter of the sixth Earl of Galloway; "she made a thousand dependants" for jobs for her friends. See Cockayne, *Complete Baronetage.*
34. *Trials of Robert,* pp. 46–47.
35. *MP,* March 16, 1775; *Mdsx J,* March 16, 1775.
36. *DNB;* Bolitho and Peel, *Drummonds,* p. 61; Leslie-Melville, *Sir John Fielding,* p. 287; *Boswell: The Great Biographer,* edited by M. Danziger and F. Brady (New York: McGraw-Hill, 1989), pp. 270–271.
37. *T&C* (1775): 37.
38. Harlan Hamilton, *Doctor Syntax* (Kent, Ohio: Kent State University Press, 1969), pp. 62–63; A. D. Harvey, *Sex in Georgian England* (New York: St. Martin's Press, 1994), pp. 91–92. "A remarkable case" from 1770 suggests the widespread acceptance of such arrangements among the polite classes. A Miss Jones filed an action against her keeper, Charles Henry Dillon, upon a bond for £3000 he had granted her. "Lord Mansfield very properly observed," noted the *Annual Register* (1770), "that if Miss Jones had been a common p—e, he would instantly have set aside the bond as void and null, but as it was granted for value, and that she had lived with the gentleman at the time, giving her company to none other, the point of law was on her side, and the bond fell to be sustained; and so the jury, without going out of court, decided in her favour, with costs of suit, and other damages" (p. 120).
39. *The Connoisseur,* 6th ed. (Oxford, 1774), 1: 33.

40. Stella Tillyard, *Aristocrats* (New York: Farrar, Straus & Giroux, 1994), pp. 183–191.

41. *T&C* (1784): 401–404; *T&C* (July 1772): 345–348.

42. D'Archenholz, *Picture*, pp. 188–194.

43. Hickey, *Memoirs*, 1: 90–92.

44. *T&C* (1775): 121–123.

45. One correspondent disparagingly argued that her father, Patrick, "took upon him-self the title of Doctor of Physic," while another pamphlet characterized him as "a rude apothecary" "who ran a primitive shop." Yet another said that her mother was fathered when Major Stewart took up with "a low creature, whilst in quarters in Ballyshannon." *MP,* June 19, 1775; *St. J's,* May 13–16, 1775; *Authentic Anecdotes of the Life and Transactions of Mrs. Margaret Rudd* (London, 1776), 1: 16–53.

46. *T&C* (October 1769): 506; *T&C* (April 1770): 44.

47. *T&C* (February 1772): 67; *T&C* (March 1774): 124; *T&C* (July 1774): 346. For Bellamy, see Cyril Hughes Hartmann, *Enchanting Bellamy* (London: Heinemann, 1956), and her own *Apologies for the Life of George Anne Bellamy* (London, 1785).

48. Jonathon Bandon, *History of Ulster* (Belfast: Blackstaff Press, 1992), pp. 179–182. The cloth was produced by an extensive network of domestic workers. This mode of production made the market towns important as depots for the collection of the material. L. M. Cullen, *Anglo-Irish Trade 1660–1800* (New York: A. M. Kelley, 1968), p. 109. The correspondence of James Adair is full of transactions relating to his estates there. A steady stream of letters from his tenants, among whom the Stewart name figured prominently, demanded his attention. Add. Ms. 50829, British Library.

49. Arthur Young, *A Tour of Ireland,* edited by A. Hutton (London, 1892), 1: 130–131; Conrad Gill, *The Rise of the Irish Linen Industry* (Oxford: Clarendon Press, 1964), pp. 28, 59; *St. J's,* May 13–16, 1775.

50. John Harrington, ed., *The English Traveller in Ireland* (Dublin: Wolfhound Press, 1991), pp. 162–163.

51. Thais was an Athenian courtesan who followed Alexander the Great. The title in eighteenth-century London identified a courtesan of intelligence and culture. At least sixteen of the sixty demi-reps discussed in *Town and Country* from 1769 through 1774 had received a good education; many more were characterized as knowledgeable, or "reading the best authors." For a scathing attack on boarding schools, see *CR* (1774): 41; *T&C* (1775): 300. The London debating societies discussed the value of boarding school education seven times between 1776 and 1779; see Andrew, *London Debating Societies,* 1994.

52. *Authentic Anecdotes,* 1: 16–53.

53. Namier and Brooke, *House of Commons,* 3: 624–626; Add. Ms. 34734, F370, F376; Add. Ms. 34735, F27, F81, F126, British Library. In one letter, Thomas Rudd warned Valentine: "I hope no disappointment will make you extravagant, because I cannot support you in it, it will be a revenge on yourself."

54. *Prudence Triumphing over Vanity and Dissipation* (London, 1776), pp. 28–37.

55. *Authentic Anecdotes,* 1: 16–53; *T&C* (1775): 300; D'Archenholz, *Picture,* p. 191.

56. *MC,* June 23, 1775; *Authentic Anecdotes,* 1: 16–55; *St. J's,* May 13–16, 1775.

57. *MC,* June 23, 1775; *Authentic Anecdotes,* 1: 16–55; *Prudence Triumphing,* pp. 97–103; *St. J's,* May 13–16, 1775.

58. *Lloyd's,* May 13–16, 1775.

59. *LM* 43 (1774): 260. For stories about the "lost years," see *MP,* March 23, 1775, March 29, 1775; *MC,* June 23, 1775. For Mrs. Gore, see *MP,* July 1, 1775.

60. *Authentic Anecdotes,* 1: 55–143; *MC,* June 23, 1775; *T&C* (1775): 457; *St. J's,* May 13–16, 1775; *WM* (October 1775): 109–110.

61. *Authentic Anecdotes,* 2: 51.

62. *T&C* (1775): 300; *Authentic Anecdotes,* 1: 55–143; *St. J's,* May 13–16, 1775. For the geography of West End prostitution, see Randolph Trumbach, *Sex and the Gender Revolution* (Chicago: University of Chicago Press, 1998), pp. 130–131, 179–180.

63. Maurice Woolfe, "Joseph Salvadore, 1716–1786," *Jewish Historical Society of England Transactions* 21 (1962–1967): 104–113; Barker, *Newspapers, Politics and English Society,* pp. 142–144; Gedalia Yogev, *Diamonds and Coral: Anglo-Dutch Jews and Eighteenth-Century Trade* (New York: Holmes & Meier, 1978), pp. 54–55, 72–73, 170–171; Todd Endelman, *Radical Assimilation in English Jewish History 1656–1945* (Bloomington: Indiana University Press, 1990), pp. 18–33; George, *London Life,* pp. 126–132. For one of the many anecdotes inspired by Kitty Fisher, see D'Archenholz, *Picture,* p. 191.

64. Mr. X lost his mistress, Mrs. Saunders, because "she took a strong dislike to his person." Mrs. Baddeley was sold by her venal husband to "an Israelite patriot Mr. M—z." Miss Fielding claimed to have been seduced from her boarding school by a bawd employed by a Mr. DaCosta, who got her drunk on champagne before he raped her. Also see the extraordinarily vile portrayal of Sir Sampson Gideon and his inamorata, the frail Alicia. *T&C* (June 1769): 284; *T&C* (May 1772): 235; *T&C* (June 1784): 290–291; *T&C* (April 1786): 172–173. Other Jewish keepers included "the insect" ([November 1788]: 487–488) and "the fugitive Israelite" ([July 1787]: 289). See also Frank Felsenstein, *Anti-Semitic Stereotypes: A Paradigm of Otherness in English Popular Culture 1660–1830* (Baltimore: Johns Hopkins University Press, 1995).

65. *Bath Journal,* March 30, 1775. In the wake of her indictment for the crime, Mrs. Rudd, recognizing how damaging these rumors of a relationship with Salvadore were to her, secured a letter from him. He could not possibly visit her, he wrote, but he thought it "just to make the declarations you desire." "I have," he began, "at several times paid and given you sums of money, and verily believe that you have received other considerable sums from other persons." Yet he denied the existence of such "an acquaintance between us" as "the world has supposed." No doubt referring to the many stories circulating about her having assumed different identities in order to fool him, he concluded that he was satisfied with the proofs "of the reality … relative to another person." In closing, Salvadore said he "was going out of town on business," but that she was free to make whatever "use" of his statement that "you may think convenient." It was a strange and enigmatic letter, one that, like so many other statements in this case, left more questions than it answered. *Mdsx J,* July 13–15, 1775.

66. *UM* (1775): 264–265; *Authentic Anecdotes,* 1: 55–143.

67. *T&C* (1775): 481–482.

68. *MC,* June 23, 1775.

69. *UM* (1775): 264–265.

70. *A Letter from Mrs. Christian Hart to Mrs. Caroline Rudd* (London, 1776), p. 73; *Authentic Anecdotes,* 2: 20–25; Valentine, *Establishment,* 2: 571–572.

71. Theodosia, *Genuine Memoirs,* pp. 119–121, 129; *Trials of Robert,* pp. 36–37. Mrs. Rudd was not alone in resorting to assumed names, especially when trying to avoid

the law. Lady Sarah Bunbury also lived under the name of Gore for a time. Till-yard, *Aristocrats,* pp. 247–248.

72. *MC,* January 19, 1776.
73. *PA,* June 16, 1775.
74. Quoted in Wendorf, *Reynolds,* p. 30.
75. Adam Smith, *The Wealth of Nations* (London: Penguin, 1986), pp. 441–442.
76. The fate of George Anne Bellamy stands as a reminder of the challenges confronting the demi-rep. Bellamy pursued a stage career while taking a succession of lovers, including John Calcraft, a wealthy ally of Henry Fox, paymaster to forty regiments. When Calcraft failed to secure her an annuity before his death, she soon found herself financially embarrassed. By 1786 she was in the Fleet, where she died "in great poverty and misery." E. J. Burford, *Wits, Wenchers and Wantons* (London: R. Hale, 1990), pp. 82–84, 176–178.
77. John Trusler, *The Way to Be Rich and Respectable* (London, 1776), p. 12; Corfield, *Power,* p. 223.

FIVE. FASHION AND ITS DISCONTENTS

1. *PA,* March 16, 1775; *Gaz,* March 16, 1775.
2. *St. J's,* March 11–14, 1775.
3. *CM,* March 18, 1775; *LC,* July 1–4, 1775; *MC,* September 18, 1775; *PA,* September 18, 1775.
4. *MP,* July 5, 1775; *Mdsx J,* March 16, 1775.
5. *PA,* September 18, 1775.
6. See Neil McKendrick, "The Commercialization of Fashion," in McKendrick et al., eds., *The Birth of Consumer Society* (London: Hutchinson, 1983), p. 47.
7. *St. J's,* June 29–July 1, 1775, August 1–3, 12–15, 1775, September 30–October 3, 1775.
8. McKendrick, "Commercialization," pp. 63–64. See Marcia Pointon, *Strategies for Showing: Women, Possession and Representation in English Visual Culture 1665–1800* (Oxford: Oxford University Press, 1997), p. 262, for more on "the head." Dress made a statement in this world for men as well. It testified to wealth, but it also advertised taste and claimed attention. Hickey's friend Robert Pott had made a name for himself as "a London rake." "He displayed peculiar taste in dress, though carried to excess in point of fashion, soon becoming the envy of all the young men of his day. I was one morning walking arm in arm with him in St. James's park, his dress then being a white coat, cut in the extremity of *ton,* lined with a Garter blue satin, edged with ermine, and ornamented with rich silver frogs; waistcoat and breeches of the same blue satin, trimmed with silver twist a la Hussar, and ermine edges." Hickey, *Memoirs,* 1: 280.
9. Quoted in Paul Langford, *A Polite and Commercial People* (Oxford: Clarendon Press, 1989), p. 405. The eponymous heroine of a serial, *The Heiress,* when told that the genteel protagonist did not have a carriage, remarked: "They do not make *quite a genteel appearance* ... as they keep no *carriage.*—People who cannot, or who will not, afford *that,* can have but small pretensions to *gentility*" (*Lady's Magazine* [January 1773]: 18).
10. *Trials of Robert,* p. 43.

11. Theodosia, *Genuine Memoirs*, p. 159.
12. *FFBJ*, July 29, 1775.
13. *Mdsx J*, July 22–25, 1775; *MP*, July 25, 1775.
14. *Gaz*, June 13, 1775.
15. It should be pointed out that, despite her many claims to be Daniel's wife in fact, if not in law, she was only able to claim "her" possessions because she had not legally married Daniel. Of course, these goods were rightly the property of Valentine Rudd, who, it was said, would later claim them.
16. *Diary of John Baker*, p. 106.
17. *St. J's*, January 6–9, 1775; *MP*, January 17, 1775. According to the information contained in Lorna Weatherill's *Consumer Behavior and Material Culture in Britain 1660–1760* (London: Methuen, 1988), the Perreaus' level of consumption put them among the very elite of society.
18. Hickey, *Memoirs*, 1: 335.
19. *MP*, July 25, 1775; *Gaz*, July 4, 1775. Belliard also said that Mrs. Rudd had never told him anything of her fortune. He sold her the jewels on the word of "one I had been acquainted with near twenty years."
20. See Pointon, *Strategies for Showing*, p. 33, for centrality of jewelry, especially for upper-class women.
21. M. Grosley, *New Observations on England and Its Inhabitants* (London, 1772), 1: 108–109. They rise late, Grosley noted, and "pass an hour at home, drinking tea with their families; about ten they go to the coffee-house, where they spend another hour: then they go home, or meet people about business." At two o'clock they go to the Exchange. "In their return, they lounge a little longer at the coffee-house, and then dine about four." Dinner ended the work day, and the rest of their time was devoted to friends and sociability. Some went to clubs; in summer people went to "the public walks." "About ten at night they go to bed, after taking a slight repast."
22. *Diary of John Baker*, p. 314.
23. Trusler, *The Way to Be Rich*, p. 12; *CR* (1774): 41.
24. How was the idea of "fashion" used by writers of the eighteenth century? A rather superficial but suggestive clue may be found in the pattern of appearance of this word and its adjectival form, "fashionable," in the *Eighteenth Century Shorter Title Catalogue*. If one eliminates duplicates, advertisements, and notices, there are 32 titles of books, pamphlets, poems, and plays with that word in its title before mid-century, and 124 after mid-century; in fact, the last three decades contain 103 of these titles.
25. *A Dictionary of Love* (London, 1777).
26. *Fashion, a Poem*.
27. Roy Porter perceptively noted that what was "particularly noteworthy however of the Georgians is how they were hoist on their own petard, both loving and hating Vanity Fair, their dreamworld of signs." "Making Faces: Physiognomy and Fashion in Eighteenth-Century England," *Etudes anglais* 4 (October–December 1985): 388.
28. See Cindy M'Creery, "Keeping up with the *Bon Ton*," in *Gender in Eighteenth Century England*, edited by Hannah Barker and Elaine Chalus (London: Addison Wesley Longman, 1997), pp. 207–229.

29. James Raven, *Judging New Wealth* (Oxford: Clarendon Press, 1992), p. 154; Langford, *Polite and Commercial People*, pp. 3–5.

30. *LM* 42 (1773): 30.

31. David Garrick, *Bon Ton,* in *Plays by David Garrick and George Colman the Elder,* edited by E. R. Wood (Cambridge: Cambridge University Press, 1982), p. 211.

32. Richard Cumberland, *The Note of Hand, or, Trip to Newmarket* (London, 1774), p. 15.

33. O'Keefe, quoted in Mrs. Clement Parsons, *Garrick and His Circle* (London: Methuen, 1906), p. 204.

34. Garrick to Hugh Kelly, October 16, 1775, *Letters of Garrick,* vol. 3. There is even some suggestion that Foote himself saw the case as "theatrical" and planned to write a play using it as the plot; see *MP,* July 15, 1775.

35. *MP,* February 8, 1775, letter from Candidus; *St. James's Magazine* 1 (October 1774): 444; *The Patriots of North America: A Sketch with Explanatory Notes* (New York and London, 1775). William Crawford, *Remarks on the Late Earl of Chesterfield's Letters to His Son* (London, 1776), pp. 79, 84.

36. Jonas Hanway, *Midnight the Signal* (London, 1776), 1: 61–63.

37. Thomas Hunter, *Reflections Critical and Moral on the Letters of Lord Chesterfield* (London, 1776), pp. 185, 260–261.

38. *CR* (1774): 41.

39. James Fordyce, *The Character and Conduct of the Female Sex* (London, 1776), pp. 55–56.

40. James Fordyce, *Sermons to Young Women,* 10th ed. (London, 1776), 1: vi–vii, 14, 2: 87.

41. *The Court of Adultery, a Vision* (London, 1778), p. 9.

42. Theodosia, *Genuine Memoirs,* pp. 119–121; Diana Donald, *The Art of Caricature: Satirical Prints in the Reign of George III* (New Haven: Yale University Press, 1996), pp. 85–89; Miles Ogborn, *Spaces of Modernity: London's Geographies 1680–1780* (New York: Guilford Press, 1998), pp. 116–157; Langford, *Polite and Commercial People,* p. 575.

43. The pre-eminent work on this topic remains Terry Castle, *Masquerade and Civilization* (Stanford: Stanford University Press, 1986). In addition to the general lessons in gentility that early periodicals like the *Tatler* and *Spectator* sought to teach, as early as 1737 T. Nivelon published *Rudiments of Genteel Behaviour* (London), which was illustrated to give pictorial representation of decorum in action. See also Peter Earle, *The Making of the English Middle Class* (Berkeley: University of California Press, 1989), p. 8; Barbara Maria Stafford, *Body Criticism* (Cambridge, Mass.: MIT Press, 1991), p. 89. Roy Porter remarks of the masquerade, "For the itch to go incognito, perhaps even cross-dressing, seemed the depths of decadence: one's appearance was no longer the proud escutcheon of self, but a device for going hidden" ("Making Faces," p. 389).

44. Porter, "Making Faces," p. 393.

45. Theodosia, *Genuine Memoirs,* pp. 78–85. As well as being of a higher social class, Francis Blake Delaval was a notorious libertine and rake.

46. Ibid., pp. 14–16.

47. Theodosia, *Genuine Memoirs,* p. 141.

48. *Mr. Daniel Perreau Narrative of His Unhappy Case* (London, 1775), p. 82.

49. *St. J's,* April 27–29, 1775.

50. Letter from "Hint" to "The Man of Pleasure," *T&C* (December 1775): 656; *LC,* December 16–19, 1775.

51. For more on Elizabeth Chudleigh, see Charles E. Pearce, *The Amazing Duchess* (London, 1911); *WM* (February 1775): 231–232; *The Newgate Calendar,* ed. Andrew Knapp and William Baldwin (London, 1828), pp. 23–27; and *St. J's,* September 8–10, 1775. The very week that it first reported on the Perreau-Rudd case, *The Weekly Magazine and Edinburgh Amusement* carried an article that offered a sympathetic portrait of Kingston, using phrases that would soon be applied to Mrs. Rudd. "This lady," the journal announced, "censured, envied, imitated, and admired, in the highest sphere of that class of people distinguished by the appellation of the beau monde… [is] graceful, elegant, and polite in manners." Superior to her critics, she possessed a "generous mind, not susceptible of spite and malice." *WM* (March 1775): 389–390.

52. Elizabeth Chatten, *Samuel Foote* (Boston: Twayne, 1980), pp. 122–127.

53. *St. J's,* September 8–10, 1775.

54. Robert Williams, *Memoirs of Hannah More* (London, 1834), p. 81.

55. Charles Neilson Gattey, *"Farmer" George's Black Sheep* (London, 1985), pp. 102–109. See also Nathaniel Wraxall, *Historical Memoirs of My Own Time* (London, 1904), p. 133. Wraxall (1751–1831), described in the *DNB* as a *novus homo* (21: 971), went to Bombay in 1769 with the East India Company. After returning to Europe, he interviewed Caroline Matilda in 1774 and became involved with a group of Danish exiles secretly planning her restoration. George III rewarded him financially and honorifically for his endeavors on her behalf. Interestingly enough, the evidence of Matilda's desire to overthrow her husband and rule in Denmark, as Catherine did in Russia, was conveyed to the King's stepmother in a forged letter, which she believed to be true. For a brief biography of Caroline Matilda, see S. W. Jackman, *Carolina, Queen of Denmark* (Lewes, England: Book Guild, 1987) p. 111.

56. *LC,* July 8–11, 1775; see also *The Vindication of Innocence; an Elegiac Poem, Sacred to the Memory of Her Majesty Queen Caroline Matilda, Late Queen of Denmark,* which appeared on June 13, 1775. The popular press started covering her story just as the Rudd-Perreau case was filling the papers; see, for example, *MC,* March 27, 1775, the long letter to *T&C* (May 1775): 257, and *GM* (July 1775): 320–322.

57. *The Trial of Miss Jane Butterfield for the Wilful Murder of William Scawen* (London, 1775), *A Letter to Mr. Sanxay* (London, 1775), *Observations on the Case of Miss Butterfield* (London, 1776), *Circumstances of the Death of Mr. Scawen* (London, 1775).

58. *Observations on the Case of Miss Butterfield,* pp. 16–17.

59. *Circumstances of the Death of Mr. Scawen,* pp. 8–10, 11–12.

60. Ibid. This pamphlet names her new purported lover to be a Captain Moss; there was certainly a Captain Moss who interested himself in her defense. The series of questions cited here is from the conclusion of this pamphlet, pp. 17–18. For the Butterfield trial , see *LC,* August 19–22, 1775; *Westminster Magazine* (August 1775): 414–419; *T&C* (July 1775): 360; *T&C* (August 1775): 418–419; Horace Walpole to Lady Ossory, 9 September 1775, in *Correspondence,* 32: 262; *WM* (September 1775): 367–368.

61. Robin Hood Debating Society, in *MC,* August 26, 1775; *St. J's,* August 3–5, 1775.

62. *St. J's,* September 7–9, 1775; also August 24–26, 1775.

63. For the Chevalier D'Eon, see Gary Kates, *Monsieur D'Eon Is a Woman: A Tale of Political Intrigue and Sexual Masquerade* (New York: Basic Books, 1995).
64. *T&C* (December 1775): 300; *LC,* December 16–19, 1775.
65. *CM,* April 8, 1775; *PA,* June 16, 1775.
66. *Remarks on a Pamphlet Lately Published by Dr. Price, Intitled, Observations on the Nature of Civil Liberty* (London, 1776). Theodosia, *Genuine Memoirs,* p. 8.
67. Stafford, *Body Criticism,* pp. 9–10.
68. Vicesmus Knox, *Essays Moral and Literary* (London, 1791), 1: 288. Knox linked the Perreaus with other "gentlemanly" criminals of his day.
69. *Bath Journal,* June 12, 1775.
70. Hunter, *Reflections,* pp. 4–8, 32–35, 43–47, 74–76, 85–86, 93; Crawford, *Remarks,* p. vii.

SIX. PRIVATE CREDIT AND PUBLIC CONFIDENCE

1. T. S. Ashton, *Economic Fluctuations in England 1700–1800* (Oxford: Clarendon Press, 1959), pp. 127–129, 152–162; *SM* (1772): 311. Five years later London still reeled from the impact of this financial disaster. "The modern method of bolstering up the great city houses," the *Morning Post* observed on February 6, 1777, "is a very dangerous custom;—productive of the ruin of numerous innocent families, and a loophole for the cunning thieves to escape thro'; this was the case in 1772."
2. *Gaz,* March 28, 1775; same accounts appeared in *CM,* April 1, 1775, and *St. J's,* April 8–11, 1775; Marcellus, *Letter,* p. 40.
3. *MP,* June 23, July 12, 1775.
4. *MP,* May 3, 1775.
5. For a description of how this system of paper circulation operated, see T. S. Wilan, *Abraham Dent of Kirby Stephen* (Manchester: Manchester University Press, 1970), pp. 112–127; *The Diary of Thomas Turner,* edited by David Vaisey (Oxford: Oxford University Press, 1985), especially appendix C; Julian Hoppit, "The Use and Abuse of Credit in Eighteenth-Century England," in *Business Life and Public Policy,* edited by N. McKendrick and R. B. Outhwaite (Cambridge: Cambridge University Press, 1986), pp. 54–78.
6. Charles Wilson, *Anglo-Dutch Commerce and Finance in the Eighteenth Century* (Cambridge: Cambridge University Press, 1941), p. 30.
7. *MP,* March 16, 1775; *Trials of Robert,* p. 14; on Frankland, see Namier and Brooke, *The House of Commons,* 2: 468.
8. Jacob Price, *Capital and Credit in British Overseas Trade* (Cambridge, Mass.: Harvard University Press, 1980), pp. 44–54; on private borrowing, see David Hancock, *Citizens of the World* (Cambridge: Cambridge University Press, 1995), pp. 247–252. Edmund Burke, desperate for money in 1769, offered Garrick a bond in order to raise £1000. Dixon Wecter, *Edmund Burke and His Kinsmen* (Boulder: University of Colorado Studies, 1939), pp. 46–47.
9. Lauchlin Macleane, according to Lucy Sutherland, raised money for Lord Shelburne without revealing his name. Macleane, along with William Burke, also speculated in East India Company stock for the Frenchman Panchard and for Lord Verney. Lucy Sutherland, *The East India Company in Eighteenth-Century Politics* (Oxford: Clarendon Press, 1952), pp. 208–212, 243.

10. *MP,* March 29, 1775.

11. Julian Hoppit, "Financial Crises in Eighteenth-Century England," *Economic History Review* 39 (1986): 39–58, especially 50–55.

12. Smith, *Wealth,* pp. 392–393, 420.

13. John Campbell, *A Political Survey of Britain* (London, 1774), 2: 238–243.

14. *GM* 42 (1772): 213.

15. *LM* (1772): 332.

16. *GM* 46 (1776): 85.

17. Isaac de Pinto, *An Essay on Circulation and Credit* (London, 1774), pp. 6–14, 17–37; Wilson, *Anglo-Dutch Commerce,* pp. 162–163.

18. De Pinto, *Essay,* pp. 37, 54, 75.

19. Hester Thrale, *Thraliana,* edited by Katherine C. Balderson (Oxford: Clarendon Press, 1942), 1: 333.

20. *GM* 44 (1774): 282; H. V. Bowen, "'The Pests of Human Society': Stockbrokers, Jobbers and Speculators in Mid-Eighteenth-Century Britain," *History* 78 (1993): 38–53.

21. "No men know better how to profit by the newspapers than the stock-jobbers. They declare war or peace at their pleasure, sign treaties of alliance, and fabricate events, which they seem to substantiate with so much address, that they have all the appearance of reality. By such arts, immense sums are lost and won every day." D'Archenholz, *Picture,* p. 43.

22. *Mrs. M. C. Rudd's Genuine Letter to Lord Weymouth with Several Authentic Anecdotes of the Late Messrs. Perreau* (London, 1776), pp. 29–30.

23. *St. J's,* January 25–27, 1776.

24. George Colman, *The Man of Business* (London, 1775), pp. 47–50.

25. P. J. Marshall, *East Indian Fortunes* (Oxford: Clarendon Press, 1976), p. 46.

26. Sutherland, *East India Company,* pp. 80–130; H. V. Bowen, "'Dipped in Traffic': East India Stockholders in the House of Commons 1768–1774," *Parliamentary History* 5 (1986): 39–53; Philip Lawson, *The East India Company* (London: Longman, 1993), pp. 92–96, 103–125.

27. *GM* (June 1769): 297. See H. V. Bowen, *Revenue and Reform: The Indian Problem in British Politics 1757–1773* (Cambridge: Cambridge University Press, 1991), pp. 36–42. A second round of speculative activity culminated in the crash of 1772–1773. Walpole wrote gloomily to Mann in 1769 that "the East India Company is all faction and gaming." "Such fortunes are made and lost every day as are past belief." The company, he complained, had richer places to dispose of than the government. "Riches, abuse, cabals, are so enormously overgrown, that one wants conceptions and words to comprehend and describe them." Walpole, *Correspondence,* 23: 133.

28. Of course, the Ayr Bank was only the most famous, or infamous, of all the private Scottish banks. See Ashton, *Economic Fluctuations,* pp. 127, 155–157; D. M. Joslin, "London Private Bankers 1720–85," *Economic History Review* 7 (1954): 167–186; Henry Hamilton, "Failure of the Ayr Bank," *Economic History Review* 8 (1956): S. G. Checkland, *Scottish Banking: A History 1695–1973* (Glasgow: Collin, 1975), pp. 124–131.

29. Ashton, *Economic Fluctuations,* p. 131.

30. Sir Nathaniel Wraxall, *The Historical and Posthumous Memoirs,* edited by Henry Wheatley (New York, 1884), 1: 348–350; *AR* (1771): 12; Julius Goebel, *The Struggle for the Falkland Islands* (New Haven: Yale University Press, 1982.)

31. *GM* 42 (1772): 311; *SM* 33 (1771): 217; Ashton, *Economic Fluctuations,* p. 127.

32. Woolfe, "Salvadore," pp. 104–113.

33. *LM* 45 (1775): 181–184, 320; Woolfe, "Salvadore," pp. 104–113. Adrien Louis de Bonnieres, Duc de Guines (1735–1806), was ambassador to England between 1770 and 1776. By 1775 he had published his memoirs and the issue had been aired in the papers and in Parliament. Walpole, *Correspondence,* 41: 299, 30: 263–264; Maza, *Private Lives,* pp. 156–165.

34. Lucy Sutherland, "Sir George Colebrooke's World Corner in Alum, 1771–73," *Economic History* (February 1936); *Thraliana,* pp. 333–334; *GM* (1773): 248. D'Archenholz offered Colebrooke as "a wonderful example of that thirst after wealth, with which some men are so unfortunately cursed." "He gave great entertainments, kept a numerous retinue of servants, and could command any sum of money." Constantly driven to search for "a new accession to his immense wealth," he engaged in the speculation that ruined him. D'Archenholz, *Picture,* pp. 127–128.

35. *DNB,* pp. 431–432; *LM* (1772): 314. His brothers were famous clergymen and doctors. *GM* (1772): 310–311.

36. Sutherland, *East India Company,* p. 223; *Letters from Mrs. Elizabeth Carter to Mrs. Montagu, between the years 1755 and 1800* (London, 1817), July 1772; Horace Walpole to Horatio Mann, in Walpole, *Correspondence,* vol. 23, 1 July 1772. In a letter to General Conway (*Correspondence,* vol. 39, 22 June 1772), Walpole confided, "It is lucky that I have had no dealings with Mr. Fordyce; for if he had ruined me, as he has half the world, I could not have *run away*"; *GM* (June 1772): 293.

37. Henrietta Fordyce, *Memoirs of the Late Mrs. Henrietta Fordyce* (London, 1823), pp. 36, 33, 292.

38. *LM* (1772): 292; Keith Feiling, *Warren Hastings* (London: Macmillan, 1966), pp. 89–90; Ashton, *Economic Fluctuations,* pp. 127–129.

39. James Boswell, *Reflections on the Late Alarming Bankruptcies in Scotland* (Edinburgh, 1772), pp. 1–7; *Thraliana,* p. 335; *GM* (September 1772): 434.

40. In British Library, Collection of Ballads and Broadsides, "A New Song on a Late Remarkable Occasion."

41. Hoppit, "Financial Crises," pp. 39–58, especially 50–55.

42. Julian Hoppit, "Attitudes to Credit in Britain 1680–1790," *Historical Journal* 33 (1990): 305–322; Hickey, *Memoirs,* 1:333; John Villette, *The Annals of Newgate* (London, 1776), 4:191–194; Hoppit, "Financial Crises," p. 54.

43. See *The Correspondence of Adam Smith,* edited by E. C. Mossner (Oxford: Clarendon Press, 1987), pp. 162–164.

44. *LM* (1773): 45; Wilson, *Anglo-Dutch Commerce,* pp. 169–182.

45. L. Sulivan writing to W. Hastings, April 28, 1773, quoted in Sutherland, "Sir George Colebrooke," p. 240, n. 5.

46. *AR* (1773): 9.

47. *MC,* June 30, 1775; *Gaz,* July 3, 1775; Sir George Colebrooke, *Retrospection or Reminiscences* (London, 1898), p. 50. The ballad on the Fordyce debacle also made snide comments on the Scots: "If there's one honest Scotchman that's Mr. F—," or "Many cries why he's just like his countrymen—," "A New Song."

48. *Gaz,* July 7, 1772. See Walpole, *Correspondence,* 23: 418, and n. 5. See also Ashton, *Economic Fluctuations,* p. 128, n. 57; Wilson, *Anglo-Dutch Commerce,* pp. 169–182.

49. *LM* 43 (1774): 300; Hoppit, "Attitudes to Credit," pp. 313–314. An article entitled "To the Opulent Jews," in the *Sussex Weekly Advertiser,* March 13, 1775, commented: "You can be no strangers to the numberless burglaries which have happened, which your people of the lower class have not only encouraged, by receiving the goods stolen, but have themselves also been engaged in committing." The author warns the Jews that they must bring all such offenders to justice, lest England withdraw "the peculiar blessings you enjoy in this nation." Perhaps in response to this extreme level of prejudice, the Great Synagogue put an advertisement in the *DA* of October 16, 1771, claiming that many London swindlers only "assume the name of Jews," and offering to provide character references for reputable Jewish merchants and brokers. For the debate, see *Gaz,* September 28, 1779. See also Felsenstein, *Anti-Semitic Stereotypes.*

50. *MP,* May 3, 1775; Namier and Brooke, *House of Commons,* 2: 658–662; *Thraliana,* 2: 355.

51. *GM* (May 1773): 248; Namier and Brooke, *House of Commons,* 2: 225–237.

52. *Thraliana,* p. 334.

53. M. C. Rudd, *Facts: Or a Plain and Explicit Narrative of the Case of Mrs. Rudd* (London, 1775), pp. 25–27. As with several other figures in this case, Kendal's identity is unclear. At the brothers' trial, a Colonel Kinder testified on their behalf. Mrs. Rudd insisted upon calling him Colonel Kendal and charged that he was behind some of the most vicious attacks upon her reputation. If her account of him is true, the Perreaus had good reasons for disguising his identity.

54. *MP,* July 1, 1775; *Gaz,* July 3, 1775; *Mrs. M. C. Rudd's Genuine Letter,* pp. 7–10; Theodosia, *Genuine Memoirs,* p. 119.

55. *Mrs. M. C. Rudd's Genuine Letter,* pp. 23–24.

56. *Calendar of Home Office Papers of the Reign of George III,* edited by R. A. Roberts (Nendeln, Liechtenstein: Kraus Reprints, 1967), 3: 285; *Prudence Triumphing over Vanity and Dissipation* (London, 1776), pp. 71–79.

57. Walpole, *Correspondence,* 23: 258.

58. David Spinney, *Rodney* (London: Allen & Unwin, 1969), pp. 238–255; Namier and Brooke, *House of Commons,* 3: 89–90. Rodney was in the clutches of Robert Mackreth, who had started life as a waiter, became manager of White's Club, and moved on to become a financier. Mackreth was "one of the most notorious usurers in London," and a dealer in landed estates. His dubious reputation and origins did little to slow his rise in society. In 1774 Lord Orford, in debt to Mackreth, sent him to Parliament. "Ruthless, shrewd and grasping," Mackreth was eventually knighted in 1795.

59. *Calendar of Home Office Papers,* 3: 312.

60. *Gaz,* April 5, 1775.

61. We have offered suggestions as to the identity of the people involved. These are, of course, just informed guesses. *MP,* July 1, 1775; *Gaz,* July 3, 1775.

62. Woolfe, "Salvadore," pp. 104–113. Salvadore's fortunes never recovered. In 1784 he left London for Charleston, South Carolina, where he went to live in what remained of an estate that had, at one time, encompassed 100,000 acres. Here he died in 1786.

63. *MP,* July 1, 1775; *Mrs. M. C. Rudd's Genuine Letter,* pp. 13–14, 40. James Adair the elder bought East India stock in order to support his son's efforts to become a player in the internal politics of the company. The younger Adair hoped that hav-

ing a stake in the company would assist his own political ambitions. In 1769 the elder Adair purchased just enough stock to qualify his son to vote in the election of the directors. He wrote to his partner asking him to advance the money or to approach the banker, Fordyce, in order to borrow it. The father expected to be a loser by the transaction, but wanted to be of service to his son. Young Adair was elected a member of the committee of proprietors on December 7, 1773, and he later became counsel for the company. He was at the center of various schemes for dealing with its accumulated problems, acting at the same time as an agent for the Rockingham interest. Add. Ms. 53808, #88, #90, British Library; Burke, *Correspondence*, 2:497; Namier and Brooke, *House of Commons*, 2:6.

64. *MP,* June 12, 1775.
65. *T&C* (1776): 41.
66. *St. J's,* January 20–23, 1776; *MC,* January 23, 1776; *Gaz,* January 23, 1776.
67. *MC,* January 25, 1776.
68. *MP,* June 17, 1775.
69. *LM* 41 (1772): 292.
70. Ibid.
71. David Hume to Adam Smith, June 27, 1772, in *Correspondence of Adam Smith,* p. 163.
72. *Gaz,* March 22, 1775; *FFBJ,* March 25, 1775.
73. *SM* (1772): 550.

SEVEN. DEBATING THE LAW

1. *Mdsx J,* June 15–17, 1775.
2. *PA,* June 16, 1775.
3. *St. J's,* June 24–27, 1775; *CM,* July 1, 1775. William Eden wrote to the Recorder soon after the brothers' trials, informing him that he need not make his report on the case if he thought "circumstances may appear in the evidence brought against her" that might be taken into account when discussing their conviction. Writing a month later, he enclosed a letter from Mr. Burgoyne on the Perreaus' behalf. At the same time, he added that "there is no reason whatever to give Mr. Robert Perreau any assurance of mercy." "He must abide the event of the report, the nature of which I cannot pretend to foresee." Eden thought, however, that in the interval, the brothers might have "a more wholesome confinement than the condemned cell." *Calendar of Home Office Papers,* 4: 355, 361, 369–370.
4. *CM,* June 16, 1775; *MP,* June 19, 1775.
5. *Mdsx J,* June 13–15, 1775; *Mrs. M. C. Rudd's Genuine Letter,* pp. 31–33.
6. *MC,* July 14, 1775.
7. The phrase suggested an earlier radical cause célèbre. The Kennedy brothers had been convicted of murdering a night watchman in 1770. They were pardoned, it was said, through the intervention of several aristocrats who were followers of Kitty Kennedy, a much-pursued courtesan. See John Brewer, "The Wilkites and the Law, 1763–74," in *An Ungovernable People,* edited by John Brewer and John Styles (New Brunswick, N.J.: Rutgers University Press, 1980), pp. 148–150.
8. *MC,* June 6, 1775; *Mdsx J,* March 16–18, 1775.

9. *Gaz*, June 24, 1775.
10. *MP*, July 8, 1775.
11. Ibid., June 16, 1775, June 22, 1775.
12. *Gaz*, June 15, 1775.
13. *MC*, June 6, 1775; *Gaz*, June 15, 1775. See also "A Country Magistrate" in *Gaz*, June 12, 1775, and "Amator Justitiae ac Veritatis" in *MP*, June 24, 1775.
14. Marcellus, *Letter*, pp. 6–12. However, "opinion without doors" was not of one mind on this question. Mrs. Rudd's evidence, some claimed, had been admitted in an attempt to discover who was the principal and who the accomplice in this confusing case. Since "her testimony has been used among other evidence as the ground-work of a Bill of Indictment; it would therefore be equally irregular and illegal to arraign her as a principal." While a correspondent to the *Morning Post* of July 8, 1775, felt that the magistrates were incorrect in admitting Mrs. Rudd as a crown witness, "A Friend to the Oppressed," writing to the *Gazetteer* of July 11, 1775, disagreed, finding Mrs. Rudd deserving of the award; *Gaz*, June 15, 1775; *MC*, June 4, 1775; *MP*, June 24, 1775.
15. *St. J's*, June 22, 1775.
16. *Gaz*, June 29, 1775; *MP*, June 19, 1775, June 22, 1775; *St. J's*, June 15–17, 1775; *MC*, June 22, 1775.
17. Beattie, *Crime and the Courts*, pp. 366–369; Leon Radzinowicz, *A History of English Criminal Law and Its Administration from 1752* (London: Stevens, 1956), 2: 33–56.
18. As the judges pointed out at the trials, this business of granting immunity from prosecution was complex. There were four ways one could receive such a promise: first, under the medieval doctrine of approvers; second, on the basis of a series of statutes, passed in the reigns of William and Mary, and of Anne, which promised immunity for impeaching confederates who committed specified crimes (the list did not include forgery); third, as part of a royal proclamation or advertisement offering immunity for assistance in solving a specific instance of a crime; and finally through the unofficial grant of the magistrate. The last was the most frequently employed grant.
19. The leading discussion of the crown witness process is John Langbein, "Shaping the Eighteenth-Century Criminal Trial: A View from the Ryder Sources," *University of Chicago Law Review* 50 (1983): 56–67, 84–96, 104.
20. David Lieberman, *The Province of Legislation Determined* (Cambridge: Cambridge University Press, 1989), pp. 99–121. Mansfield's reputation led to his house being destroyed in the Gordon riots of 1780.
21. *Boswell for the Defence*, edited by W. K. Wimsatt and F. Pottle (New York, McGraw-Hill, 1959), p. 176; *The Mansfield Manuscripts and the Growth of English Law in the Eighteenth Century* (Chapel Hill: University of North Carolina Press, 1992), 1: 5–6, 117–118, and in general chapters 1 and 2; James Roscoe, *Lives of Eminent British Lawyers* (London, 1830), pp. 217–18; John Campbell, *The Lives of the Chief Justices* (Philadelphia, 1851), 2: 338–339.
22. *MP*, July 4, 1775; *Mansfield*, 1: 5.
23. *Gaz*, July 4, 1775; *MC*, July 4, 1775; *CM*, July 8, 1775; *MP*, July 5, 1775, July 7, 1775; *Leeds Mercury* July 11, 1775.
24. *MC*, July 5, 1775.
25. *Mdsx J*, July 1–4, 1775.

26. It is worth noting that Robert's testimony also contained this ambiguity.

27. *Mdsx J,* July 1–4, 1775.

28. Ibid., July 4–6, 1775.

29. Ibid.; *Gaz,* July 4, 1775; *MP,* July 5, 1775. It could be argued that Mrs. Rudd was twice lucky, first in being made a crown witness, and then in not being called at the trials of Daniel and Robert Perreau. If she had testified in either case, and then had told a lie that could be exposed as such, the case for depriving her of her protection would have been stronger. At the very least, she could have been prosecuted for perjury. As it was, much of the evidence of her lies emerged in contexts that the judges, in strict propriety, could not, as Justice Aston observed, "take cognizance of." *Gaz,* September 18, 1775.

30. *MC,* July 5, 1775; Lieberman, *Province of Legislation,* p. 88, and more generally, pp. 71–143; Brewer, "Wilkites and the Law," pp. 156–168; *Mansfield,* 1: 6, 99–108, 196–205.

31. R v. Rudd, *English Reports* (Edinburgh, 1900–1930), 168: 160–164; *MC,* July 5, 1775. Langbein demonstrates that Mansfield misrepresented practice at this point, for the magistrates did not pardon. Rather the justice gave a promise not to prosecute. Yet this is a technical distinction that contemporaries seemed to ignore. In the debate that followed his decision, no one characterized the practice as other than a pardon, despite the fact that no official pardon was issued. On discretion, see King, *Crime, Justice and Discretion,* chapter 7.

32. R v. Rudd, *English Reports,* 168: 160–164; *MC,* July 5, 1775.

33. *Gaz,* July 14, 1775. At the request of her counsel, the judges agreed to delay her trial so that she could locate an important witness in Scotland.

34. *PA,* September 18, 1775.

35. Edward Foss, *The Judges of England* (New York: AMS Press, 1966), 8: 294–295; Valentine, *Establishment* 1: 376. During the Gordon riots, Gould declined the offer of troops to protect his house. *Gaz,* September 19, 1775.

36. *Gaz,* September 19, 1775; *MC,* September 18, 1775.

37. *Gaz,* September 19, 1775. The press noted again Mrs. Rudd's conduct during the hearing. "Though at her Entrance and during the Arguments, she possessed a decent composure and steady Firmness that baffles all description," on being once again sent back to Newgate, she "trembled much, and seemed greatly affected with her situation." *GEP,* September 15, 1775; *PA,* September 18, 1775.

38. R v. Rudd, *English Reports,* 168: 165.

39. It is worth noting that, despite the intensity of the controversy and the wide publicity accorded Mansfield's decision, it had no discernible impact on magistrates' practice. They continued to act as they had before these deliberations, and the courts respected their grants of crown witness status.

40. The ninety letters published between June and December 1775 that deal exclusively with the case range in length and interest. In order to get some idea of a comparison with "typical" correspondence, we counted the length of fifty letters, twenty-five in the *Morning Chronicle* of November 1775 and twenty-five in the *Gazetteer* of July 1775, and compared them with the letters dealing with the Perreau-Rudd case. Interestingly, the most significant differences emerge only with the very long letters. Whereas the sample letters contain no correspondence longer than 199 column lines, there are eight case letters longer than that. Seven letters are between 202 and 293

lines, but one massive letter is 549 column lines, filling one half of the first and more than one half of the second page of the *Public Advertiser* for August 21, 1775. In another measure of the case's appeal, the popular debating society, the Robin Hood, took up the question: "Whether it is consistent with justice and equity, to bring a person to trial, after his or her being admitted an evidence for the crown." The decision was in the affirmative. *MC,* August 26, 1775.

41. *PA,* August 21, 1775.

42. Ibid.

43. Quoted in Brewer, "Wilkites and the Law," p. 158; see Henry Dagge, *Considerations on Criminal Law* (London, 1772), p. 134, where he announced that vesting power in judges is dangerous.

44. *MP,* June 9, 1775. Lieberman notes that "Mansfield's innovations have often appeared as a foreign-inspired assault on English orthodoxies" (*Province of Legislation,* pp. 87, 131); Brewer, "Wilkites and the Law," p. 159.

45. *MC,* June 8, 1775.

46. *Gaz,* December 6, 1775.

47. *St. J's,* September 19–21, 1775.

48. *MP,* June 9, 1775, August 30, 1775, October 12, 1775; *PA,* July 12, 1775. Another correspondent wrote that the pardon should not be "clogged" with conditions. The overly strict imposition of the rule laid down by the judges would defeat the purpose of the grant. If a criminal feared that because he forgot to mention one in a hundred of his crimes he might be tried and executed, he would never cooperate. *Gaz,* September 24, 1775.

49. *MP,* June 9, 1775, September 20, 1775; *Gaz,* July 15, 1775. The same disagreement about the relation of equity and common law appeared in the decisions offered by the judges in September. Judge Gould, voting against withdrawing immunity, argued for allowing it to Mrs. Rudd "in the spirit and genius of the common law." Justice Ashurst, voting for withdrawing the immunity, said Mrs. Rudd's trial was necessary "if justice be the thing to be sought, if the laws are meant to be fairly enforced and equitably executed." *OBSP,* (September 1774): 496–497.

50. *MP,* June 9, 1775.

51. Ibid., August 30, 1775.

52. *MC,* June 8, 1775.

53. *PA,* July 12, 1775; A Barrister, *The Case of Margaret Caroline Rudd* (London, 1775), p. 70.

54. *MC,* November 24, 1775.

55. *CM,* September 23, 1775; *St. J's,* September 21–23, 1775; *MC,* September 23, 1775.

56. *MP,* July 10, 1775.

57. *PA,* July 12, 1775.

58. Ibid.

59. Ibid., July 10, 1775.

60. "Taking all property crimes together," John Beattie has written, "the treatment of women was substantially different from that of men, for women were more likely to be acquitted and, if convicted, to be found guilty of a less charge than that stated in the indictment." *Crime and the Courts,* pp. 437–438; King, *Crime, Justice and Discretion,* pp. 196-207.

61. *PA,* August 21, 1775.

1. *MP*, March 29, 1775, for an early doubt about her authorship of the "Case."
2. *Gaz*, April 11, 1775.
3. Rudd, *Facts*, pp. 11, 23.
4. *MP*, March 27, 1775. The only other case we have come across was an appeal by the famous demi-rep Kitty Fisher, asking the public not to buy, or believe, a scurrilous pamphlet that had appeared, purporting to be her life story. See Horace Bleackley, *Ladies Fair and Frail* (London: John Lane, Bodley Head, 1925), pp. 61–62. For glimpses of other scandalous women and their writings, see Margaret Ann Doody, "The Law, the Page, and the Body of Woman: Murder and Murderesses in the Age of Johnson," *The Age of Johnson* 1 (1987): 127–160; Clare Brant, "Speaking of Women: Scandal and the Law in the Mid-Eighteenth Century," in *Women, Texts and Histories 1575–1760,* edited by C. Brant and D. Purkis (London: Routledge, 1992), pp. 242–270; Felicity Nussbaum, "Heteroclites: The Gender of Character in the Scandalous Memoirs," in *The New Eighteenth Century,* edited by F. Nussbaum and L. Brown (New York: Methuen, 1987), pp. 144–167.
5. *MP*, July 8, 1775, April 12, 1775.
6. *PA*, July 20, 1775, *Gaz*, April 5, 1775.
7. *MP*, May 29, 1775.
8. *Lloyd's,* March 15–17, 1775; *MP*, March 16, 1775; Rudd, *Facts*, p. 7.
9. *Gaz*, April 5, 1775.
10. *MP*, May 18, 1775, May 15, 1775. See Auditor, in *MP*, June 19, 1775, for a purportedly "real" genealogy of her family of origin.
11. She later said she thought that Rudd had died abroad. He had not. *Gaz*, April 5, 1775.
12. See, for example, *MP*, July 1, 1775.
13. *Lloyd's,* May 13–16, 1775. For stories about the "lost years" see *MP*, March 23, 1775, March 29, 1775, March 31, 1775, June 10, 1775; *MC*, June 23, 1775. For Mrs. Gore, see *MP*, July 1, 1775.
14. *MP*, June 12, 1775.
15. Rudd, *Facts*, pp. vi, 8, 20.
16. *MP*, March 27, 1775, *Gaz*, March 28, 1775.
17. *MP*, July 1, 1775.
18. Ibid., March 27, 1775, *Gaz*, March 28, 1775.
19. *MP*, April 12, 1775; also appeared in *St. J's*, April 11–13, 1775.
20. Rudd addressed the two as "sisters," stressing their affinity. The correspondence was filled with confidences concerning her plans and activities, especially her efforts to advance the interests of the brothers. In this letter she concluded by telling the sisters of her dream that one day soon she would be "Lady P—." Folger Library, Ms. M.b. 37; *MP*, March 27, 1775; *Gaz*, March 28, 1775.
21. See Rudd, *Facts*, pp. 25–27.
22. *MP*, July 10, 1775.
23. Ibid., June 12, 1775, June 17, 1775.
24. *Gaz*, April 5, 1775, *MP*, April 4, 1775.
25. Rudd, *Facts*, pp. vi, 47; R. F. Brissenden, *Virtue in Distress: Studies in the Novel of Sentiment from Richardson to Sade* (London: Macmillan, 1974), pp. 129–130, 91; La

Belle Assemblee in *LC,* March 6, 1780; *LC,* April 22–25, 1775. For more on this theme, see G. J. Barker-Benfield, *The Culture of Sensibility* (Chicago: University of Chicago Press, 1992), John Mullan, *Sentiment and Sociability* (Oxford: Oxford University Press, 1988), and Ann Jessie Van Sant, *Eighteenth Century Sensibility and the Novel* (Cambridge: Cambridge University Press, 1993).

26. *MP,* April 13, 1775.

27. Ibid., May 29, 1775.

28. Mrs. Rudd's benevolence could sometimes take on a sinister, threatening quality, as in her letter addressed to the Messrs. P—, in which she remarked that "from an inherent humanity and tenderness, and in consideration of the light she stood in as wife and sister-in-law, she has hitherto acted with the greatest lenity and forbearance towards them," but she would not continue to be kind if her reputation continued to be attacked by their supporters. *GEP,* April 20, 1775.

29. *MP,* May 6, 1775, June 12, 1775.

30. *Gaz,* April 5, 1775, March 28, 1775.

31. *MP,* May 17, 1775.

32. *Boswell: The Ominous Years,* pp. 357–358. On April 15, 1779, the society at Coachmakers' Hall debated the following question: "Which is most likely to produce happiness, the nice feelings of extreme sensibility, or the apathy of cold indifference?" *Gaz,* April 13, 1779.

33. *Gaz,* March 28, 1775, April 5, 1775, July 17, 1775; *MP,* July 3, 1775. "Moral weeping is the sign of so noble a passion" [1755], quoted in Brissenden, *Virtue in Distress,* p. 83.

34. Phrases from a letter written in her behalf, perhaps by she herself, in *MP,* May 17, 1775. For more on the sentimentality of this period, see Langford, *A Polite and Commercial People,* chapter 10.

35. Henry Mackenzie, quoted in Brissenden, *Virtue in Distress,* p. 126; *MP,* June 13, 1775, for Selini; for Eve, *PA,* June 16, 1775, and reference in debate, *MC,* July 3, 1776; for Millwood, *MP,* May 15, 1775.

36. The line is from a poem, "A Poetical Billet from Captain R[oche] to Mrs. R[udd]," which imagined a mock-courtship between these two people on trial for their lives. Captain Roche was tried and let free for killing a man in a duel (*GM* [September 1775]: 443); and for a reply, "To the Author of a Poetical Billet," see *GM* (October 1775): 492. The second part of this subtitle echoes Greg Dening's fine book, *Mr Bligh's Bad Language* (Cambridge: Cambridge University Press, 1992).

37. *MP,* May 29, 1775; *Mdsx J,* May 27–30, 1775.

38. *LC,* March 16–18, 1775; Brissenden, *Virtue in Distress,* pp. 92, 94. From Jonah Barrington's *Personal Sketches of His Own Time* (London, 1830), 1: 144–145, we get the following story of Lady M., a woman married against her will to a man she despised and to whom she was later unfaithful: "Nature had formed me for all the pleasures and the pains which are alike inseparable from sensibility. I found a glow in every thought—an enthusiasm in every action. My feelings were always *in earnest.* I could love to excess, and hate to rancour! but I could do neither with mediocrity. I could be the best or the worst of wives. I could endure any thing with a man I loved, but could not sit upon a throne with one whom I detested."

39. Ann Radcliffe, *The Italian or the Confessional of the Black Penitents* (1797; reprinted Oxford: Oxford University Press, 1998), pp. 68, 32; for Mrs. Macaulay, *Letters on Ed-*

ucation [1790] part 1, letter 24, "Chastity," see Vivien Jones, *Women in the Eighteenth Century* (London: Routledge, 1990). Macaulay claimed that the result of her method of education would be a woman who was "a careless, modest beauty, grave, manly, noble, full of strength and majesty" (p. 116).

40. *Boswell: The Ominous Years*, p. 356.

41. William Duncan, *The Elements of Logic* (London, 1787), pp. 1–4; Isaac Watts, *The Improvement of the Mind* (London, 1782), 1: 4–6.

42. *Gaz*, April 11, 1775; *MP*, May 12, 1775; *Gaz*, July 3, 1775.

43. Shakespeare, in *GEP*, August 8, 1775; Young in *MC*, June 10, 1775; Mason's Elfrida, also in *GEP*, August 8, 1775; Sir William Draper, *MC*, August 19, 1775. Not only do these anonymous letters sound like hers, but the Shakespeare quote comes from the same play, *The Merchant of Venice*, as the quote in her letter.

44. *Mrs. M. C. Rudd's Genuine Letter*, p. 43; *The Letters of Junius*, edited by John Cannon (Oxford: Oxford University Press, 1978).

45. *MP*, June 12, 1775.

46. Ibid., April 12, 1775; *PA*, July 6, 1775, July 20, 1775.

47. *MP*, May 26, 1775, May 15, 1775; *MC*, June 4, 1775; *St. J's*, May 13–15, 1775.

48. *Authentic Anecdotes*, p. 43; *MP*, May 20, 1775, May 18, 1775, July 4, 1775.

49. *Mdsx J*, April 1–4, 1775.

50. *Mrs. Stewart's Case, Written by Herself* (London, 1789), pp. 8–9.

51. See Richard Holmes, *Dr. Johnson and Mr. Savage* (London: Hodder and Stoughton, 1993).

52. Ibid., pp. 1, 14, 20–26, 34, 36.

53. "Justice," in *MP*, January 9, 1789. Sir William Musgrave wrote on the flyleaf: "Upon no better foundation than her mother's name being Stewart she imposed on the Herald's College in Scotland to make out a pedigree that allied her to a great Number of noble Families. This pedigree she enclosed in her first letter to Lord Rawdon and because he did not give credit to it afterwards—she has taken occasion to abuse him in the following pamphlet."

54. In the postscript to *Mrs. Stewart's Letter*, Rudd remarked that she could not "but give my enemies a smile of defying contempt when I reflect that my fate rests with a discerning Public—with ENGLISH RECTITUDE and ENGLISH HUMANITY" (p. 30).

55. The *Gentleman's Magazine* revealed the authorship of the novel. "It may gratify curiosity to be informed, that the 'Belle Widows' is the production of the celebrated Mrs. Rudd, alias Stewart. While the lady was confined in the Fleet Prison in 1787, experiencing a misery of extreme want, she wrote this novel, ... to answer a *private* purpose. It was revised by another author" (*GM* [1790]: 68). William West confirmed the attribution in *Fifty Years' Recollection of an Old Bookseller* (1835, reprinted New York: Garland Publishing, 1974), p. 21.

56. *The Belle Widows* (London, 1789), 2: 258, 70, 125, 128–129, 139.

57. Ibid., 1: 195, 201.

58. Ibid., 2: 1–2. Rudd's character sketch of Clive is interesting: "The General was the quintessence of eastern pomposity. He mistook ostentation for dignity; glare for splendour; superficial smattering for literature; and farrago observation, gleaned from his former motley situations [Clive started out life as a clerk for the East India Company], for correct and extensive knowledge of life. Yet he had some good sense,

and some good qualities, and was one of the least exceptionable of our *Asiatic quality.*" It was rumored that Rudd had been kept by Clive; there is a strong hint in *Authentic Anecdotes* (p. 22) that the "King of Nabobs" gave Mrs. Rudd her pension.

59. See John Sainsbury, "Wilkes and Libertinism," *Studies in Eighteenth-Century Culture* 26 (1996): 151–174. Boswell was also a friend of Wilkes's and the two men frequently discussed the women they were keeping, or had kept.

60. *Belle Widows,* 1: 13.

61. Ibid., 2: 199–200.

62. *MP,* March 29, 1775; Folger Library, Ms. M.b. 37.

63. Theodosia, *Genuine Memoirs,* pp. 124, 138.

NINE. MRS. RUDD ON TRIAL

1. *MP,* September 19, 1775.

2. Ibid., December 10, 1775, December 11, 1775; *St. J's,* December 7–12, 1775; *PA,* December 9, 1775; *Mdsx J,* December 7–9, 1775.

3. *Reminiscences of Henry Angelo* (London, 1830; reprinted New York: Benj Blom,
1969), 1: 468–471. Angelo composed his memoirs more than fifty years after the
event. He had little doubt of her "deep-designing wickedness, which had wrought
the ruin of these unhappy brothers, and destroyed the peace of a once happy and
virtuous family."

4. *CM,* July 15, 1775.

5. *Mdsx J,* December 7–9, 1775; *PA,* December 9, 1775.

6. *GEP,* December 12, 1775.

7. *Mdsx J,* March 25–28, 1775, April 1–4, 1775.

8. Ibid., May 27–30, 1775.

9. Ibid., June 13–15, 1775.

10. *MC,* December 4, 1775. The defense must have long known that Henrietta Perreau
would testify against Mrs. Rudd. The first criticism of her appearing in this capacity came in a letter to *CM,* July 22, 1775.

11. *MC,* September 9, 1775.

12. *Trials of Robert,* pp. 68–72; *PA,* December 9, 1775. This volume included the trial
of Mrs. Rudd, although the report was imperfect. See *Gaz,* December 11, 1775, as
well as *Monthly Miscellany* (1776): 12.

13. *Reminiscences of Angelo,* 1: 469.

14. *Trials of Robert,* pp. 71–74.

15. *DNB.*

16. *Trials of Robert,* pp. 72–78; *PA,* December 9, 1775; *Gaz,* December 11, 1775; *Reminiscences of Angelo,* 1: 469.

17. *Reminiscences of Angelo,* 1: 469; *PA,* December 9, 1775; *MP,* December 11, 1775. Only
the *Morning Post* offered a less critical review of Davy's examination. While Mrs.
Perreau was so upset during the interrogation, Davy, "observing her distress, spoke
to her with extreme tenderness, and assured her he meant nothing personal, or ill-
natured." The servant Moody once again testified to Mrs. Rudd's "feigned hand."
Cowper, however, elicited from him the admission that he had never actually seen
Mrs. Rudd sign Adair's name. Even more fatally, he confessed that he could not

identify her "common hand." After remarking that in his testimony Moody "sung the same song over again," one paper added that it was "induced to doubt of this man's memory, or integrity" because he so waffled in his account of what he had and had not seen. *Gaz,* December 11, 1775.

18. Namier and Brooke, *The House of Commons,* 2: 468–469; Lewis Namier, *England in the Age of the American Revolution* (London: Macmillan, 1970), p. 222.

19. *Gaz,* April 11, 1775.

20. *MP,* April 11, 1775, May 6, 1775.

21. Ibid., May 12, 1775; *St. J's,* May 11–13, 1775. Even the *Morning Post* finally expressed a reluctance to publish an additional letter that contained "some severe reflections on a worthy baronet" (May 17, 1775).

22. *MP,* May 12, 1775.

23. *Mdsx J,* June 13–15, 1775.

24. Hickey, *Memoirs,* 1: 334–37; Phillips, *Mid-Georgian London,* p. 269. Belliard told of Daniel coming to him three months before the case broke, saying he wanted to purchase a ring. While the jeweler had one made according to Daniel's design, he loaned him another, asking only that when Daniel wore the ring, he should mention that it was for sale for £2000.

25. *CM,* July 22, 1775; *St. J's,* July 22, 1775; *MP,* July 26, 1775, August 7, 1775; *MC,* August 16, 1775.

26. *Gaz,* July 4, 1775.

27. *MP,* August 29, 1775.

28. Ibid., July 13, 1775.

29. *MP,* September 27, 1775; *MC,* October 13, 1775.

30. *Gaz,* October 26, 1775; *MC,* October 27, 1775; *MP,* October 27, 1775.

31. *Gaz,* October 31, 1775.

32. *MP,* December 10, 1775; *Gaz,* December 11, 1775; *Trials of Robert,* pp. 78–82.

33. *Mdsx J,* December 7–9, 1775; *Trials of Robert,* pp. 78–82; *Gaz,* December 11, 1775.

34. *Trials of Robert,* pp. 82–83; *Gaz,* December 11, 1775.

35. *She Is and She Is Not, a Fragment of the True History of Miss C. De Grosberg* (London, 1776), pp. iv, 106.

36. *CR* (1776): 160; *MR* (1776): 490.

37. *Letter from Mrs. Christian Hart,* pp. 38–39, 66.

38. *Trials of Robert,* pp. 92–96. John Bailey "was a native of Ireland" who came to London about 1760 to study English law. Never particularly successful as a practitioner, he was unable to escape from what contemporaries snidely referred to as the "lower branch" of the profession. His adoption of "a genteel manner" soon exhausted his small fortune. He attended the Old Bailey looking for employment, and it was there that he encountered Mrs. Rudd. One report claimed that she paid his fees "by her transferring her person to him." This relationship continued for some time after her trial, but finally ended when he became jealous of her other admirers. Addicted to drink, unsuccessful as a lawyer, he was said to have died in extreme poverty. *Nocturnal Revels* (London, 1779), 2: 244–251; Corfield, *Power,* pp. 80–83.

39. Ibid., pp. 98–101, 106–107.

40. Ibid., pp. 102–108. Bailey was no doubt aware of the damage this charge represented to his career. He too responded with a pamphlet; he wrote, he said, out of an obligation "to preserve a character unimpeached and unsullied as the snow drop's

flower." The character he sought to preserve was not only Mrs. Rudd's but his own as well. [John Bailey], *The Trial at Large of Mrs. Margaret Caroline Rudd* (London, 1775), p. i.

41. *Gaz*, December 11, 1775; *MP*, December 10, 1775; *CR* (1776): 248; *MR* (1776): 334; *Trials of Robert*, pp. 102–111; *Letter from Mrs. Christian Hart*, p. 39.

42. "We have only to lament," the *Gazetteer* opined, that the instigator "should be permitted to live in human society; because, on the one hand, if the prisoner was the inventress, she would have purchased the life of an antediluvian at much too high a price; on the other hand, if fabricated by Sir Thomas Frankland and Mrs. Perreau, we think the best husband in Britain, and the most valuable Eastern Paraphanalia, thus obtained, much too dear." *Gaz*, December 11, 1775.

43. *Gaz*, December 11, 1775; *MP*, December 10, 1775.

44. *St. J's*, December 7–12, 1775.

45. *Gaz*, December 11, 1775; *St. J's*, December 7–12, 1775.

46. *Trials of Robert*, p. 101.

47. *Mrs. M. C. Rudd's Genuine Letter*, pp. 47–48. This work also claimed that Nightingale was in reality "the well-known Polly H—s—m" and implied that she had been paid by someone for her testimony. *Gaz*, December 11, 1775; *St. J's*, December 7–12, 1775.

48. *Gaz*, December 11, 1775; *MP*, December 10, 1775; *Mdsx J*, December 7–9, 1775.

49. *MP*, December 11, 1775.

50. *Reminiscences of Angelo*, 1: 469–71; *Gaz*, December 11, 1775; *PA*, December 9, 1775; *Mdsx J*, December 7–9, 1775.

51. *Mdsx J*, December 7–9, 1775.

52. *MP*, December 10, 1775, December 11, 1775.

53. *PA*, December 27, 1775.

54. *Gaz*, January 15, 1776.

55. *PA*, December 29, 1775.

TEN. "IF INNOCENTS SHOULD SUFFER"

1. *Gaz*, January 15, 1776.

2. Beattie, *Crime and the Courts*, p. 431; Douglas Hay, "Property, Authority and the Criminal Law," in *Albion's Fatal Tree*, edited by D. Hay et al. (New York: Pantheon, 1975), pp. 40–49; King, *Crime, Justice and Discretion*, especially chapter 9; Gatrell, *The Hanging Tree*, chapter 16.

3. *MC*, January 11, 1776; Lord Deloraine, "who has figured upon the horizon of gaiety and dissipation for upwards of twenty years ... married a widow-lady, Mrs. Knight, for her money." *Nocturnal Revels*. For the accusation of a link between Rudd and Deloraine, see *MP*, March 23, 1775, September 2, 1775; Walpole, *Correspondence*, 23: 511.

4. K. Morgan, ed., *An American Quaker in the British Isles* (Oxford: Oxford University Press, 1992), p. 263.

5. *Nocturnal Revels*, 2: 245–46.

6. *American Quaker*, p. 263; Thomas Frost, *The Life of Thomas, Lord Lyttelton* (London, 1876), p. vii; *DNB*; Alan Valentine, *The British Establishment 1760–1784* (Norman:

University of Oklahoma Press, 1970), 2: 562. The Regatta was an event that filled the papers for days in late June. Great sums were spent to design elaborate displays for the barges. The aristocracy eagerly participated in the preparations, and the Regatta enjoyed royal patronage. It culminated in feasting and dancing at Ranelagh. The event also produced much complaint about how frivolous activities distracted the nation at a time of crisis. It was perhaps symbolically appropriate that low tide and rain turned the day into a rout.

7. Walpole, *Correspondence,* 24: 464–465. Lyttelton came to an early and bad end. He died at the age of thirty-five, in the midst of extravagance and debauchery. Walpole wrote after his death: "What a pity it was that such extraordinary talents as Lord Lyttelton was endowed with, were accompanied with so vicious and infamous a disposition of every kind" (25: 2). *LC,* November 27–30, 1779.

8. *The Autobiography and Correspondence of Mary Granville, Mrs. Delany,* edited by Lady Landover, 2nd ser. (London, 1862), 2: 188; Pearce, *The Amazing Duchess,* p. 188.

9. Yale University Library, Ms. (L 174).

10. *Gaz,* December 25, 1775.

11. *MC,* January 12, 1776. It is worth remarking again that Woodfall and the *Morning Chronicle* took a leading role in the assault on Mrs. Rudd's reputation.

12. *MC,* January 17, 1776.

13. Ibid., January 13, 1776.

14. Ibid., January 15, 1776.

15. Ibid., January 12, 1776.

16. *PA,* January 16, 1776; *MC,* January 16, 1776; *Gaz,* January 13, 1776.

17. *MP,* December 18, 1775, December 19, 1775.

18. Ibid., December 19, 1775, December 20, 1775, December 23, 1775.

19. Ibid., December 20, 1775, December 23, 1775.

20. Ibid., December 23, 1775, December 26, 1775.

21. *PA,* January 4, 1776.

22. *MC,* January 12, 1776.

23. *PA,* January 16, 1776.

24. *Gaz,* January 16, 1776.

25. *MC,* January 13, 1776.

26. *PA,* January 17, 1776.

27. Ibid., January 11, 1776.

28. Ibid., January 9, 1776.

29. Blackstone, *Commentaries,* 1: 234, 243, 257, 2: 390–391; King, *Crime, Justice and Discretion,* pp. 304–333.

30. William Paley, *Principles of Moral and Political Philosophy* (1785; reprinted Houston: St. Thomas Press, 1977), p. 376. Paley's book originated in lectures he gave at Cambridge between 1768 and 1776. Beattie, *Crime and the Courts,* p. 586.

31. *Gaz,* January 15, 1776.

32. *Mdsx J,* June 1–3, 1775.

33. The debate took place on June 26, 1775. *MC,* July 3, 1775.

34. *CM,* January 13, 1776; *MC,* July 17, 1775, January 22, 1776.

35. *MC,* January 15, 1776; *MP,* January 17, 1776; see "Humanus," *MC,* June 19, 1775, June 29, 1775, January 15, 1776, January 16, 1776.

36. *MR* (1767): 387.
37. *Gaz,* June 29, 1775. For citations of Blackstone, Beccaria, and Montesquieu, see *MP,* October 12, 1775.
38. *PA,* January 8, 1776; *MC,* January 8, 1776; *Gaz,* January 15, 1776.
39. *MC,* January 15, 1776; *PA,* January 16, 1776.
40. *MC,* January 25, 1776.
41. *Mrs. M. C. Rudd's Genuine Letter,* pp. 5–7. Mrs. Rudd continued to take an interest in reports relating to the case even after the brothers' execution. In 1777 a newspaper illustrating a stock-jobbing trickery referred to Daniel Perreau's masterminding a drop on the Exchange that resulted in his pocketing "no less a sum than two thousand pounds." Mrs. Rudd's furious response lambasted the anecdote's author and instead insisted that it had been Col. Kendal who, when in the service of the French ambassador in England, Chatelet, had used the trick to enrich himself. *MP,* November 17, 1777, November 10, 1777.
42. *Mrs. M. C. Rudd's Genuine Letter,* pp. 1–9, and see chapter 6 for a fuller discussion of the Perreau dealings.
43. *Mrs. M. C. Rudd's Genuine Letter,* pp. 17–23.
44. Ibid., pp. 38, 32–37.
45. Ibid., pp. 37–40.
46. Ibid., pp. 12–13; Villette, *Genuine Account,* p. 15.
47. *PA,* January 17, 1776; *Gaz,* January 16, 1776.
48. *MC,* January 15, 1776.
49. Quoted in Linda Colley, *Britons: Forging the Nation 1707–1837* (New Haven: Yale University Press, 1992), p. 208.
50. *PA,* January 4, 1776.
51. Ibid., January 17, 1776; *Gaz,* January 16, 1776.
52. *MC,* January 8, 1776.
53. *Gaz,* June 12, 1775; *MC,* June 14, 1775; *MP,* June 20, 1775.
54. *Gaz,* January 15, 1776.
55. *PA,* June 12, 1775. Only "Neitherside" agreed with this author, noting that "a petty forger would long since have been exhibited at Tyburn." *MP,* September 25, 1775.
56. *MC,* June 14, 1775.
57. *CM,* January 20, 1776.
58. *PA,* January 22, 1776.
59. *Cumberland Pacquet,* February 1, 1776.
60. *CM,* January 13, 1776; *FFBJ,* January 13, 1776.
61. *Manchester Mercury,* January 30, 1776.
62. *MC,* January 16, 1776.
63. J. Heneage Jesse, *Memoirs of the Life and Reign of George the Third* (London, 1867), 2: 250.
64. *Gaz,* January 18, 1776. Boswell was in Edinburgh when he read an account of the executions. He was much "affected" and "could not fall asleep for a long time after going to bed." *Boswell: The Ominous Years,* p. 223.
65. *PA,* January 8, 1776.
66. *CM,* January 20, 1776.
67. Ibid.

68. *PA,* January 22, 1776, January 23, 1776.
69. Ibid.
70. *Gaz,* January 18, 1776; *MP,* January 18, 1776; *MC,* January 22, 1776.
71. *Gaz,* January 20, 1776.
72. *PA,* January 22, 1776.
73. Ibid., January 23, 1776.
74. Ibid., January 16, 1776, January 25, 1776; *MP,* January 26, 1776.
75. *MC,* January 31, 1776.
76. *MP,* January 27, 1776.
77. *Gaz,* January 28, 1776; *MC,* February 9, 1776.
78. *MC,* January 25, 1776; *WM* (January 1776): 156–157.
79. *Gaz,* January 24, 1776.
80. Ibid.
81. *MP,* January 30, 1776.
82. *Gaz,* January 24, 1776.
83. *St. J's,* January 23–25, 1776.
84. *SM* (1776): 105, 143; *MR* (1776): 244–245.
85. Ibid.
86. *MC,* January 25, 1776.
87. *PA,* January 24, 1776.
88. *MC,* January 23, 1776.
89. *CR* (1776): 160.
90. *MC,* February 10, 1776, February 15, 1776, February 21, 1776.
91. *GM* (1776): 45–46.

ELEVEN. LOOKING BACK

1. *Prudence Triumphing,* pp. 67, 13, 102; *Authentic Anecdotes,* introduction; *Observations on the Trial of Mr. Robert Perreau,* p. 32.
2. *The Diary and Letters of Thomas Hutchinson,* 2: 6–7; see also Bernard Bailyn, *The Ordeal of Thomas Hutchinson* (Cambridge, Mass.: Harvard University Press, 1974), especially pp. 343–347.
3. *The Journal of Samuel Curwen,* 1: 106–107.
4. We would like to thank Amanda Vickery for these references. Amanda Vickery, *The Gentleman's Daughter: Women's Lives in Georgian England* (New Haven: Yale University Press, 1998), p. 339, n. 36.
5. After Mrs. Rudd passed from popular memory, she lived on in scholarly works. The standard editions of Boswell and Walpole continue this tradition. See Gordon Turnbull, "Criminal Biographer: Boswell and Margaret Caroline Rudd," *Studies in English Literature* 26 (1986): 512.
6. *The Diabo-Lady* (London, 1777), pp. 3–4.
7. *A Particular Account of the Dreadful and Shocking Apparitions of the Two Unfortunate Perreaus* (London, 1776).
8. *Gaz,* December 28, 1775.
9. *MC,* December 30, 1775.

10. *T&C* (1776): 258. See 16 George III c. 122.

11. Feiling, *Hastings*, p. 181.

12. *LM* (1771): 477. "Masquerades, Ranelagh, Concerts, and many other diversions take up the town," Hutchinson lamented in June 1775. "Never was a time when so great a part of the people spend so great a portion of their time and estates in amusements and dissipations." Hutchinson, *Diary*, 2: 36.

13. *Observations on the Trial of Mr. Robert Perreau*, p. 38; *PA*, September 22, 1775; *GEP*, September 21, 1775.

14. *MC*, June 20, 1775.

15. *St. J's*, January 23–25, 1776.

16. Dror Wahrman, "Percy's Prologue: From Gender Play to Gender Panic in Eighteenth-Century England," *Past and Present* 159 (1998): 113–160; Joanna Innes, "Politics and Morals: The Reformation of Manners Movement in the Eighteenth Century," in *The Transformation of Political Culture: England and Germany in the Late Eighteenth Century*, edited by E. Hellmuth (London: Oxford University Press, 1990), pp. 57–118; John Money, "The Masonic Moment; or, Ritual, Replica and Credit: John Wilkes, the Macaroni Parson, and the Making of the Middle Class Mind," *Journal of British Studies* 32 (1993): 358–395; Wilson, *The Sense of the People*, pp. 185–89, 246, 254, 269; Donna T. Andrew, *Philanthropy and Police* (Princeton: Princeton University Press, 1989), pp. 155–177.

EPILOGUE

1. For reports of Mrs. Robert Perreau, see *GEP*, January 20, 1776, *MC*, January 22, 1776, and *GM*, 79 (1809): 893.

2. *GM*, 79 (1809): 893; *GM*, 80 (1810): 596; *The Record of Old Westminsters*, edited by G. F. Russell Baker and A. Stenning, vol. 3 (London: Chiswick Press, 1928), India Office Records, J/1/9234. William Hickey, the son of Daniel's attorney, met Perreau in India. Robert Samuel Perreau prospered at first, Hickey wrote, "until a natural disposition to embark on every sort of speculation led him to engage in the indigo line, in which either from a want of sufficient knowledge of the business, or from some unknown disasters, he finally and utterly failed." Despite these reverses, Perreau continued to enjoy the support of "the principal persons in the Settlement." In 1790 he was appointed secretary to the Calcutta Insurance Company. A discovery of "a very considerable deficiency" in the cash of the company was repaired by his friends, but his situation was so embarrassed that he fled the colony, leaving many creditors unpaid, among them Hickey himself. The only "satisfaction" he received from Perreau was in telling him that "he was a despicable scoundrel and deserved quite as much if not more than his father and uncle." Hickey, *Memoirs*, 3: 245–256, 4: 324, 447–449.

3. *GM*, 104 (1834): 318.

4. Mrs. Thrale reported that when Boswell spoke of his visit, he said that Mrs. Rudd, upon hearing his name, replied, "Oh Sir ... pray sit down—I have often heard of you, we are *both characters*—pray sit down." Thrale, *Thraliana*, pp. 358–359.

5. Boswell, *The Life of Johnson*, Advertisement to Second Edition, p. 8.

6. Turnbull, "Criminal Biographer, p. 512.

7. Boswell, *Life of Johnson*, p. 776.

8. *Boswell: The Ominous Years,* p. 358.
9. Ibid.
10. Ibid., p. 359.
11. Hickey, *Memoirs,* I: 15. William Hickey, describing another demi-rep, remarked that while "in her youth she had been an extraordinarily fine woman," at the time of her death she was "rather on the decline, and nearly approaching to her fortieth year."
12. James Boswell, *The English Experiment,* edited by Irma S. Lustig and Frederick A. Pottle (New York: McGraw-Hill, 1986), p. 47.
13. Frank Brady has argued that Mrs. Rudd was Margaret Boswell's "first serious rival." *James Boswell, The Later Years 1769–1795* (New York: McGraw-Hill, 1984), p. 382.
14. This warning came from his old friend, Sir Joshua Reynolds. *Boswell: The Applause of the Jury* (New York: McGraw-Hill, 1981), p. 339.
15. *The Correspondence of James Boswell,* edited by Charles N. Fifer (London: Heinemann, 1976), p. 297.
16. Boswell, *The English Experiment,* p. 50.
17. Ibid., pp. 60–61.
18. Ibid., pp. 137–138.
19. See Turnbull, "Criminal Biographer," p. 511.
20. *SM* (1779): 341; *Notes and Queries,* 10 S VIII, p. 361; IX, p. 114.
21. *Times,* February 4, 1797; *GM* 70 (1800): 483.
22. *GM* 79 (1809): 581.
23. The indefatigable Horace Bleackley ended a note on the trial with a plea for information: "Can any reader of "N & Q" inform us when and where this clever, beautiful and wicked woman drew her last breath?" *Notes and Queries,* 10 S VIII, p. 361. No one seems ever to have replied.
24. Horace Walpole, *Correspondence* (New Haven: Yale University Press, 1965), February 26, 1791, II: 208.

BIBLIOGRAPHY

PRIMARY SOURCES

Addington, William. *An Abridgement of Penal Statutes.* London, 1775.

Angelo, Henry. *The Reminiscences of Henry Angelo.* 2 vols. London, 1830; reprinted New York: Benj Blom, 1969.

Authentic Anecdotes of the Life and Transactions of Mrs. Margaret Rudd. London, 1776.

The Autobiography and Correspondence of Mary Granville, Mrs. Delany, edited by Lady Landover. 2nd series. London, 1862.

[Bailey, John]. *The Trial at Large of Mrs. Margaret Caroline Rudd.* London, 1775.

Baker, John. *Diary of John Baker,* edited by Philip C. Yorke. London: Hutchinson, 1931.

Barrington, Jonas. *Personal Sketches of His Own Time.* 2nd ed. 2 vols. London, 1830.

A Barrister, *The Case of Margaret Caroline Rudd.* London, 1775.

Bellamy, George Anne. *Apologies for the Life of George Anne Bellamy.* London, 1785.

Blackstone, William. *Commentaries on the Laws of England.* 4 vols. Chicago: University of Chicago Press, 1979.

Boswell, James. *The Correspondence of James Boswell,* edited by Charles N. Fifer. London: Heinemann, 1976.

——. *Life of Samuel Johnson.* Oxford: Oxford University Press, 1976.

——. *Reflections on the Late Alarming Bankruptcies in Scotland.* Edinburgh, 1772.

Boswell: The Applause of the Jury, edited by Irma S. Lustig and F. A. Pottle. New York: McGraw-Hill, 1981.

Boswell: The English Experiment, edited by Irma S. Lustig and Frederick A. Pottle. New York: McGraw-Hill, 1986.

Boswell: The Great Biographer, edited by M. Danziger and F. Brady. New York: McGraw-Hill, 1989.

Boswell: The Ominous Years 1774–1776, edited by C. Ryskamp and F. Pottle. New York: McGraw-Hill, 1963.

Boswell for the Defence, edited by W. K. Wimsatt and F. Pottle. New York: McGraw-Hill, 1959.

Boswell's London Journal 1762–1763, edited by F. Pottle. New York: McGraw-Hill, 1950.

Burke, Edmund. *Correspondence of Edmund Burke,* edited by Lucy Sutherland, et al. 10 vols. Cambridge: Cambridge University Press, 1960.

Calendar of Home Office Papers of the Reign of George III, edited by R. A. Roberts. Nendeln, Liechtenstein: Kraus Reprints, 1967.

Campbell, John. *A Political Survey of Britain.* 2 vols. London, 1774.

Campbell, R. *The London Tradesman.* London, 1747; reprinted New York: A.M. Kelley, 1969.

Carter, Elizabeth. *Letters from Mrs. Elizabeth Carter to Mrs. Montagu, between the Years 1755 and 1800.* London, 1817.

Circumstances of the Death of Mr. Scawen. London, 1775.

Colebrooke, Sir George. *Retrospection or Reminiscences.* London, 1898.

Colman, George. *The Man of Business.* London, 1775.

The Court of Adultery, a Vision. London, 1778.

Crawford, William. *Remarks on the Late Earl of Chesterfield's Letters to His Son.* London, 1776.

Cumberland, Richard. *Memoirs of Richard Cumberland.* 2 vols. London, 1804.

———. *The Note of Hand, or, Trip to Newmarket.* London, 1774.

Curwen, Samuel. *The Journal of Samuel Curwen Loyalist,* edited by Andrew Oliver. 2 vols. Cambridge, Mass.: Harvard University Press, 1972.

Dagge, Henry. *Considerations on Criminal Law.* London, 1772.

D'Archenholz, M. *A Picture of England.* Dublin, 1790.

De Pinto, Isaac. *An Essay on Circulation and Credit.* London, 1774.

The Diablo-Lady. London, 1777.

A Dictionary of Love. London, 1777.

Duncan, William. *Elements of Logic.* London, 1787.

The English Reports. 176 vols. Edinburgh, 1900–1930.

An Explicit Account of the Lives and Trials of the Twin Brothers. London, 1775.

Fashion, a Poem. Bath, 1775.

Female Artifice, or Charles James F-x Outwitted. London, 1774.

Female Forgery. London, 1775.

Fielding, John. *A Brief Description of the Cities of London and Westminster.* London, 1776.

[———]. *Forgery Unmasked.* London, 1775.

Foote, Samuel. *The Table Talk and Bon Mot of Samuel Foote,* edited by William Cooke. London: Meyers & Rogers, 1902.

Fordyce, Henrietta. *Memoirs of the Late Mrs. Henrietta Fordyce.* London, 1823.

Fordyce, James. *The Character and Conduct of the Female Sex.* London, 1786.

———. *Sermons to Young Women.* London, 1776.

Free Thoughts on Apothecaries and Empirics. London, 1773.

Garrick, David. *Bon Ton.* In *Plays by David Garrick and George Colman the Elder,* edited by E. R. Wood. Cambridge: Cambridge University Press, 1982.

———. *Letters of David Garrick,* edited by David Little and George Kahrl. 3 vols. Cambridge, Mass.: Belknap Press, 1963.

Gentleman of the Inner Temple. *Law Observations Relating to the Case of Mrs. Rudd.* London, 1776.

Genuine Memoirs of the Messrs. Perreau. London, 1775.

Grosley, M. *New Observations on England and Its Inhabitants.* London, 1772.

Gurney, Joseph. *An Account of the Arguments of Counsel with the Opinions at Large of the Hon. Mr. Justice Gould, Mr. Justice Ashurst, and Mr. Baron Hotham.* London, 1775.

Hanway, Jonas. *Midnight the Signal.* 2 vols. London, 1776.

Harrison, Walter. *A New and Universal History, Description and Survey of the Cities of London and Westminster.* London, 1775.

Hickey, William. *Memoirs,* edited by Alfred Spencer. 4 vols. London: Hurst and Blankett, 1923–1925.

Hunter, Thomas. *Reflections Critical and Moral on the Letters of Lord Chesterfield.* London, 1776.

Hutchinson, Thomas. *The Diary and Letters of Thomas Hutchinson,* edited by Peter Hutchinson. London, 1883.

Jesse, J. Heneage. *Memoirs of the Life and Reign of George the Third.* 3 vols. London, 1867.

Junius. *Letters of Junius,* edited by John Cannon. Oxford: Oxford University Press, 1978.

Knox, Vicesmus. *Essays Moral and Literary.* 2 vols. London, 1776; 2nd ed. 1791.

Laws Respecting Women. London, 1777.

A Letter from Mrs. Christian Hart to Mrs. Caroline Rudd. London, 1776.

A Letter to Mr. Sanxay. London, 1775.

Lichtenberg's Visits to England, translated by M. Mare and W. Quarrell. Oxford: Clarendon Press, 1938.

The Life, Trials and Dying Words of the Two Unfortunate Twin Brothers. London, 1776.

Lillo, George. *The London Merchant,* edited by William McBurney. Lincoln: University of Nebraska Press, 1965.

The Mansfield Manuscripts and the Growth of English Law in the Eighteenth Century, edited by James Oldham. Chapel Hill: University of North Carolina Press, 1992.

Marcellus. *A Letter to the Earl of Suffolk.* London, 1775.

Memoirs of the Life of Robert Adair. London, 1790.

Memoirs of Hannah More, edited by Robert Williams. London, 1834.

Mr. Daniel Perreau's Narrative of His Unhappy Case. London, 1775.

The Newgate Calendar, edited by Andrew Knapp and William Baldwin. London, 1828.

Nivelon, T. *Rudiments of Genteel Behavior.* London, 1737.

Nocturnal Revels. 2 vols. London, 1779.

Observations on the Case of Miss Butterfield. London, 1776.

Observations on the Trial of Robert Perreau. London, 1775.

Paley, William. *Principles of Moral and Political Philosophy.* [1785]; reprinted Houston: St. Thomas Press, 1977.

A Particular Account of the Dreadful and Shocking Apparitions of the Two Unfortunate Perreaus. London, 1776.

The Patriots of North America: A Sketch with Explanatory Notes. New York and London, 1775.

Piguerit, C. D. *An Essay on the Art of Newspaper Defamation.* London, 1775.

Prudence Triumphing over Vanity and Dissipation. London, 1776.

Radcliffe, Ann. *The Italian or the Confessional of the Black Penitents* [1797]; reprinted Oxford: Oxford University Press, 1998.

Remarks on a Pamphlet lately Published by Dr. Price, Intitled, Observations on the Nature of Civil Liberty. London, 1776.

Roscoe, James. *Lives of Eminent British Lawyers.* London, 1830.

[Rudd, M. C.]. *The Belle Widows.* 2 vols. London, 1789.

Rudd, M. C. *Facts: Or a Plain and Explicit Narrative of the Case of Mrs. Rudd.* London, 1775.

——. *Mrs. M. C. Rudd's Genuine Letter to Lord Weymouth, with Several Authentic Anecdotes of the Late Messrs. Perreau.* London, 1776.

——. *Mrs. Stewart's Case, Written by Herself, and Respectfully Submitted to the Enlightened Part of the Public.* London, 1789.

She Is and She Is Not, a Fragment of the True History of Miss C. De Grosberg. London, 1776.

Smith, Adam. *The Correspondence of Adam Smith,* edited by E. C. Mossner. Oxford: Clarendon Press, 1987.

——. *The Wealth of Nations.* London: Penguin, 1986.

Theodosia. *Genuine Memoirs of the Mess. Perreau.* London, 1775.

Thrale, Hester. *Thraliana,* edited by Katherine C. Balderson. 2 vols. Oxford: Clarendon Press, 1942.

The Trial of Miss Jane Butterfield for the Wilful Murder of William Scawen. London, 1775.

The Trials of Robert and Daniel Perreau. London, 1775.

The True and Genuine Lives and Trials of the Two Unfortunate Brothers, Robert and Daniel Perreau. London, 1775.

Trusler, John. *The Way to Be Rich and Respectable.* London, 1776.

Turner, Thomas. *The Diary of Thomas Turner,* edited by David Vaisey. Oxford: Oxford University Press, 1985.

Villette, John. *The Annals of Newgate.* 4 vols. London, 1776.

——. *A Genuine Account of the Behavior and Dying Words of Daniel Perreau and Robert Perreau.* London, 1776.

The Vindication of Innocence; An elegiac poem sacred to the memory of Her Majesty Queen Caroline Matilda, late Queen of Denmark. 1775.

Walpole, Horace. *Correspondence.* 48 vols. New Haven: Yale University Press, 1965.

Watts, Isaac. *The Improvement of the Mind.* London, 1782.

Whole Trials at Large of Robert and Daniel Perreau and Margaret Caroline Rudd. London, 1776.

Wraxall, Nathaniel. *The Historical and Posthumous Memoirs,* edited by Henry Wheatley. 5 vols. New York, 1884.

——. *Historical Memoirs of My Own Time.* London, 1904.

Young, Arthur. *A Tour of Ireland,* edited by A. Hutton. London, 1892.

SECONDARY SOURCES

Andrew, D. T. *London Debating Societies, 1776–1799.* London: London Record Society, 1994.

——. *Philanthropy and Police.* Princeton: Princeton University Press, 1989.

Ashton, T. S. *Economic Fluctuations in England 1700–1800.* Oxford: Clarendon Press, 1959.

Aspinall, Arthur. *Politics and the Press c. 1780–1850.* London: Home & Van Thal, 1949.

Bailyn, Bernard. *The Ordeal of Thomas Hutchinson.* Cambridge, Mass.: Belknap Press, 1974.

Baker, Russell G. F., and A. Stenning. *The Record of Old Westminsters.* London: Chiswick Press, 1928.

Bandon, Jonathan. *History of Ulster.* Belfast: Blackstaff Press, 1992.

Barker, Hannah. *Newspapers, Politics and English Society 1695–1855.* Harlow: Longman, 2000.

———. *Newspapers, Politics and Public Opinion in Late Eighteenth-Century England.* Oxford: Clarendon Press, 1998.

Barker-Benfield, G. J. *The Culture of Sensibility.* Chicago: University of Chicago Press, 1992.

Barry, Jonathan. "The Press and the Politics of Culture in Bristol, 1660–1775." In J. Black and J. Gregory, eds., *Culture, Politics and Society in Britain, 1660–1800,* pp. 49–81. Manchester: Manchester University Press, 1991.

Beattie, J. M. *Crime and the Courts in England 1660–1800.* Princeton: Princeton University Press, 1986.

———. "The Criminality of Women in Eighteenth-Century England." *Journal of Social History* 8 (1975): 80–116.

———. "Scales of Justice: Defense Counsel and the English Criminal Trial in the Eighteenth and Nineteenth Centuries." *Law and History Review* 9 (1991): 221–267.

Bleackley, Horace. *Ladies Fair and Frail.* London: John Lane, Bodley Head, 1925.

———. *The Life of John Wilkes.* London: John Lane, Bodley Head, 1917.

Bolitho, Hector, and Derek Peel. *The Drummonds of Charing Cross.* London: Allen & Unwin, 1967.

Bowen, H. V. "'Dipped in Traffic': East India Stockholders in the House of Commons 1768–1774." *Parliamentary History* 5 (1986): 39–53.

———. "'The Pests of Human Society': Stockbrokers, Jobbers and Speculators in Mid-eighteenth-century Britain." *History* 78 (1993): 38–53.

———. *Revenue and Reform: The Indian Problem in British Politics 1757–1773.* Cambridge: Cambridge University Press, 1991.

Bradley, James. *Popular Politics and the American Revolution.* Macon, Ga.: Mercer University Press, 1986.

Brady, Frank. *James Boswell, The Later Years 1769–1795.* New York: McGraw-Hill, 1984.

Brant, Clare. "Speaking of Women: Scandal and the Law in the Mid-Eighteenth Century." In C. Brant and D. Purkis, eds., *Women, Texts and Histories 1575–1760,* pp. 242–270. London: Routledge, 1992.

Brewer, John. "Commercialization and Politics." In N. McKendrick et al., eds., *The Birth of Consumer Society,* pp. 197–262. London: Hutchinson, 1983.

———. *Party Ideology and Popular Politics at the Accession of George III.* Cambridge: Cambridge University Press, 1981.

———. "The Wilkites and the Law, 1763–74." In John Brewer and John Styles, eds., *An Ungovernable People,* pp. 128–171. New Brunswick, N.J.: Rutgers University Press, 1980.

Brissenden, R. F. *Virtue in Distress: Studies in the Novel of Sentiment from Richardson to Sade.* London: Macmillan, 1974.

Brown, Peter. *The Chathamites.* London: Macmillan, 1967.

Burford, E. J. *Wits, Wenchers and Wantons.* London: R. Hale, 1990.

Campbell, John. *The Lives of the Chief Justices.* Philadelphia, 1851.

Castle, Terry. *Masquerade and Civilization*. Stanford: Stanford University Press, 1986.

Chatten, Elizabeth. *Samuel Foote*. Boston: Twayne, 1980.

Checkland, S. G. *Scottish Banking: A History 1695–1973*. Glasgow: Collin, 1975.

Christie, Ian. *British "Non-Elite" MPs 1715–1820*. Oxford: Oxford University Press, 1995.

———. *Myth and Reality in Late-Eighteenth-Century British Politics*. London: Macmillan, 1970.

Cockayne, G. E. *The Complete Baronetage of England*. 6 vols. Exeter: W. Pollard, 1900–1909.

Colley, Linda. *Britons: Forging the Nation 1707–1837*. New Haven: Yale University Press, 1992.

Corfield, Penelope. *Power and the Professions in Britain 1700–1850*. London: Routledge, 1995.

Cranfield, G. A. *The Press and Society*. London: Longman, 1978.

Cullen, L. M. *Anglo-Irish Trade 1660–1800*. New York: A. M. Kelley, 1968.

Dening, Greg. *Mr. Bligh's Bad Language*. Cambridge: Cambridge University Press, 1992.

Devereaux, Simon. "The City and the Sessions Papers: 'Public Justice' in London 1770–1800." *Journal of British Studies* 35, no. 4 (1996): 466–503.

Donald, Diana. *The Age of Caricature: Satirical Prints in the Reign of George III*. New Haven: Yale University Press, 1996.

Doody, Margaret Ann. "The Law, the Page, and the Body of Woman: Murder and Murderesses in the Age of Johnson." *The Age of Johnson* 1 (1987): 127–160.

Dunn, Richard. *Sugar and Slaves: The Rise of the Planter Class in the English West Indies, 1624–1713*. Chapel Hill: University of North Carolina Press, 1972.

Earle, Peter. *The Making of the English Middle Class*. Berkeley: University of California Press, 1989.

Emsley, Clive. *Crime and Society in England, 1750–1900*. London: Longman, 1987.

Endelman, Todd. *Radical Assimilation in English Jewish History 1656–1945*. Bloomington: Indiana University Press, 1990.

Feiling, Keith. *Warren Hastings*. London: Macmillan, 1966.

Felsenstein, Frank. *Anti-Semitic Stereotypes: A Paradigm of Otherness in English Popular Culture 1660–1830*. Baltimore: Johns Hopkins University Press, 1995.

Foss, Edward. *The Judges of England*. 9 vols. New York: AMS Press, 1966.

Frost, Thomas. *The Life of Thomas, Lord Lyttelton*. London, 1876.

Gatrell, V. A. C. *The Hanging Tree: Execution and the English People 1770–1868*. Oxford: Oxford University Press, 1994.

Gattey, Charles Neilson. *"Farmer" George's Black Sheep*. Bourne End, England: Kelsal, 1985.

George, M. Dorothy. *London Life in the Eighteenth Century*. New York: Capricorn, 1963.

The Georgian Era: Memoirs of the Most Eminent Persons. 2 vols. London, 1833.

Gill, Conrad. *The Rise of the Irish Linen Industry*. Oxford: Clarendon Press, 1964.

Gloag, John. *Georgian Grace*. London: A. & G. Black, 1956.

Goebel, Julius. *The Struggle for the Falkland Islands*. New Haven: Yale University Press, 1982.

Gwynn, Robin. *Huguenot Heritage*. London: Routledge & Kegan Paul, 1985.

Hamilton, Harlan W. *Doctor Syntax*. Kent, Ohio: Kent State University Press, 1969.

Hamilton, Henry. "Failure of the Ayr Bank." *Economic History Review* 8 (1956): 405–417.

Hammer, Stephanie Barbe. *The Sublime Crime*. Carbondale: Southern Illinois University Press, 1994.

Hampden, John. *An Eighteenth-Century Journal, Being a Record of the Years 1774–1776*. London: Macmillan, 1940.

Hancock, David. *Citizens of the World*. Cambridge: Cambridge University Press, 1995.

Harrington, John, ed. *The English Traveller in Ireland*. Dublin: Wolfhound Press, 1991.

Hartmann, Cyril Hughes. *Enchanting Bellamy*. London: Heinemann, 1956.

Harvey, A. D. *Sex in Georgian England*. New York: St. Martin's Press, 1994.

Hay, Douglas. "Property, Authority and the Criminal Law." In D. Hay et al., eds., *Albion's Fatal Tree*, pp. 17–63. New York: Pantheon, 1975.

Healey, Edna. *Coutts and Company 1692–1992: The Portrait of a Private Bank*. London: Hodder & Stoughton, 1992.

Hellmuth, Eckhart. "'The Palladium of All Other English Liberties': Reflections on the Liberty of the Press in England during the 1760s and 1770s." In E. Hellmuth, ed., *The Transformation of Political Culture: England and Germany in the Late Eighteenth Century*, pp. 467–501. London: Oxford University Press, 1990.

Hindle, Wilfred. *The Morning Post 1772–1937*. London: Routledge, 1937.

Hoare, H. P. R. *Hoare's Bank*. London: Collins, 1955.

Holmes, G., and D. Szechi. *The Age of Oligarchy*. London: Longman, 1993.

Holmes, Geoffrey. *Augustan England*. London: Allen & Unwin, 1982.

Holmes, Richard. *Dr. Johnson and Mr. Savage*. London: Hodder & Stoughton, 1993.

Hoppit, Julian. "Attitudes to Credit in Britain 1680–1790." *Historical Journal* 33 (1990): 305–322.

———. "Financial Crises in Eighteenth-Century England." *Economic History Review* 39 (1986): 39–58.

———. "The Use and Abuse of Credit in Eighteenth-Century England." In N. McKendrick and R. B. Outhwaite, eds., *Business Life and Public Policy*, pp. 54–78. Cambridge: Cambridge University Press, 1986).

Innes, Joanna. "Politics and Morals: The Reformation of Manners Movement in the Eighteenth Century." In E. Hellmuth, ed., *The Transformation of Political Culture: England and Germany in the Late Eighteenth Century*, pp. 57–118. London: Oxford University Press, 1990.

Jackman, S. W. *Carolina, Queen of Denmark*. Lewes: Book Guild, 1987.

Jones, Vivien. *Women in the Eighteenth Century*. London: Routledge, 1990.

Joslin, D. M. "London Private Bankers 1720–85." *Economic History Review* 7, 2nd series (1954): 167–186.

Kates, Gary. *Monsieur D'Eon Is a Woman: A Tale of Political Intrigue and Sexual Masquerade*. New York: Basic, 1995.

Kernan, Alvin. *Samuel Johnson and the Impact of Print*. Princeton: Princeton University Press, 1987.

King, Peter. *Crime, Justice and Discretion: Law and Social Relations in England 1740–1820*. Oxford: Oxford University Press, 2000.

Korobkin, Laura H. *Criminal Conversations: Sentimentality and Nineteenth-Century Legal Stories of Adultery*. New York: Columbia University Press, 1998.

Langbein, John. "Shaping the Eighteenth-Century Criminal Trial: A View from the Ryder Sources." *University of Chicago Law Review* 50 (1983): 1–136.

Langford, Paul. *A Polite and Commercial People.* Oxford: Clarendon Press, 1989.

Lawson, Philip. *The East India Company.* London: Longman, 1993.

Leslie-Melville, Ronald. *The Life and Work of Sir John Fielding.* London: L. Williams, 1934.

Lieberman, David. *The Province of Legislation Determined.* Cambridge: Cambridge University Press, 1989.

Lutnick, Solomon. *The American Revolution and the British Press 1775–1783.* Columbia: University of Missouri Press, 1967.

Marshall, P. J. *East Indian Fortunes.* Oxford: Clarendon Press, 1976.

Maxted, Ian. *The London Book Trades 1775–1800.* Folkestone, England: Dawson, 1977.

Maza, Sarah. *Private Lives and Public Affairs: The Causes Célèbres of Prerevolutionary France.* Berkeley: University of California Press, 1993.

McGowen, R. "The Body and Punishment in Eighteenth Century England." *Journal of Modern History* (December 1987): 651–679.

———. "Forgery Discovered, or the Perils of Circulation in Eighteenth-Century England." *Angelaki* 1 (1993–1994): 113–129.

———. "From Pillory to Gallows: The Punishment of Forgery in the Age of the Financial Revolution." *Past and Present* 165 (1999): 107–140.

———. "Knowing the Hand: Forgery and the Proof of Writing in Eighteenth-Century England." *Historical Reflections/Reflexions Historiques* 24 (1998): 385–414.

McKendrick, Neil. "The Commercialization of Fashion." In Neil M. McKendrick et al., eds., *The Birth of Consumer Society*, pp. 34–99. London: Hutchinson, 1983.

M'Creery, Cindy. "Keeping Up with the *Bon Ton.*" In Hannah Barker and Elaine Chalus, eds., *Gender in Eighteenth Century England*, pp. 207–229. London: Addison Wesley Longman, 1997.

Money, John. *Experience and Identity: Birmingham and the West Midlands 1760–1800.* Montreal: McGill-Queen's University Press, 1977.

———. "The Masonic Moment; or, Ritual, Replica and Credit: John Wilkes, the Macaroni Parson, and the Making of the Middle Class Mind." *Journal of British Studies* 32 (1993): 358–395.

Morgan, K., ed. *An American Quaker in the British Isles.* Oxford: Oxford University Press, 1992.

Mullan, John. *Sentiment and Sociability.* Oxford: Oxford University Press, 1988.

Namier, Lewis. *England in the Age of the American Revolution.* London: Macmillan, 1970.

Namier, Lewis, and John Brooke. *The House of Commons.* 3 vols. London: Oxford University Press, 1968.

Nussbaum, F. "Heteroclites: The Gender of Character in the Scandalous Memoirs." In F. Nussbaum and L. Brown, eds., *The New Eighteenth Century*, pp. 144–167. New York: Methuen, 1987.

Ogborn, Miles. *Spaces of Modernity: London's Geographies 1680–1780.* New York: Guilford Press, 1998.

Parsons, Mrs. Clement. *Garrick and His Circle.* London: Methuen, 1906.

Pearce, Charles E. *The Amazing Duchess.* London: Paul, 1911.

Phillips, Hugh. *Mid-Georgian London.* London: Collins, 1964.

Plomer, H. R. *A Dictionary of the Printers and Booksellers Who Were at Work in England 1726–1775.* Oxford: Oxford University Press, 1932.

Pointon, Marcia. *Strategies for Showing: Women, Possession and Representation in English Visual Culture 1665–1800.* Oxford: Oxford University Press, 1997.

Porter, Roy. "Making Faces: Physiognomy and Fashion in Eighteenth-Century England." *Etudes anglais* 4 (October–December 1985): 385–396.

Price, Jacob. *Capital and Credit in British Overseas Trade.* Cambridge, Mass.: Harvard University Press, 1980.

Radzinowicz, Leon. *A History of English Criminal Law and Its Administration from 1752.* 5 vols. London: Stevens, 1948–1986.

Raven, James. *Judging New Wealth.* Oxford: Clarendon Press, 1992.

Rea, Richard. *The English Press in Politics 1760–1774.* Lincoln: University of Nebraska Press, 1963.

Rudé, George. *Hanoverian London.* London: Secker & Warburg, 1971.

———. *Wilkes and Liberty.* Oxford: Oxford University Press, 1962.

Sainsbury, John. *Disaffected Patriots: London Supporters of Revolutionary America 1769–1782.* Kingston: Queens University Press, 1987.

———. "Wilkes and Libertinism." *Studies in Eighteenth-Century Culture* 26 (1996): 151–174.

Schwarz, L. D. *London in the Age of Industrialisation, Entrepreneurs, Labour Force and Living Conditions 1700–1850.* Cambridge: Cambridge University Press, 1992.

Sheridan, R. B. "The Rise of a Colonial Gentry: A Case Study of Antigua, 1730–1775." *Economic History Journal* (April 1961): 342–357.

———. *Sugar and Slavery.* Baltimore: Johns Hopkins University Press, 1974.

Spinney, David. *Rodney.* London: Allen & Unwin, 1969.

Stafford, Barbara Maria. *Body Criticism.* Cambridge, Mass.: MIT Press, 1991.

Stone, L., and J. F. Stone. *An Open Elite?* Oxford: Clarendon Press, 1986.

Straub, Kristina. *Sexual Suspects: Eighteenth-Century Players and Sexual Ideology.* Princeton: Princeton University Press, 1992.

Styles, John. "Sir John Fielding and the Problem of Criminal Investigation in Eighteenth-Century England." *Transactions of the Royal Historical Society,* 5th ser., 33 (1983): 127–149.

Sutherland, Lucy. *The East India Company in Eighteenth-Century Politics.* Oxford: Clarendon Press, 1952.

———. "Sir George Colebrooke's World Corner in Alum, 1771–73." *Economic History* (February 1936): 237–258.

Tillyard, Stella. *Aristocrats.* New York: Farrar, Straus & Giroux, 1994.

Trumbach, Randolph. *Sex and the Gender Revolution.* Chicago: University of Chicago Press, 1998.

Turnbull, Gordon. "Criminal Biographer: Boswell and Margaret Caroline Rudd." *Studies in English Literature* 26 (1986): 511–535.

Valentine, Alan. *The British Establishment 1760–1784.* 2 vols. Norman: University of Oklahoma Press, 1970.

Van Sant, Ann Jessie. *Eighteenth Century Sensibility and the Novel.* Cambridge: Cambridge University Press, 1993.

Vickery, Amanda. *The Gentleman's Daughter: Women's Lives in Georgian England.* New Haven: Yale University Press, 1998.

Wahrman, Dror. "*Percy's* Prologue: From Gender Play to Gender Panic in Eighteenth-Century England." *Past and Present* 159 (1998): 113–160.

———. "The Problem of English Identity in the American Revolution." *American Historical Review* (in press).

Weatherill, Lorna. *Consumer Behavior and Material Culture in Britain 1660–1760*. London: Methuen, 1988.

Wecter, Dixon. *Edmund Burke and His Kinsmen*. Boulder: University of Colorado Studies, 1939.

Welsh, Alexander. *Strong Representations*. Baltimore: Johns Hopkins University Press, 1992.

Wendorf, Richard. *Sir Joshua Reynolds: The Painter in Society*. Cambridge, Mass.: Harvard University Press, 1998.

Werkmeister, Lucyle. *The London Daily Press, 1772–1792*. Lincoln: University of Nebraska Press, 1963.

Wheatley, Henry B. *London Past and Present*. 3 vols. London, 1891.

Wilan, T. S. *Abraham Dent of Kirby Stephen*. Manchester: Manchester University Press, 1970.

Wilson, Charles. *Anglo-Dutch Commerce in the Eighteenth-Century*. Cambridge: Cambridge University Press, 1941.

Wilson, Kathleen. *The Sense of the People: Politics, Culture and Imperialism in England, 1715–1785*. Cambridge: Cambridge University Press, 1998.

Woolfe, Maurice. "Joseph Salvadore 1716–1786." *Jewish Historical Society of England Transactions* 21 (1962–1967): 104–113.

Yogev, Gedalia. *Diamonds and Coral: Anglo-Dutch Jews and Eighteenth-Century Trade*. New York: Holmes & Meier, 1978.

Carpenter, Lady Almeira, 214

Carter, Mrs. (translator), 151

"Case" (Mrs. Rudd), 63, 189, 191

Cassidy, David, 264

Castle, Terry, 303n43

Chamberlain, Lord, 129

Character witnesses. *See* Witnesses

Charlotte (queen of George III), 130;
    pardon appeal to, 253–54

Chatelet, Count de, 159

Chesterfield, Lord, 134–35

Childs family, 98

Christian VII (king of Denmark), 129

Chudleigh, Elizabeth. *See* Kingston,
    Duchess of

Churchill, John, 96

Cliffords (investment firm), 155

Clive, Robert, 148, 161; and East India
    Company, 140, 146–47, 155; in Mrs.
    Rudd's novel, 214, 315–16n58

Coachmakers Hall debating society, 156

Colebrooke, Sir George, 93, 94; impunity
    of, 157; speculative ventures of, 149–50,
    154, 155, 307n34

Colman, George, 144–45

Combe, William, 101, 272

Commentaries on the Laws of England
    (Blackstone), 253

Considerations on Criminal Law (Dagge),
    253

Cooper, Elizabeth, 79

Courtesans. *See* Demi-reps

Cowper (attorney), 220, 223, 316–17n17

The Cozeners (Foote), 272

Craftsman, 82

Crane, Reverend, 161

Crash of 1772: causes of, 147–50; and
    credit system, 136, 163–64, 305n1; and
    East India Company, 154–55; Fordyce's
    contribution to, 150–52; Perreaus linked
    to, 137–38

Crawford, William, 123, 134–35

Credit system: and crash of 1772, 136,
    150–52, 305n1; de Pinto's defense of, 142;
    mistrust in, 153–54, 164; private transac-
    tions of, 17, 140–41, 153, 305nn8,9; repu-
    tation's importance to, 18, 138–40, 141;
    signature feature of, 18, 23; speculation's

abuse of, 137–38, 142–43, 148–50, 163,
    307n34

Critical Review, 68, 233

Crown witness protection: authority to
    grant, 170–71, 172, 175, 311n39; eligibility
    for, 173; Fielding's accountability for,
    168–69; four ways to receive, 310n18;
    gendered view of, 186; Gould's
    arguments for, 177–78; legal controversy
    over, 165–67, 309nn3,7; Mansfield's hear-
    ings on, 172–76, 311n29; pardon versus,
    175, 311n31; Robert Perreau's request for,
    14; public concerns over, 179–80, 182–84,
    310n14, 311–12n40, 312nn48,49; for Mrs.
    Rudd, 28–29, 46; Mrs. Rudd
    disqualified from, 49–50, 165, 178–79

Cumberland, George, 293n18

Cumberland, Richard, 37, 96–97, 122,
    290–91n49, 293n18

Cumberland Pacquet, 53

Cummyng, James, 230

Curwen, Samuel, 7, 117, 271, 293n17,
    298–99n5

Dagge, Henry, 14, 167, 253, 290–91n49; in
    pardon campaign, 251; professional repu-
    tation of, 288n2; Mrs. Rudd on, 199;
    trial conduct of, 187

Dagge, James, 290–91n49

Daily Advertiser, 60, 308n49

Dalboux, Francis, 64

Dalboux, Hannah, 45, 64–65, 294n28

D'Archenholz, M.: on Colebrooke's specu-
    lation, 307n34; on demi-reps, 101; on
    English press, 78, 293n19; on London's
    attractions, 104–5; on West End status,
    88

Davenport, Thomas, 172, 174, 220, 235;
    and Frankland's testimony, 230–32

Davy, William, 220, 223, 224–25, 235,
    316–17n17

Death penalty, criticism of, 252–53

Dekker, Thomas, 4

Deloraine, Lord, 244, 318n3

Demi-reps, 301n76; and Jews, 108, 300n64;
    marriage to, 100–101, 298n38;
    origins/backgrounds of, 102–3, 299n51

Denbigh, Earl of, 260

20–22, 26–27, 30–31, 186–87; of Mrs. Rudd's pedigree, 229–30; Rudd trial's testimony on, 40–42; speculation tied to, 143, 145, 306n21; uttering versus, 28, 35, 221

Forgery Unmasked (pamphlet), 68, 69

Fountain, Peter, 288n2

Fox, Charles James, 79, 100

Fox, Henry, 301n76

Francis, Sir Philip, 142, 148

Frankland, Sir Thomas, 60, 99, 137, 189; background of, 87, 225–26; bond trans-actions with, 74, 75, 139–40; death of, 279; dispossession of Mrs. Rudd by, 116, 118, 226–29, 230–31, 317n24; forgery losses of, 25; at Robert Perreau's trial, 42; pretrial testimony of, 27; as prosecutor of Mrs. Rudd, 50; Mrs. Rudd's portrayal of, 167, 226–27, 229–30; at Mrs. Rudd's trial, 230–32

Freedom of the press, debates on, 54–55, 292n5

Free Society of Artists exhibition (1776), 220

Galloway, Lord, 102, 210

Galloway family, 281, 298n33

Garrick, David, 61, 113, 121–22, 288n2, 290–91n49, 305n8

Gazetteer: circulation of, 56; on Mrs. Hart's charges, 318n42; letters in, on Rudd case, 311–12n40; on pardon decision, 265–66; on Perreaus' execution, 9–10; on Perreaus' forgery, 164; on Robert Perreau's innocence, 263–64; on scandal focus, 59; on Scottish notes, 155–56; se-lective coverage by, 65, 294n30

Gemmells (creditor), 137

General Evening Post, 67

Gentleman's Magazine, 32, 53, 141; on Alexander Adair, 279–80; on *Belle Wid-ows,* 315n55; on Fordyce scandal, 151; on Mrs. Rudd's death, 284; on unresolved outcome, 267–68

Genuine Memoirs of the Messrs. Perreau (pamphlet), 68–69

George III (king of England), 2, 57, 75; and Caroline Matilda, 130, 304n55; par-don appeals to, 251–52, 253–54, 258, 260–61; public criticism of, 265–66

Germain, Lord George, 83, 106, 260, 261

Gideon, Sir Sampson, 107, 300n64

Gisborne, Thomas, 87

Gloucester, Duke of, 75

Gould, Justice, 177–78, 311n35, 312n49

Gower family, 75, 281, 298n33

Graft (merchant), 137

Greenfield (broker), 137

Greville, W. W., 101

Grey, de, Lord Chief Justice, 178

Grieve, Elizabeth Harriet, 78–79

Grieve, Harriot. *See* Grieve, Elizabeth Har-riet

Grindal, Dr., 96

Grosley, M., 118, 302n21

Guadeloupe (West Indies), 94–95

Guines, Count de, 149, 307n33

Hanway, Jonas, 123

Harman, Samuel, 264

Harrison, Walter, 290n43

Hart, Christian, 233–36, 318n42

Hart, John, 234–35

Hastings, Warren, 273

Hawkins, Caesar, 96

Hawkins, William, 34

Hickey, Joseph, 87, 94, 154–55, 228

Hickey, William, 94, 101, 298n29, 322n2, 323n11

Hillsborough, Lord, 24

Hilton, Vaugh (Perreaus' brother-in-law), 262

Hoare family, 98

Holtke, Count von, 129

Horneck, Mrs. (demi-rep), 103

Hotham, Judge, 167, 178

Howarth, Henry, 220

Hume, David, 154, 163

Humphreys, Polly, 100

Hunter, Sophia, 103

Huske, John, 138, 156

Hutchinson, Thomas, 61, 271, 322n12

Immunity from prosecution. *See* Crown witness protection

Irish linen trade, 103, 299n48

illegitimacy/adultery among, 99–100; kinship networks of, 89, 91–92; lifestyle of, 116, 301n9, 302n21; magazines' coverage of, 114, 120–21; marriage alliances of, 93–94; and pardon entitlement debate, 259–60, 261, 320nn55,57; Perreaus' posthumous restoration to, 263–64; theatrical representation of, 121–22

London Magazine, 114, 120, 121, 275, 277

The London Merchant (Lillo), 48

London Packet, 249

"The London Tragedy" (broadsheet), 273

Lucas, William, 36, 220, 223

Lucy, Sir Berkeley, 100

Lumley, Miss (Lord Scarborough's daughter), 100

Lurgan (Ireland), 103

Lyttelton, Earl of, 244–46, 319n7

Lyttelton, Lady, 42, 97

Mackreth, Robert, 308n58

Macleane, Lauchlin, 109, 305n9

Macqueen, Robert, 281

Magazines, 114–15, 120–21

Magistrates. See Bow Street magistrates

Manchester Mercury, 53

Mann, Horace, 151, 155, 245, 307n36

Manningham, Dr., 162

The Man of Business (Colman), 144–45

Mansfield, Lord, 2, 87, 223; crown witness hearings of, 172–76, 311nn29, 31,39; Gould's opinion versus, 177–78; public criticism of, 181–82, 312n44; traits/attitudes of, 171–72, 174–75, 310n20

Marriage: to demi-reps, 100–101, 298n38; as strategic alliance, 93–94

Masquerade, 124–25, 303n43. See also Fashion

Matrimonial Magazine, 120

Matthews, Miss (demi-rep), 102

Mawbey, Joseph, 98

Medina family, 107

Melville, General, 97

Middlesex Journal, 33, 52, 57–58, 83, 239

Mills (banker), 74

Mistresses. See Demi-reps

Monthly Miscellany, 114

Monthly Review, 68, 233, 236

Moody, John, 40–41, 256, 316–17n17

Moore, Sir John, 96

More, Hannah, 129

Moriencourt, Countess of, 149, 158

Morning Chronicle, 44, 184–85; coverage terminated by, 267; on execution of Perreaus, 9; first forgery reports in, 51–52, 60, 293n18; on forged news problem, 276; letters in, on Rudd case, 311–12n40; on letter to Weymouth, 254–55; on Mrs. Rudd, 66–67, 239, 294n33; on Scottish notes, 155

Morning Post, 52; circulation of, 56, 67; on crash of 1772, 305n1; on Davy's cross-examination tactics, 316–17n17; on execution of Perreaus, 9, 10; gossip/misinformation in, 58–59, 61–62; Harriot Grieve's letter in, 78–79; on Mrs. Rudd, 114, 239, 283; Mrs. Rudd's use of, 63, 65–66, 81

Moss, Captain, 304n60

Mrs. Stewart's Case (Mrs. Rudd), 209–12, 315nn53,54

Musgrave, Sir William, 212, 315n53

Neale, James, Fordyce and Downe (firm), 149, 150–52

Neale, William, 118

Newcastle, Duke of, 18, 86, 104, 107, 261

Newgate Calendar, 129

Newgate prison, 3, 8, 11

Newnham, Sheriff, 11

Newspapers: circulation of, 55–56; debates on value of, 54–55, 292n5; on execution of Perreaus, 7, 9–10; first Perreau-Rudd reports in, 51–52, 59–60, 293n18; gossip/scandal focus of, 58–59; inaccuracies in, 60–62, 264–65, 276, 293n17; letters in, 77–78; moralistic criticism of, 83–84, 295n67; pamphlets reprinted in, 67; political content of, 56–58; prejudicial impact of, 53, 81–83; Mrs. Rudd's use of, 63–66, 81; selective coverage by, 65–67, 294nn30,33; staff/sources of, 61, 293n19; terminated coverage by, 267. See also Letters to the press; names of specific newspapers

Rudd, Mrs. *(continued)*
    gendered defense of, 184–87, 312n60;
    Lyttelton linked to, 244, 246; magazine
    illustrations of, 114–15; marriage of, to
    Rudd, 104–5, 194–95; newspaper attacks
    on, 66–67, 78–80, 246–47, 294n33;
    pamphlet ascribed to, 68; Daniel
    Perreau's introduction to, 70, 109,
    124–25; Daniel Perreau's union with, 30,
    194, 195–97, 198, 201; Robert Perreau's
    testimony on, 14, 37–39; Perreau trial's
    strategy against, 36, 39–43, 46–47, 219;
    portrait etching of, 220; pretrial
    testimony of, 14–15, 29–31; promises to
    Perreaus by, 71–75, 85–86, 99, 248–49;
    public fascination with, 2, 215–17; resi-
    dence location of, 89; revisionist charac-
    terization of, 271–74, 277–78, 321n5;
    Salvadore's relations with, 72, 79, 102,
    108–9, 162, 300n65; as sentimental
    heroine, 200–203, 216, 314nn28,32,33;
    terminated press coverage of, 267. *See
    also* Rudd, Mrs., writings of; Trial of
    Mrs. Rudd
Rudd, Mrs., writings of: after execution of
    Perreaus, 320n41; authorship of, 189; au-
    tobiographical novel, 212–15, 315nn55,58;
    birth/breeding claims in, 193–94,
    197–98; books/letters influencing,
    206–7, 315n43; competing elements of,
    208–9; on Dagge's evil, 199; on Mrs.
    Dalboux, 64–65, 294n28; on Frankland,
    226–27, 228–30; during imprisonment,
    210–15, 315nn53–55, 315–16n58; on
    Kendal's influence, 158; on Kinder's evil,
    198–99; on marital circumstances,
    194–95; masculine language/style of,
    205–6, 208, 211–12, 314nn38,39; money
    theme of, 195–97; pardon campaign's
    provocation of, 254–57; on Henrietta
    Perreau, 202, 222; to Perreau sisters, 198,
    215, 276, 313n20; public response to,
    204–5, 208, 209, 212, 215–17; for public
    vindication, 63–64, 190, 191–92, 203,
    313n4; sentimental self-portrait in,
    200–205, 216, 314nn28,32,33; on specula-
    tion, 144; on speculation by Perreaus,

137–38, 158, 160, 161–62; to Weymouth,
    254–55, 266; wife/mother theme of, 198,
    199–200, 256–57
Rudd, Thomas (Mrs. Rudd's father-in-
    law), 104, 299n53
Rudd, Valentine (Mrs. Rudd's husband),
    31, 70, 104–5, 194–95, 284, 299n53

Sadleir (insurance broker), 137
Salvadore, Joseph, 142; and Falkland
    Islands scheme, 148–49, 158; family
    background of, 106–7; financial ruin of,
    155, 160–61, 308n62; financial success of,
    107; Mrs. Rudd's relations with, 72, 79,
    102, 108–9, 162, 300n65
Sandwich, Lord, 74–75, 245
Sanxay (druggist), 130, 137
Sapertas (creditor), 137
Savage, Richard, 210
Savoir Vivre club, 245
Scawen, William, 130, 131, 132
Schomberg, Dr., 96
The Scotchman, 57
Scot's Magazine, 136
Scottish notes, 155–56, 307n47
Seaforth, Duke of, 100
Sentimentalism: criticism of, 204–5;
    hero trope of, 47–48; inappropriate
    expression of, 205, 216, 314nn36,38; of
    Mrs. Rudd's writings, 200–203,
    314nn32,33
Shackleton, Elizabeth, 271
Shee, Captain, 106
"She Is and She Is Not" (pamphlet), 232
Shelburne, Lord, 305n9
Sibelius (Dutch engraver), 220
Signatures on notes, 18, 23
Sir Charles Grandison (Richardson), 107
Skinner (auctioneer), 117
Smith, Adam, 110, 141
Somerset, James, 224
Speculation: in alum, 149–50, 307n34;
    Isaac de Pinto on, 142; in East India
    Company, 146–48, 150, 306n27; during
    Falklands crisis, 148–49, 158–60; by
    Alexander Fordyce, 150–51, 152–53; by
    the Perreaus, 137–38, 160, 161–62, 196,